A HANDBOOK FOR PROFESSIONAL FUTURES AND OPTIONS TRADERS

A HANDBOOK FOR PROFESSIONAL FUTURES AND OPTIONS TRADERS

JOSEPH D. KOZIOL

JOHN WILEY & SONS
New York • Chichester • Brisbane • Toronto • Singapore

Library of Congress Cataloging in Publication Data:

Koziol, Joseph D.
    A handbook for professional futures and options traders.

    Bibliography: p.
    Includes index.
    1. Commodity exchanges.   2. Financial futures.
3. Option (Contract) I. Title.
HG6024.A3K68 1987   332.64′4   87-8180
ISBN 0-471-87423-X

Printed in the United States of America

10 9 8 7 6 5 4 3 2 1

Dedicated to Marjorie
and our family

Preface

The purpose of this handbook is to present a framework that emphasizes the probabilistic nature of decision making for trading and hedging programs. Equally, the text strives to quantify criteria that in many organizations are often assessed qualitatively for actual trading situations. It details various analytical approaches by offering applications-oriented techniques. While the book distinguishes between historical results and expected values, it demonstrates the critical interdependence between the two as well.

JOSEPH D. KOZIOL

Bedford, New York
June 1987

Acknowledgments

The following organizations deserve special acknowledgement: the Chicago Board of Trade, the Chicago Mercantile Exchange, the Comex, the New York Mercantile, the New York Cotton Exchange, the Coffee, Sugar, & Cocoa Exchange, the Kansas City Board of Trade, and the Commodity Research Bureau, Inc. Their aid during the data compilation and graphic assembly of this text was very helpful.

I am very grateful to the people at John Wiley & Sons for their indulgences, particularly the granted extensions of time. Steve Kippur, Mike Hamilton, Nettie Bleich, and Karl Weber deserve special thanks.

Last, though not in importance, I extend my appreciation to my colleagues, friends, family, and to the professional staff at John Wiley & Sons for their support, helpful criticisms, editing, typing, and everything else that transforms a manuscript into a cohesive book.

J.D.K.

CONTENTS

A HANDBOOK FOR PROFESSIONAL FUTURES AND OPTIONS TRADERS

1

Introduction

FUTURES TRADING AS A BUSINESS

Futures trading is a business. Whether you are a speculator, manager, or hedger you cannot afford to view risk and reward as notions. Instead, these two key words must be quantified into meaningful concepts. By so doing, you can answer questions such as: How great is the risk? What are the rewards? How many contracts should be positioned?

Banking, insurance, sports, and other economic endeavors use computers to collect data and transform it into valuable information. Corporate strategies or game plans then emerge. This is also the case in futures. Many professional traders employ the services of computer support. Since you are competing against these individuals, among others, you cannot neglect this aspect.

For example, the insurance industry utilizes actuarial tables which were derived from a statistical analysis of historical data. So it is the case with the futures markets. Market data, simulated trades, and actual trades lend themselves to the same type of analysis.

RISKS AND REWARDS

Risk is the potential loss one will suffer if a given position is not successful. Reward is the potential profit if it is successful. Historical analysis of previous conditions is one of the better ways to assess both concepts.

At the elementary level, risk can be viewed as the extent of a daily range move, daily limit move. Daily range move refers to the established amount a commodity price is permitted to vary during one market session. For example, the ordinary daily limit for Chicago Treasury bonds is 3 points per contract. This means that a session's price cannot exceed the previous settlement price by more than 3 points, or be more than 3 points under it. Therefore the permissible range of price swings from the previous session is 6 points per contract.

In the worst possible daily case, a position's entry price is at one extreme and the settlement price is at the other extreme; the settlement price is in direct opposition to the intended action. Continuing with the Chicago Treasury bond example, take a contract, purchased at a limit-up price, that settled limit down. If the position were held for the session and "carried overnight," the loss for the day would be 6 points or $6,000 per contract. As can be seen, the initial day's risk can potentially be the greatest. On subsequent days the potential loss is only 50 percent of the range, or one limit move. A more sophisticated presentation of risk is described in Chapter 12, Testing.

An elementary view of reward is the converse case of the previous example. On the initial day of the position, a Treasury bond contract was sold at the limit-up price, and the market declined to settle at the lower limit. Thus the first day's profits would be 6 points or $6,000 per contract. If the market continued to move downward, the subsequent days profits would be 3 points or $3,000 per contract. A more sophisticated presentation of reward is described in Chapter 12, Testing.

THE NECESSITY OF DEFINING GOALS AND HAZARDS

Often this topic is overlooked. "Trading programs" may be pursued with little or no thought given to the goals and hazards. Rather, they warrant scrutiny as the fundamental basis for a strategy.

Critical questions that have a material bearing on the successful outcome of a trading program must be answered here. Examples for a sample checklist are:

1. How conservative, aggressive, or somewhere in between the two is the trading program to be?
2. Is the trading to be hedging, speculative, or a combination of the two?
3. What commitment is to be given to the trading program?
   a. How much time?
   b. Total investment?
   c. Dollar amount or percentage loss of total investment before revision or termination?
4. What are the profit or hedging objectives?
   a. Are expected profits twice the risk capital (not necessarily the total capital—see Chapter 12, Testing) acceptable?
   b. Or is another ratio satisfactory?
5. Does an individual or organization make the final trading decision, or is another party authorized to act?

6. What place does futures trading have in the personal portfolio or corporate operations?

7. What other factors important to the trading program must be considered?

    a. Legal limitations?

    b. Corporate charter?

    c. Position limits?

By addressing these points, among others, the scope of the trading program will be defined, and the operator can then proceed to test and implement strategies.

RANDOMNESS OR WORKABLE DATA

"Price changes" have been demonstrated to be primarily motivated by random influences; however, the same body of literature does not dispute the

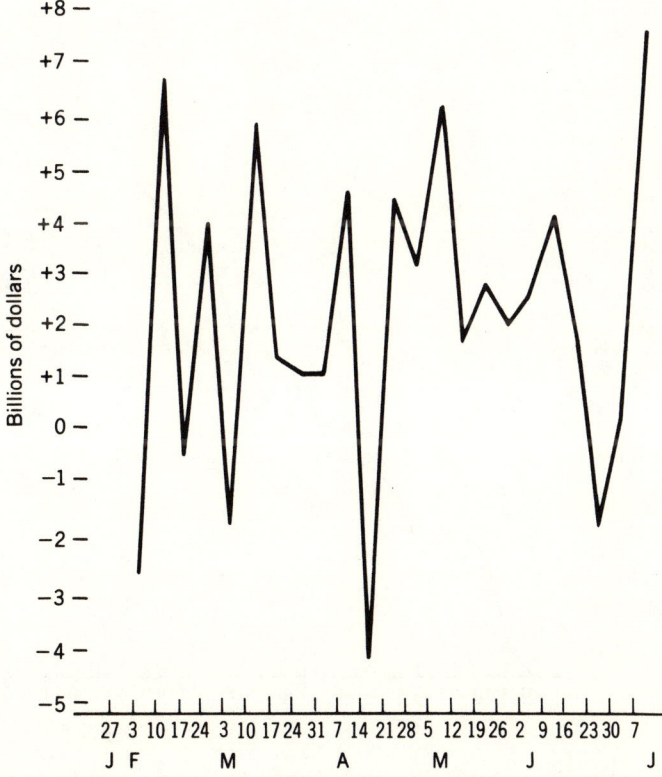

CHART 1.1 Money supply—weekly changes (*Source:* Federal Reserve Bank of St. Louis, *U.S. Financial Data*)

correlation of one price to another within a time series. In fact, there are tendencies toward strong autocorrelations and serial correlations. These correlations are very important points because they permit operators not only to assume the presence of trends, or at the very least interdependence among the observations, but also to actually test for them. This enhances the confidence level in the application of the tested program.

This concept is best illustrated by a graphic presentation. For example, in recent years there has been an increasing focus on the money supply, however defined. A great deal of time and effort are expended attempting to predict the weekly changes for that series. By examining Charts 1.1 and 1.2, it can be seen that the former presents an erratic picture, while the latter displays greater order and seeming predictability.

Reinforcing this valuable idea are Charts 1.3 and 1.4. They present the monthly changes in gold prices and a time series constructed of the monthly prices. Again, the former chart portrays erratic behavior while the latter suggests correlative pricing tendencies. With this knowledge of randomness, correlation, and workable data we will explore various analytical methodologies.

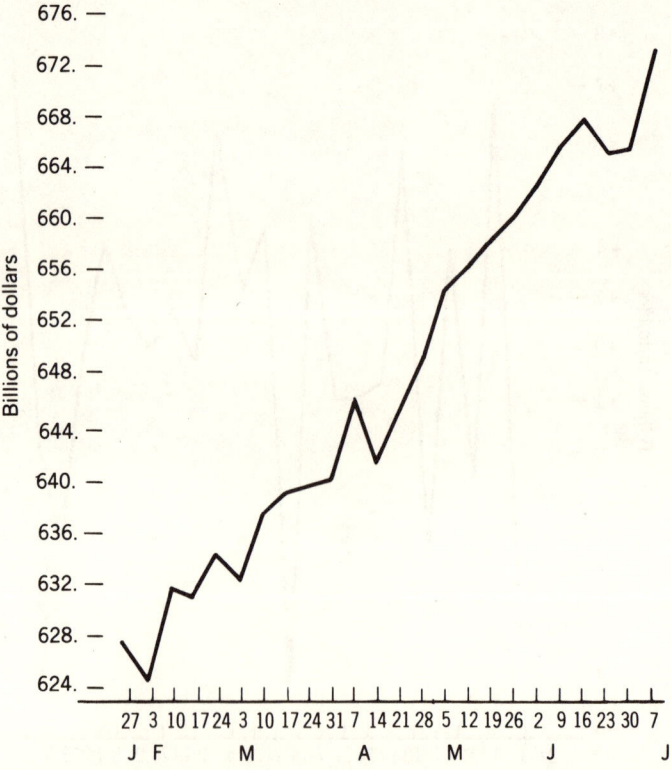

CHART 1.2 Money supply—cumulative total (*Source:* Federal Reserve Bank of St. Louis, *U.S. Financial Data*)

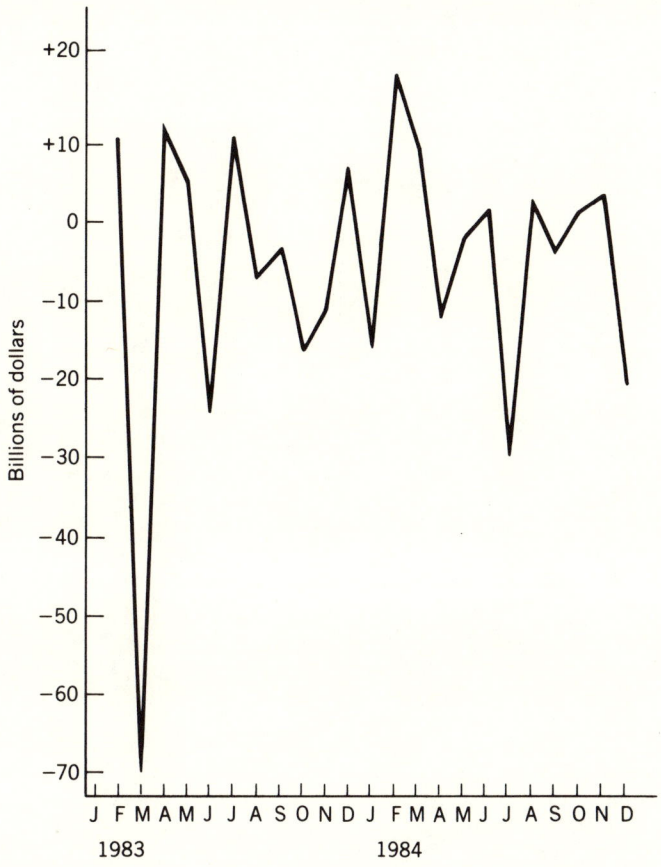

CHART 1.3 Monthly changes in gold prices (*Source:* Commodity Research Bureau Yearbooks)

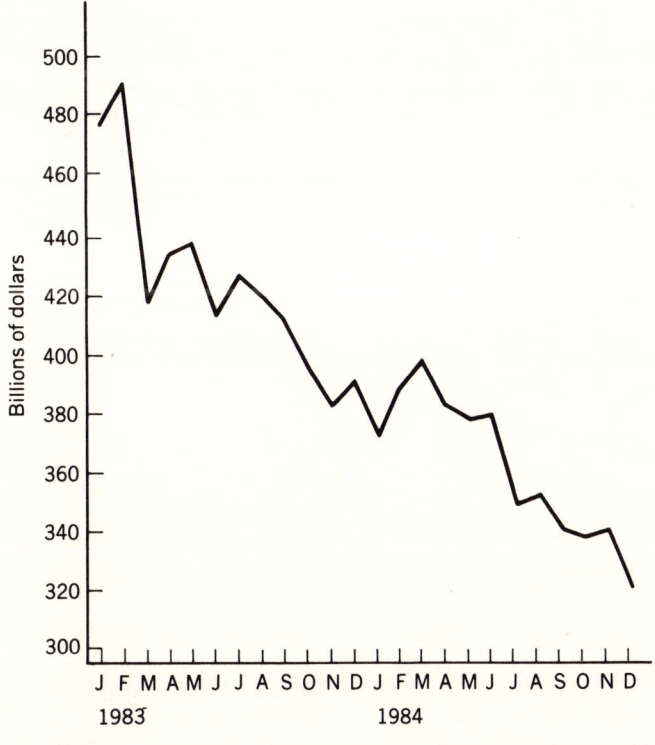

CHART 1.4 Gold price time series (*Source:* Commodity Research Bureau Yearbooks)

2
Technical Analysis

COMMENTARY

Perhaps no other topic of commodity trading has received as much attention as technical analysis. It is the focus of numerous random walk studies as well as being the basic approach for many speculators. One of the main premises for this course of action is the belief that the study of past price behavior is suitable for application to trading operations in the marketplace. Although many authors include chart reading in the realm of technical analysis, this book will explore the specialized subject of chart analysis in Chapter 3, Chart Analysis.

PRICES

Prices are the key to technical analysis. Since they consist of a stream of readily available numbers, they lend themselves very easily to quantitative analysis. One can average, compare, and otherwise statistically assess prices. Technicians not only consider the resultant numbers per se but also evaluate their behavior. Technicians do not ordinarily rely on only one technique but usually blend several into their approaches. This means that the manager can use a moving average coupled with a consideration of a reversal or other technical phenomena.

AVERAGING PROCESSES

One simple technique is to construct a moving average series. These averages smooth out a data series. Consider the following five pieces of data:

21.55, 21.34, 21.47, 21.62, and 21.55. In this case, a 5-day simple average would be:

$$\frac{21.55 + 21.34 + 21.47 + 21.62 + 21.55}{5} = 21.51$$

The most recent 3-day (last three items) average would be:

$$\frac{21.47 + 21.62 + 21.55}{3} = 21.55$$

Note: In both cases, the simple average was rounded to maintain the two decimal integrity of the data series.

The concept of moving averages arises from the movement of the averaging process over time. Returning to the five-item data series, one can generate two other 3-day simple averages. The 3-day simple averages are:

$$\frac{21.34 + 21.47 + 21.62}{3} = 21.48$$

and

$$\frac{21.55 + 21.34 + 21.47}{3} = 21.45$$

Table 2.1 lists the dates, prices, and the 2-, 3-, 4-, and 5-day simple moving averages for the five-item data series.

As can be seen, the longer the specified time span for a moving average, the fewer moving averages for a given data series. Also, the longer-term moving averages react more slowly or show greater stability than the shorter-term moving averages. To determine the number of possible simple averages from a data series, use the formula $D - (L - 1)$ where: D is the number of data observations in the series, and L is the length of the specified average. Returning to Table 2.1, we have five data items and we want to know how many 2- and 4-day moving averages are possible. We determine that there are:

$$5 - (2 - 1) = 4$$

possible 2-day moving averages and

$$5 - (4 - 1) = 2$$

TABLE 2.1. SIMPLE MOVING AVERAGES

Date	Close	2-Day Moving Average	3-Day Moving Average	4-Day Moving Average	5-Day Moving Average
January 26	21.55				
January 27	21.34	21.50			
January 28	21.47	21.41	21.45		
February 1	21.62	21.55	21.48	21.50	
February 2	21.55	21.59	21.55	21.50	21.51

Source: This table is based on Chicago Board of Trade data.

possible 4-day moving averages. When performing analysis, this formula will indicate how many moving averages to expect.

Table 2.2 expands the listing of data items for July soybean oil while Chart 2.1, graphically portrays the averages against the background of the daily price action.

Advocates of moving averages point out that they are not so much interested in the individual daily action but rather the trend in the prices. By averaging the daily prices they expect to smooth out tolerably acceptable random variations (see Chapter 12, Testing) and be set to capitalize on an unusually large price movement. It is in the area of technical analysis and mechanical system trading that the trader finds a significant departure between the mathematical concept of moving averages and their application.

Before proceeding to explore several applications of the ordinarily used moving averages, a survey of the textbook variety will be presented. The latter type tends to be more useful (and common) in the assessment of other economic data, and it will be helpful not only in subsequent chapters but also will provide another perspective for this chapter. Table 2.3 lists 50 days of price history with the attendant moving average series. Note that while the moving averages require several days before getting on line, they do not make it to the end of the price data as in the previous tables.

Once again using July soyoil data, Chart 2.2 visually presents the application of the textbook moving averages.

Trading Applications

The most straightforward trading application of the moving average is the crossover technique. The operator specifies the lengths for the moving averages and determines buy/sell signals from their relationship. In the simplest form, a strict mechanical application of this technique provides the operator with a method that is always in the marketplace; that is, no neutral or standaside condition exists.

TABLE 2.2. ILLUSTRATIVE JULY SOYBEAN OIL DATA

Date	High	Low	Close
November 20	22.40	22.10	22.20
November 23	22.10	21.90	22.00
November 24	22.04	21.06	21.68
November 25	22.00	21.08	21.80
November 27	21.95	21.80	21.92
November 30	21.99	21.75	21.75
December 1	22.17	21.65	22.16
December 2	22.15	21.95	21.95
December 3	22.02	21.90	21.99
December 4	22.45	22.05	22.32
December 7	22.25	21.90	21.95
December 8	22.05	21.55	21.55
December 9	21.75	21.50	21.70
December 10	21.70	21.45	21.53
December 11	21.65	21.30	21.53
December 14	21.50	21.20	21.30
December 15	21.35	21.00	21.05
December 16	21.00	20.32	20.97
December 17	21.20	20.92	21.00
December 18	21.00	20.65	20.73
December 21	20.70	20.50	20.52
December 22	20.60	20.32	20.45
December 23	20.55	20.25	20.54
December 24	20.90	20.54	20.81
December 28	21.00	20.82	20.94
December 29	20.84	20.47	20.60
December 30	20.70	20.53	20.60
December 31	20.60	20.38	20.38
January 4	20.40	20.29	20.40
January 5	20.40	20.32	20.32
January 6	20.67	20.45	20.62
January 7	20.98	20.63	20.87
January 8	20.93	20.73	20.74
January 11	20.83	20.60	20.65
January 12	20.58	20.47	20.56
January 13	20.61	20.54	20.60
January 14	20.69	20.63	20.69
January 15	20.73	20.58	20.61
January 18	20.78	20.60	20.70
January 19	20.65	20.58	20.58
January 20	20.71	20.52	20.68
January 21	20.87	20.72	20.78
January 22	20.88	20.74	20.87
January 25	21.10	20.81	21.01
January 26	21.49	21.07	21.48
January 27	21.60	21.45	21.55
January 28	21.52	21.32	21.34
January 29	21.58	21.38	21.47
February 1	21.68	21.26	21.62
February 2	21.72	21.48	21.55

Source: This table is based on Chicago Board of Trade data.

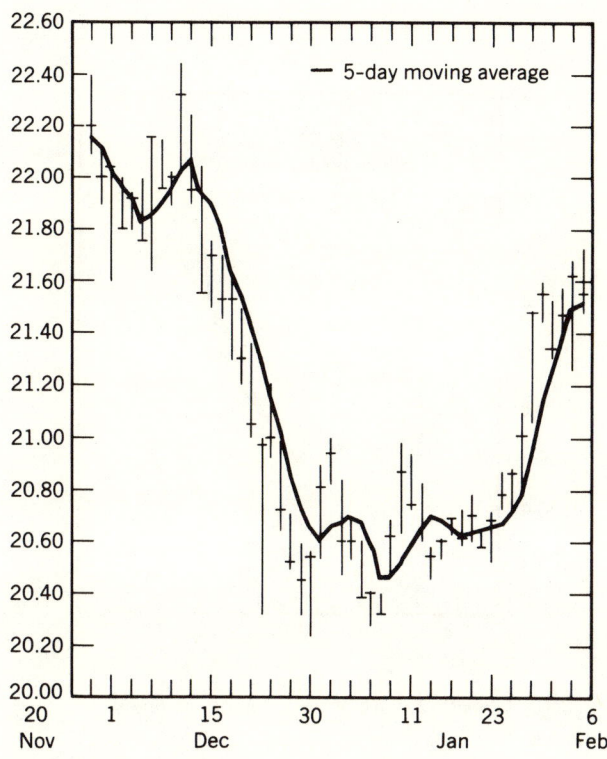

CHART 2.1 Averages superimposed against daily price action

TABLE 2.3. MATHEMATICAL OR TEXTBOOK MOVING AVERAGES

Date		Close	5-Day Moving Average	15-Day Moving Average
January	6	20.62		
January	7	20.87		
January	8	20.74	20.69	
January	9	20.65	20.68	
January	12	20.56	20.65	
January	13	20.60	20.62	
January	14	20.69	20.63	
January	15	20.61	20.64	20.76
January	18	20.70	20.65	20.82
January	19	20.58	20.67	20.86
January	20	20.68	20.72	20.90
January	21	20.78	20.78	20.97
January	22	20.87	20.96	21.04
January	25	21.01	21.14	
January	26	21.48	21.25	
January	27	21.55	21.37	
January	28	21.34	21.49	
January	29	21.47	21.51	
February	1	21.62		
February	2	21.55		

Source: This table is based on Chicago Board of Trade data.

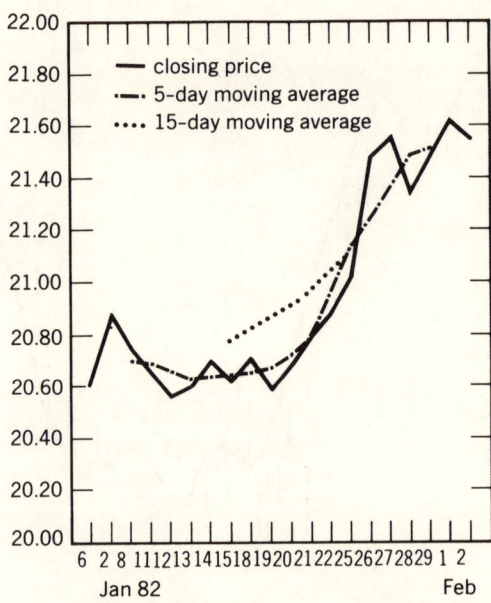

CHART 2.2 Textbook moving averages

The general trading rules for this approach are:

1. Buy if the short-term average is greater than the long-term average.
2. Sell if the short-term average is less than the long-term average.

Situations may arise where the two moving averages, both short and long term, are equal, and at that point the system can maintain the prevailing buy or sell position until there is a complete crossover. The actual buy/sell criteria can vary from trader to trader according to the definitions and requirements of each. Sometimes, the trader may use the direction of the longer-term average as the deciding factor. For example, if the short-term average exceeded the long-term average, a buy situation would be indicated. Then if the averages become equal, provided the most recent long-term moving average value exceeded the immediately preceding long-term moving average value, the technique would continue to indicate a buy situation.

To visualize the crossover concept, examine Charts 2.3 and 2.4. As can be seen, Chart 2.3 is a 5- and 20-day moving average arrangement superimposed over the daily price action (a relatively short-term oriented arrangement) while Chart 2.4 is a 10- and 40-day moving average arrangement superimposed over the daily price action (a relatively long-term oriented arrangement). The data for these Charts are provided by Tables 2.2 and 2.4.

As can be seen in Chart 2.3, and 5- and 20-day moving average arrangement generated a number of transactional signals. These occurred on January 13, 14, 15, and 18. From November 20 to January 12, the 5-day average was

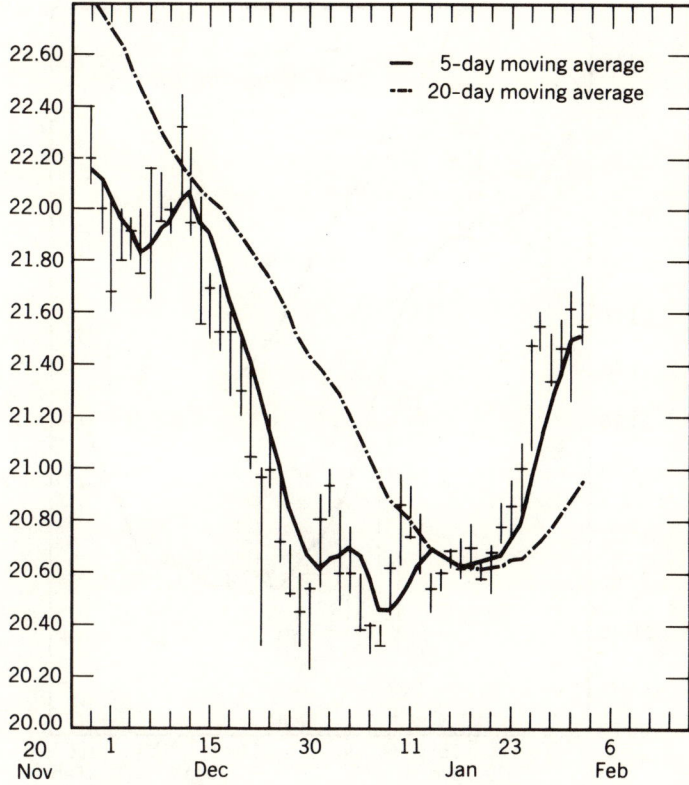

CHART 2.3 5- and 20-day moving average arrangement

always less than the 20-day average (a sell situation), while from January 19 to February 2, the 5-day average was always greater than the 20-day average (a buy situation). To examine these events in tabular form see Table 2.5.

Similarly, Chart 2.4 depicts the 10- and 40-day moving average arrangement. It generated only one fresh transactional signal, since prior to January 29 the short-term average (10-day) was always less than the long-term average (40-day); and from February 1 the short-term average was always greater than the long-term average. This course of events is listed in Table 2.6.

Weighted Moving Averages

Depending on the decision maker's judgment, a variety of moving average arrangements can be constructed. Some of the more common will be presented. In general form, a weighted moving average is constructed by applying the generalized weighting expression:

$$\frac{P_i w_i + \cdots + P_n W_n}{\sum\limits_{i}^{n} W_i}$$

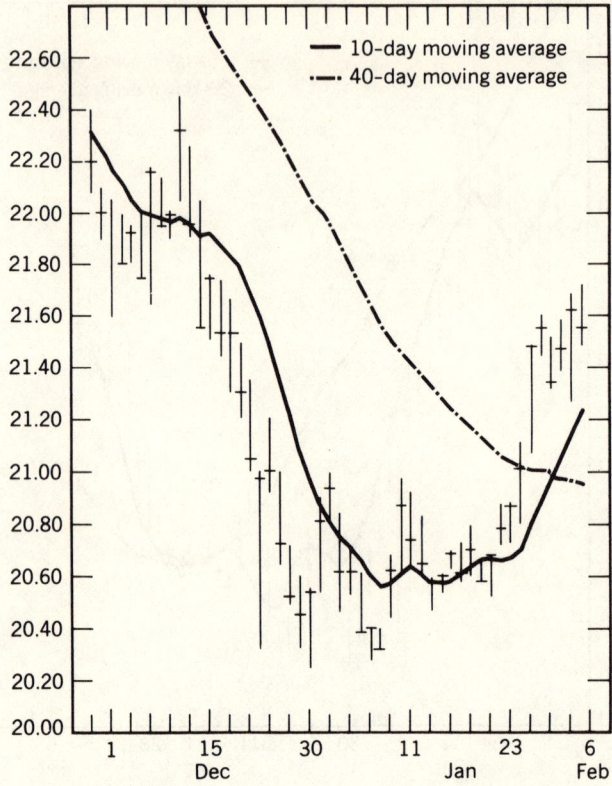

CHART 2.4 10- and 40-day moving average arrangement

In the simplest case, the weights are equal to one and the solution is a simple moving average as presented earlier. To see this, let us return to the July soyoil data.

$$\frac{(1 \times 21.55) + (1 \times 21.34) + (1 \times 21.47) + (1 \times 21.62) + (1 \times 21.47)}{1 + 1 + 1 + 1 + 1}$$

$$= \frac{107.45}{5} = 21.51$$

The following sections will present weighting parameters other than those equal to one.

Arithmetic Progression Averages

For an arithmetic progression average, the weights increase by constant increments, such as: 1, 2, 3, 4, 5, and so on. In the case of increments of 4,

TABLE 2.4. 10- AND 40-DAY MOVING AVERAGE ARRANGEMENTS

Date		Close	10-Day Moving Average	40-Day Moving Average
November	20	22.20	22.32	23.35
November	23	22.00	22.24	23.32
November	24	21.68	22.17	23.28
November	25	21.80	22.11	23.23
November	27	21.92	22.05	23.20
November	30	21.75	22.00	23.15
December	1	22.16	21.99	23.10
December	2	21.95	21.98	23.04
December	3	21.99	21.96	22.97
December	4	22.32	21.98	22.92
December	7	21.95	21.95	22.86
December	8	21.55	21.91	22.79
December	9	21.70	21.91	22.71
December	10	21.53	21.88	22.64
December	11	21.53	21.84	22.58
December	14	21.30	21.80	22.52
December	15	21.05	21.69	22.46
December	16	20.97	21.59	22.40
December	17	21.00	21.49	22.33
December	18	20.73	21.33	22.27
December	21	20.52	21.19	22.20
December	22	20.45	21.08	22.13
December	23	20.54	20.96	22.06
December	24	20.81	20.89	22.01
December	28	20.94	20.83	21.94
December	29	20.60	20.76	21.87
December	30	20.60	20.72	21.79
December	31	20.38	20.66	21.71
January	4	20.40	20.60	21.64
January	5	20.32	20.56	21.56
January	6	20.62	20.57	21.51
January	7	20.87	20.61	21.46
January	8	20.74	20.63	21.42
January	11	20.65	20.61	21.37
January	12	20.56	20.57	21.33
January	13	20.60	20.57	21.28
January	14	20.69	20.58	21.24
January	15	20.61	20.61	21.21
January	18	20.70	20.64	21.17
January	19	20.58	20.66	21.13
January	20	20.68	20.67	21.09
January	21	20.78	20.66	21.06
January	22	20.87	20.67	21.04
January	25	21.01	20.71	21.02
January	26	21.48	20.80	21.01
January	27	21.55	20.90	21.01
January	28	21.34	20.96	20.99
January	29	21.47	21.05	20.97
February	1	21.62	21.14	20.97
February	2	21.55	21.24	20.95

Source: This table is based on Chicago Board of Trade data.

TABLE 2.5. 5- AND 20-DAY MOVING AVERAGES TRANSACTIONAL ANALYSIS

Date	5-Day Moving Average	20-Day Moving Average	Position/Action
Prior to January 13	Less than 20-day moving average	Greater than 5-day moving average	Short (or awaiting fresh signal)
January 13	20.68	20.67	Go long (or reverse from short)
January 15	20.62	20.63	Go short (or reverse from long)
January 18	20.63	20.62	Go long (or reverse from short)
After January 18	Greater than 20-day moving average	Less than 5-day moving average	Stay long (or await fresh signal)

TABLE 2.6. 10- AND 40-DAY MOVING AVERAGES TRANSACTIONAL ANALYSIS

Date	10-Day Moving Average	40-Day Moving Average	Position/Action
Prior to January 29	Less than 40-day moving average	Greater than 10-day moving average	Short (or awaiting fresh signal)
January 29	21.05	20.97	Go long (or reverse from short)
After January 29	Greater than 40-day moving average	Less than 10-day moving average	Long (or awaiting fresh signal)

with 2 as a departure weight, the weights are: 2, 6, 10, 14, 18, and so on. Applying the first case to the data we have:

$$\frac{(1 \times 21.55) + (2 \times 21.34) + (3 \times 21.47) + (4 \times 21.62) + (5 \times 21.47)}{1 + 2 + 3 + 4 + 5}$$

$$= \frac{322.47}{15} = 21.50$$

The premise for this approach is that the most recent prices are considered more indicative of the underlying price movement than are prior prices; hence the most recent prices are assigned the greatest weights. As in the case of simple moving averages, a short-term average can be weighted one way, while the longer-term average can be weighted another. Again, the crossover principles are used as far as transactional decision making is concerned.

Fibannoci Weighted Averages

There is nothing mystical about the Fibannoci series. Its progression follows: 1, 1, 2, 3, 5, 8, 13, 21. . . . As can be seen, subsequent values are the result of adding the two immediately preceding values. Applying these weights to the generalized expression and data, we obtain:

$$\frac{(1 \times 21.55) + (1 \times 21.34) + (2 \times 21.47) + (3 \times 21.62) + (5 \times 21.47)}{1 + 1 + 2 + 3 + 5}$$

$$= \frac{258.04}{12} = 21.50$$

Exponentially Weighted Averages

There are numerous weighting techniques called exponential. We will explore only one here. Generally, most exponential averages consider all the data in the series, with each subsequent average being influenced by those

TABLE 2-7. EXPONENTIAL AVERAGES

Day	Close	e = .40		e = .10	
		XA_t	XA_{t-1}	XA_t	XA_{t-1}
1	21.55	21.55	21.55	21.55	21.55
2	21.34	21.47	21.55	21.53	21.55
3	21.47	21.47	21.47	21.53	21.53
4	21.62	21.53	21.47	21.54	21.53
5	21.55	21.54	21.53	21.55	21.54

Source: This table is based on Chicago Board of Trade data.

TABLE 2.8. COMPARATIVE VALUES[a]

Day	Close	e = .40		e = .10		e = .05	
		XA_t	XA_{t-1}	XA_t	XA_{t-1}	XA_t	XA_{t-1}
1	21.55	21.55	21.55	21.55	21.55	21.55	21.55
2	21.34	21.47S	21.55	21.53S	21.55	21.54S	21.55
3	21.47	21.47PE	21.47	21.53S	21.53	21.53S	21.54
4	21.62	21.53L	21.47	21.54L	21.53	21.53L	21.53
5	21.55	21.54L	21.53	21.55PE	21.54	21.53L	21.53

[a]L = long
S = short
PE = possible exit point
Source: This table is based on Chicago Board of Trade data.

averages calculated previously. Thus these averages do not lose or drop data as they move along in time as did the previous moving averages.

The generalized expression is:

$$XA_t = eP_t + (1 - e) XA_{t-1}$$

where

XA_t = the exponentially smoothed average for the most recent session
e = the smoothing weight
P_t = the closing price
$(1 - e)$ = the smoothing factor for the previous session's average
XA_{t-1} = the previous session's exponential average

Before substituting data from Table 2.1, one conventional way of starting up the series is to assume that $XA_t = XA_{t-1}$ at the departure point, since there is no previously established value for XA_{t-1} at that point.

Table 2.7 presents XA_t and XA_{t-1} values for two different e (smoothing) weights. As a rule, the greater the responsiveness the trader wants the average to possess the higher the assigned weight to the price. Also, the weight value is greater than zero but less that one, or $0 < e < 1$.

Note: This technique is very useful for fundamental analysis and forecasting studies as well.

Comparisons

The results for the examined moving averages are presented in Table 2.8. Note the values and their variations. These are important since different transactions may be indicated by the techniques followed. In other words, it can occur that one technique is long while another is short in a given market.

GEOMETRIC MEAN

The geometric mean can be either less than or equal to the arithmetic mean—it is never greater than it. The Value Line Index is based on the geometric mean; whereas the Standard & Poors (S & P) and New York Stock Exchange (NYSE) indexes are adjusted weighted averages. The geometric mean is widely used for determining averages of rates of change, price indexes, and ratio analyses. It should be noted that it is suitable only for positive numbers, but this is not a major drawback as relative pricing can be implemented. Two methods are used to calculate the geometric mean. The first calculates the nth root of the multiplicative product of the series, or $\sqrt[n]{p_1 \times p_2 \times \ldots \times p_n}$.

The second approach is:

$$\text{Geometric mean} = \frac{\Sigma \log p}{n}$$

Though both produce identical results, the second approach is more frequently used for large series due to its computational ease.

FILTERS

Filters are also known as bands, channels, windows, or corridors. They are lines surrounding the path of a series of data, be they actual or smoothed. In a way, they are surrogates for support and resistance lines. Figures 2.1 and 2.2 represent two examples of this.

This technique is similar to the crossover principle. Should prices penetrate the upward band, a buy condition occurs; if prices go below the lower band, a sell condition occurs. The premise of this technique is that the bands permit prices to vary within tolerable limits; however, a movement through a band causes the system to generate a transaction: buy, sell, go neutral. Typically, bands are constructed on a percentage basis of a smoothed price series. Actual prices then dictate market posture relative to where actual prices are to the bands or smoothed series. Table 2.9 lists four bands representing two cases.

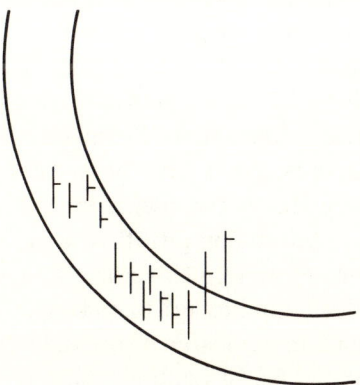

FIGURE 2.1 Filter example

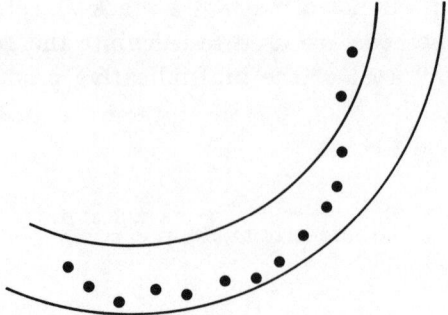

FIGURE 2.2 Filter example

TABLE 2.9. LISTING OF BANDS

Day	Smoothed Series	Upper Band	Lower Band	Upper Band	Lower Band
1	21.55	21.77	21.33	22.20	20.90
2	21.47	21.68	21.26	22.11	20.83
3	21.47	21.68	21.26	22.11	20.83
4	21.53	21.75	21.31	22.18	20.88
5	21.54	21.76	21.32	22.19	20.89

Source: This table is based on Chicago Board of Trade data.

OSCILLATORS

These analytical tools arise from the differences of two price series. The series may be actual prices themselves minus a moving average series of the difference between two moving average series. It is most useful in trying to determine overbought/oversold conditions. Table 2.10 presents the closing prices, the 5- and 10-day moving averages, and the oscillator values.

The previous sections of this chapter presented smoothing and filtering techniques. Oscillators consider another facet of price action—the rate of price change. Usually this technique is used to sensitize the operator to potential turning points in a series as it measures the speed or departure of one series to another. The premise here is, generally, the greater the departure from the benchmark series the more likely the occurrence of a reactionary phase to return to the benchmark. One major pitfall to a reliance on this simplistic technique is the occurrence of an explosive or climactic move in prices, particularly if the trader used such indicators to dictate the market posture taken. This can lead to being short an explosive bull market or long a panic decline. This tool tends to be more useful in trading affair markets which do not exhibit strong trending characteristics.

TABLE 2.10. AN OSCILLATOR EXAMPLE

Date	Close	5-Day Moving Average	10-Day Moving Average	Oscillator
November 20	22.20	22.16	22.32	−.16
November 23	22.00	22.12	22.24	−.12
November 24	21.68	22.04	22.17	−.13
November 25	21.80	21.97	22.11	−.14
November 27	21.92	21.92	22.05	−.13
November 30	21.75	21.83	22.00	−.17
December 1	22.16	21.86	21.99	−.13
December 2	21.95	21.92	21.98	−.06
December 3	21.99	21.95	21.96	−.01
December 4	22.32	22.03	21.98	+.05
December 7	21.95	22.07	21.95	+.12
December 8	21.55	21.95	21.91	+.04
December 9	21.70	21.90	21.91	−.01
December 10	21.53	21.81	21.88	−.07
December 11	21.53	21.65	21.84	−.19
December 14	21.30	21.52	21.80	−.28
December 15	21.05	21.42	21.69	−.27
December 16	20.97	21.28	21.59	−.31
December 17	21.00	21.17	21.49	−.32
December 18	20.73	21.01	21.33	−.32
December 21	20.52	20.85	21.19	−.34
December 22	20.45	20.73	21.08	−.35
December 23	20.54	20.65	20.96	−.31
December 24	20.81	20.61	20.89	−.28
December 28	20.94	20.65	20.83	−.18
December 29	20.60	20.67	20.76	−.09
December 30	20.60	20.70	20.72	−.02
December 31	20.38	20.67	20.66	+.01
January 4	20.40	20.58	20.60	−.02
January 5	20.32	20.46	20.56	−.10
January 6	20.62	20.46	20.57	−.11
January 7	20.87	20.52	20.61	−.09
January 8	20.74	20.59	20.63	−.04
January 11	20.65	20.64	20.61	+.03
January 12	20.56	20.69	20.57	+.12
January 13	20.60	20.68	20.57	+.11
January 14	20.69	20.65	20.58	+.07
January 15	20.61	20.62	20.61	+.01
January 18	20.70	20.63	20.64	−.01
January 19	20.58	20.64	20.66	−.02
January 20	20.68	20.65	20.67	−.02
January 21	20.78	20.67	20.66	+.01
January 22	20.87	20.72	20.67	+.05
January 25	21.01	20.78	20.71	+.07
January 26	21.48	20.96	20.80	+.16
January 27	21.55	21.14	20.90	+.24
January 28	21.34	21.25	20.96	+.29
January 29	21.47	21.37	21.05	+.32
February 1	21.62	21.49	21.14	+.35
February 2	21.55	21.51	21.24	+.27

Source: This table is based on Chicago Board of Trade data.

VOLUME

Volume refers to the amount of trading activity. Usually, it means the total trading for all the months for a given commodity. In Example 1, the volume activity for the Chicago Board of Trade T-note futures for the trading session of July 23, 1986 is shown.

Example 1

Delivery Months	Volume
September 1986	19,149
December 1986	1,519
March 1987	14
June 1987	0
Total	20,682

Source: This table is based on Chicago Board of Trade data.

In this case, the total volume was 20,682 contracts, though each futures month had a different activity. Guidelines for analyzing volume are presented in Table 2.11.

On Balance Volume

On balance volume (OBV) is a quantitative approach of the analysis of volume. It compares similar prices to their respective OBV statistics. Its purpose is to identify phases of accumulation/distribution. It tends to be particularly useful for phases prior to breakouts (upside thrust) and breakdowns (downside thrusts). Two numerical examples of this are shown in Tables 2.12 and 2.13.

The first example presents a situation of accumulation (rising OBV) while the latter presents distribution (declining OBV). As can be seen, the September British pound futures contract displayed accumulation, particularly from

TABLE 2.11. GUIDELINES FOR ANALYZING VOLUME

Price Action	Volume	Interpretation
Slight rise	Unusually heavy	Bearish
Rising	Increasing	Bullish
Rising	Steady	Bullish
Rising	Decreasing	Bearish
Declining	Increasing	Bearish
Declining	Steady	Bearish
Declining	Decreasing	Bullish
Slight decline	Unusually heavy	Bullish

TABLE 2.12. OBV UPSIDE BREAKOUT: ACCUMULATION BRITISH POUND

Date	Price	Change	Volume	OBV
May 11	202.60	−1.60	−3,231	−3,231
May 14	203.40	.80	+1,970	−1,261
May 15	205.80	2.40	+2,619	+1,358
May 16	205.10	−.70	−1,006	+352
May 17	204.90	−.20	−1,071	−719
May 18	204.50	−.40	−1,025	−1,744
May 21	203.55	−.95	−990	−2,734
May 22	204.10	.55	+903	−1,831
May 23	204.90	.80	+991	−840
May 24	204.60	−.30	−512	−1,352
May 25	204.10	−.50	−502	−1,854
May 29	204.95	.85	+785	−1,069
May 30	205.40	.45	+837	−232
May 31	206.35	.95	+3,174	+2,942
June 1	207.25	.90	+2.088	+5,030
June 4	207.20	−.05	−1,396	+3,634
June 5	207.45	.25	+1,815	+5,449
June 6	206.75	−.70	−2,203	+3,246
June 7	205.95	−.80	−1,368	+4,614
June 8	205.40	−.55	−2,183	+2,431
June 11	206.35	.95	+996	+3,427
June 12	208.50	2.15	+4,484	+7,911
June 13	208.80	.30	+4,259	+12,170
June 14	208.10	−.70	−2,334	+9,836
June 15	209.55	1.45	+2,518	+12,354

TABLE 2.13. OBV DOWNSIDE BREAKDOWN: DISTRIBUTION OF HEATING OIL

Date	Price	Change	Volume	OBV
November 2	101.40	.30	+4,789	+4,789
November 3	101.45	.05	+3,410	+8,199
November 4	101.60	.15	+3,449	+11,648
November 5	101.35	−.25	−6,550	+5,098
November 6	101.60	.25	+4,243	+9,341
November 9	101.55	−.05	−2,515	+6,826
November 10	101.60	.05	+4,183	+11,009
November 11	101.35	−.25	−4,334	+6,675
November 12	101.25	−.10	−3,355	+3,320
November 13	101.00	−.25	−3,341	−21
November 16	100.65	−.35	−3,708	−3,729
November 17	100.50	−.15	−4,295	−8,024
November 18	100.30	−.20	−4,436	−12,460
November 19	100.65	.35	+3,648	−8,812
November 20	100.40	−.25	−4,095	−12,907
November 23	100.20	−.20	−3,813	−16,720
November 24	100.15	−.05	−2,482	−19,202
November 25	100.07	−.08	−2,853	−22,055
November 27	99.97	−.10	−3,447	−25,502
November 30	99.80	−.17	−6,251	−31,753

May 11 to mid-June. Notice how the OBV statistics generally increase in value for similar prices as time goes on. It is this strengthening in values which is suggestive of an accumulation phase prior to an upside breakout (see Chart 2.5).

Conversely, the formidable breakdown in May heating oil futures was suggested by the rapid deterioration in its OBV statistics, particularly from November 1 to the end of that month. Chart 2.6 graphically portrays the collapse following the distribution phase.

To calculate OBV, one assigns a plus value to the daily volume for an up-change in price, a minus to the daily volume for a down-change in price, and

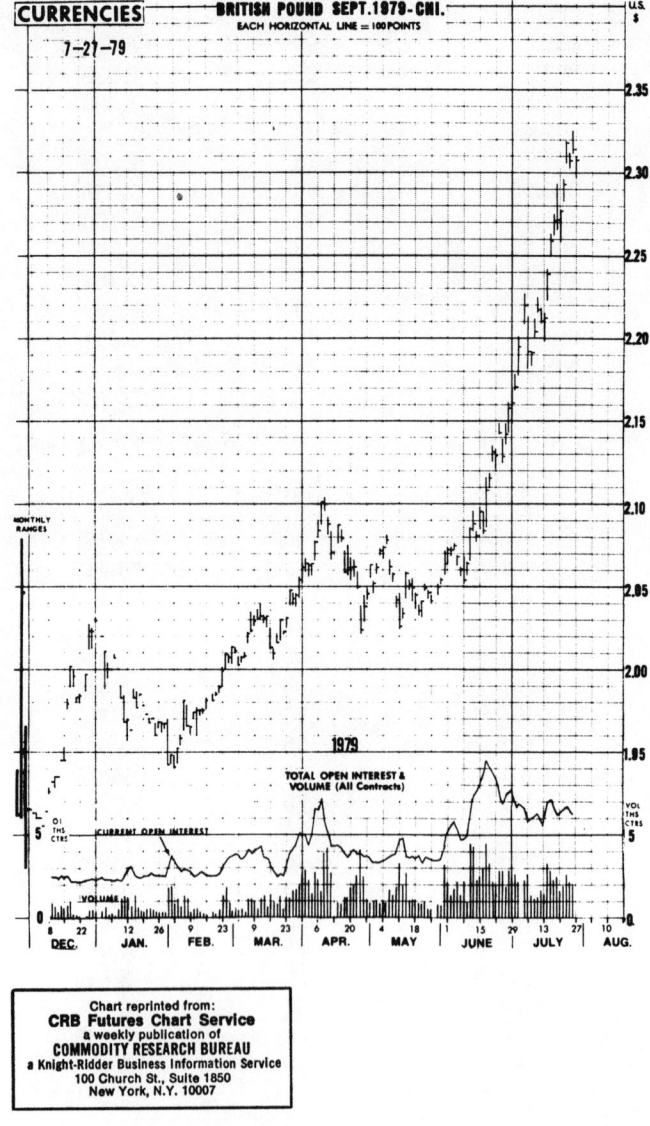

CHART 2.5 Accumulation

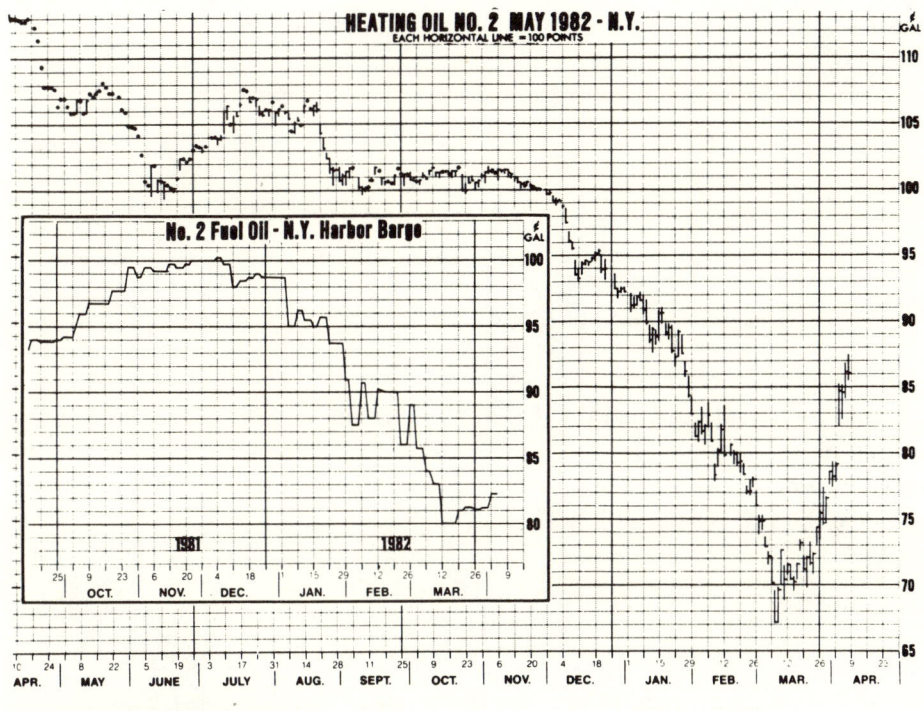

CHART 2.6 Distribution

no assignment for an unchanged session. For the last step, that session's volume is essentially omitted.

Variations in determining OBV include:

1. Use moving average total values, such as: 40, 80, 100 OBV statistics.
2. Once an OBV statistic is determined, continue to add/subtract to that series with no dropping or deleting of any former value.
3. Use only volume assigned to a particular futures contract month.
4. Use total volume assigned to a commodity even though focus is on one specific month.
5. Use a series of the nearby spot futures months.

OPEN INTEREST

The open interest statistic reflects the open commitment for a given commodity. It has two components. The first is the individual futures month; the second is the total open interest for all active months for the given commodity.

TABLE 2.14. GUIDELINES FOR ANALYZING OPEN INTEREST

Prices	Open Interest	Interpretation	Rationale
Up	Up	Bullish	Greater potential Shortcovering
Up	Down	Bearish	Shortcovering
Down	Up	Bearish	Greater potential Liquidation
Down	Down	Bullish	Liquidation

By open commitment it is meant that the number of contracts open or yet to be liquidated long equals the number of positions open or yet to be covered short. Example 2 lists the open interest as of the close of business on July 22, 1986 for the Chicago Board of Trade T-note futures.

Example 2

Delivery Months	Open Interest	Change
September 1986	61,870	+621
December 1986	6,231	+410
March 1987	270	+4
June 1987	2	0
Total	68,373	+1,035

Source: This table is based on Chicago Board of Trade data.

The general interpretation for assessing open interest behavior is in Table 2.14.

Other methods analyze open interest to determine if it is experiencing seasonal growth or decline; or if it is displaying contraseasonal tendencies. Also, there is a great deal of research as to the participant composition, such as small speculators, large traders, and hedgers. This latter analysis seeks to determine whether there are unusual advances or declines in participant percentage holdings both from long and short perspectives.

GAPS

Among the more potent phenomena in technical analysis are the gaps. They occur in a variety of ways. Depending on the situation, traders may respond in a way expecting the gap to be filled (short-term view) and take a

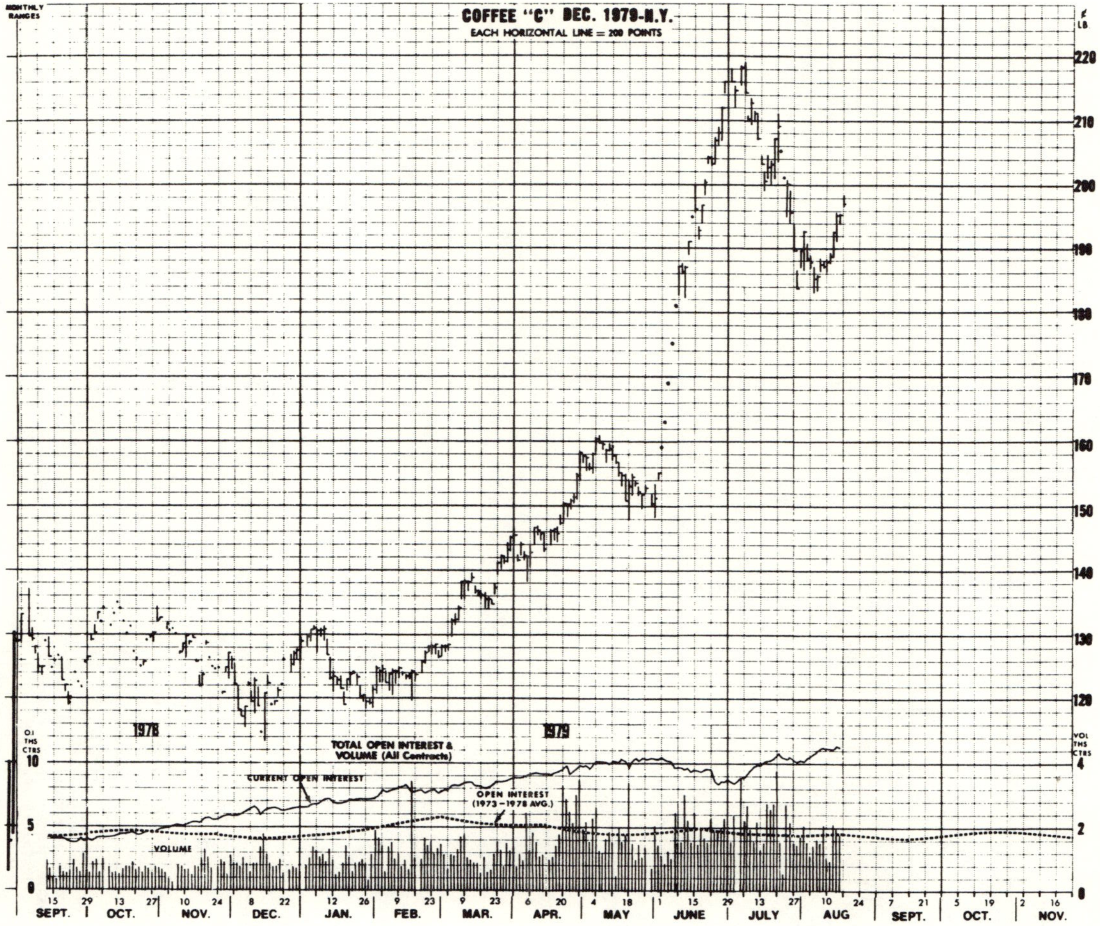

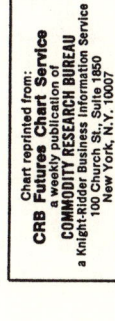
Chart reprinted from:
CRB Futures Chart Service
a weekly publication of
COMMODITY RESEARCH BUREAU
a Knight-Ridder Business Information Service
100 Church St., Suite 1850
New York, N.Y. 10007

COFFEE "C" DEC. 1979-N.Y.
EACH HORIZONTAL LINE = 200 POINTS

CHART 2.7 Dynamic gap

position opposite to the direction of the gap's price action. Other traders respond with the gap and prefer to position themselves with its price action. Here, they do not expect the gap to be filled soon. Generally, gaps occurring within a congestion (consolidation) area tend to be filled within a short time, while those occurring outside a congestion area tend to require more time to be filled and the subsequent move is more dynamic. In fact, the greater the initial gap size, the larger the subsequent move tends to be.

This text will focus on dynamic gaps. Gaps tend to occur when the market did not adequately discount a particular event or prospect. This event may be

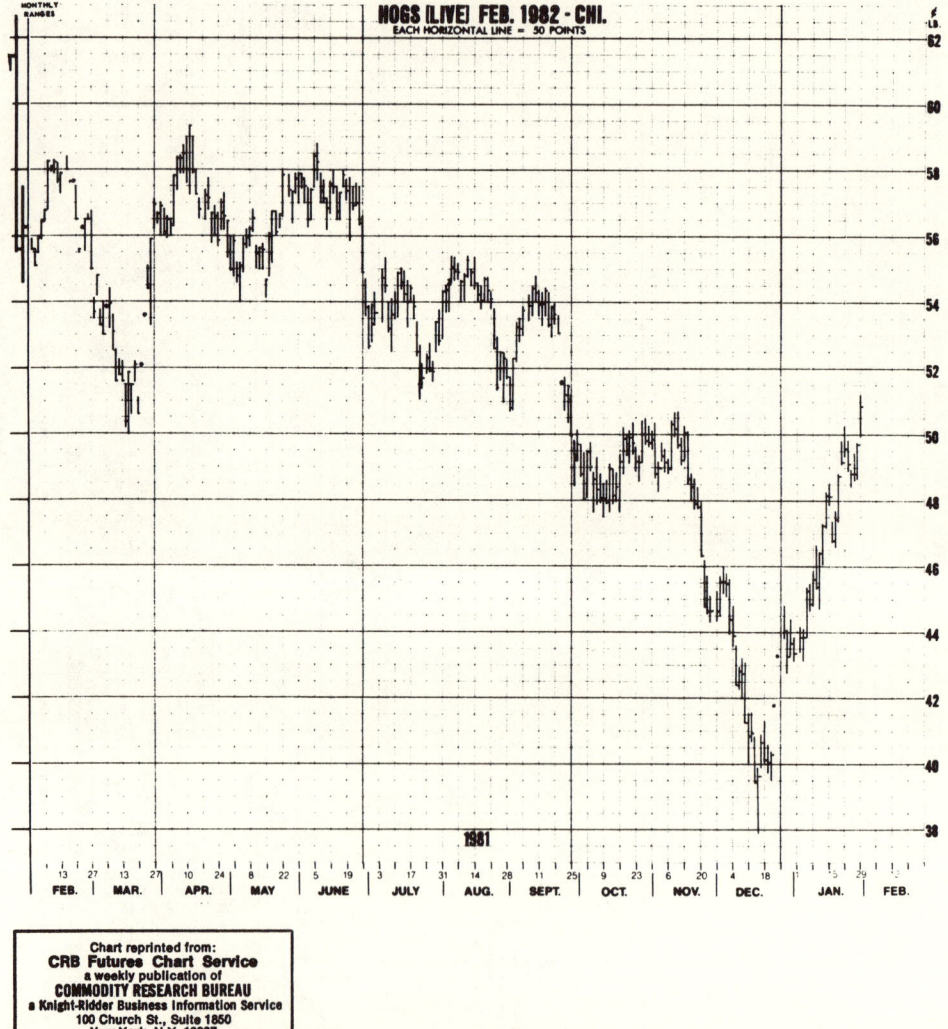

CHART 2.8 Dynamic gap

an embargo declaration, a significant agricultural freeze in a major growing region, an unexpected economic report, or massive currency intervention. For the market not to discount these events prior to the fact makes sense since they are extremely unpredictable and extraordinary in economic importance. Once given the extraordinary event, the market swiftly tries to evaluate its impact. Consider the following four examples: (1) the coffee market, (2) the hog market, (3) the pork belly market, and (4) the orange juice market. Charts 2.7, 2.8, 2.9, and 2.10 respectively represent these four situations.

Chart 2.7 highlights the power of a dot-gap situation. The dots represent limit-up pricing given a reported freeze in Brazil. Notice that once the market started to trade again, it approximately doubled the value of the dot-gap area. In other words, from the point of resumed trading the market continued to move upward to the extent of the effectively nontraded (or minimal activity) area. This phenomenon has tended to be fairly common in such situations.

Chart 2.8 presents the case of February 1982 live hogs. Notice the March 1981 and December 1981 advances. Both were ignited by dot-gap sparks. Also, the prolonged decline that developed during the summer months tended to

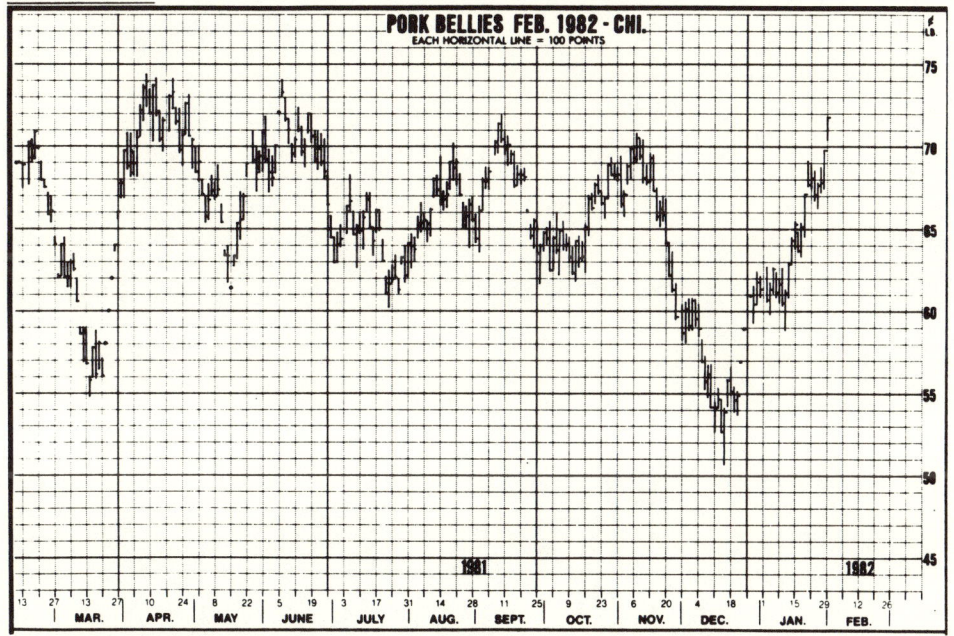

CHART 2.9 Dynamic gap

accelerate once a dot-gap occurred in September. These gaps coincided with pig crop reports.

Chart 2.9 presents the case of February 1982 pork bellies. Notice the similarities between sparked advances and dot-gap suggested declines. This chart also responded to the pig crop reports.

Chart 2.10 presents the case of May 1981 frozen concentrated orange juice futures. As depicted in chart 2.7, the freeze provoked run up and prompted a series of limit-up days, which started at approximately 85 cents per pound and continued to the $1.18 area. Again, the market resumed trading and climbed another 30 cents, which is approximately the value extent of the series of limit-up moves.

One interpretation for this phenomenon is that in this abrupt attempt to discount an extraordinary event, the market does not actively trade until

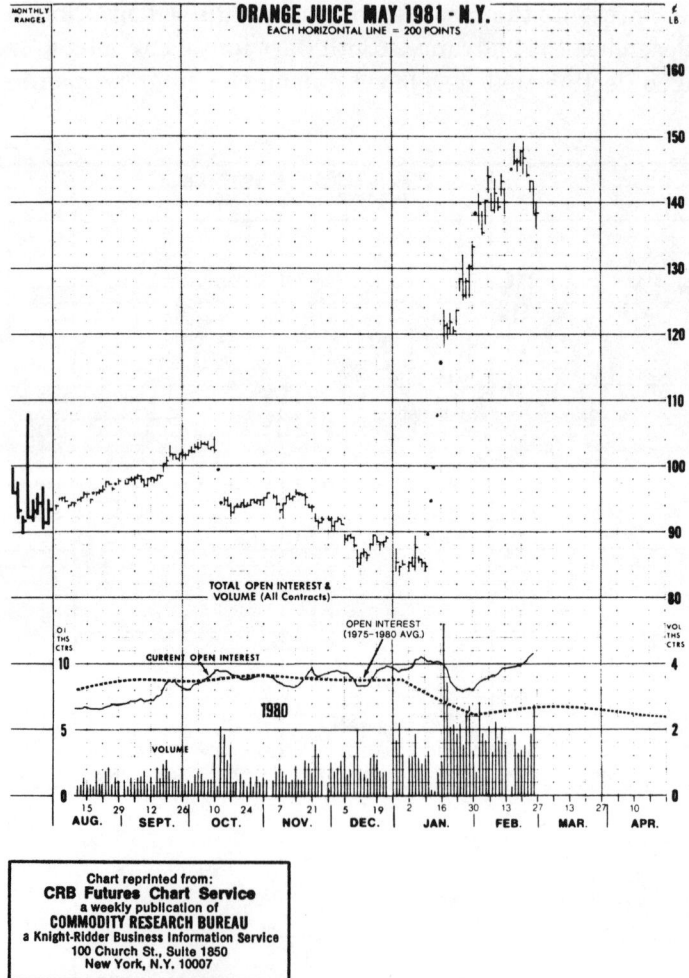

CHART 2.10 Dynamic gap

prices reach the first economically feasible area. This area is established not only by speculator actions but by hedgers. In a sense, when the market effectively resumes trading, it is giving a hint that this may be the low point of the new fundamentally justified equilibrium pricing area. In fact, prices tend to oscillate between the point of initial resumption of normal activity and the estimated extension of the move. This remains the case until another important news item occurs or the market reacts to new supply/demand influences dramatically.

TIME INTERVAL TECHNIQUES

Although prices are intrinsic to these techniques, selection of acceptable time intervals is the primary consideration. Like averaging processes, their purpose is trend identification; however, there is no smoothing algorithm. Instead of generating average prices, the time interval techniques focus on absolute price action for a specified time frame. This concept is related to the range statistic. For a given time series and selected time interval, the decision maker locates the maximum value and the minimum value and computes the range. The expression is:

$$\text{Maximum value} - \text{minimum value} = \text{range}$$

Here, the maximum value is the highest price, the minimum value is the lowest price, and the range is the difference between the two prices. Going one step further, the range provides an indication of risk size. Contrary to a popular Wall Street axiom, this technique operates on buy the (new) highs, and sell the (new) lows.

There are three basic techniques:

Daily

Weekly

Monthly

For all three time interval techniques, the transactional conditions are the same.

1. Buy the commodity if it makes a high greater than the high contained by the specified time interval.
2. Sell the commodity if it makes a low less than the low contained by the specified time interval.

There are variations for these transactional conditions. One requires the purchase or sale of the commodity on a penetration of the appropriate high or low. Another variation requires the purchase or sale only if the price closes above or below the appropriate high or low (whether absolute or on a closing basis).

Daily Interval

A daily interval is predetermined, be it 2 days, 5 days, 21 days, or whatever number of days the decision maker determines to be adequately reliable. Since markets do not usually fulfill their move in one leg, these techniques try to estimate the ordinary holding or consolidating periods. When the market makes a movement outside the given price range as defined by the time frame, then a transaction will occur. To illustrate this concept, consider Chart 2.11. It shows the June 1986 Kansas City value line with several buy/sell points.

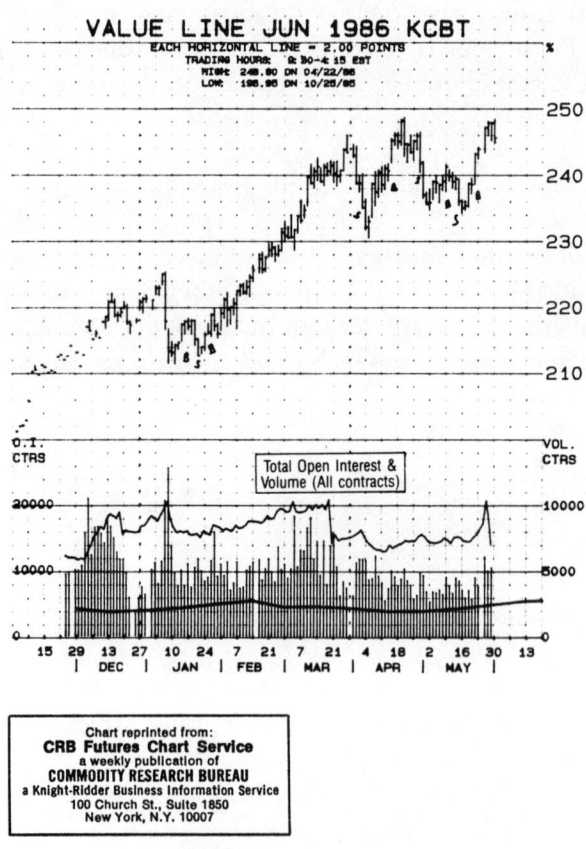

CHART 2.11 Daily interval

Weekly Interval

The weekly interval examines price-behavior-basis calendar week intervals. These intervals can be: 1, 2, 3, 4, 5 . . . weeks. Application is similar to that of the daily interval. Chart 2.12 shows the case of June 1986 MMI maxi contract.

Variations of this technique are:

1. Monday through Friday calendar week basis

2. Tuesday through following Monday calendar week basis

3. Wednesday through following Tuesday calendar week basis

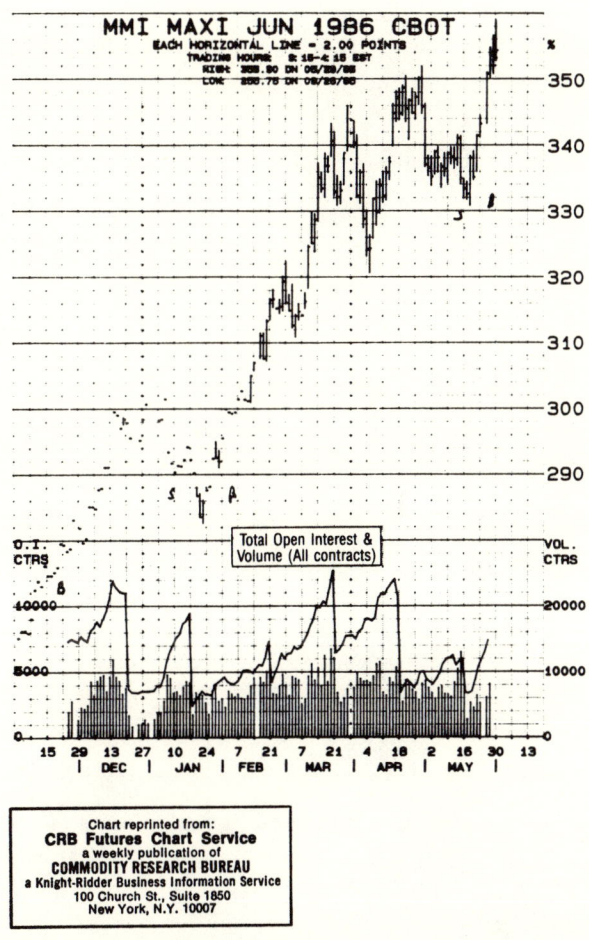

CHART 2.12 Weekly interval

4. Thursday through following Wednesday calendar week basis

5. Friday through following Thursday calendar week basis

If the market is not open for transactions on a given day due to a holiday that day would still be included in the determination of the calendar week interval, however, there would be no prices associated with it.

Monthly Interval

The monthly interval technique requires the use of calendar months instead of days or weeks. It is seldom directly applied in a strict mechanical trading system beyond a 3-month horizon because of the potential for rapidly expanding risk parameters. Nonetheless, its value is important. It can alert the trader to major moves and support/resistance levels. Also, it is amenable to long-term wave analysis such as the Elliott wave approach. Charts 2.13 and 2.14 demonstrate its power to predict major markets while highlighting its propensity toward escalating risk.

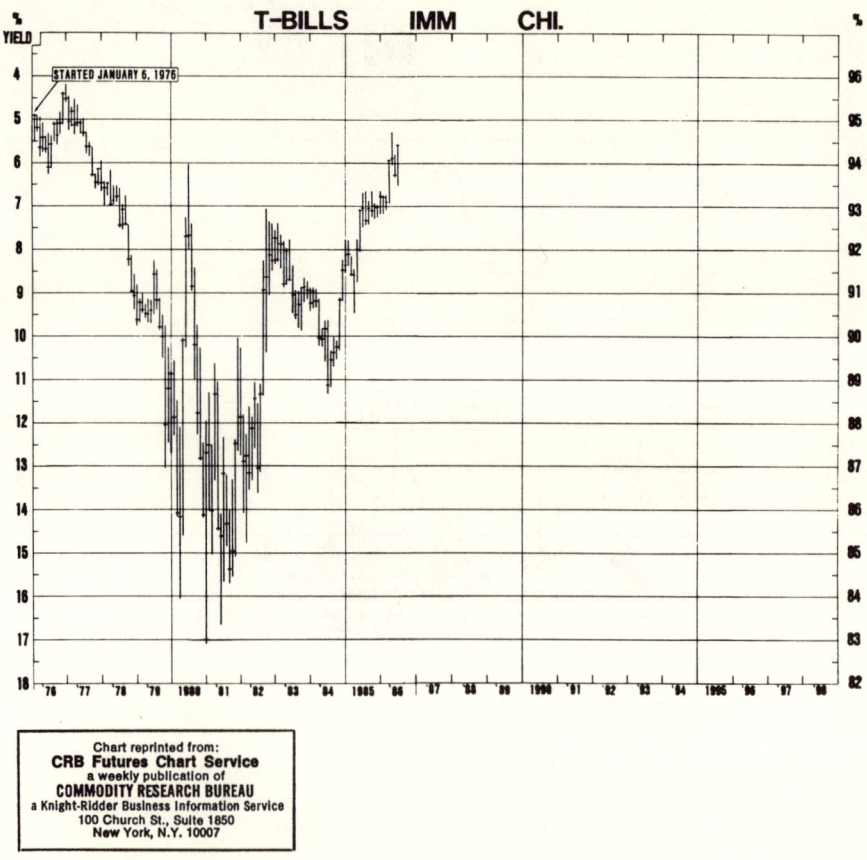

CHART 2.13 Monthly interval

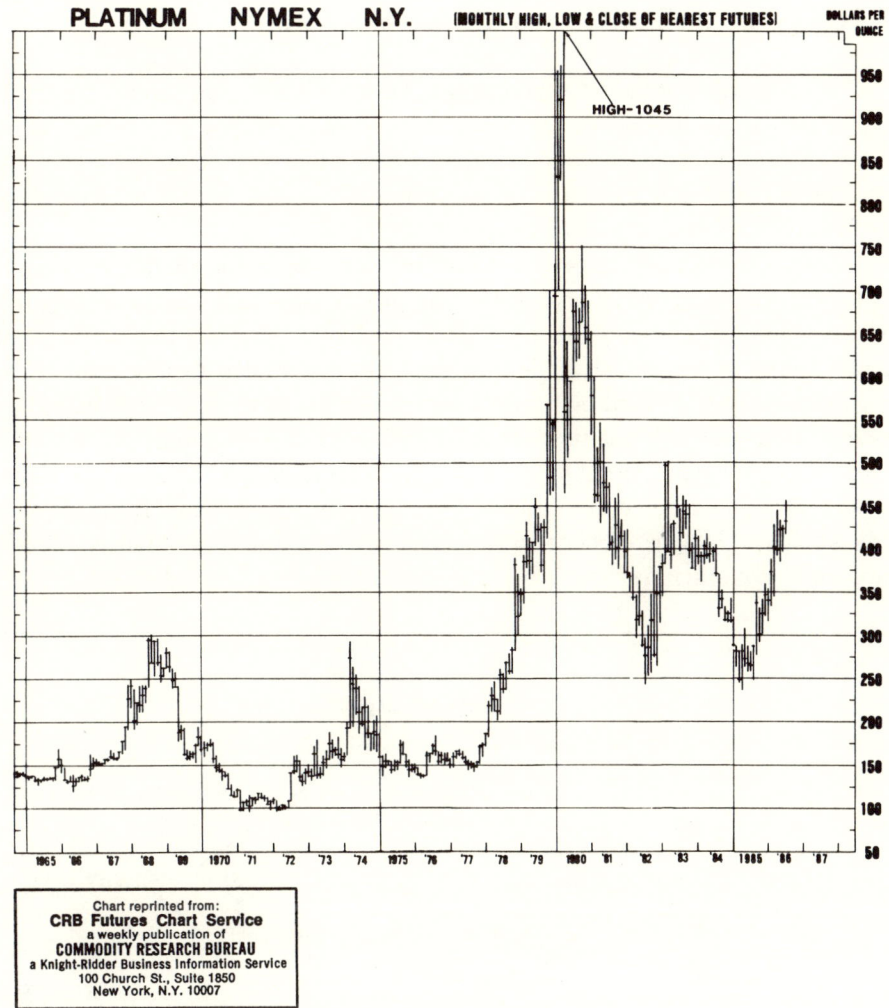

PLATINUM   NYMEX   N.Y.   (MONTHLY HIGH, LOW & CLOSE OF NEAREST FUTURES)

HIGH-1045

CHART 2.14 Monthly interval

Unequal Interval Arrangements

Unequal interval arrangements are applicable to the daily, weekly, and monthly interval techniques. Unlike the single parameter case for any of the aforementioned situations, unequal arrangements (two parameters) permit a neutral mode. The simple unitary case does not: It is either long or short once an initial transaction signal is generated. For the daily composite case, with 7- and 15-day parameters, initiating a trade requires a close outside the 15-day highs or lows; but to go neutral would require an appropriate close outside only the 7-day highs or lows. On a weekly basis a 1, 3 parameter arrangement means that to go either long or short, the market must close outside the 3-week high or low, however, to go neutral would require a close outside only the 1-week low or high.

FORECASTING MODELS COMMENTARY

The interdependence of observations for time series can cause substantial mathematical problems for certain methods while being advantageous for others. The former methodologies assume randomly independent data, the latter group does not. For this second group, the existence of lag dependency has fostered the emergence of adaptive modeling.

Incorporated into this adaptive methodology are differencing, moving average, and autoregressive processes. The procedures vary in complexity from simple exponential models to more elaborate ones such as Box-Jenkins. Although many exponential models assume independence in the error terms, they are still widely applied on an adaptive basis; however, the Box-Jenkins models make no such assumption, but rather their development tries to remove those incongruities by various differencing steps. Diagram 2.1 illustrates a decision tree comparison of five common approaches. It employs criteria such as: length of observation series, seasonality, volatility of data, peaks, and nonstationarity.

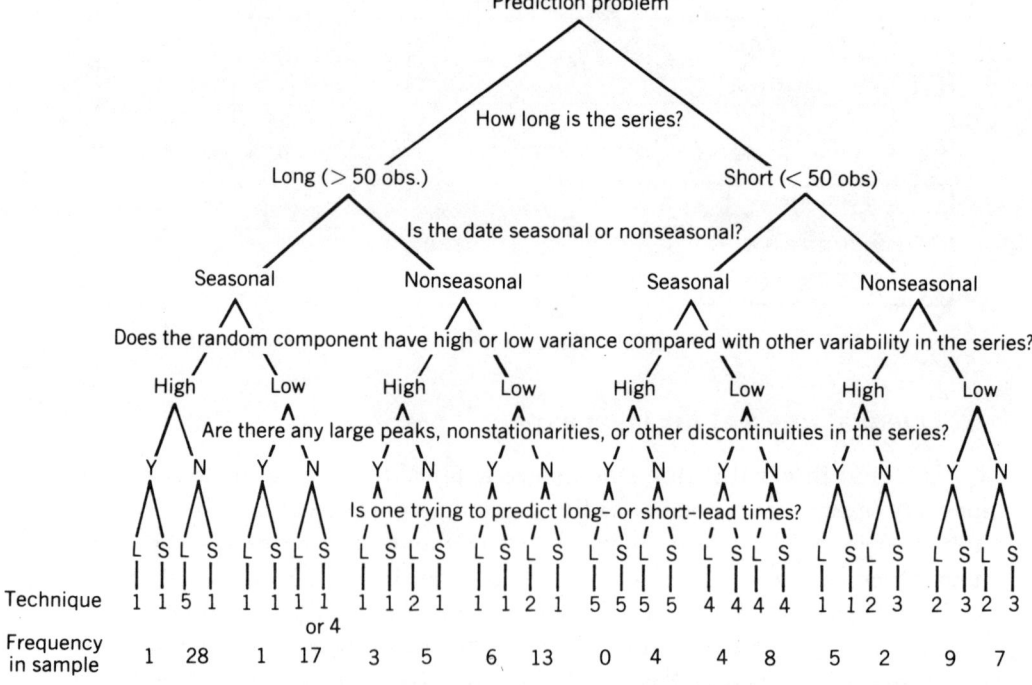

DIAGRAM 2.1 Time-series approaches; A method of choosing a time series prediction technique. Key to techniques: 1: Box-Jenkins; 2: Brown; 3: Modified Brown; 4: Holt-Winters; 5: Harrison. (*Source:* Reproduced by permission of the publishers, Charles Griffin & Company Ltd., of London, from Kendall, *Time Series*, 2nd Ed., 1976)

3
Chart Analysis

ART AND SCIENCE

Chart reading is one of the art forms of market analysis. Although it possesses a greater degree of subjective interpretation, quantitative tools are still applicable as will be seen in this chapter and others.

Art can be seen as one analogy to chart analysis. The prices are the artist's colors and the drawn chart is the picture on the canvas. Expectationally, it presents a useful picture. Chartists believe their charts represent supply and demand, support and resistance. By studying the configuration, one may detect a probable movement in price. Experienced chartists anticipate not only the next direction of the market but also its likely extent.

Chart analysis is founded on the premise that the chart's configurations depict all known information—technical, fundamental, political, and weather-related—for the commodity in question. On unknown information, chartists think the existing configuration may provide helpful hints to the nature of the next important news item and its attendant impact on the market.

As in other professions, chartists may not have a definitive opinion at all times. Rather, most wait for those situations that allow them to act on what appears to be a strong conditional case. The rest of the time, they assume a wait-and-see attitude.

IMPORTANT FORMATIONS

The following sections examine the more common and powerful chart formations. This is not an exhaustive presentation, but rather a generalized one. The subsequent sections classify formations according to their more dominant characteristics.

Congestion or Consolidation Formations

Congestion and consolidation are the most frequently observed formations. They occur at many stages within bull and bear markets. Whenever a market hesitates or seems to be holding within a trading pattern, the congestion or consolidation pattern emerges. Also, the first leg of a move can be assimilated into a consolidation formation. The duration, shape, and reliability of each formation varies considerably. Some of the more popular varieties are:

Triangles

Pennants

Rectangles

Occasionally, these formations appear at the culmination of a major move and thus become top or bottom formations.

Triangles

Triangles develop certain characteristics depending on whether the market is ready to rally or react. Some exhibit bullish tendencies, bearish tendencies, or neutral tendencies. Figures 3.1, 3.2, and 3.3 respectively represent these. Other names for these figures are: ascending triangle, descending triangle, and symmetric triangle.

Charts 3.1, 3.2, and 3.3 depict three actual cases with the formation outlined. Notice the subsequent price movements which developed from the apex points highlighted by the arrows.

FIGURE 3.1 Ascending triangle

FIGURE 3.2 Descending triangle

FIGURE 3.3 Symmetric triangle

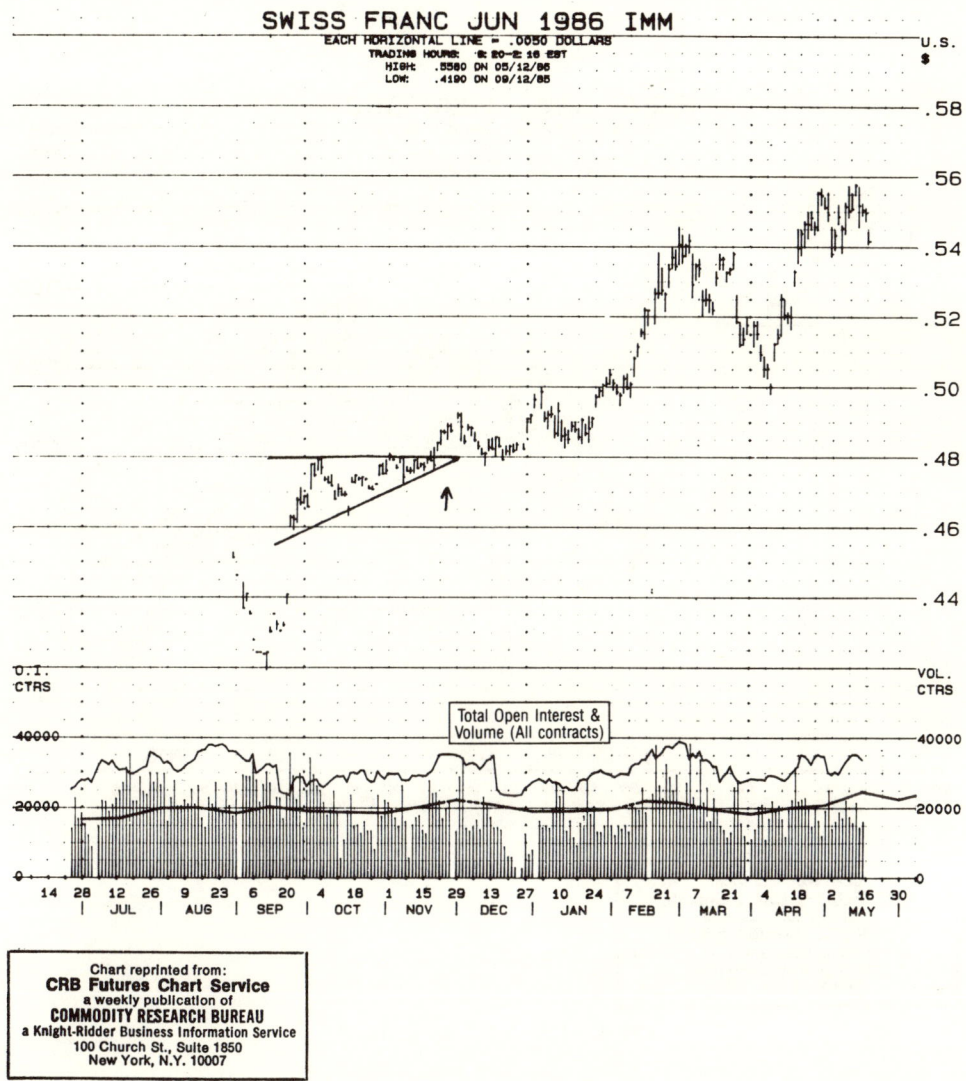

SWISS FRANC JUN 1986 IMM

EACH HORIZONTAL LINE = .0050 DOLLARS
TRADING HOURS: 8:20–2:16 EST
HIGH: .5580 ON 05/12/86
LOW: .4190 ON 09/12/85

Total Open Interest &
Volume (All contracts)

CHART 3.1 Ascending triangle

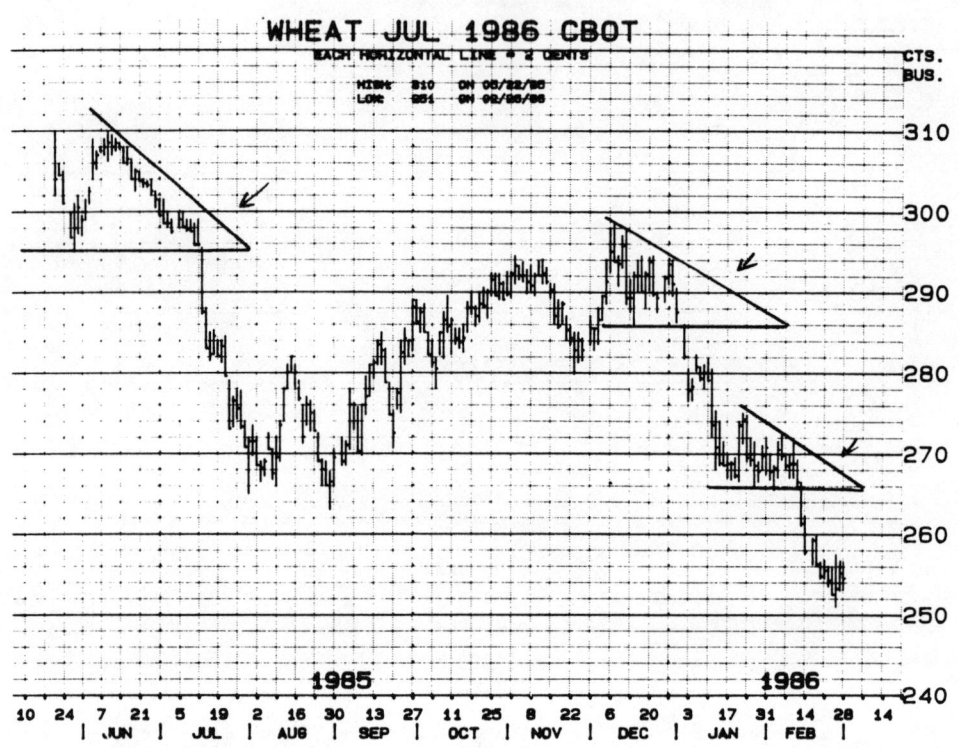

WHEAT JUL 1986 CBOT

EACH HORIZONTAL LINE = 2 CENTS

HIGH 310 ON 05/22/86
LOW 251 ON 02/05/86

CHART 3.2 Descending triangle

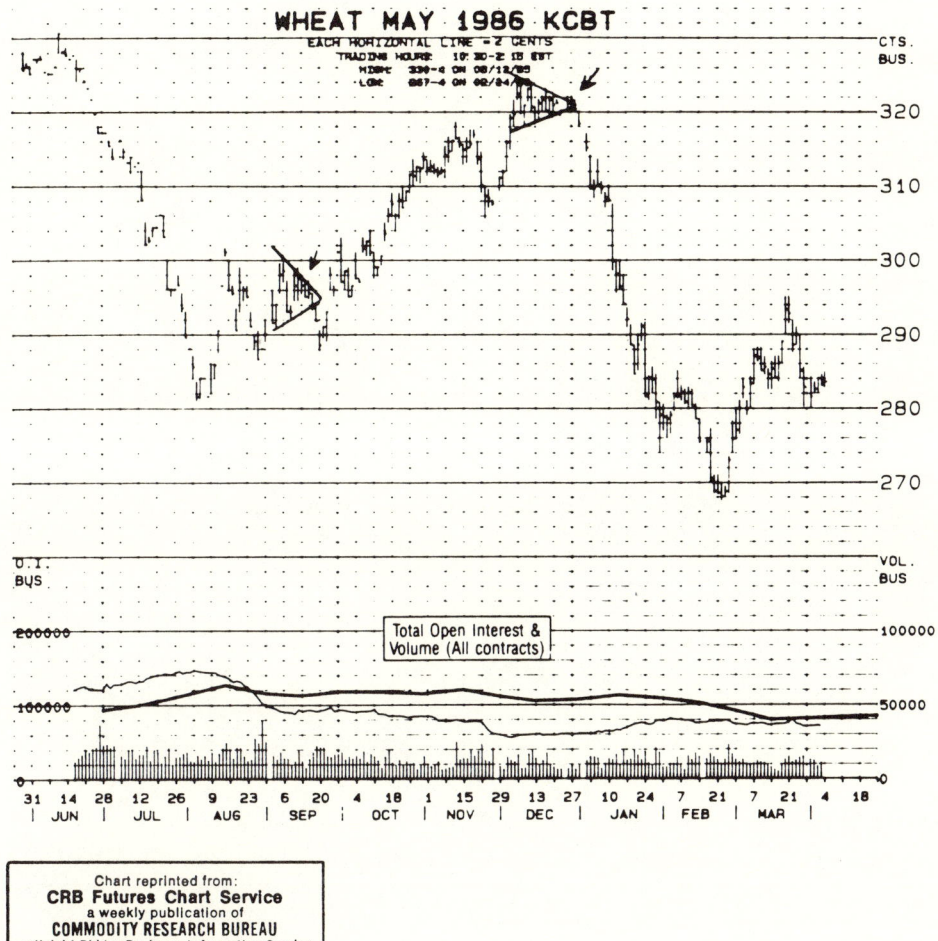

CHART 3.3 Symmetric triangle

Pennants

As pennant patterns develop, the price range displays constancy or a tendency toward a progressive narrowing. Figures 3.4, 3.5, 3.6, and 3.7 present the generalized cases. Actual cases are represented by Charts 3.4, 3.5, 3.6, and 3.7.

FIGURE 3.4 Pennant

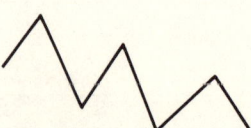

FIGURE 3.5 Pennant

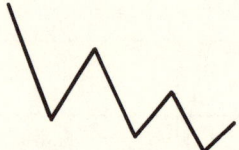

FIGURE 3.6 Pennant

FIGURE 3.7 Pennant

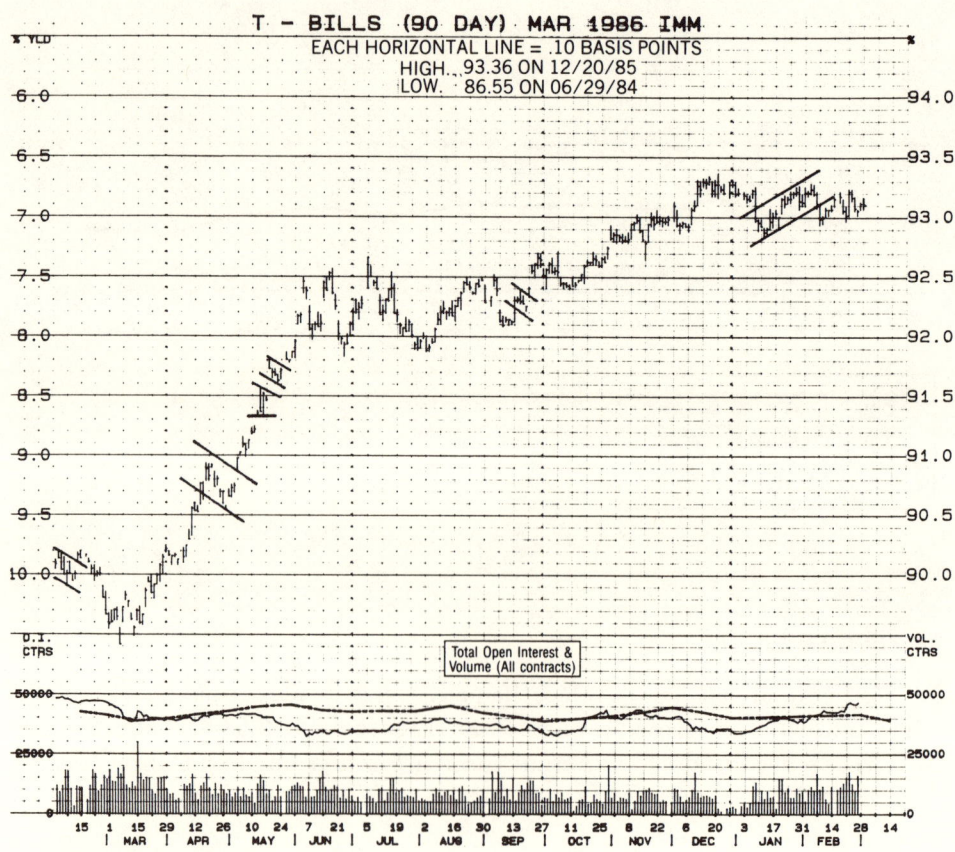

CHART 3.4 Pennant

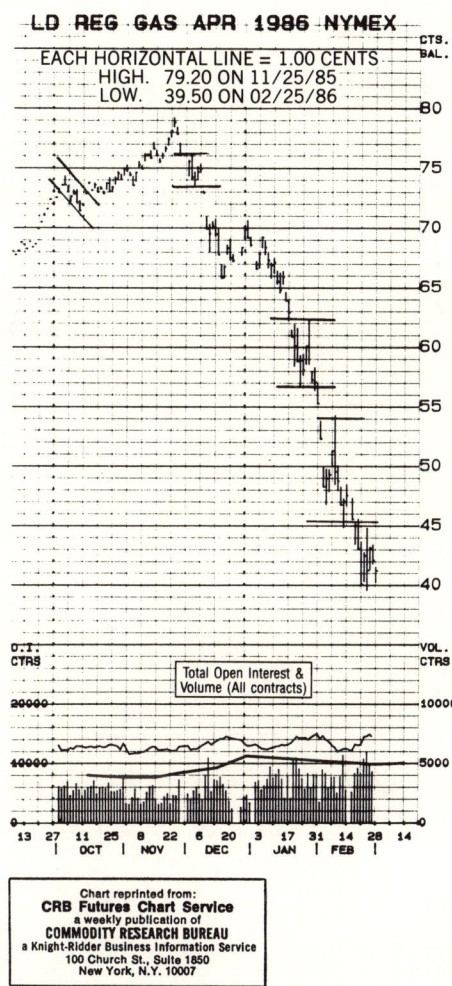

LD REG GAS APR 1986 NYMEX

EACH HORIZONTAL LINE = 1.00 CENTS
HIGH.   79.20 ON 11/25/85
LOW.   39.50 ON 02/25/86

Total Open Interest &
Volume (All contracts)

CHART 3.5 Pennant

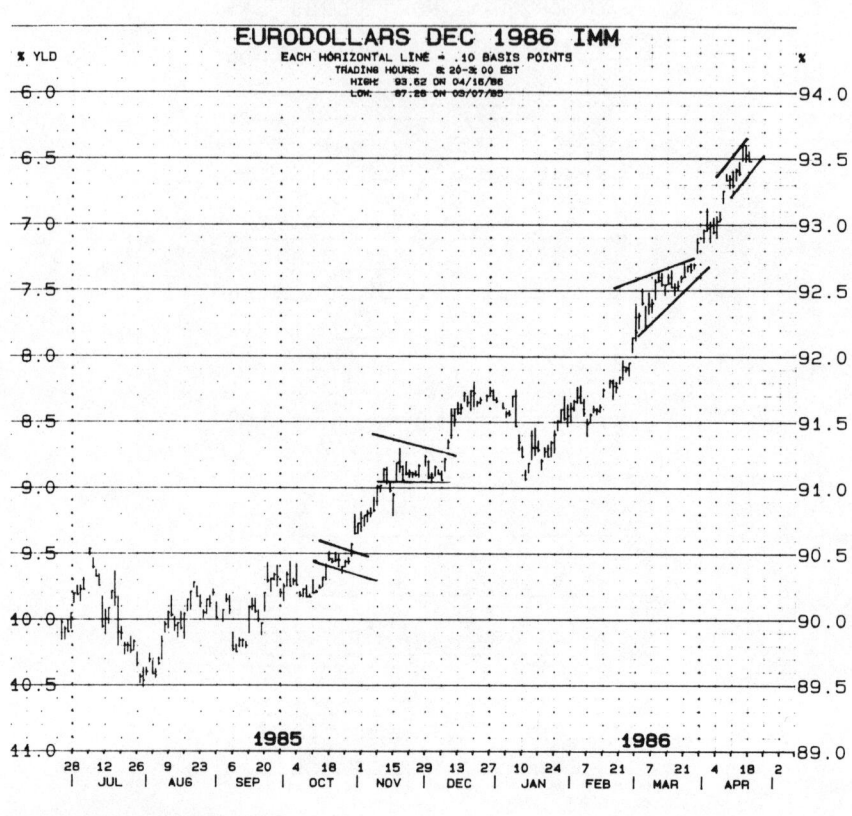

EURODOLLARS DEC 1986 IMM
EACH HORIZONTAL LINE = .10 BASIS POINTS
TRADING HOURS: 8: 20-3: 00 EST
HIGH: 93.62 ON 04/16/86
LOW: 87.26 ON 03/07/85

CHART 3.6 Pennant

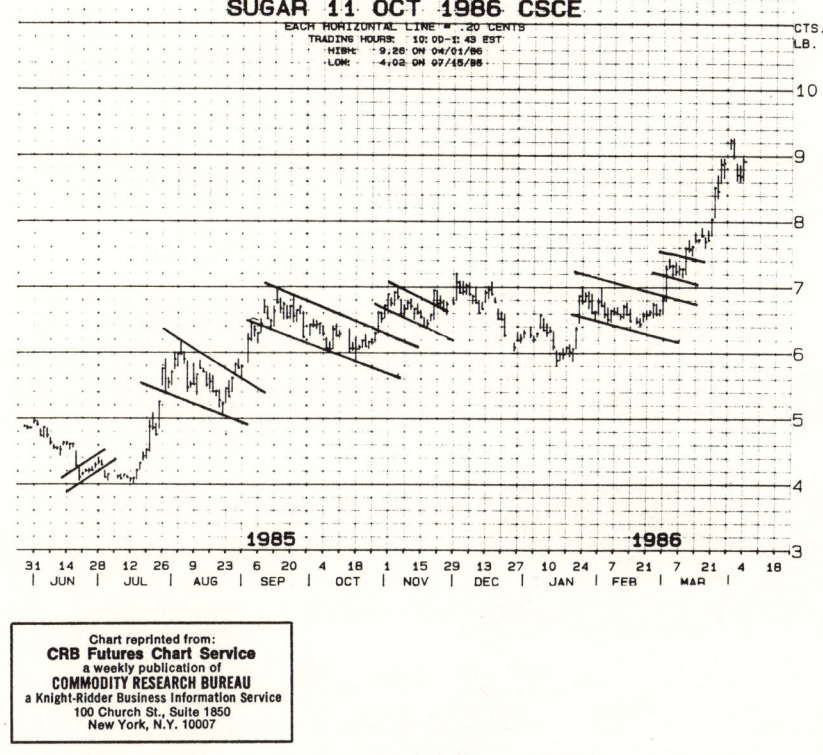

CHART 3.7 Pennant

Rectangles

These formations appear as their geometric name indicates. Their occurrence suggests an equality between the bearish and bullish elements in the marketplace. Upon the release of a news item or strong anticipation of an important development, prices depart from this pattern. Figures 3.8 and 3.9 provide generalized representations.

Two case histories are shown by Charts 3.8 and 3.9. Table 3.1 provides interpretive comments for price movements which depart from the three primary congestion formations.

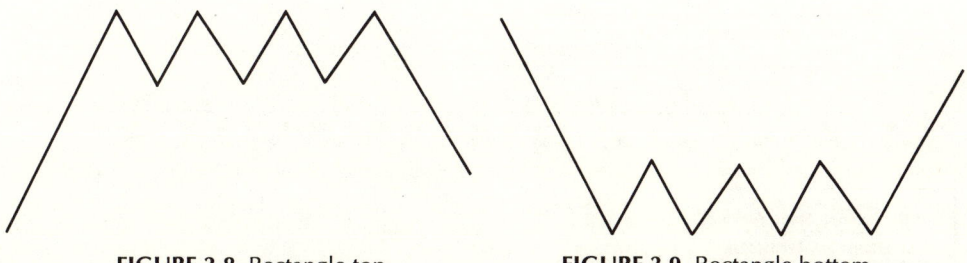

FIGURE 3.8 Rectangle top   **FIGURE 3.9** Rectangle bottom

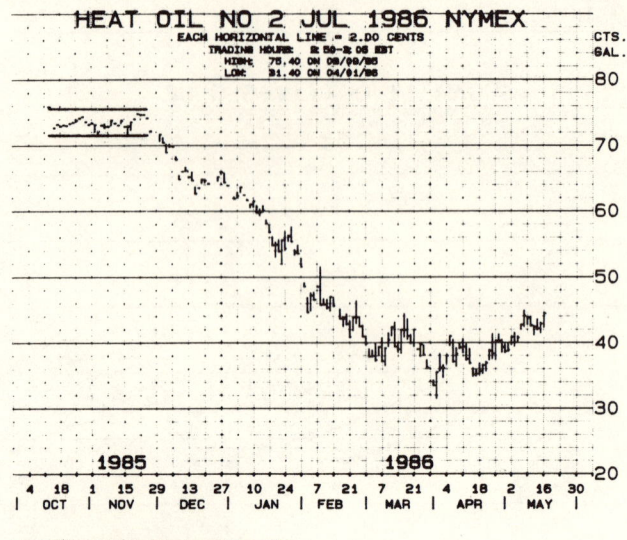

CHART 3.8 Rectangle top

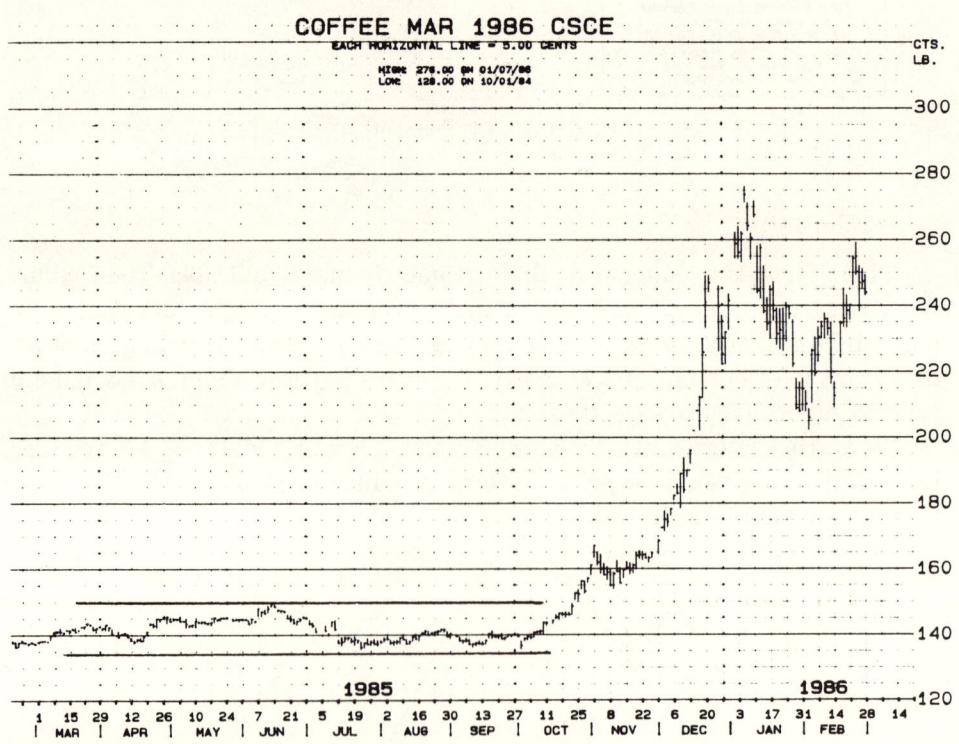

CHART 3.9 Rectangle bottom

TABLE 3.1. INTERPRETIVE TABLE FOR CHART FORMATIONS[a]

Consolidation Pattern	Price Range and Action	Awaited News Development	Subsequent Price Action	Rationale
Ascending triangle	Dampening and rising	Apparently bullish	Upward	News item confirms bullish sentiment
Ascending triangle	Dampening and rising	Apparently bullish	Downward	News item negates bullish sentiment
Descending triangle	Dampening and declining	Apparently bearish	Upward	News item negates bearish sentiment
Descending triangle	Dampening and declining	Apparently bearish	Downward	News item confirms bearish sentiment
Symmetric triangle	Dampening and leveling	Apparently neutral	Downward	News item indicates bearish situation
Symmetric triangle	Dampening and leveling	Apparently neutral	Upward	News item indicates bullish situation

[a]Rectangles, pennants, or wedges can be substituted for triangles for interpretative purposes.

Tops and Bottoms

These patterns occur at the culmination of significant moves. Their size, variety, and speed of completion vary widely. Regarding speed, they may be abrupt, such as island or key reversals; moderately swift, such as head and shoulders, double tops and bottoms; or slow, such as broadening tops and bottoms, and triple tops and bottoms.

Abrupt Formations

Islands and key reversals tend to occur in climatic moves. Sometimes, for a given commodity on a specific day, one contract month may display a reversal. For example, after a prolonged advance during which the shorts found it difficult to cover their positions, the market tended towards limit-up action. After the turning point, the downside collapse was just as dramatic, but now the longs found it difficult to liquidate. Usually, these developments coincide with force majeure type actions by exchanges or governmental bodies, or serious changes in market expectations. Charts 3.10 and 3.11 depict an island reversal top and bottom, while Charts 3.12 and 3.13 depict a key reversal top and bottom, respectively.

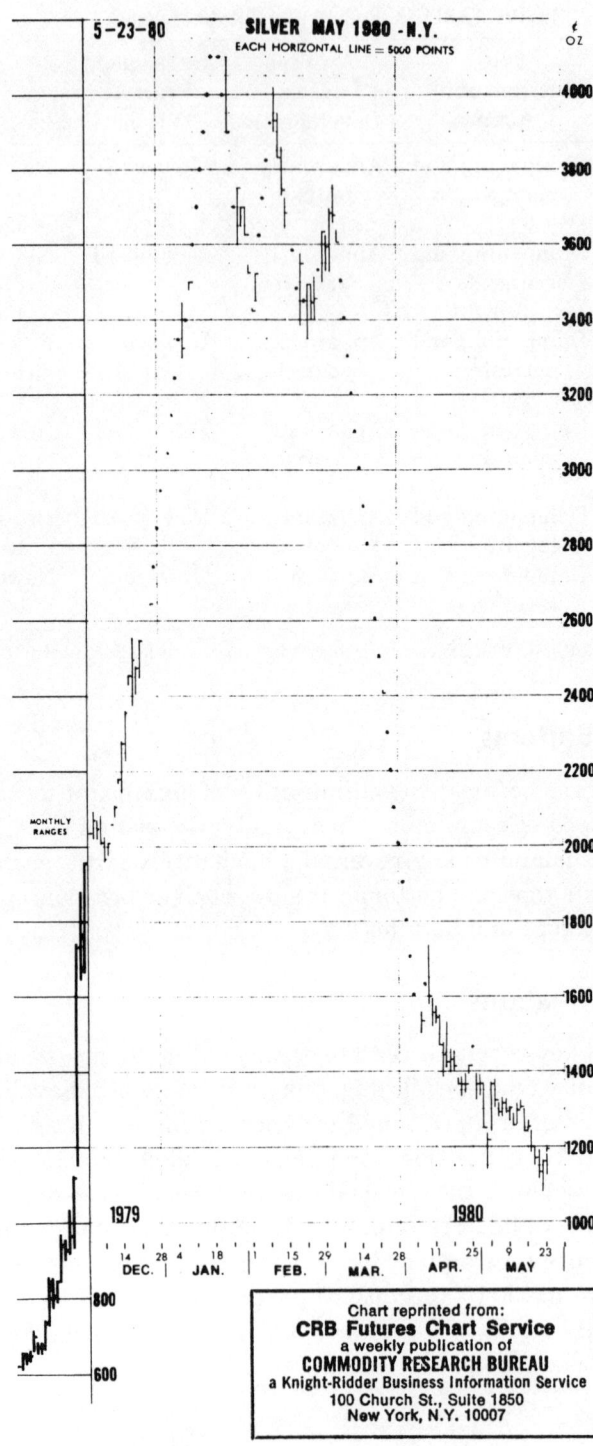

CHART 3.10 Island reversal top

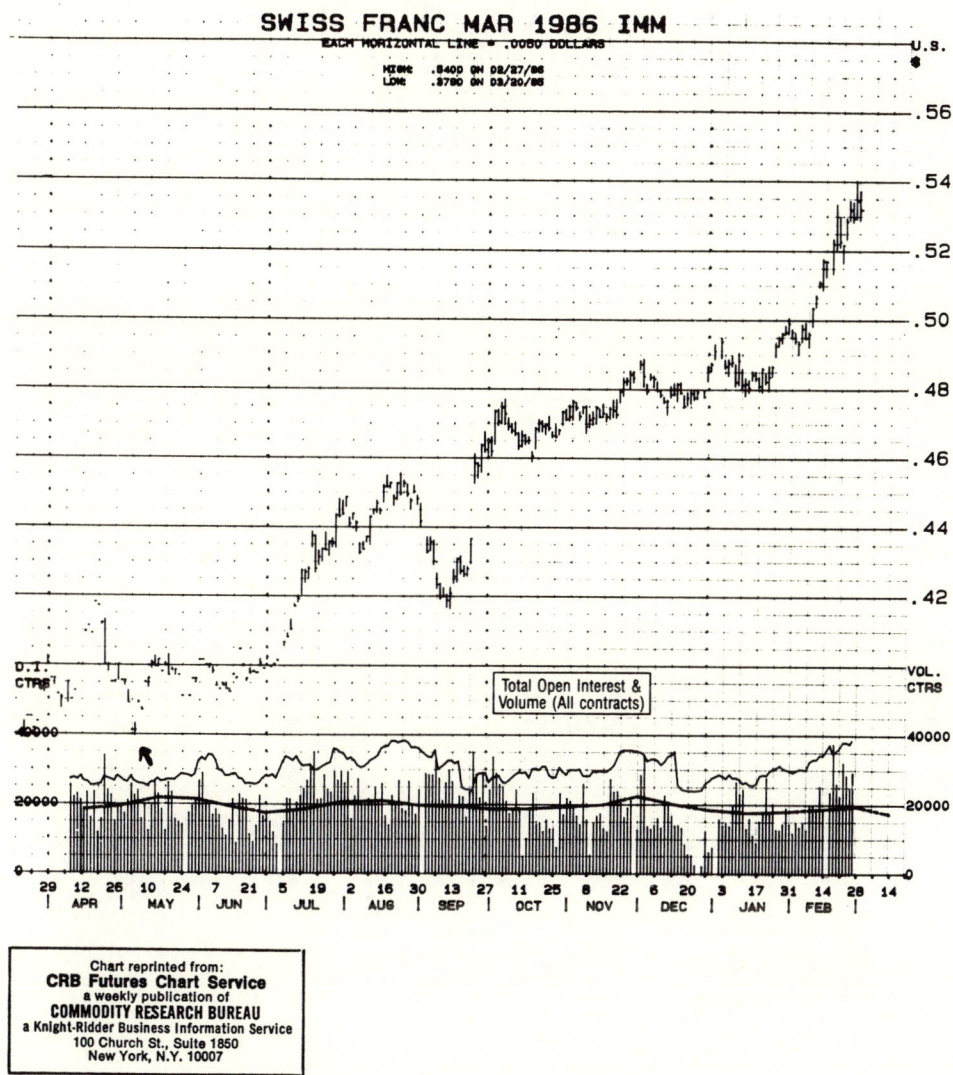

CHART 3.11 Island reversal bottom

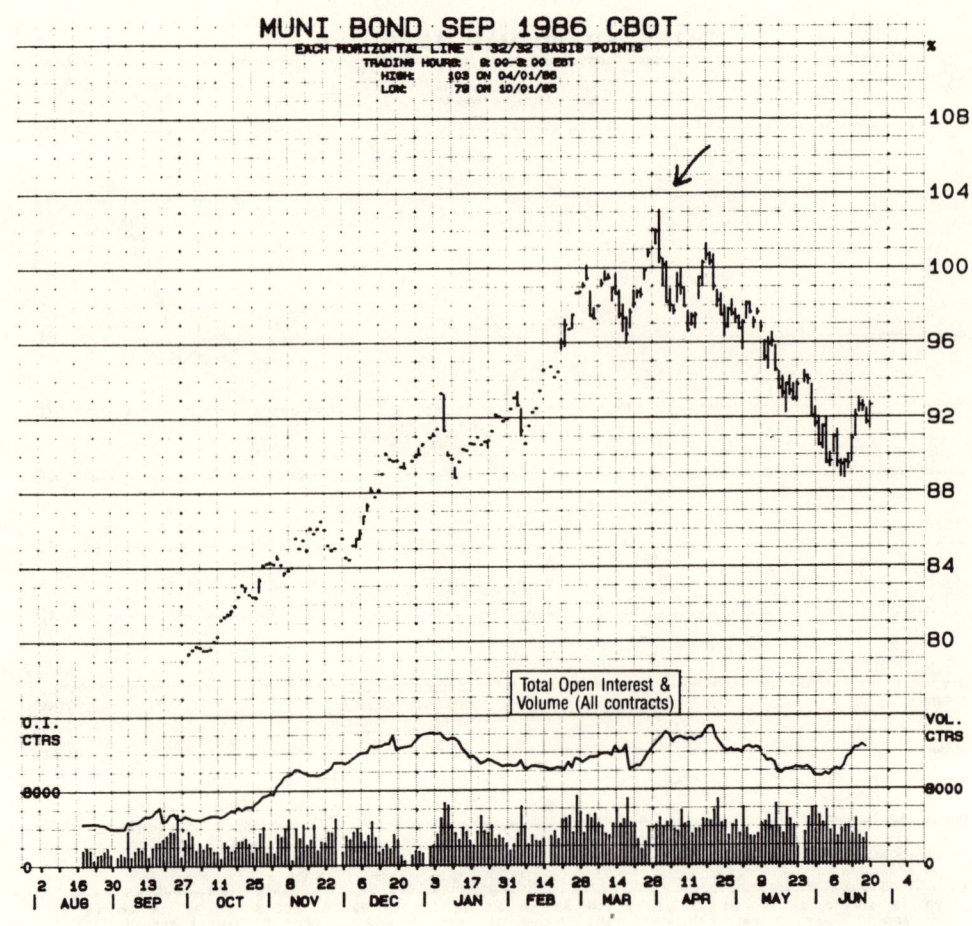

CHART 3.12 Key reversal top

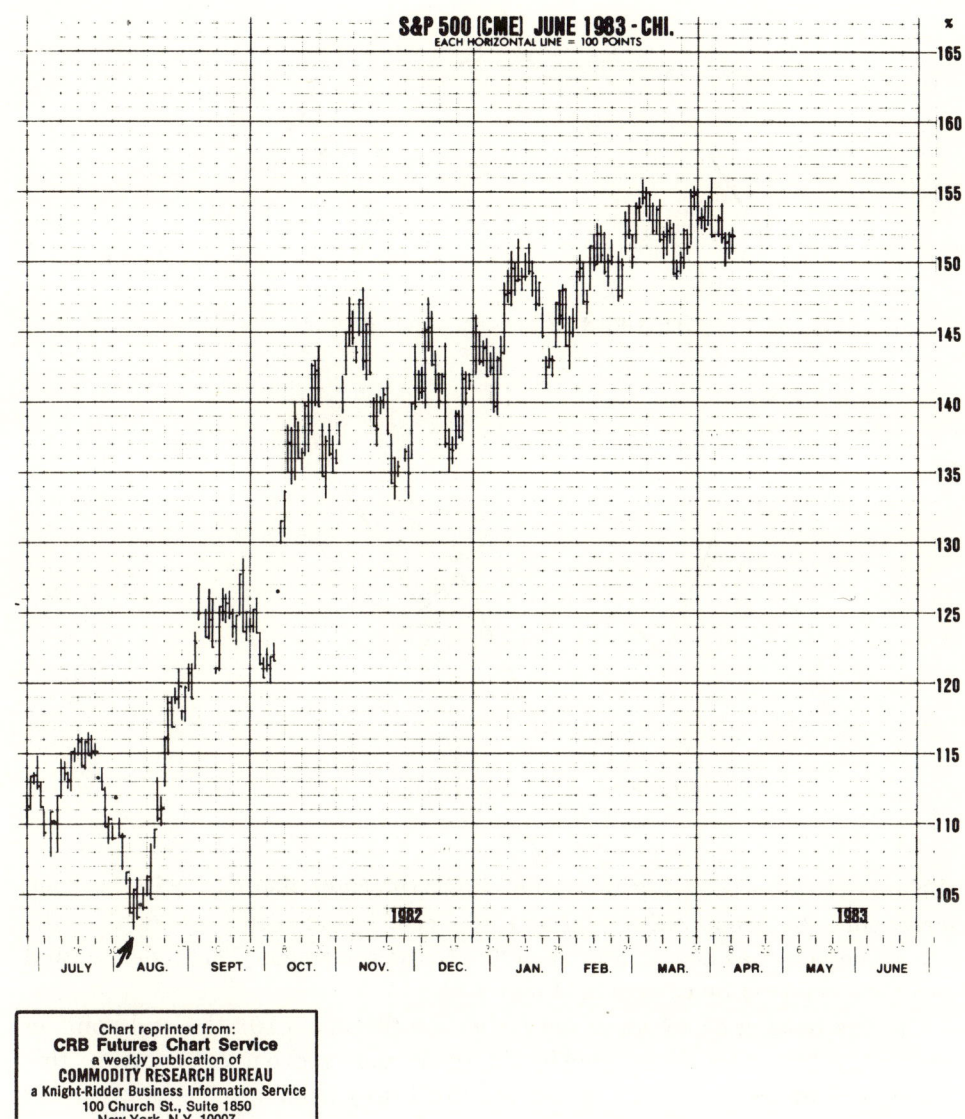

CHART 3.13 Key reversal bottom

Moderate Formations

The head-and-shoulders formation is among the most publicized. It can be indicative of a top (see Figure 3.10) or a bottom (see Figure 3.11). In each figure, the lowercase letters *a*, *c*, and *e* represent the left shoulder, the head, and the right shoulder, respectively. These figures are only guidelines; other, more complicated patterns occur, which are referred to as complex head-and-shoulders formations. The uppercase *E* represents another possible right shoulder point. In theory, the lower the right shoulder is in a top formation,

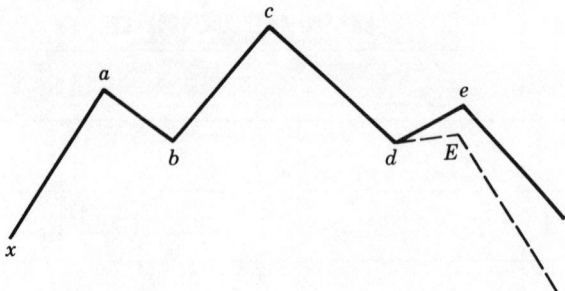

FIGURE 3.10 Head and shoulders top

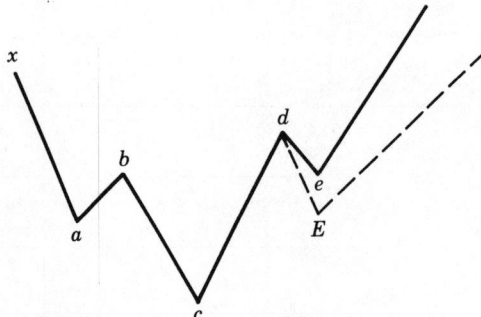

FIGURE 3.11 Head and shoulders bottom

the greater the expected decline; the higher the right shoulder is in a bottom formation, the greater the expected advance. It can also be seen that the chart's potency has been diminished due to the uppercase E shoulder. Actual cases are depicted by Charts 3.14 and 3.15.

In the head-and-shoulders top formation (Figure 3.10), the end point in the first rally, a, was superseded by the subsequent move to c. Generally, this move exhibits less volume. Finally, the third rally from d to e not only failed to penetrate point c, but failed to surpass point a. Generally, the rally from d to e (E) occur on less volume than either x to a or b to c.

In the head-and-shoulders bottom formation (Figure 3.11), the end point a in the x to a decline was penetrated by point c; however, points a and c were not penetrated on the downside by the final decline, which terminated at point e (E). Volume is an important consideration. Ideally, it would be relatively the heaviest on the x to a decline, less heavy on the b to c decline. Moreover, the volume should increase progressively on each rally within the configuration.

Double tops and bottoms require a moderate amount of time to evolve. Typically, in the top formation the secondary top is somewhat lower than the

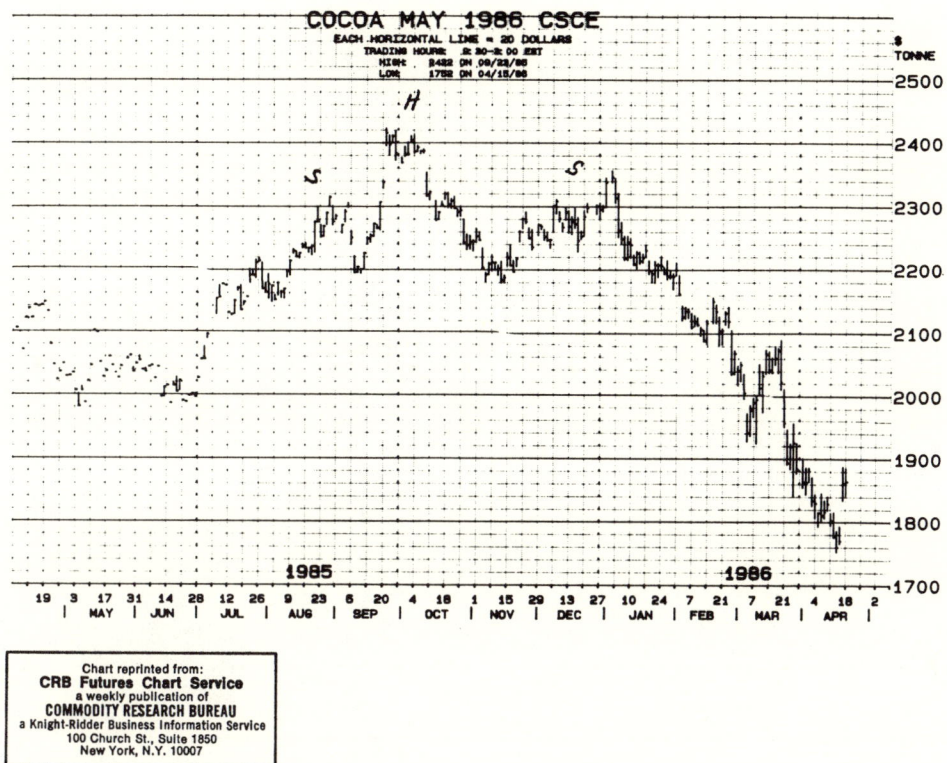

CHART 3.14 Head and shoulders top

primary (previous) high. Conversely, in the bottom formation the secondary bottom is higher than the primary (previous) low. Figures 3.12 and 3.13 depict the generalized top and bottom formation.

In the ideal double-top case, the c to d upswing's high is less than the a to b high. However, it can happen that the c to d upswing high is equal to the a to b upswing high, or the c to d upswing high is greater than the a to b upswing high. Nevertheless, the latter two cases can just as well be double-top formations. As in head-and-shoulders formations, volume plays an important role. The volume on the secondary advance is usually less than on the primary advance. Also, one can find the volume increasing on each subsequent sell-off.

In the ideal double-bottom case, the f and g downside usually achieves the lowest price. However, it can happen that the h to i downswing low is equal to the previous low; or the h to i downswing low is less than the previous low. By introducing volume analysis, generally the heaviest downside volume is witnessed on the primary low, and the subsequent sell-off experiences increased volume. Charts 3.16 and 3.17 depict actual double-top and double-bottom histories.

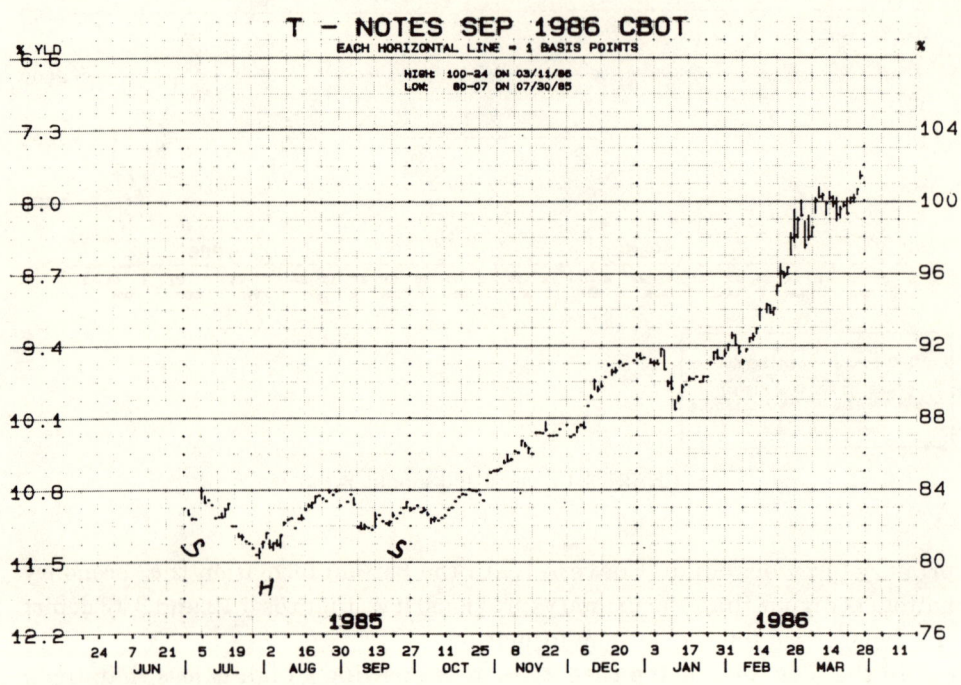

CHART 3.15 Head and shoulders bottom

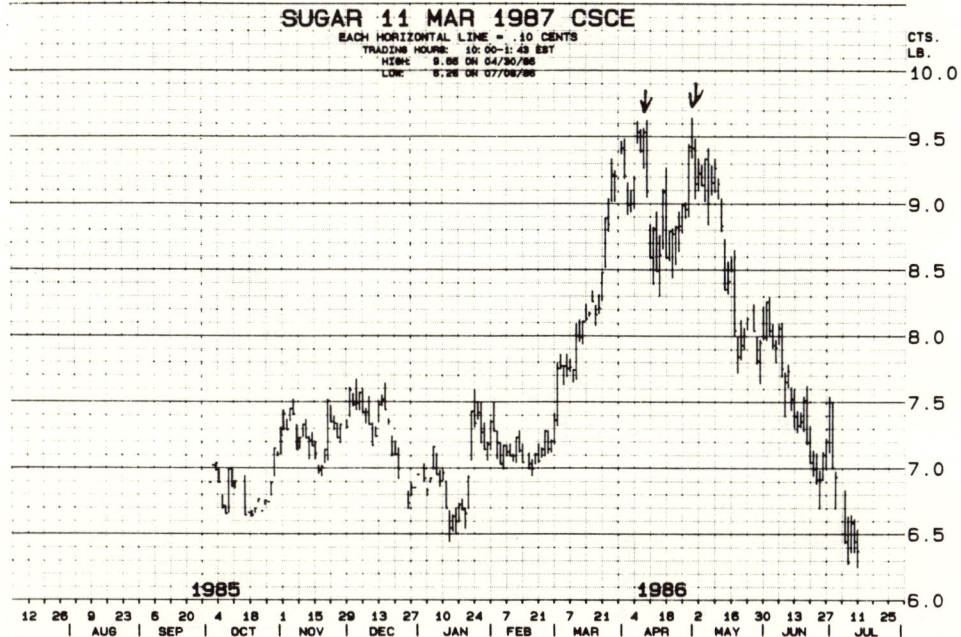

CHART 3.16 Double top

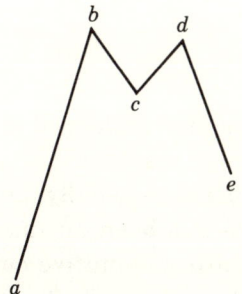

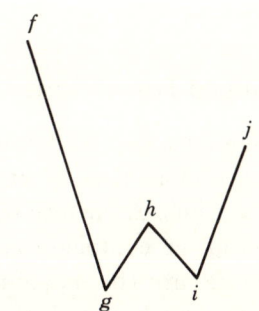

FIGURE 3.12 Double top

FIGURE 3.13 Double bottom

57

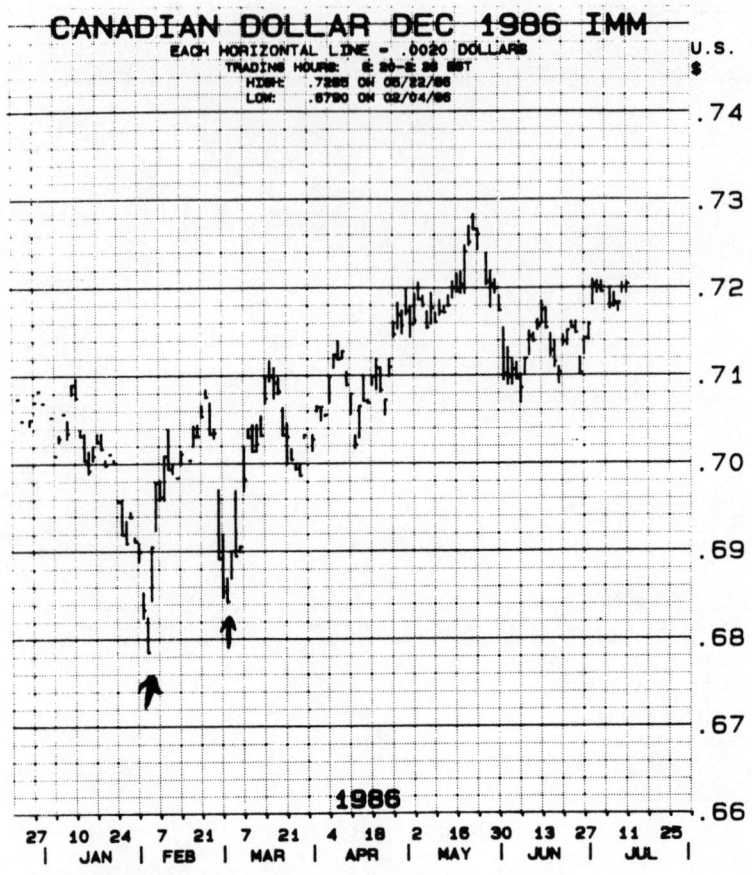

CHART 3.17 Double bottom

Prolonged Formations

Broadening tops and triple tops and bottoms are prolonged formations. They require more time to evolve than the formations described in the two previous sections. A variety of conflicting information—usually old crop versus new crop—or confusion as to whether there has been an unannounced policy change, are the major influences here. Until a definitive outlook materializes, the market tends to sway between rather wide and often increasing boundaries. The better examples of this are the broadening formations. Figures 3.14, 3.15, 3.16, and 3.17 represent the generalized patterns for the broadening bottom, triple top, and triple bottom.

These four figures have time horizons denoted by *t*, to emphasize the time factor. Charts 3.18, 3.19, 3.20, and 3.21 present actual cases.

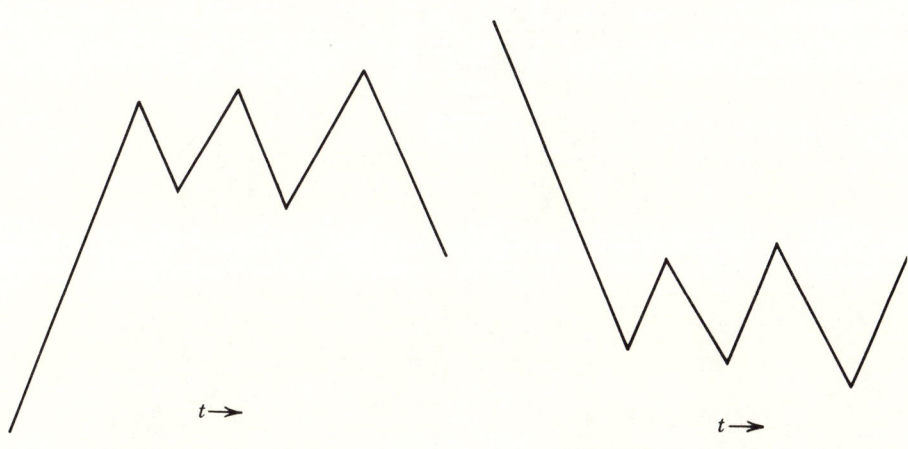

t→

FIGURE 3.14 Broadening top

FIGURE 3.15 Broadening bottom

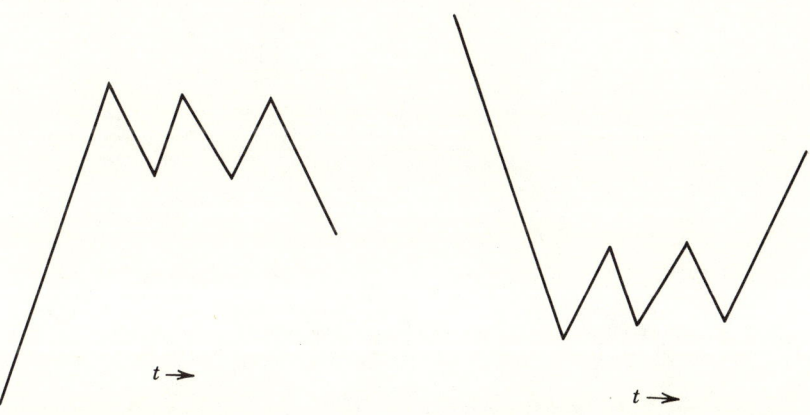

t→

FIGURE 3.16 Triple top

FIGURE 3.17 Triple bottom

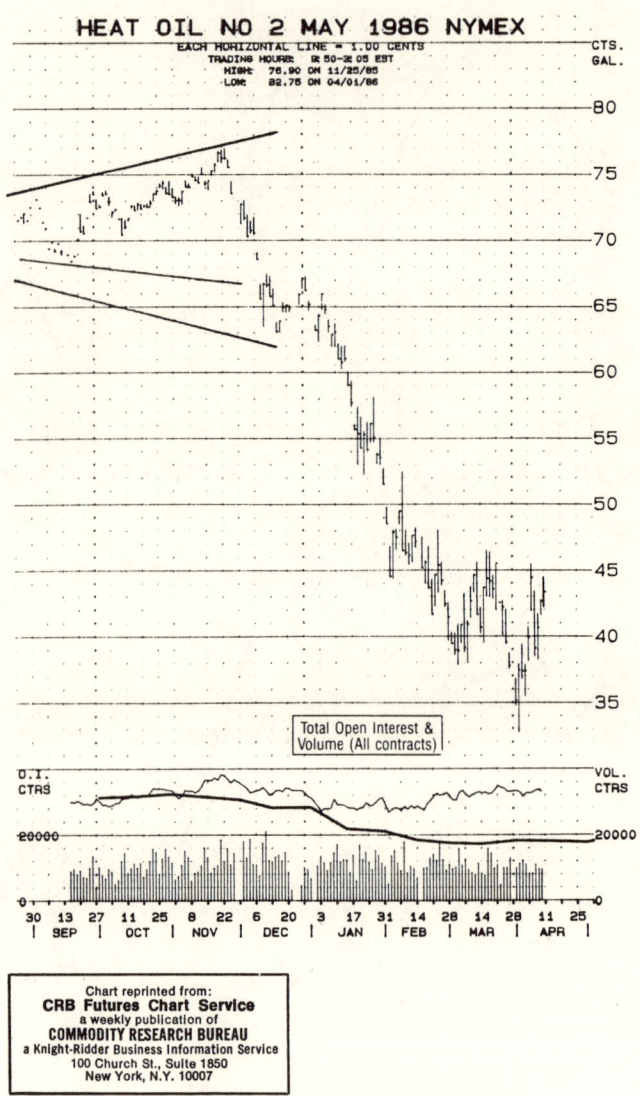

HEAT OIL NO 2 MAY 1986 NYMEX

EACH HORIZONTAL LINE = 1.00 CENTS
TRADING HOURS: 9:50-3:05 EST
HIGH: 76.90 ON 11/25/85
LOW: 32.75 ON 04/01/86

Total Open Interest & Volume (All contracts)

CHART 3.18 Broadening top

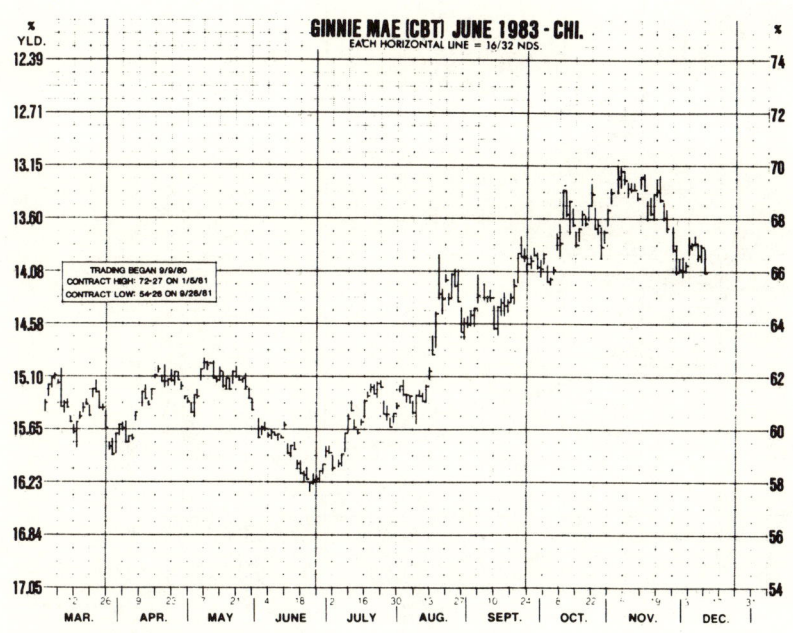

CHART 3.19 Broadening bottom

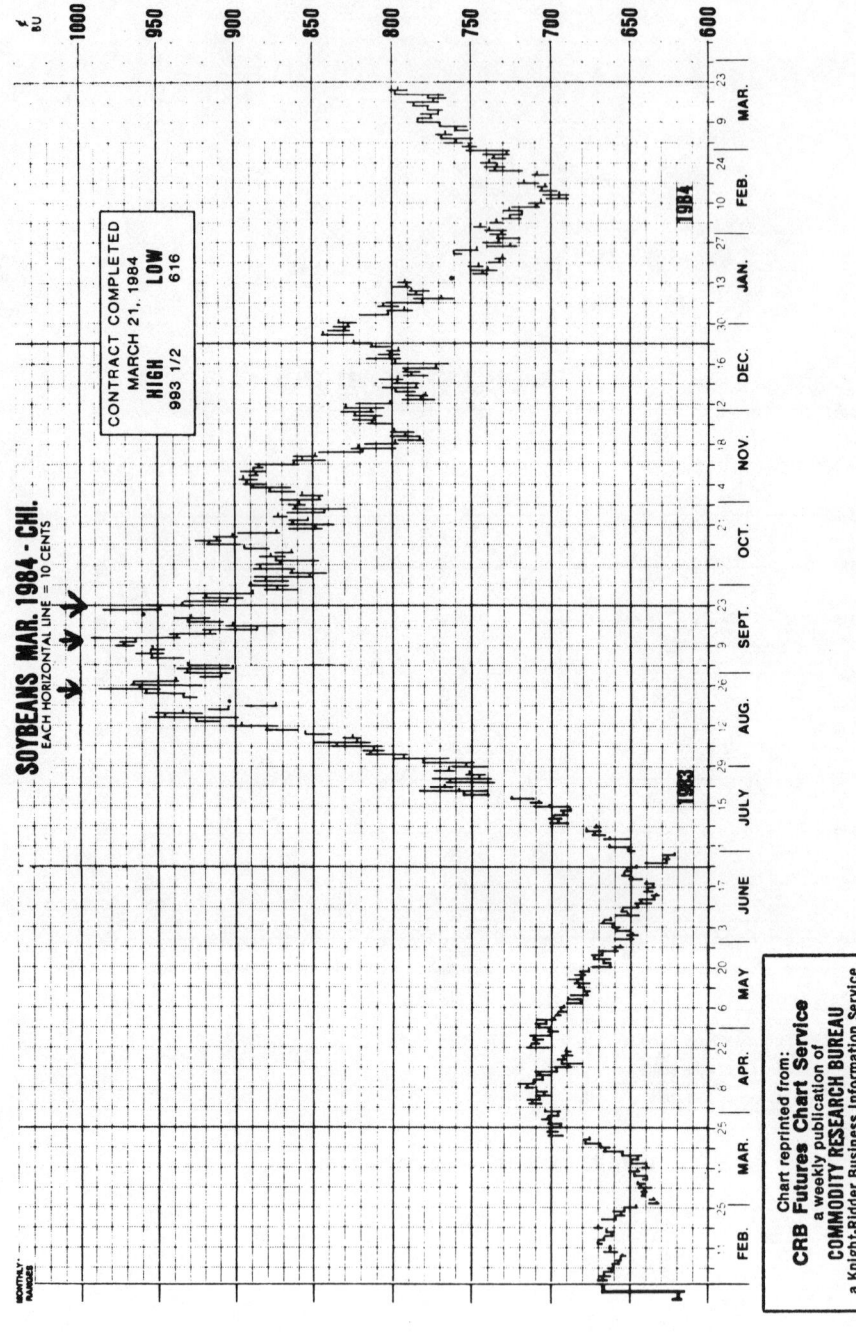

SOYBEANS MAR. 1984 - CHI.
EACH HORIZONTAL LINE = 10 CENTS

CONTRACT COMPLETED
MARCH 21, 1984
HIGH   LOW
983 1/2   616

MONTHLY RANGES

Chart reprinted from:
CRB Futures Chart Service
a weekly publication of
COMMODITY RESEARCH BUREAU
a Knight-Ridder Business Information Service
100 Church St., Suite 1850
New York, N.Y. 10007

CHART 3.20 Triple top

62

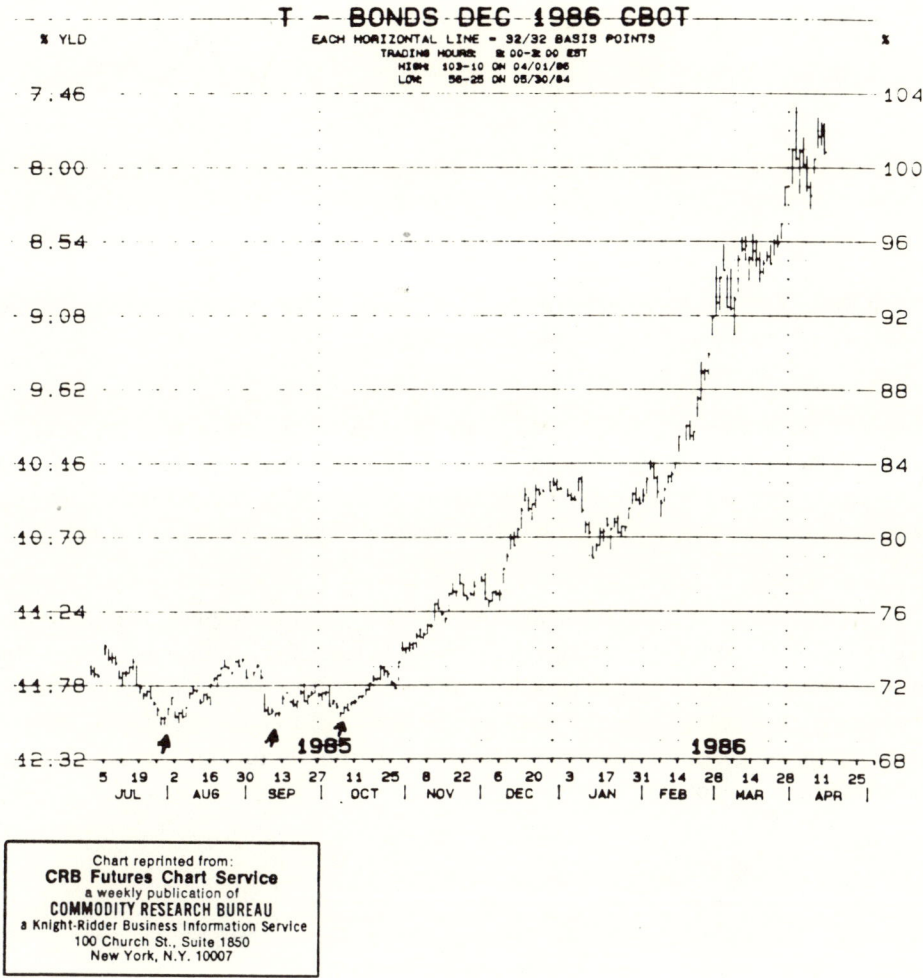

CHART 3.21 Triple bottom

Perverse Formations

Unlike the pennant, triangular, and rectangular formations presented earlier, these perverse formations expand in trading range magnitude over time. To compare these formations visually, see Figures 3.18, 3.19, and 3.20. The reason for the perversity is that the formations represented by Figures 3.18 and 3.19 maintain a constant or, better still, declining level of risk with the passage of time, while Figure 3.20 presents a formation whose risk expands with the passage of time.

Since the magnitudes of the prices remain constant or diminish in the two previous figures, their risk is more readily definable and manageable. Additionally, they are more amenable to trend-following techniques. Figure 3.20

FIGURE 3.18 Constant risk influences

FIGURE 3.19 Declining or dampening risk influences

is not favorable for such techniques. It requires those which are contratrend, or a careful use of oscillators (see Chart 3.22).

RATIONALE 1. Pennants, triangles, and rectangles exhibit essentially constant-to-dampening price range action over time, since market participants on both sides (long and short) are causing the price to gravitate toward its equilibrium point. Market information is basically in agreement among the longs and shorts, and the formations reflect this efficient discounting effort.

RATIONALE 2. Perverse formations exhibit expansive price range action over time, since market participants on both sides act with increasing anxiety due to widely conflicting information. Moreover, the information becomes increasingly less reliable over time. In mathematical economics these formations would represent explosive situations. Ordinarily formations act calmly, perverse ones do not.

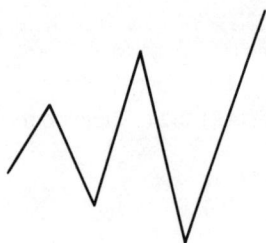

FIGURE 3.20 Perverse or expanding risk influences

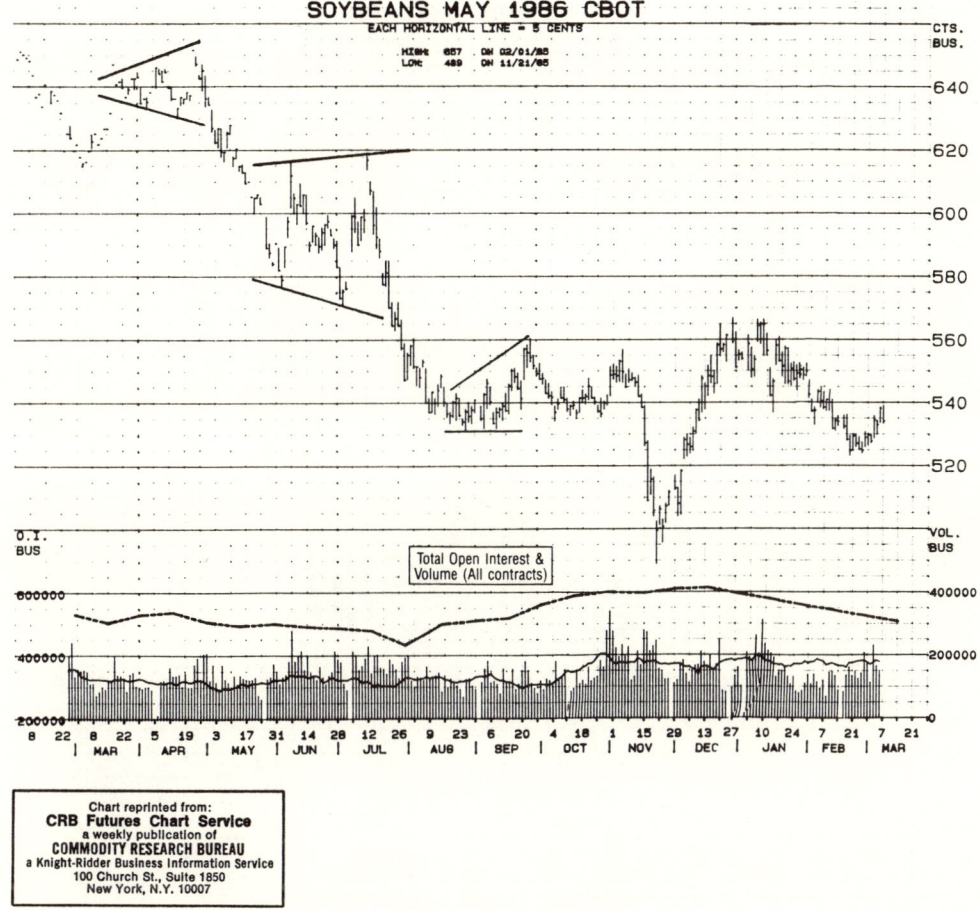

SOYBEANS MAY 1986 CBOT
EACH HORIZONTAL LINE = 5 CENTS

HIGH 657 ON 02/01/85
LOW 489 ON 11/21/85

Total Open Interest & Volume (All contracts)

Chart reprinted from:
CRB Futures Chart Service
a weekly publication of
COMMODITY RESEARCH BUREAU
a Knight-Ridder Business Information Service
100 Church St., Suite 1850
New York, N.Y. 10007

CHART 3.22 Perverse formation

COMMENTARY

Charts can be constructed with trade-by-trade, hourly, daily, weekly, monthly, or yearly data. The analysis remains the same. The subsequent price movements tend to be the greatest in the formations which required a longer time to evolve. For example, the sugar market on a weekly basis was confined between 6 to 10 cents per pound between 1977 to 1979, but once it broke out of this range a major upswing occurred (see Chart 3.23).

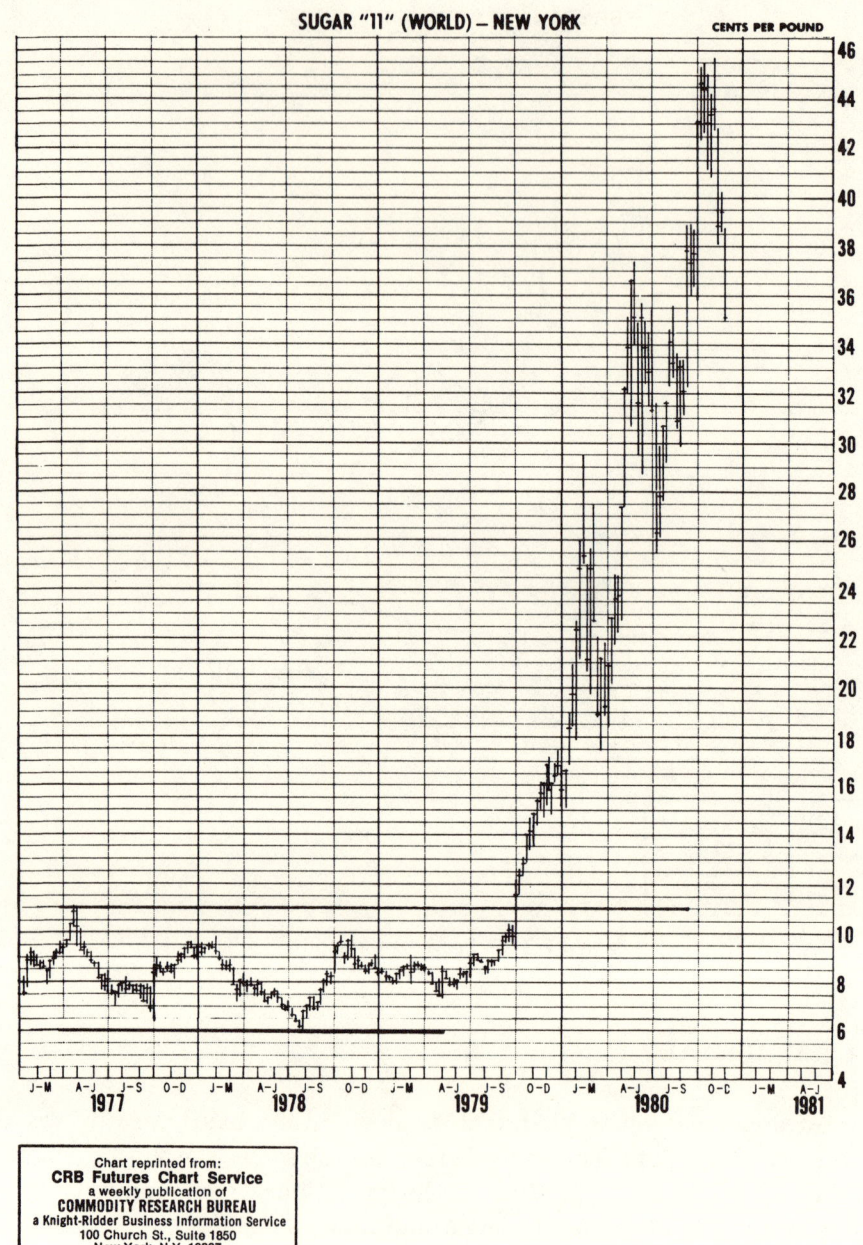

SUGAR "11" (WORLD) — NEW YORK

CENTS PER POUND

CHART 3.23 Sugar market—weekly chart

ELLIOTT WAVE ANALYSIS

This approach concerns longevity of a move and the sequencing of waves. In its expansive form, it sums up the various Elliott waves into movements of almost cosmic dimensions. Some authors refer to these as grand super-cycles. This text is concerned with the elemental process of analyzing a move.

Figures 3.21 and 3.22 reflect two such movements. Notice that each figure consists of five waves. These five waves represent one move. In theory, moves can be added until the entire extent of an advance or decline is traced. Once a wave is identified, the analyst can expect four other waves. Similarly, if three waves have occurred, two more need to be completed. This technique does not so much consider timing or precise price extent of a move but rather determines what phase the market is in. Chart 3.24 shows the weekly basis case of New York copper futures. Each wave is denoted by 1, 2, 3, 4, and 5.

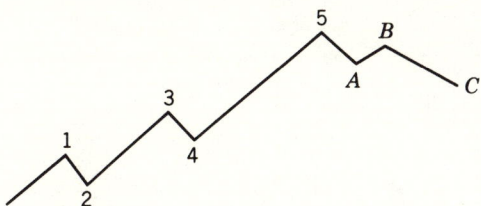

FIGURE 3.21 Elliott wave up movement

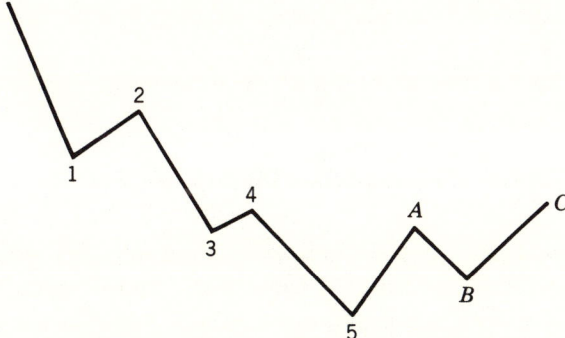

FIGURE 3.22 Elliott wave down movement

CHART 3.24 New York copper—Weekly chart

QUANTITATIVE CONSIDERATIONS

This is the scientific aspect of charts. In an empirical sense, the analyst can measure the time duration between peaks and troughs, the duration of an upswing, and the duration of a downswing. Additionally, the magnitude of a move and its range can be discerned quickly. Once these statistics have been compiled, it is up to the analyst to determine the minimum, maximum, and average values for all aspects as well as other descriptive statistics. For greater detail, the analyst can examine similar statistics for each wave component in a price move. By doing so, the manager leaves the realm of an intuitively based analysis and enters into one which has quantitative guidelines. This graphic, empirical approach has other benefits. It serves as a benchmark for more sophisticated analysis. When statistics are constantly generated, an analyst can lose visual perception of the task. As in navigation, the coordinates are important but so is a map of the terrain.

One example of this scientific approach to chart analysis is the examination of seasonal tendencies. By viewing a chart, an analyst can detect a seasonal behavior in prices. If the analyst is working with monthly data, there are 12 components to a yearly series. Sophisticated techniques can be employed to obtain seasonal factors for each month and test their reliability. Quantitative testing of these data can then determine whether visual and intuitive observations are statistically supportable.

Another example is the application of decision theory and payoff matrices. By testing expectations against the marketplace's realities, the analyst can ascertain the expectational values of the perceived recognition of important chart formations.

GAP CONSIDERATIONS

The occurrence of gaps, which are breaks in price continuity, at or about trendlines, usually alerts the analyst that major movements are incipient. The failure of the gap to fill quickly (within one to six sessions) suggests a serious fundamental and technical event. Subsequent behavior may retrace a reactionary move, but if this fails to close the gap, another major price phase is probable.

ACCELERATION/DECELERATION OF TRENDS

Generally, an acceleration is witnessed by the change in the slope of the price movement. A sudden increase in slope is indicative of a climactic run in prices, the occurrence of an important fundamental influence, or both. This acceleration tends to culminate in explosive tops and panic bottoms.

A deceleration or gradual reduction in slope or price variability suggests waning interest or the full assimilation of fundamental information. For up-trends, the action is characterized as heavy or sluggish, whereas for down-trends the action would be viewed as slow or stale. In either case, the market's price path is more likely to be influenced by new information in a direction opposite that which had been the primary trend.

THEORY OF CHART ANALYSIS

Many chartists consider charts indispensable to market analysis. A quick look at a chart provides insight not only to the historic variation and level in prices, but also to how those movements evolved. For example, an analyst can determine whether movements have been slow or swift, tight or wide, smooth or erratic. In a very important sense, these additional facts assist in the formulation of a market strategy. How prices behaved is just as important as how they achieved current levels.

A more careful examination of a chart can indicate the presence of recognizable and significant patterns, such as: major reversals, pronounced treadlines, and gaps. By quantifying the impact and expected values and risks or these phenomena, a chartist is better prepared to measure type, extent, and duration of subsequent movements.

Trendlines and Channels

Trendlines refer to the specific segments of a commodity's price history. Depending on how detailed the chart's configurations are, they can indicate short-, intermediate-, and long-term characteristics. A chart need not pose just the primary trend; it can also present contrary and secondary trend movements. Charts 3.25 and 3.26 represent uptrend and downtrend situations, respectively.

Channels are formed by delineating a price movement along its highs and lows. Typically, it is a parallel presentation of the trend. It defines the boundaries of the price path. Departures from this defined region are to be viewed as indicators of potential change. Chart 3.27 highlights the channel concept. Channels are one technique to determine support and resistance levels.

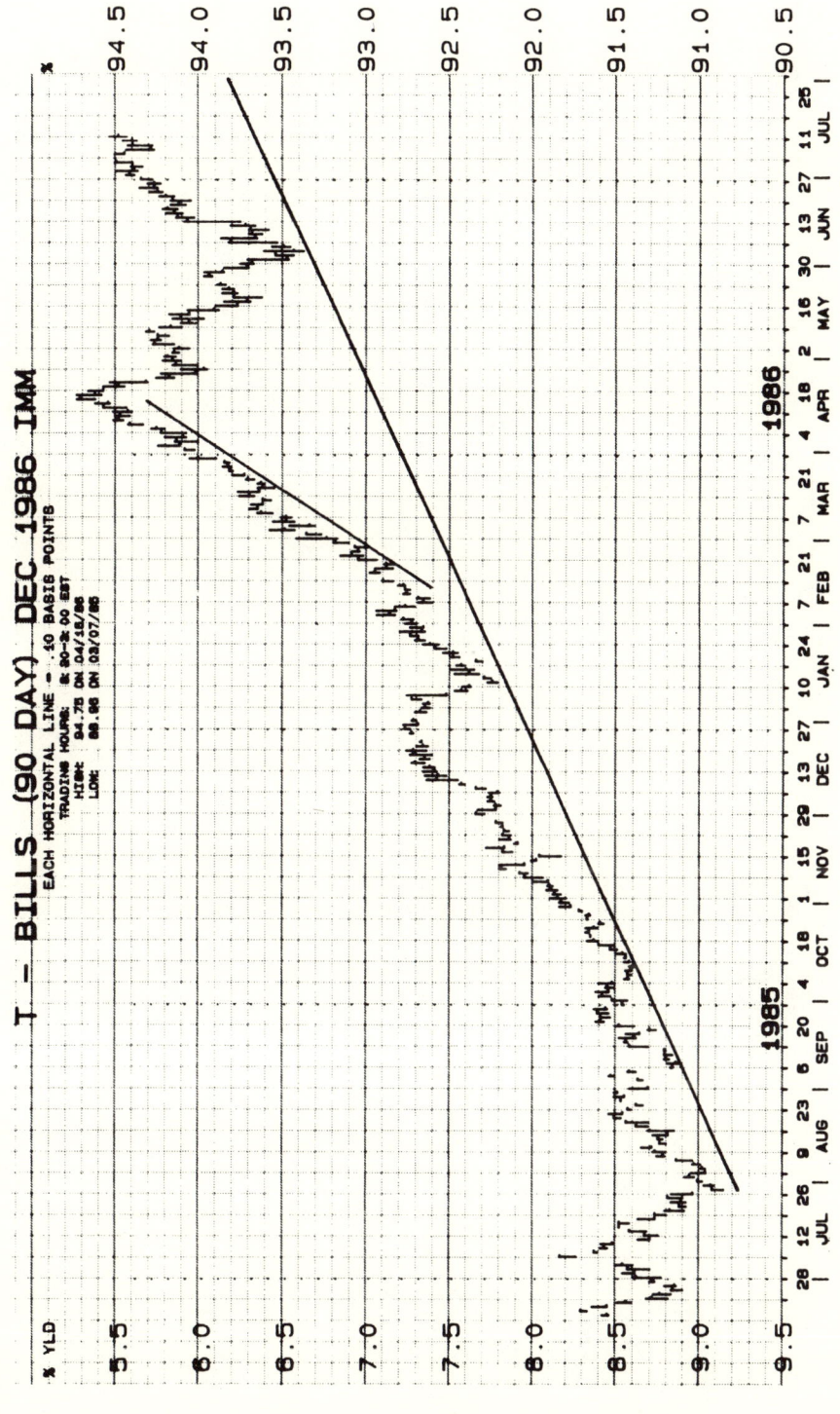

CHART 3.25 Uptrend

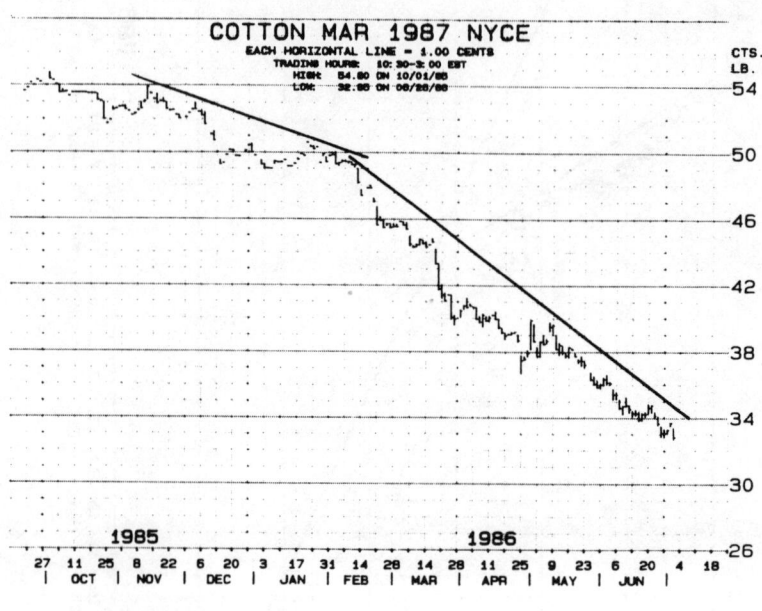

COTTON MAR 1987 NYCE

EACH HORIZONTAL LINE = 1.00 CENTS
TRADING HOURS: 10:30-3:00 EST
HIGH: 54.60 ON 10/01/85
LOW: 32.95 ON 06/26/86

CTS.
LB.

1985   1986

27 11 25 8 22 6 20 3 17 31 14 28 14 28 11 25 9 23 6 20 4 18
| OCT | NOV | DEC | JAN | FEB | MAR | APR | MAY | JUN |

CHART 3.26 Downtrend

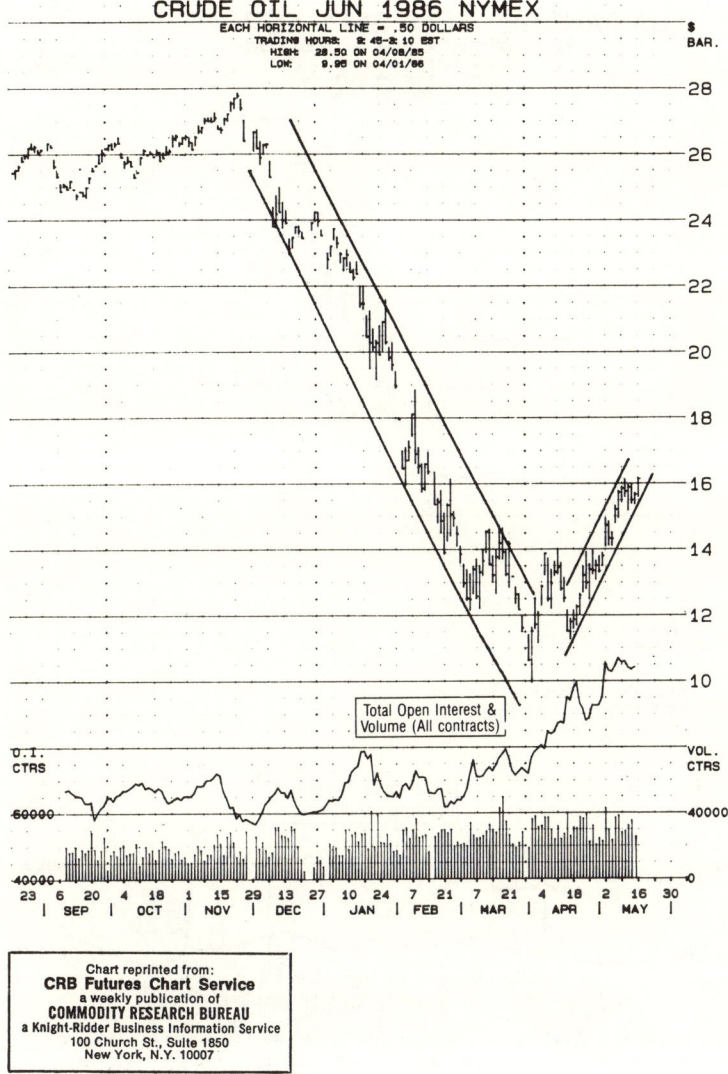

CHART 3.27 Channels

Support and Resistance

The upper limits of a pattern indicate resistance levels, whereas the lower levels of a pattern indicate support levels. Most formations reflect both concepts, though abrupt formations usually pinpoint the extreme value (support or resistance) which must be assessed against other formations to find its complement. It should be noted that support and resistance areas change over time. Chart 3.28 demonstrates a number of support and resistance levels.

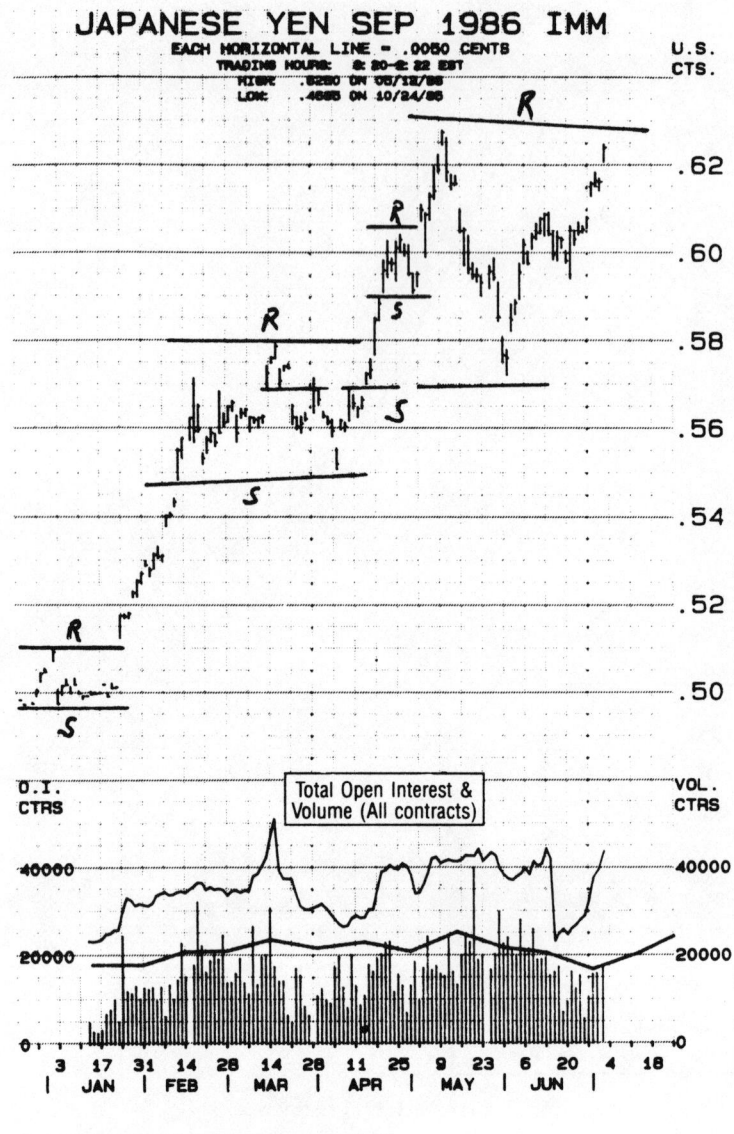

CHART 3.28 Support and resistance

4
Fundamental Analysis

DEFINING THE PROCESS

Fundamental analysis starts with an assessment of supply and demand; it then continues through the market evaluation of governmental, exchange, and other political—regulatory body—constraints. By developing an understanding of the fundamentals, the decision maker enhances his or her capacity to test and to act. As is seen in Figure 4.1 fundamental analysis is the third facet to market analysis. Fundamental analysis runs the gamut from qualitative studies through statistical analysis to econometric modeling.

SUPPLY

Supply is one word which represents several concepts. It can refer to:
Current crop production
Current inventory
Current inventory and expected production
Possible substitutes
Weather conditions
Governmental reserves, rationing actions, and so forth
Fiscal and monetary policies
Foreign exchange rates
Cost of production or issuance
Institutional and public holdings

Depending on commodity, the list can also consider known reserves, potential reserves, cost analysis of recycling, production capacity, and anything else of importance to the given situation.

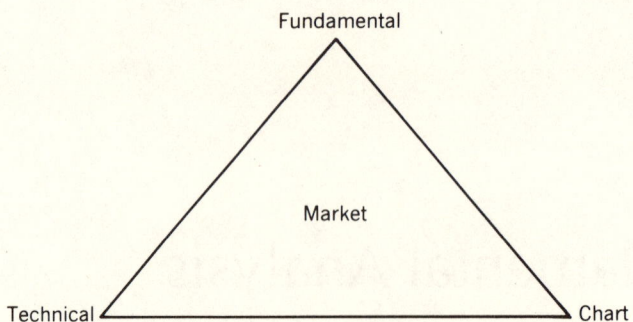

FIGURE 4.1 Three primary analytic methods

DEMAND

Demand is more than the desired quantity of a commodity for a given price. For market analysis, it is the wanted quantity of a commodity over a continuance of price, for a specified time period. It can refer to:

Consumption

Quantity sought for inventory

Consumption and quantity sought for inventory

Substitutions

Stockpiling efforts by governments or trade organizations

Supply and Demand Interactions

Supply and demand are represented by various time series, yet their applications are generally of a qualitative nature. Why is this so? Perhaps it is the transition from current (reported) statistics to anticipated ones. By their nature, reported statistics are representations of the past. They require time to collect, compile, and present. Often the actual situations can vary widely from the statistically reported one. This can be empirically the case, when the time series is released over a longer period. Consider a quarterly or monthly report versus a weekly or daily report. An important event could have occurred which is not reflected in the numbers yet. These events can be infrequent but profound—such as nuclear disasters—whereby anticipations are only best made by qualitative means, as insufficient data are available for even small sample testing. By their name, futures suggest an anticipatory element. Not only do they seemingly reflect the known data, but behave as if they anticipate future or unknown events.

Examples of this phenomenon are markets which responded to potential dramatic production changes. The events at the Chernobyl power plant caused abrupt expectational revisions in supply/demand estimates, not only for the Soviet Union but globally as well. See Charts 4.1 and 4.2.

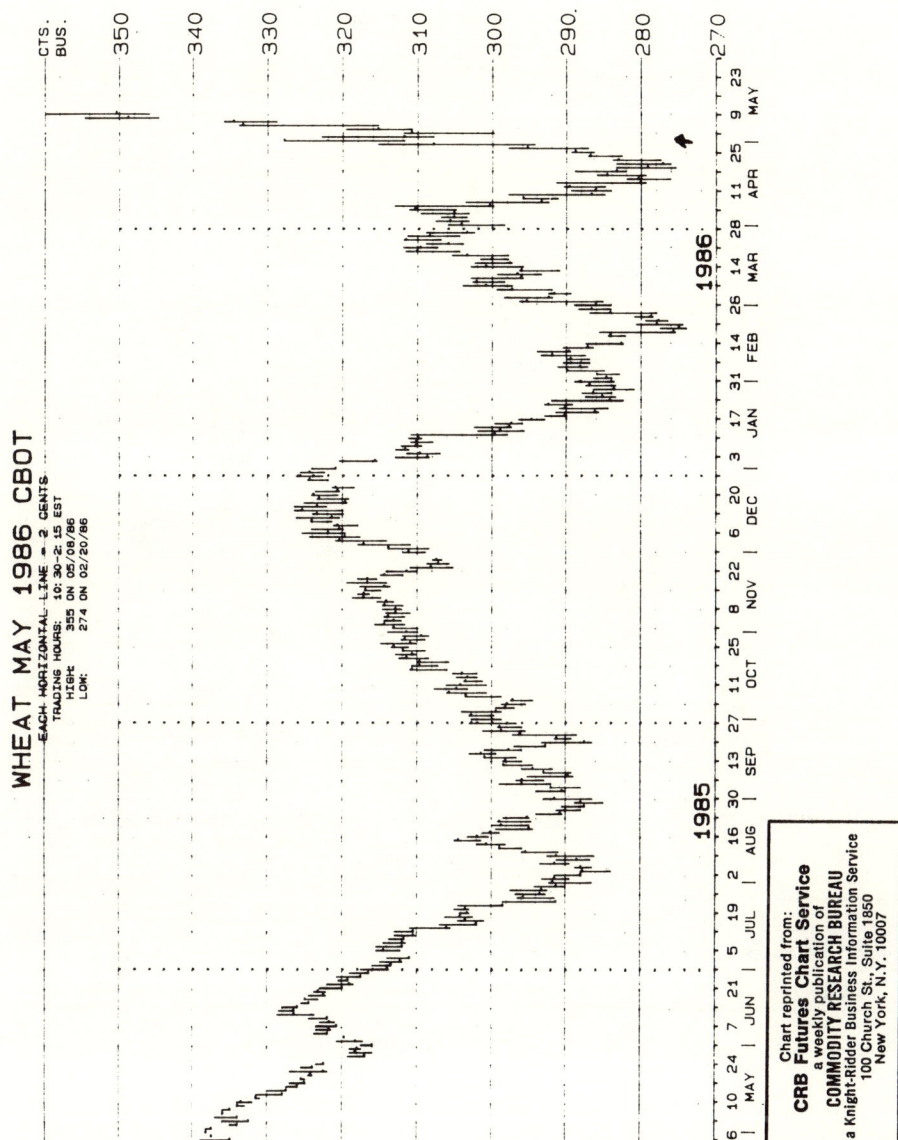

CHART 4.1 Response reaction to Chernobyl incident

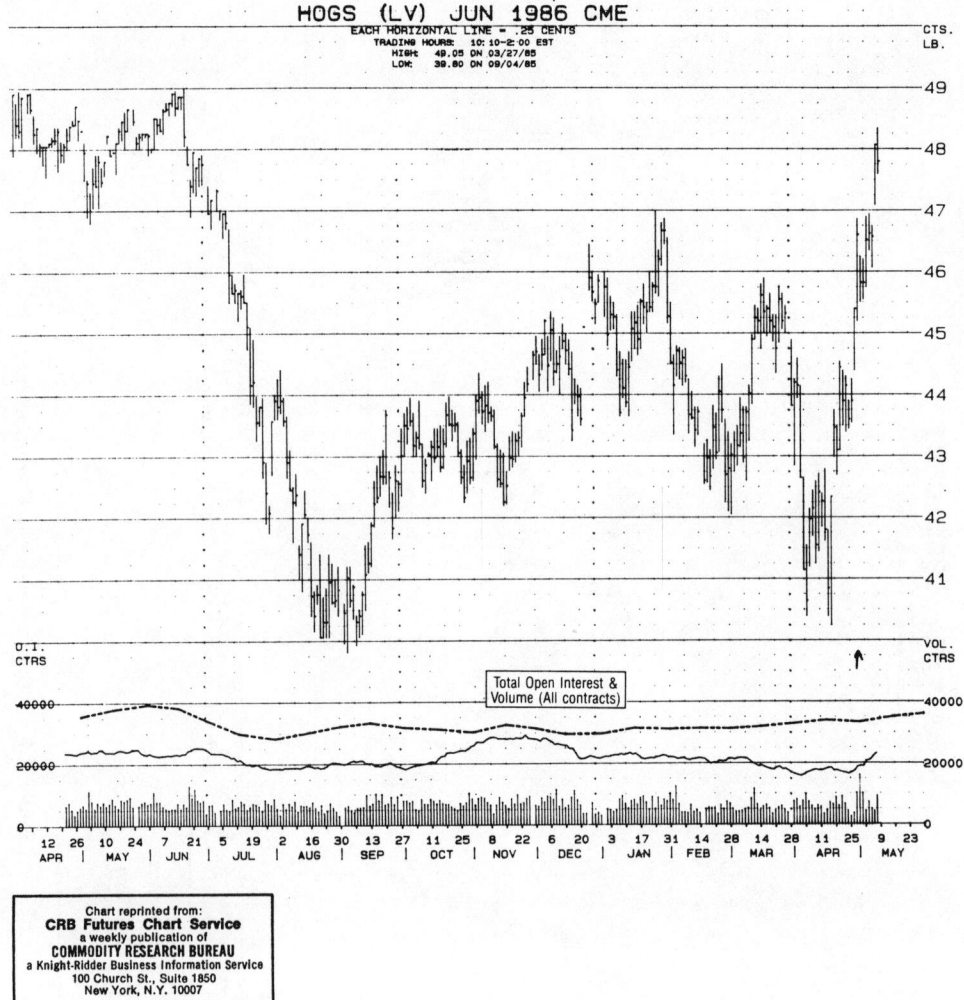

CHART 4.2 Response to Chernobyl incident

Supply Curve

Supply curve is one phrase which conveys several concepts. Typically it refers to: (1) quantity offerings at various prices at one particular time, or (2) quantity offerings at various prices for multiple periods in time. Figure 4.2 depicts the concept of a supply curve. Notice that the quantity offered for sale increases with price.

Demand Curve

Demand curve is another phrase which conveys several concepts. It can refer to: (1) the amount of a commodity sought at various prices at a particular

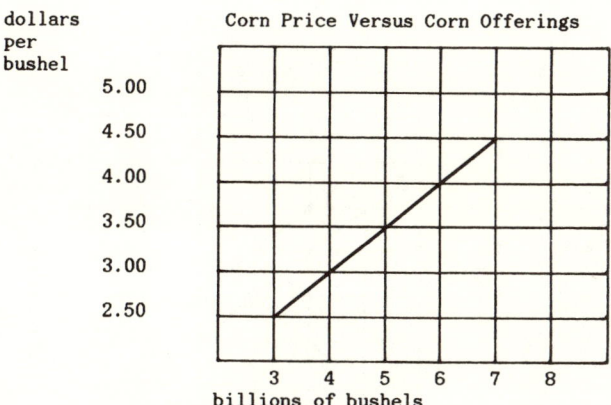

FIGURE 4.2 Hypothetical supply curve

point in time, or (2) the amount of a commodity sought at various prices for multiple points in time. Figure 4.3 depicts a hypothetical demand curve. As can be seen in this figure, the quantity sought is inversely related to the price. The lower the price, the greater the quantity sought.

Supply and Demand Curves

By superimposing Figure 4.3 on Figure 4.2, the interaction of supply and demand can be seen (see Figure 4.4). Notice the intersection point, E, is the equilibrium price for the depicted curves, S and D. It indicates that 5 billion bushels of corn will exchange hands at $3.50 per bushel, since both suppliers and demanders consider those quantities and prices to be agreeable. Figure 4.4 also presents a shift in demand D to D_i, and a shift in supply S to S_i. These changes cause the emergence of three potential equilibrium points: E_1, E_2, E_3.

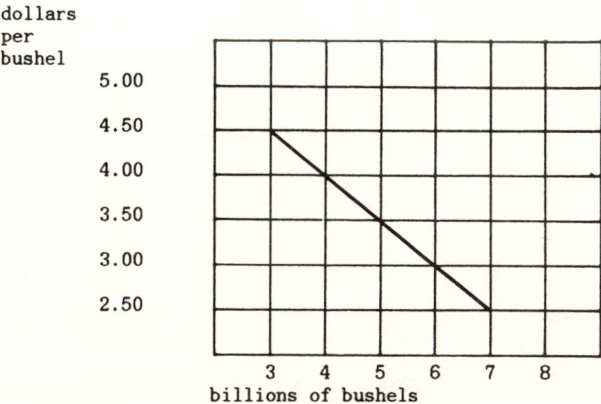

FIGURE 4.3 Hypothetical demand curve for corn

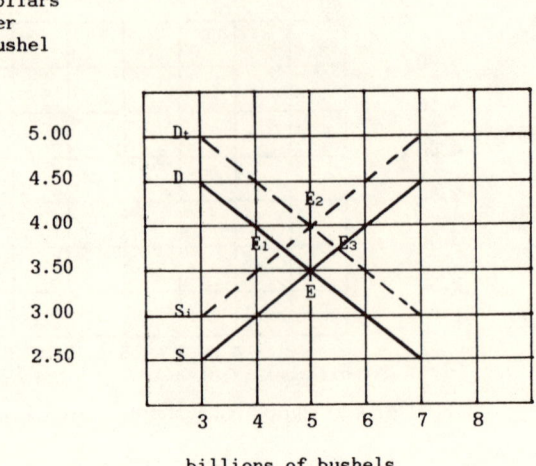

billions of bushels

FIGURE 4.4 Intersection of supply and demand curves

In the case of a supply shift S to S_i, notice that at the 3 billion bushel level the suppliers are now seeking $3.00 per bushel instead of $4.50. With no change in the demand curve, the new equilibrium point is E_1. The result is a higher equilibrium price, but reduced quantity is transacted. Point E_3 represents the case of a shift in demand (increase) with no change in the supply curve. Here, not only is the equilibrium price higher (than E) but more quantity is transacted at the new equilibrium point. Point E_2 represents the case of a shift in both supply and demand. According to this particular example, there is no change in transacted quantity between E and E_2, rather the equilibrium price rose from $3.50 to $4.00.

Elasticities

Elasticity is applied to supply and demand to assess responsiveness. The measurement tool for this is the coefficient of elasticity. It relates percentage changes in price to percentage changes in quantity. One expression of this is:

$$C = \frac{\dfrac{\text{change in } Q_1}{\text{quantity}}}{\dfrac{\text{change in price}}{\text{price}}} \qquad \text{(Expression 1)}$$

while another expression is:

$$C = \frac{\text{price} \times \text{change in quantity}}{\text{quantity} \times \text{change in price}} \qquad \text{(Expression 2)}$$

TABLE 4.1. DEMAND CURVE DATA

	a	b	c	d	e
Price ($/bushel)	4.50	4.00	3.50	3.00	2.50
Quantity de- manded (billions of bushels)	3	4	5	6	7

Table 4.1 provides data for a calculation of the elasticity of demand for the hypothetical corn example. The numbers in column c represent the price and quantity statistics, while the blocks adjacent to it (b and d) will be used to determine the change statistics. The coefficient is calculated (using Expression 2) as follows:

$$C = \frac{3.50 \times 2}{5 \times 1} = \frac{7}{5}$$

or

$$C = 1.4$$

Here, the coefficient of elasticity is 1.4. Coefficients greater than 1 are said to be elastic, those equal to 1 are called unitary, and those less than 1 are inelastic.

APPLYING MANAGEMENT THEORY

There are four basic steps in fundamental analysis. They are:

1. Define the problem/objective
2. Determine the important variables
3. Consider the constraints
4. Generate possible solutions.

Defining the Situation

The first step of the analysis is to define the problem. Considerations can be:

The probable average price for a particular time frame

The maximum or minimum values

Other factors

Once the problem and objective have been defined, the decision maker can proceed with the analyses.

Determining the Important Variables

What variables are necessary to generate a satisfactory solution set? They must make economic sense and be available on a timely basis. This availability may be on an actual reporting or estimating basis. The greater the divergence in expectations, the greater the prospect for larger profits or losses. The value of collecting salient information, making good estimates, and placing the appropriate trades should be less than or equal to the expected value.

Constraints. What are the boundaries not only in terms of availability of data but actual limitations in implementing the trading program? Considerations may include:

Position limits

Size and liquidity of the marketplace

Government or exchange regulations

Corporate or organizational charters

Budget limits on trading research and trading costs

Capital limitations for trading program

Other factors

Generating Possible Solutions. Since the decision maker is operating in a probabilistic world there is a tendency toward multiple solutions. One explanation for this is "change." As trading programs are implemented, the marketplace is subject to a variety of radical developments and changing outlooks. This

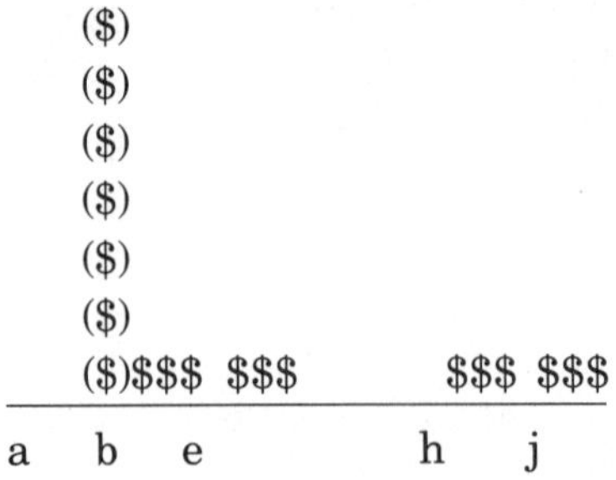

```
($)
($)
($)
($)
($)
($)
($)$$$  $$$        $$$ $$$
a   b   e        h   j
```

Note: ($) represent the proverbial eggs

FIGURE 4.5 Investment opportunity horizons

can modify the decision maker's strategy or even prompt a reversal in market posture.

Also, multiple solutions offer a wider breadth of potential success, since the opportunity horizon is no longer dependent on the attainment of only one event. In other words, "Don't put all your eggs in one basket" (see Figure 4.5).

As shown, column B places all seven investment eggs ($) on the possible occurrence of event B. This is an all-or-nothing strategy, whereas rows B–E and H–J offer a number of potential payoff situations.

INFORMATION AND ESTIMATES

For fundamental analysis, the greater benefits tend to occur when the decision maker possesses better information than his or her competitors. Such information contains two critical parts. The first is the monitoring of given (reported) statistics. There tends to be little disagreement here among the participants. It is the second part, estimates, that sparks the widest variation in outlooks while proffering the better potential returns or variations thereof.

Information is Relative

Expression 3 presents information as a relationship:

$$\text{Information} = \frac{\text{expected value}}{\text{cost}} \qquad \text{(Expression 3)}$$

This says that information has expected value but that value is related to its cost. As in other economic ventures, the value should be greater than the cost. So too in the case of variable and data selection for trading programs. It is not profitable to pursue those research and analytical projects where the cost of attaining better or more nearly complete information exceeds its value. To highlight this, a decision maker may spend $500 per average trade and may even buy the proverbial lows and sell the proverbial highs, yet the expected value per trade may only be $400. Hence every time such a trade is conducted, though seemingly exact and correct, it actually loses money.

This concept of cost effectiveness versus information is best demonstrated in business functions of reliability and sampling. Both government and business organizations employ statistical sampling techniques to estimate the size or quality of a particular population. To count every soybean, certificate of deposit, or consumer item is too expensive and unnecessary. By using suitable statistical techniques, one can gain a reasonable knowledge of how much and how good.

TABLE 4.2. IMPACT OF MONEY SUPPLY CHANGES ON NEXT DAY'S SPECIFIED INTEREST RATE MARKET

| | | Interest Rate Change | | |
		Down	None	Up
Weekly changes in the money supply	Down	10	4	7
	None	2	3	1
	Up	8	3	14

Total: 52 observations in year

Estimates

Good estimates are generally more valuable than reported statistics, for it is the estimate component of information which separates successful programs from others.

Quantifying Estimates. The decision maker has a wide latitude in constructing research models. These models may vary from one decision maker to another because of different objectives, risks, and constraints. For example, a supplier or underwriter may pursue one trading plan while a consumer or money management firm may pursue a greatly different one. To see how quantification emerges, examine Table 4.2.

These arrangements need not be confined to agricultural commodities. For example, Table 4.2 records the impact of a reported change in money supply to the subsequent day's change in interest rates.

The arrangements can be greater in size and complexity than the 3 × 3 matrix shown. The research designs should be adapted to suit the decision maker's requirements. Other statistical arrangements, both similar and dissimilar, can be constructed.

SCATTER DIAGRAMS

Scatter diagrams are visual aids in assessing the relationship between the variables. By plotting the x and y values, a feel for the raw statistics can be developed. Moreover, if a and b values were known, the regression function could be plotted. As it is, a freehand approximation can usually suffice to ascertain visually the responsiveness between variables.

Chart 4.3 depicts the world's production of corn and maize versus an average U.S. corn price. As can be seen, the two paired factors acted inversely, as one would expect. The diagram also points out that there was not a directly proportional response between the two factors, which indicates the presence

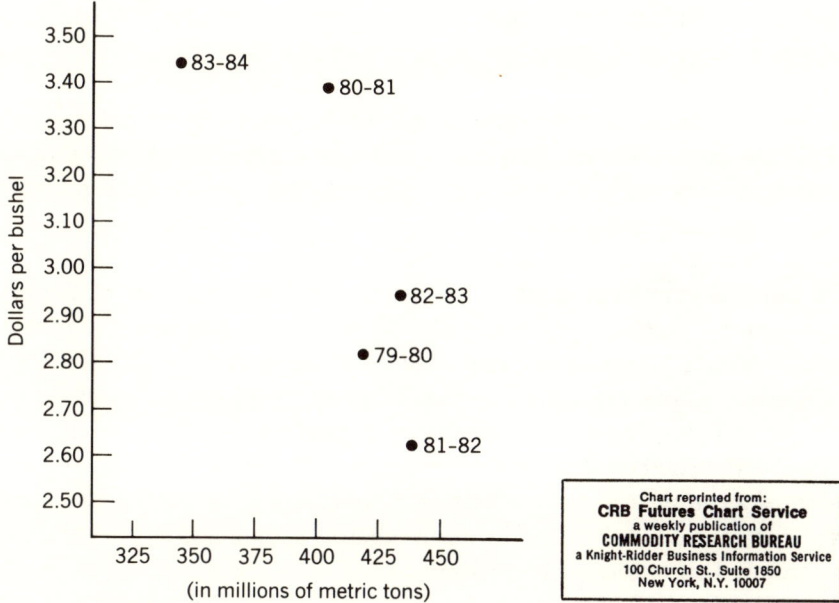

CHART 4.3 World production of corn and maize versus U.S. corn prices

of other influences. These influences could be: trade-weighted dollar values, livestock numbers in the United States and elsewhere, competitive feed grain prices, and so forth.

This approach is not limited to the presentation of absolute prices and production. It can just as easily portray the association between relative supplies or the relationship of demands to relative prices.

For the financial markets, the relative size of the National Short-Term Debt relative to the National Long-Term Debt can provide insights as to relative interest rates or the structure of the yield curve. Additionally, these relative sizes can be applied to municipal versus federal debts and their relative interest rates.

REGRESSION ANALYSIS

Regression analysis is a popular quantification tool since it will readily show the reaction in variable y, given a value for variable x. In its generalized form $a + bx = y$, a denotes the constant value (the intercept), b refers to the regression coefficient, x is the independent variable, and y is the dependent variable. This technique has three principal drawbacks.

First, many actual time-series data tend to produce misleadingly strong regression and correlation results, though in actuality the relationships are not as strong. Conditions known as serial and autocorrelation are the general drawbacks, as is multicollinearity.

In other words, one would probably find a higher degree of relationship between actual data for the Consumer Price Index and the Wholesale Price Index, but a more meaningful one would be the relative change in these two indexes.

Second, it is assumed the data are normally distributed independent values. This need not be the case. In fact, numerous studies have found that stock market returns as well as other economic data are distributed in nonnormal and interdependent fashions. Moreover, there tends to be greater occurrence of events away from the mean expected value than would normally be expected. Several empirical studies have suggested that the tails of the probability functions contain approximately 10 percent of the density and not 5 percent as would be normally expected. Expressed differently, this "fatter tails" condition does not imply only a 5 percent higher chance of dramatic returns—it indicates a potential doubling of the likelihood of the outliers.

Finally, the relationship need not be linear. There may not be a constancy in the slope as defined by the b statistic. Sometimes, data transformations can approximate this, but it must be remembered that nonlinear relationships often confound simple regression analysis.

The following will highlight some of the strengths of this technique, which is also known as least-squares analysis, so called because the technique seeks the linear relationship where the variations about the computed line are at a minimum. The simplicity of design lends strong intuitive appeal while facilitating further computations. For stable models, once the intercept and coefficients have been determined, straightforward calculations generate new projections on the substitution of additional x values. Since the approach is founded on the normal distribution, it has extensive and well-documented statistical properties. Moreover, extensions of this process permit additional analytical approaches as demonstrated in the following equation.

The equation (model) $a + bx = y^p$ is solved as follows, where y^p is the predicted value.

$$a = \frac{\left(\Sigma y\right)\left(\Sigma x^2\right) - \left(\Sigma x\right)\left(\Sigma xy\right)}{n\left(\Sigma x^2\right) - \left(\Sigma x\right)^2} \tag{1}$$

$$b = \frac{n\left(\Sigma xy\right) - \left(\Sigma x\right)\left(\Sigma y\right)}{n\left(\Sigma x^2\right) - \left(\Sigma x\right)^2} \tag{2}$$

The symbol Σ (summation sign) means that all the values in the specified series are summed, or added together; n refers to the number of observations; and a and b are constants whose values remain to be determined.

For example, an analyst may seek the statistical relationship—not necessarily the causal one—between rates of change in the money supply and rates of change in inflationary expectations. Other relationships could be: the changes in federal funds to Treasury bill yields, or rainfall to crop production.

Multiple Regression Analysis

This approach seeks the optimal linear combination of independent x variables which best describes the reaction in the y variable. The expression becomes:

$$y^P = a + b_1x_1 + b_2x_2 + \cdots + b_ix_i$$

where the i subscript refers to the last specified variable. While the simple linear case related money supply changes to changes in inflationary expectations, a more comprehensive model now includes changes in U.S. dollar values versus a basket of currencies of the principal trading partners of the United States and changes in the price of crude oil. Ascertaining the appropriate lag relationships for the independent variables would enhance the predictive power of such a model. Sometimes, variable changes do not correspond day by day or month by month. Yet groups of variables may exhibit strong associative tendencies given the proper lead-lag relationships.

CORRELATION ANALYSIS

There are a number of correlation tests. They indicate the degree of association of one variable with another variable. In regression analysis, a correlation coefficient can be determined which is parametric in nature. Later in the text, a method which is nonparametric will be presented. The importance of this means that the underlying generating function can be of any type with no assumption of normalcy as it focuses on ordinal pairings and not cardinal values. Its worth is in the establishment of the statistical association between two time series. It does not provide a parametric prediction as to which way or to what extent one variable will go, given a value of another variable; rather, it generalizes expected direction or association.

DISCRIMINANT ANALYSIS

Regression analysis is related to discriminant analysis, but here the procedure attempts to discern whether there are significant differences between populations or means. This methodology has been used to discriminate among variables underlying the creditworthiness for borrowers and to categorize scores for quantifying the risk characteristics of bankrupt firms versus solvent firms.

The discriminant function is:

$$Z = L_1 x_1 + L_2 x_2 + \cdots + L_i x_i$$

where Z is the index or scoring statistic of the linearly combined x_i variables. Though familiar in form to the regression equation, this procedure searches for the maximum differences between the groups and not the minimum ones. Because of the relatively large statistical variations, distinctions between classifications can be isolated.

For market analysis, the test can be used to differentiate between bullish and bearish scenarios, favorable and unfavorable hedging outlooks, or to determine the prevalence of tight versus accommodative monetary policy. The Z score or statistic is computed and viewed as a predictive indicator. The procedure attempts to determine a linear path between two sets of data or situations. By examining subsequent sets of data, the analyst can infer whether the new situations have quantitative characteristics more nearly akin to one set of conditions versus another set.

SEQUENTIAL ANALYSIS

Often this terminology refers to the progressive estimation of expected values and events in the construction of decision trees. It also refers to a dynamic sampling approach which continues until a hypothesis is statistically proved or refuted. Unlike many other sampling techniques in which the sample size is fixed and denoted as the constant n, the sequential approach views sample size as a variable m (to avoid misunderstandings about its size). The technique is especially important for assessing the ongoing performance of trading and hedging programs as it permits continuance of trades until the previously established termination criteria are violated. Moreover, the technique is a powerful testing device as its statistical characteristics frequently enable the analyst to use smaller sample sizes than those which would be required for many other sampling techniques. It should be noted that m is now a random variable and its size continues to grow until a termination point is reached.

The sequential approach is particularly suitable for situations where the costs of being wrong are extremely high, the analyst does not have the luxury of numerous observations, or resources are valuable. Money management firms and hedging organizations often face these circumstances.

The sequential probability ratio test places numerical boundaries around a trading program. Depending on the defined criteria, such as probability of up and down changes, winning versus losing trades, steady or improving basis relationships versus worsening ones, the technique will continue to function until a definitive statistical result is attained.

The expressions for these are:

$$LR = \frac{LF_2}{LF_1}$$

where LR is the likelihood ratio, LF_2 is the second likelihood function, and LF_1 is the first likelihood function. The upper and lower boundaries are established by applying:

$$UB = \frac{1 - B}{A} \quad \text{and} \quad LB = \frac{B}{1 - A}$$

where UB is the upper boundary, LB is the lower boundary, and A and B refer to the specified tolerance levels for errors. For example: A trader is uncertain of the outlook, but he thinks positive changes can occur either 45 or 55 percent of the time, and the remainder is the representative negative change percentages. These changes can be in price, basis, or other considerations. Once the correct situation is ascertained, the appropriate trades can be initiated.

Substituting .10 and .30 for A and B, it is determined that:

$$UB = \frac{1 - .30}{.10} = 7 \quad \text{and} \quad LB = \frac{.30}{1 - .10} = .33$$

Since this is a success–failure or binomial arrangement, "1" will be assigned to positive changes and "0" for negative changes. Therefore, the evaluation of the first likelihood ratio, given an initial positive change, is:

$$\frac{(.55)^1 (.45)^0}{(.45)^1 (.55)^0} = 1.22$$

The numerator reflects the hypothesis that 55 percent of changes are expected to be positive and 45 percent to be negative, while the denominator has the converse assignment of probabilities. If the second change was also positive, the ratio would advance to 1.49; otherwise it would drop to 1.00 since the likelihoods are multiplicatively updated. For a second positive change, the arithmetic would have been $1.22 \times 1.22 = 1.49$ whereas a positive and negative sequence would have been $1.22 \times .82 = 1.00$. This sampling procedure continues until either previously established termination boundary is violated. For ordinary sampling techniques, the procedure would terminate on the attainment of the prior to testing specified sample size, be it the 10th, 30th, 100th, or whatever other designated sample observation size.

5

Seasonal Analysis

RECURRING INFLUENCES

Seasonal factors are influences that tend to recur on a reasonably consistent basis. They can be: harvest activities, grain movements, retail sales, and similar recurrent economic data. This analysis empirically defines important time periods for price run ups, sell-offs, or stability. It can provide guidelines for relative price factors attendant to each period. These periods can represent monthly seasonal factors for a 12-month year—which need not be a calendar year. For example, the crop year for corn is October to September; for soybeans, September to August. The crop year analogy in the financial world would be the fiscal year. Seasonally, there are money flows into the Treasury (income tax payment dates) and outflows for various benefit payments. Other examples would be: housing starts, the clustering of dividend payment dates, and quarterly refundings.

The seasonal process need not be limited to a 12-month period. It can be 6 months, 18 months, or whatever time frame is required to complete the seasonal process. Some livestock expansion/contraction processes are very short (for broilers), moderately longer (for hogs), or lengthy (for beef). Beet sugar crops have 12-month periods while cane sugar crops tend to average between 18 and 24 months.

The time units which comprise the entire seasonal process in its broader sense need not be months. They can be hours, days, weeks, or even quarters. Examples of these would be hourly trading patterns on the New York Stock Exchange, daily slaughter numbers, weekly monetary statistics, or quarterly coffee roastings. Generally, periods of duration greater than quarters are assigned to cyclical analysis, but many of the precepts underlying both approaches are the same.

WEEKLY ANALYSIS

The flow into and out of storage for pork bellies is one example of defining a seasonal pattern on a weekly basis. The data and factors are listed in Table 5.1 and graphically portrayed by Chart 5.1. As can be seen in this table and chart, the seasonal pork belly storage peaks in the 21st week (week of May 23) and seasonally bottoms during the 39th through 41st weeks. In the unadjusted data given in Table 5.1, the peaks occurred during the 21st and 23rd weeks, and the lowest storage occurred during the 39th and 41st weeks for the 1980 and 1981 years, respectively.

Of course, these dates may not be hard and fast; additional data years may cause variations among the seasonal factors. Nonetheless, the procedure is the same.

Before examining other seasonal examples, an explanation of the procedure will now be given. First, a specification of the seasonal time period is required. In the above weekly data example, each year was decomposed into 52 time periods; hence the analysis is searching for 52 seasonal factor values. To determine the value of each seasonal factor, a columnar summation was 3,302.7 for 1980 and 3,357.5 for 1981. Next a weekly (seasonal time period) average is calculated. For 1980 it was 63.5 and 64.6 for 1981. These averages were simply calculated by 3,302.7/52 and 3,357.5/52, respectively. Each raw data value was divided by that year's weekly average factor times 100. For example, the seasonal factor for the first week in 1980 was determined by:

$$\frac{62.8}{63.5} \times 100 = 99$$

which is exactly the value shown in Table 5.1. Note that seasonal factors are often represented by integers, thus rounding may be required. This procedure is continued for the remainder of the data for the year. The summations of each year's seasonal factors should equal the number of factors multiplied by 100. For 1980, this statistic was 5,202 while 1981 was 5,369 or 169 greater than its theoretical value. The greater the variations of the computed summations from the theoretical summation, the greater the need to adjust the seasonal factors. In this case, the variation is primarily due to rounding. Finally, each corresponding seasonal period's values are averaged across the data years. Since there are only two data years in this example, the grand (across years) seasonal factor for week 1 is:

$$\frac{99 + 127}{2} = 113$$

TABLE 5.1. WEEKLY PORK BELLY STORAGE

Week	1980 Raw	1981 Raw	Seasonal Factor 1980	Seasonal Factor 1981	Grand Seasonal Factor
1	62.8	82.2	.99	1.27	1.13
2	63.8	81.8	1.00	1.27	1.14
3	65.5	82.8	1.03	1.28	1.16
4	64.3	79.4	1.01	1.23	1.12
5	62.0	76.1	.98	1.18	1.08
6	61.1	74.5	.96	1.15	1.06
7	60.0	74.8	.94	1.16	1.05
8	59.5	76.5	.94	1.18	1.06
9	60.9	79.4	.96	1.23	1.10
10	63.4	82.4	1.00	1.28	1.16
11	66.5	85.2	1.05	1.32	1.19
12	70.7	87.8	1.11	1.36	1.24
13	75.4	89.7	1.19	1.39	1.29
14	80.2	90.6	1.26	1.40	1.33
15	84.0	94.5	1.32	1.46	1.39
16	87.0	100.0	1.37	1.55	1.46
17	89.8	105.3	1.41	1.63	1.52
18	91.9	110.5	1.45	1.71	1.58
19	93.2	116.4	1.47	1.80	1.64
20	95.5	121.0	1.50	1.87	1.69
21	97.6	122.2	1.54	1.89	1.72
22	99.1	120.0	1.56	1.86	1.71
23	100.2	118.0	1.58	1.83	1.71
24	100.1	114.8	1.58	1.78	1.68
25	98.2	110.7	1.55	1.71	1.63
26	92.1	106.4	1.45	1.65	1.55
27	86.1	101.7	1.36	1.58	1.47
28	79.4	93.9	1.25	1.45	1.35
29	72.9	85.8	1.15	1.33	1.24
30	67.6	74.0	1.06	1.15	1.11
31	61.4	63.7	.97	.99	.98
32	54.7	55.0	.86	.85	.86
33	48.1	47.0	.76	.73	.75
34	37.2	38.9	.59	.60	.60
35	30.4	30.4	.48	.47	.48
36	25.3	26.1	.40	.40	.40
37	21.4	21.7	.34	.34	.34
38	20.6	18.1	.32	.28	.30
39	19.2	14.5	.30	.22	.26
40	20.3	12.5	.32	.19	.26
41	22.2	11.0	.35	.17	.26
42	26.3	11.1	.41	.17	.29
43	30.2	12.7	.48	.20	.34
44	34.5	13.8	.54	.21	.38
45	39.7	15.9	.63	.25	.44
46	45.9	18.3	.72	.28	.50
47	52.7	24.0	.83	.37	.60
48	59.9	28.4	.94	.44	.69
49	67.6	34.7	1.06	.54	.80
50	74.8	40.3	1.18	.62	.90
51	78.5	44.9	1.24	.70	.97
52	81.0	46.6	1.28	.72	1.00

Source: CRB Yearbooks, CRB Futures Charts service, a publication of Commodity Research Bureau. A Knight-Ridder Business Information Service ⓒ CRB.

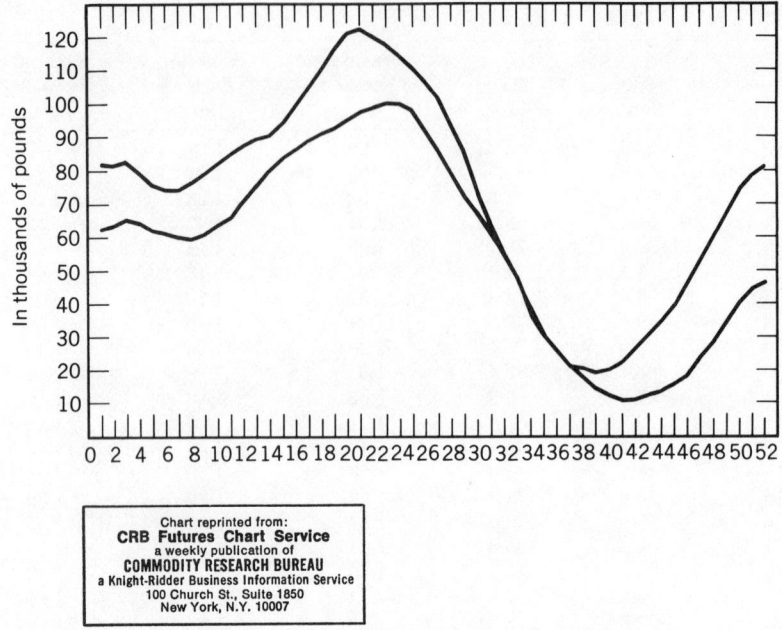

CHART 5.1 Weekly pork belly storage (*Source:* CRB Yearbooks, CRB Futures Charts Service, a publication of Commodity Research Bureau. A Knight-Ridder Business Information Service © CRB)

and

$$\frac{118 + 62}{2} = 90$$

for week 50.

Occasionally the number of reporting weeks varies across the evaluation years as there can be either 52 or 53 such periods. This aberration must be taken into account.

MONTHLY ANALYSIS

Cash No. 2 yellow corn at Chicago is seasonally analyzed by month in Table 5.2 and graphically by Chart 5.2. This example illustrates the method on a crop year—not a calendar year—basis. Nevertheless, there are 12 seasonal time periods (months) which require seasonal factors. As in the previous example, averages were calculated for each year. The statistics were: 295, 312, 275, 231, 226, 254, and 281. To arrive at the seasonal factor for October

TABLE 5.2. CASH CORN PRICES NO. 2 YELLOW, CHICAGO

Year	Oct	Nov	Dec	Jan	Feb	Mar	Apr	May	June	July	Aug	Sept	Totals	Mean Price
1973–1974	2.37	2.50	2.68	2.90	3.13	2.99	2.69	2.70	2.93	3.35	3.63	3.55	35.42	2.95
1974–1975	3.74	3.48	3.47	3.19	2.96	2.90	2.96	2.82	2.89	2.95	3.12	2.99	37.47	3.12
1975–1976	2.74	2.59	2.59	2.62	2.70	2.68	2.68	2.84	2.96	2.96	2.87	2.77	33.00	2.75
1976–1977	2.49	2.33	2.44	2.53	2.54	2.52	2.50	2.41	2.27	2.05	1.78	1.80	27.66	2.31
1977–1978	1.84	2.14	2.19	2.19	2.21	2.36	2.51	2.57	2.51	2.28	2.17	2.13	27.10	2.26
1978–1979	2.22	2.28	2.27	2.29	2.35	2.42	2.53	2.66	2.83	3.00	2.82	2.78	30.45	2.54
1979–1980	2.73	2.59	2.69	2.54	2.65	2.65	2.60	2.61	2.70	3.08	3.36	3.44	33.69	2.81

Seasonal Factors

Year	Oct	Nov	Dec	Jan	Feb	Mar	Apr	May	June	July	Aug	Sept
1973–1974	80	85	91	98	106	101	91	92	99	114	123	120
1974–1975	120	112	111	102	95	93	95	90	93	95	100	96
1975–1976	100	94	94	95	98	97	97	103	108	108	104	101
1976–1977	108	101	106	110	110	109	108	104	98	89	77	78
1977–1978	81	95	97	97	98	104	111	114	111	101	96	94
1978–1979	87	90	89	90	93	95	100	105	111	118	111	109
1979–1980	97	92	96	90	94	93	93	96	96	110	120	122
Sum	673	669	684	682	694	692	695	704	716	733	731	720
Grand	96	96	98	97	99	99	99	101	102	105	104	103

Adjusted Seasonal Factors

(deleted 1974–1975)	Oct	Nov	Dec	Jan	Feb	Mar	Apr	May	June	July	Aug	Sept
Sum	553	557	573	580	599	599	600	614	623	640	631	624
Aver.	92	93	96	97	100	100	100	102	104	107	105	104

Source: CRB Yearbooks, CRB Futures Charts Service, a publication of Commodity Research Bureau. A Knight-Ridder Business Information Service © CRB.

1973–1974, that month's price was divided by that year's one average monthly price multiplied by 100, or

$$\frac{237 \times 100}{295} = 80$$

This process was continued for all months and years. It is important to rec-

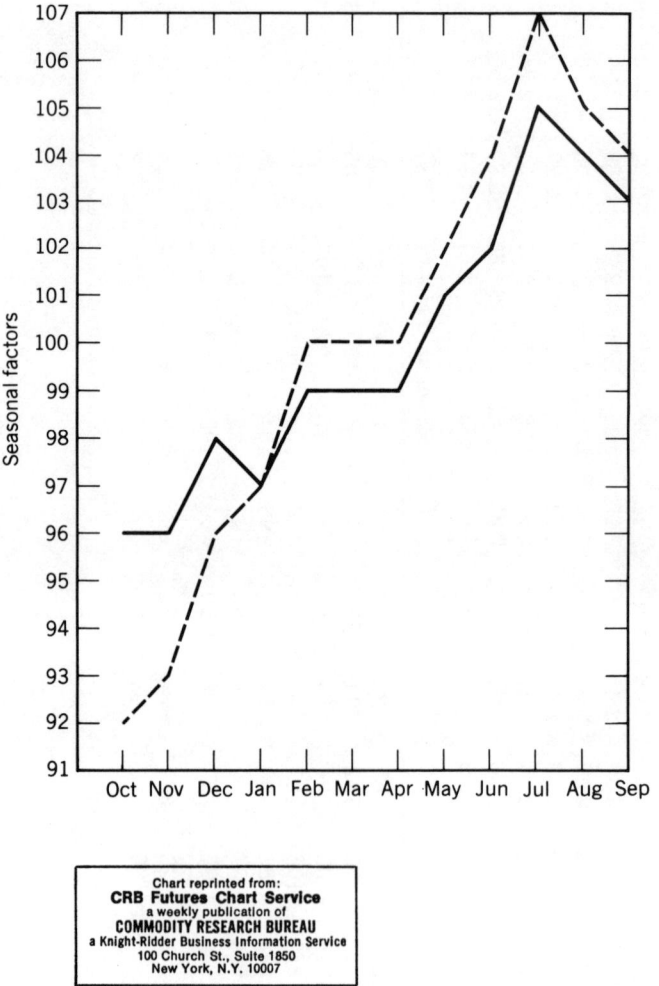

CHART 5.2 Grand and adjusted seasonal factors for corn prices (*Source:* CRB Yearbooks, CRB Futures Charts Service, a publication of Commodity Research Bureau. A Knight-Ridder Business Information Service © CRB)

TABLE 5.3. AVERAGE PRICE OF NO. 2 RED WINTER WHEAT AT CHICAGO (DOLLARS PER BUSHEL)

Year	Jun	Jul	Aug	Sep	Oct	Nov	Dec	Jan	Feb	Mar	Apr	May
1978-1979	3.18	3.22	3.32	3.42	3.51	3.68	3.68	3.73	3.88	3.79	3.60	3.86
1979-1980	4.36	4.39	4.23	4.28	4.30	4.13	4.26	2.36	4.39	4.18	3.96	4.04
1980-1981	3.96	4.17	4.21	4.38	4.70	4.92	4.54	4.57	4.34	4.15	4.18	3.80
1981-1982	3.60	3.70	3.70	3.87	3.97	4.08	3.86	3.77	3.57	3.59	3.70	3.43
1982-1983	3.31	3.36	3.35	3.18	2.98	3.33	3.23	3.32	3.40	3.36	3.51	3.55
1983-1984	3.53	3.59	3.71	3.62	3.56	3.42	3.55	3.47	3.34	3.57	3.65	3.65
X =	3.66	3.74	3.75	3.79	3.84	3.93	3.85	3.87	3.82	3.77	3.77	3.72

Source: CRB Yearbooks, CRB Futures Charts Service, a publication of Commodity Research Bureau. A Knight-Ridder Business Information Service © CRB.

ognize that this table calculated the adjusted grand seasonal factors. In other words, data for one or more years were selectively omitted since there may have been stratification in the data. This stratification manifests itself as atypical behavior and the 1974–1975 crop year appears to be such a period, particularly as its October monthly seasonal factor is at its yearly maximum at a time when there tends to be the greatest seasonal weakness. By performing the grand seasonal calculations omitting the 1974–1975 crop year, it can be seen that the seasonal factors have become somewhat more pronounced. This is graphically depicted by the broken line series in Chart 5.2.

The average price of No. 2 red winter wheat at Chicago is listed in Table 5.3 and portrayed by Chart 5.3. Its seasonal factors are listed in Table 5.4 while Table 5.5 presents an analysis of the seasonal factors.

Seasonally, this particular type of wheat experiences lows in June and highs in November; but from an absolute variation perspective as determined by range, the greatest variability is in May and the lowest is in December. The variability concept is important as it isolates those periods which exhibit potentially large or small departures from expectations. In other words, it highlights risk. By using this concept, the analyst is furnished with information about time periods more prone to extraordinary event occurrence, which has importance for the possible emergence of contraseasonal behavior. Therefore the trading program can be modified to approach the marketplace

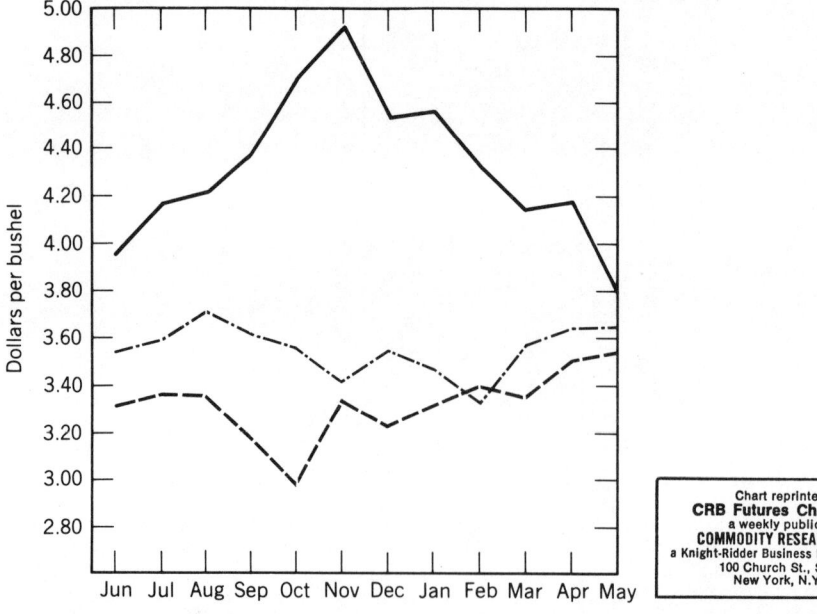

CHART 5.3 Selective display of No. 2 red winter wheat at Chicago (*Source:* CRB Yearbooks, CRB Futures Charts Service, a publication of Commodity Research Bureau. A Knight-Ridder Business Information Service © CRB)

TABLE 5.4. SEASONAL FACTORS FOR AVERAGE PRICE OF NO. 2 RED WINTER WHEAT AT CHICAGO

Year	Jun	Jul	Aug	Sep	Oct	Nov	Dec	Jan	Feb	Mar	Apr	May
1978–1979	89.08	90.20	93.00	95.80	98.32	103.08	103.08	104.48	108.68	106.16	100.84	108.12
1979–1980	102.83	103.54	99.76	100.94	101.42	97.41	100.47	102.83	103.54	98.58	93.40	95.28
1980–1981	91.45	96.30	97.23	101.15	108.55	113.63	104.85	105.54	100.23	95.84	96.54	87.76
1981–1982	96.26	98.93	98.93	103.48	106.15	109.09	103.21	100.80	95.45	95.99	98.93	91.71
1982–1983	99.70	101.20	100.90	95.78	89.76	100.30	97.29	100.00	102.41	101.20	105.72	106.93
1983–1984	99.16	100.84	104.21	101.69	100.00	96.07	99.72	97.47	93.82	100.28	102.53	102.53

Source: CRB Yearbooks, CRB Futures Charts Service, a publication of Commodity Research Bureau. A Knight-Ridder Business Information Service © CRB.

TABLE 5.5. ANALYSIS OF WHEAT SEASONAL FACTORS (DESCRIPTIVE STATISTICS)

	Jun	Jul	Aug	Sep	Oct	Nov	Dec	Jan	Feb	Mar	Apr	May
Sum	578.48	591.01	594.03	598.84	604.20	619.58	608.62	611.12	604.13	598.05	597.96	592.33
Index	96.41	98.50	99.01	99.81	100.70	103.26	101.44	101.85	100.69	99.68	99.66	98.72
High	102.83	103.54	104.21	103.48	108.55	113.63	104.85	105.54	108.68	106.16	105.72	108.12
Low	89.08	90.20	93.00	95.78	89.76	96.07	97.29	97.47	93.82	95.84	93.40	87.76
Range	13.75	13.34	11.21	7.70	18.79	17.56	7.56	8.07	14.86	10.32	12.32	20.36

Source: CRB Yearbooks, CRB Futures Charts Service, a publication of Commodity Research Bureau. A Knight-Ridder Business Information Service © CRB.

on a conditional basis and not an unconditional one where strategies are instituted in a strictly mechanical manner.

QUARTERLY ANALYSIS

Seasonal variations in U.S. cocoa grindings are assessed by the data in Tables 5.6, 5.7, 5.8, and 5.9 and graphically by Chart 5.4. Tables 5.6 and 5.7 represent the years 1971–1980 while Tables 5.8 and 5.9 represent 1981–1984. The year is divided into 4 quarters, each representing one seasonal factor. Table 5.6 lists the early raw data while Table 5.7 lists the early seasonal factors. Going through the arithmetic, the seasonal factor for the first quarter of 1971 was determined by:

$$\frac{65.3}{69.7} \times 100 = 94$$

and the fourth quarter of 1979 was determined by:

$$\frac{37.0}{40.1} \times 100 = 92.$$

The grand seasonal factor for the second quarters across the years for Tables 5.6 and 5.7 was simply the average of all second-quarter factors, or

$$\frac{97 + 91 + 105 + 102 + 99 + 98 + 102 + 94 + 103 + 88}{10} = 105$$

TABLE 5.6. UNITED STATES QUARTERLY COCOA GRINDINGS (IN THOUSANDS OF METRIC TONS)

Year	1Q	2Q	3Q	4Q	Total	Average
1971	65.3	67.9	66.8	78.9	278.9	69.7
1972	79.3	66.1	63.2	80.4	289.0	72.3
1973	77.9	73.4	60.7	66.5	278.5	69.6
1974	67.6	58.8	54.5	48.7	229.6	57.4
1975	43.7	51.7	53.2	59.3	207.9	52.0
1976	60.9	55.0	55.0	54.5	225.4	56.4
1977	56.5	46.9	40.9	39.4	183.7	45.9
1978	42.0	38.4	36.9	45.3	162.6	40.7
1979	40.5	41.4	41.4	37.0	160.3	40.1
1980	33.5	31.5	34.9	42.4	142.3	35.6
	567.2	531.1	507.5	552.4	column totals	
	56.7	53.1	50.8	55.2	column averages	

Source: CRB Yearbooks, CRB Futures Charts Service, a publication of Commodity Research Bureau. A Knight-Ridder Business Information Service © CRB.

TABLE 5.7. SEASONAL FACTORS FOR U.S. COCOA GRINDINGS (FOR 1971 TO 1980)

Year	1Q	2Q	3Q	4Q	Average
1971	94	97	96	113	100
1972	110	91	87	111	100
1973	112	105	87	96	100
1974	118	102	95	85	100
1975	84	99	102	114	100
1976	108	98	98	97	100
1977	123	102	89	86	100
1978	103	94	91	111	100
1979	101	103	103	92	100
1980	94	88	98	119	100
	1047	979	946	1024	column totals
	105	98	95	102	column averages

Source: CRB Yearbooks, CRB Futures Charts Service, a publication of Commodity Research Bureau. A Knight-Ridder Business Information Service © CRB.

TABLE 5.8. UNITED STATES QUARTERLY COCOA GRINDINGS (IN THOUSANDS OF METRIC TONS)

Year	1Q	2Q	3Q	4Q	Total	Average
1981	48.4	46.0	48.8	47.1	190.3	47.6
1982	47.7	50.6	50.1	50.7	199.1	49.8
1983	45.9	46.7	47.8	53.2	193.6	48.4
1984	42.4	41.6	40.9	39.5	164.4	41.1

Source: CRB Yearbooks, CRB Futures Charts Service, a publication of Commodity Research Bureau. A Knight-Ridder Business Information Service © CRB.

TABLE 5.9. SEASONAL FACTORS FOR U.S. COCOA GRINDINGS (FOR 1981 TO 1984)

Year	1Q	2Q	3Q	4Q	
1981	1.02	.97	1.03	.99	
1982	.96	1.02	1.01	1.02	
1983	.95	.96	.99	1.10	
1984	1.03	1.01	1.00	.96	
	3.96	3.96	4.03	4.07	column totals
	.99	.99	1.01	1.02	column averages

Source: CRB Yearbooks, CRB Futures Charts Service, a publication of Commodity Research Bureau. A Knight-Ridder Business Information Service © CRB.

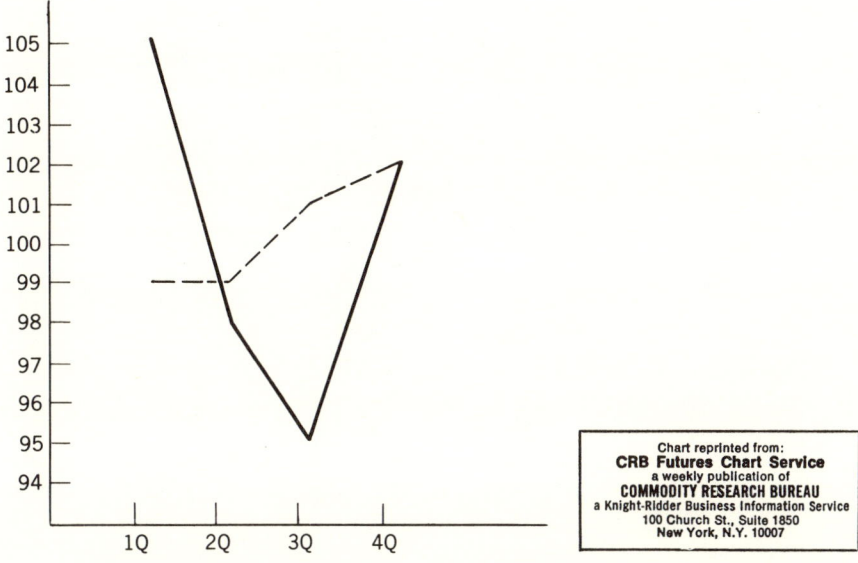

CHART 5.4 Seasonal factors for 2 periods for U.S. cocoa grindings

Thus, on a seasonal basis, Tables 5.6 and 5.7 indicate the greatest grinding period is the first quarter and slowest is the third quarter. However, the more recent tabular data suggest a shift away from this behavior as the first two quarterly factors are the minimums while the second half of the year reflects increased grinding activity. Therefore it is necessary to ascertain whether there has been a change in the overall seasonal process which can impact the reliability of the simple application of seasonal factors.

SEASONAL COMPARISONS

This section reexamines the value of detecting greater-than or less-than seasonal occurrences. As mentioned previously, atypical behavior can suggest the presence of other dominant forces. Returning to the data provided in Table 5.2, corn acted in a stronger than normally expected manner, particularly from the July of 1973–1974 year through the first 4 months of the 1974–1975 year. This can be seen by comparing those specific seasonal factors against the corresponding grand seasonal factors. For example, the July 1973–1974 seasonal factor was 114 versus a grand seasonal factor of 105, or an adjusted grand seasonal factor of 107. By similarly comparing the other months in this fashion it can be seen that corn was acting stronger than one would usually expect.

Another variation to this approach is through deseasonalized statistics. Essentially, these statistics indicate what prices would have been if there were no seasonal factors at work. Tables 5.10 and 5.11 illustrate this concept.

TABLE 5.10. DESEASONALIZED SERIES (IN CENTS PER BUSHEL)

	Feb 1974	Mar 1974	Apr 1974	May 1974	Jun 1974	Jul 1974	Aug 1974	Sep 1974	Oct 1974	Nov 1974	Dec 1974	Jan 1975
Actual prices	313	299	269	270	293	335	363	355	374	348	347	319
Grand seasonal factors	99	99	99	101	102	105	104	103	96	96	98	97
Deseasonalized factors	316	302	272	267	287	319	349	345	390	363	354	329

Source: CRB Yearbooks, CRB Futures Charts Service, a publication of Commodity Research Bureau. A Knight-Ridder Business Information Service © CRB.

TABLE 5.11. DESEASONALIZED SERIES (IN CENTS PER BUSHEL)

	Feb 1974	Mar 1974	Apr 1974	May 1974	Jun 1974	Jul 1974	Aug 1974	Sep 1974	Oct 1974	Nov 1974	Dec 1974	Jan 1975
Actual prices	313	299	269	270	293	335	363	355	374	348	347	319
Grand seasonal factors	100	100	100	102	104	107	105	104	92	93	96	97
Deseasonalized factors	313	299	269	265	282	313	346	341	407	374	361	329

Source: CRB Yearbooks, CRB Futures Charts Service, a publication of Commodity Research Bureau. A Knight-Ridder Business Information Service © CRB.

In Table 5.10, the price change between July and August 1974 was 28 cents; however, the deseasonalized data show the change to be 30 cents or somewhat greater. A large deviation was the September-to-October 1974 change. For actual prices there was a 19-cent gain, but on a deseasonalized basis it translated into a substantial 45-cent increase. Table 5.11 dramatizes this state of affairs even more. Examining the same two monthly changes, it is seen that the deseasonalized gains were 33 and 66 cents, respectively.

Table 5.11 highlights a less-than situation. Although actual prices dropped only 1 cent from November 1974 (348) to December 1974 (347), the deseasonalized data suggest a 13-cent decline. Returning to Table 5.2, it can be seen that soon thereafter a major sell-off occurred.

Critical Considerations

It is critical to identify the length of the entire seasonal process before dissecting it into separate time units that will represent the relatively consistent behavior patterns. The analysis need not commence at the beginning of the week or month, since the important departure dates can vary from those derived from a casual glance at a calendar. Moreover, the entire process can be partitioned into seemingly irregular time units, but the definition of their factor periods should be consistent for each process year. For example, a 6-period year can be comprised of the following factors:

Factor 1 = January & February

Factor 2 = March & April

Factor 3 = May & June

Factor 4 = July, August, & September

Factor 5 = October & November

Factor 6 = December

Note that not all the factors consist of 2 months; rather, most were 2 months in length but for explanatory purposes Factor 4 was designated a 3-month period and Factor 6 a 1-month period. Nevertheless, if this arrangement is identified as a reasonable partition, it should be applied throughout the analysis across the various years. As in most rules, there are exceptions, and this is no different. Due to marketplace anticipations, the exact arrival of an important departure date can be earlier or later than usual. Additionally, structural shifts in the economic variables can alter the timing of departure dates. For example, structural shifts in agricultural production can encourage more double cropping or productivity in less climate-vulnerable areas. Similarly, construction activity would be less prone to weather conditions in the Southwest than in the Northeast, affecting regional construction statistics differently.

INTERACTIONS AMONG TIME SERIES COMPONENTS

Seasonal analysis is influenced not only by the underlying cyclical and trend movements in the given time series but by cyclical and trend properties within the seasonal factors themselves. These interactions can generate either more widely varying or dampening seasonal values over time.

By reviewing the seasonal factor tables presented earlier, it is easy to see that seasonality exists, but its behavior is not identical in amplitude or periodicity over time. Applying further refinements to the seasonal factors can produce improved forecasts and explanations of time-series behavior.

A Word of Caution

Many time series, particularly those for the economic-financial markets, are released on a seasonally adjusted basis. This basis can be somewhat problematical as the seasonal adjustment methods must be acquired in order to assess more accurately not only those data but their relationship to nonseasonally adjusted series. As demonstrated previously, the two perspectives on data provide complementary insights to the behavior of the specified time series.

6
Cyclical Analysis

A QUANTITATIVE APPROACH

Cycles are one of the components of a time series, the others being: trend, seasonality, and irregular movements. Some researchers include waves or extremely long-term price behavior as a final element in the analysis of a time series. Cycles can be short-, intermediate-, or long-term in nature. Examples of this would be: intraday, daily, weekly, monthly, or yearly swings or some combination thereof. The most readily obvious ones are those which are seasonal. Harvest pressures on prices, accumulation and distribution of stocks, demand flows, monetary activities, and a broad list of other economic items demonstrate this feature. Methods used for seasonal analysis can be adapted to the study of cycles, and there are other techniques particularly developed for cyclical analysis.

The dissection of a time series usually begins by detrending the series, leaving the seasonal, irregular, and cyclical components. Proceeding with this extraction of forces, the next step is the removal of seasonality. Typically the irregular component is viewed as a broadly defined "error" component, leaving the last major factor, the cyclical influence.

Series are often described as either periodic or oscillatory in behavior. The easiest to analyze are the periodic series. In periodic series the duration or time length of the cyclical component is fairly regular; optimally it is also fairly constant in amplitude, which is the difference between its maximum (peak) and its minimum (trough). As most price series tend to lack this regularity and constancy, other approaches are necessary. The application of higher mathematical techniques such as Fourier analysis and spectrum analysis can generally refute the existence of many economic cycles that do exist. The primary rationale is that the last two techniques require certain periodic characteristics not usually present. Although these techniques are rather powerful and can decipher hidden periodic action, they are ill-equipped to do so when either the amplitude or duration, or both, is highly erratic.

The problem becomes one of operator identification. Though many mathematical purists would be uncomfortable with this, statisticians would not. The application of curve-fitting techniques, especially higher order polynomials, usually lacks sufficiently tolerable predictability as well as being inordinately difficult to solve. Sometimes the optimal approach is the simple one, particularly if it is more suitable to the problem. For example, the basic measurement of previous time lengths of cycles and their amplitudes provides the analyst with a basic historical background for the specified series. Though series have behaved within definable boundaries, they have also varied among themselves. Although series are not expected to repeat in a precise fashion, they are expected to recur in an approximate manner.

Departures from past tendencies generally indicate other abnormally powerful forces acting on the series, and they should become the focal points of the analysis. For example, greater-than-normal or even contracyclical behavior suggests that something out of the ordinary is taking place in the market. Systematic trend followers savor such situations, for they are generally exploitable on their expected value basis. These situations can also indicate a more powerful confluence of cyclical factors.

The first step is to surmise the expected time frame from peak to trough. Then the measurement continues to determine the length from peak to peak and from trough to trough. Since these series tend to be irregular in length, the significance of these additional measurements is to isolate some sort of stable duration for the life of the cycle. These differences occur since the typical culmination of a large move is followed by a period of relative stagnation or dampened amplitude. The simple addition of the peak to trough time frame is unsatisfactory. The reason: Such an additive component would strongly suggest a mathematically periodic nature to the series when this is not frequently the case. For example, demand for certain items can manifest itself differently for some months depending on how long the Christmas shopping season is; or, in which month Easter occurs. Everyone recognizes the retail orientation of these two events, yet a nonadaptive approach for observation and analysis of these two occurrences would be inaccurate.

Similarly, the occurrence of a mild or harsh winter in the Northeast would cause a substantial difference in the demand structure for heating oil.

The following decomposition of soybean stocks at U.S. mills on the first of the month (Table 6.1) will define the terms used and provide data for a nonparametric analysis for the presence of cycles. This approach makes no assumptions about the distribution characteristics of a given time series, and it does not require a strict regularity in time or amplitude. Its greatest weakness is the lack of a projection or point predictability of a series, but other techniques presented throughout this handbook tackle that issue.

TABLE 6.1. SOYBEAN STOCKS AT U.S. MILLS ON FIRST OF MONTH[a] (IN MILLIONS OF BUSHELS)

Crop Year	Sept	Oct	Nov	Dec	Jan	Feb	Mar	Apr	May	Jun	Jul	Aug
1973–1974	N30.7	−13.5	+89.5	+125.8	−115.8	+119.0	+123.0	−112.3	−95.5	−81.5	−66.5	−57.0
1974–1975	−41.6	−23.0	+93.9	+123.0	−102.5	−83.2	−79.2	−65.3	−55.4	−44.3	−37.7	−35.4
1975–1976	−27.4	−26.8	+116.6	+137.2	−131.5	−121.1	−109.8	−101.3	−92.8	−79.4	−80.5	−66.3
1976–1977	−48.7	+63.0	+127.5	+159.8	−154.2	−147.5	−146.5	−140.3	−126.8	−108.6	−83.4	−50.9
1977–1978	−23.4	−20.3	+101.5	+123.9	−113.0	−94.4	−87.3	+102.8	−90.2	−76.3	−54.5	−44.6
1978–1979	−37.9	−31.9	+138.4	+149.4	−127.3	−112.4	+124.0	−120.9	−96.7	−71.1	+73.0	−55.6
1979–1980	−37.5	+39.2	+166.5	+184.5	−163.3	−145.4	−130.7	−118.6	−95.8	−79.7	−75.7	−73.9
1980–1981	−56.9	+80.4	+166.0	+172.0	−138.7	−125.9	−105.4	−97.2	−84.4	−67.8	−49.2	−43.9
1981–1982	−33.4	−31.5	+105.8	+135.2	−114.5	−99.8	−84.6	−79.2	−72.2	−60.8	−51.2	−43.6
1982–1983	−30.0	−29.0	+114.2	+145.5	−125.1	−116.2	−98.5	−96.2	−84.6	−69.8	−62.0	−55.4
1983–1984	−58.6	+63.9	+124.5	+142.3	−124.0	+125.3	−114.8	−105.3	−94.2	+101.7	−83.4	−57.7

[a]N represents no change sign available for data as given.

Source: CRB Yearbooks, CRB Futures Charts Service, a publication of Commodity Research Bureau. A Knight-Ridder Business Information Service © CRB.

111

MEASUREMENT OF CYCLES

The time distance between a peak and trough or trough and peak is referred to as a phase: It is the duration between two consecutive turning points. This concept of phase is relevant to the nonparametric study of cycles.

The time distance between two consecutive peaks or two consecutive lows is a cycle. It reflects the two phases, upward and downward. It should be noted that the duration of the upward movement need not be equal to the downward movement. In fact, for most futures and their underlying cash markets, there is a significant difference between the duration, depending on phase type.

The first step is to identify the phase length, or the duration from peak to trough and from trough to peak. This dual measurement is necessary since the cyclic components share certain commonality in up-phases versus the commonalities present during down-phases. Table 6.1 lists the soybean stock data per crop year. Preceding each column is a plus or minus sign, which represents the difference in stock levels between successive calendar months. It shows that stocks have always increased between October 1 through December 1, while always declining during September, December, April, and July. For the other months there were mixed patterns, though some were more heavily weighted in favor of one type versus the other. Chart 6.1 graphically portrays this series.

Observationally, the series peaks in December and troughs either in September or October. It reflects a pattern of stock accumulation during harvest and subsequent distribution during the marketing year.

Examining Table 6.1 by going along row one, the first phase is down of length 1, from September 1 to October 1, 1973. This is followed by an up phase of length 2. Therefore, the first complete cycle for these data is represented by a 3-month length. Proceeding with this analysis, the December 1973 to January 1974 period is a down phase of length 1, while the subsequent up phase is of length 2. Again, a completed cycle is of a 3-month length. The third down phase is of length 7 and the subsequent up phase is of length 2 for a cycle length of 9. This procedure continues for the remainder of the data.

Table 6.2 compositely lists the lengths of monthly sign phase runs, regardless of direction. It indicates a total of 35 phases. Table 6.3 further refines these runs as to upward (+) or downward (−). There were 17 up phases and 18 down phases for a total of 17 completed cycles.

Table 6.3 points out that all up phases have terminated by the end of the third month while only one-half of the down phases terminated by the end of the third month. Thus a distinct difference exists between these particular phase lengths by type. As there are 132 observations, n equals 132. The beginning and ending points impact the study since by definition the number of turning points requires neighboring values for comparison.

Mathematically, a goodness-of-fit test is required since the problem be-

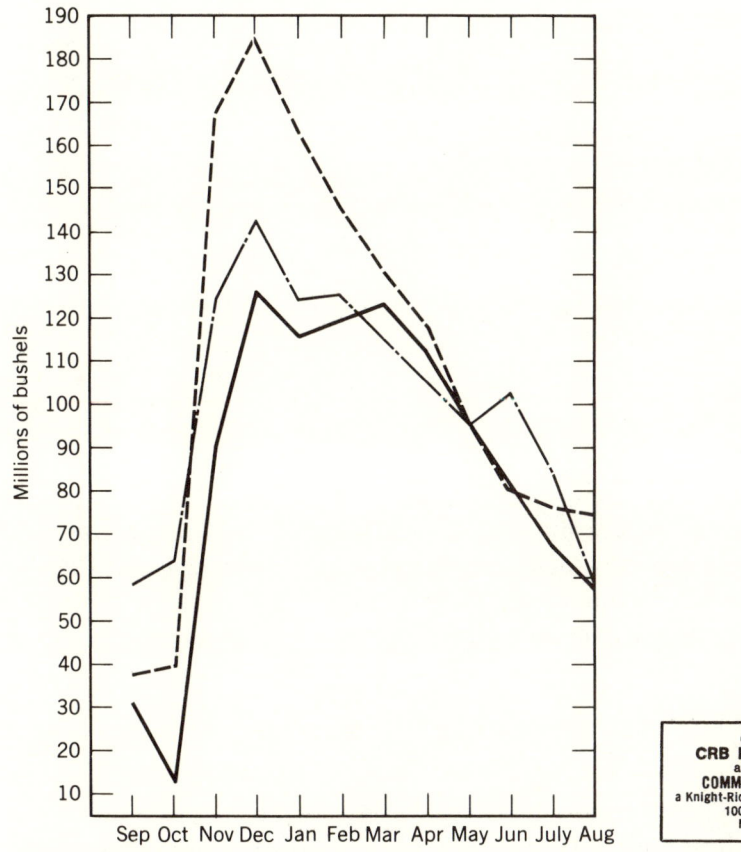

CHART 6.1 Selective presentation of soybean stocks at U.S. mills on first of month (*Source:* CRB Yearbooks, CRB Futures Charts Service, a publication of Commodity Research Bureau. A Knight-Ridder Business Information Service © CRB)

comes one of hypothesis testing. There are two hypotheses: (1) the series acts as an independently random one; (2) the series is characterized by cyclical fluctuations. The goodness-of-fit test is readily tested. The solution requires the determination of the theoretically expected phase run lengths versus the observed phase run lengths. The formulas for these are:

$$EL_1 = \frac{5(n-3)}{12}$$

$$EL_2 = \frac{11(n-4)}{60}$$

and

$$EL_3 = \frac{4n-21}{60}$$

TABLE 6.2. NONDIFFERENTIATED PHASE LENGTHS

Length	1	2	3	4	5	6	7	8	9	10	11	12
Number of phases	8	11	7	0	0	1	1	0	3	4	0	0

TABLE 6.3. PHASE LENGTHS DIFFERENTIATED BY TYPES

Length	1	2	3	4	5	6	7	8	9	10	11	12
Number of up $(+)$	5	8	4	0	0	0	0	0	0	0	0	0
Number of down $(-)$	3	3	3	0	0	1	1	0	3	4	0	0

Total: 17 up phases
       18 down phases

Expectationally, EL_1 represents all the expected phase runs of length 1, EL_2 represents all the expected phase runs of length 2, and EL_3 represents all the expected phase runs which are greater than 2. Table 6.4 lists the expected versus the observed phase run lengths.

The goodness-of-fit statistic is evaluated by:

$$\chi_P^2 = \frac{\left(A_1 - EL_1\right)^2}{EL_1} + \frac{\left(A_2 - EL_2\right)^2}{EL_2} + \frac{\left(A_3 - EL_3\right)^2}{EL_3}$$

where χ_P^2 is the chi-square phase run statistic, A_1, A_2, and A_3, are the actual observations for phase runs of lengths 1, 2, and 3 or more, respectively. Here, the χ_P^2 is 52.32 or substantially greater from the accept hypothesis one statistic of 10.28 for a desired significance level of .01. In other words, this series does not behave as an independently random one, rather it manifests cyclical attributes in a statistical sense.

It should be noted that the expectation of brief phase runs such as those equal to 1 or 2 have the highest expected values. Moreover, these expectations diminish with increasing phase run lengths. This is clearly not the case here. In fact, just the opposite occurred with the frequency of observed phase values increasing with the extended lengths.

Although the conclusion seems obvious from the raw data and their attendant plot, this test is extremely sensitive for detecting the absence or ex-

TABLE 6.4. PHASE LENGTH RUNS

Length	Observed	Expected
1	8	53.75
2	11	23.47
3 or more	16	8.45

istence of cyclical fluctuations in time series which are observationally devoid of readily apparent cyclical behavior. Similarly, the potency of this test helps to differentiate between illusory and statistically significant cyclical forces.

The aforementioned demonstration was a three-fold classification. W. A. Wallis and G. H. Moore have suggested that the ordinary application of the χ_P^2 test should be supplanted by values predicated on 2.5 degrees of freedom for values greater than or equal to 6.3. For lesser values, $\frac{6}{7} \chi_P^2$ with 2 degrees of freedom is recommended.

For higher degrees of classification, the formula for expected phase run length frequencies is:

$$E(L) = \frac{2(L^2 + 3L + 1)(n - L - 2)}{(L + 3)!}$$

where $E(L)$ represents the expected number of phase run lengths of a designated size L.

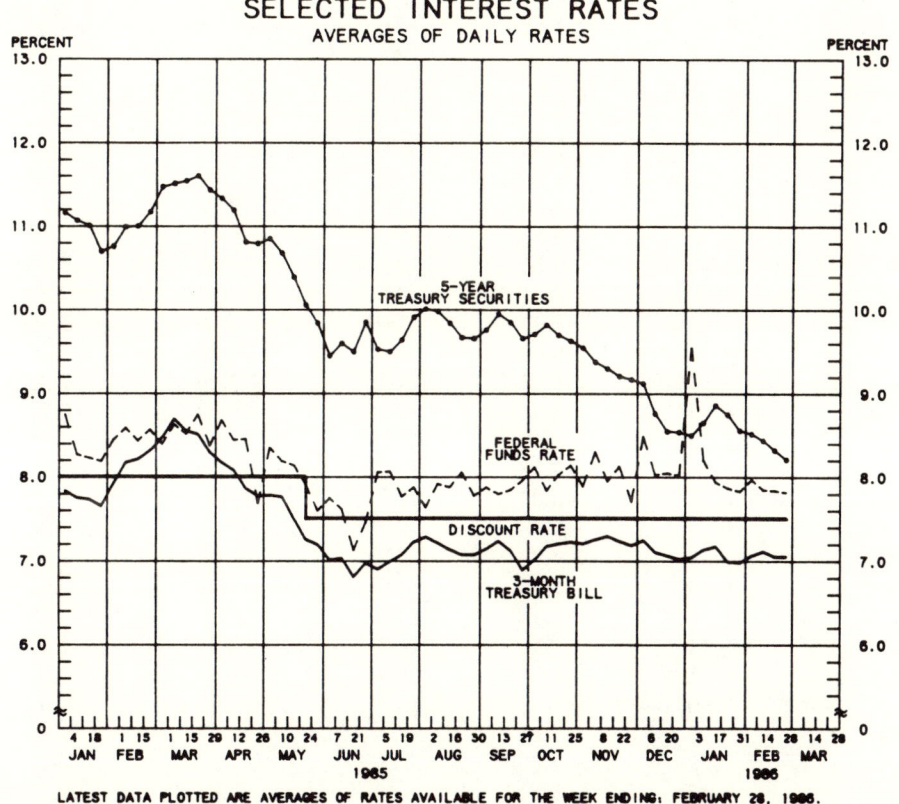

LATEST DATA PLOTTED ARE AVERAGES OF RATES AVAILABLE FOR THE WEEK ENDING: FEBRUARY 28, 1986.

CHART 6.2 Selected interest rates (*Source: U.S. Financial Data*, Federal Reserve Bank of St. Louis)

It should be noted, as in the case of many other nonparametric tests, cardinal classifications and analyses are dispensed with by transforming the data into more general ordinal classifications. These generalized methods function equally as well with periodic series or oscillatory ones.

Chart 6.2 depicts federal funds and 3-month Treasury bill yields which are listed in Table 6.5. Although both of these markets are short term, the two series behave differently. As shown in Table 6.6, both series exhibit cyclic

TABLE 6.5. FED FUNDS AND T-BILL DATA[a]

Date	Federal Funds	3-Month Treasury Bill	Date	Federal Funds	3-Month Treasury Bill
11/2/84	N9.73	N9.10	7/05	+8.06	−6.90
11/09	+9.87	−8.65	7/12	+8.07	+6.99
11/16	−9.55	+8.68	7/19	−7.77	+7.07
11/23	−9.47	−8.55	7/26	+7.88	+7.25
11/30	−9.00	−8.41	8/02	−7.64	+7.28
12/07	−8.83	+8.44	8/09	+7.92	−7.21
12/14	−8.70	−8.27	8/16	−7.88	−7.13
12/21	−7.99	−7.81	8/23	+8.06	−7.07
12/28	−7.95	−7.67	8/30	−7.78	N7.07
1/04/85	+8.75	+7.83	9/06	+7.88	+7.08
1/11	−8.27	−7.75	9/13	−7.80	+7.23
1/18	−8.23	−7.72	9/20	+7.85	−7.16
1/25	−8.19	−7.65	9/27	+7.96	−6.89
2/01	+8.45	+7.92	10/04	+8.12	+7.01
2/08	+8.59	+8.15	10/11	−7.84	+7.17
2/15	−8.44	+8.21	10/18	+8.03	+7.20
2/22	+8.57	+8.31	10/25	+8.14	+7.22
3/01	−8.40	+8.47	11/01	−7.89	−7.20
3/08	+8.63	+8.69	11/08	+8.30	+7.25
3/15	−8.52	−8.54	11/15	−7.95	+7.29
3/22	+8.75	−8.51	11/22	+8.13	−7.23
3/29	−8.38	−8.29	11/29	−7.71	−7.18
4/05	+8.18	−8.17	12/06	+8.49	+7.24
4/12	−8.45	−8.08	12/13	−8.03	−7.14
4/19	+8.46	−7.86	12/20	+8.05	−7.06
4/26	−7.69	−7.73	12/27	−8.02	−7.02
5/03	+8.35	+7.78	1/03/86	+9.55	+7.04
5/10	−8.19	−7.76	1/10	−8.20	+7.13
5/17	−8.14	−7.58	1/17	−7.94	+7.17
5/24	−7.91	−7.25	1/24	−7.87	−6.99
5/31	−7.60	−7.19	1/31	−7.83	−6.97
6/07	+7.75	−7.01	2/07	+7.97	+7.06
6/14	−7.62	+7.03	2/14	−7.85	+7.11
6/21	−7.13	−6.81	2/21	−7.84	−7.05
6/28	+7.46	+7.05	2/28	−7.82	N7.05

[a]N represents no change sign available for data as given.
Source: U.S. Financial Data, Federal Reserve Bank of St. Louis.

TABLE 6.6. EXPECTED VERSUS ACTUAL RUNS

Length	Federal Funds		Treasury Bills	
	Expected	Actual	Expected	Actual
L_1	11.25	18	11.25	3
L_2	4.77	1	4.77	5
L_3	1.65	3	1.65	5

Source: U.S. Financial Data, Federal Reserve Bank of St. Louis.

tendencies; but the federal funds series was fluctuating more rapidly than theoretically expected while the Treasury bill series fluctuated significantly less rapidly than theoretically expected.

This approach can be used with hourly, daily, quarterly, and yearly data. Even though the test proved the existence of cyclic behavior in all three time series here, the presence of a trend, particularly a pronounced one, can influence the reliability of the test since the clustering of phase length runs could be misconstrued as a cyclic phenomenon.

The detrending of the data by one of the popular methods, such as moving averages, would reduce the distortive impact of the trend effect.

It should be recognized that the analyst's assessment of the warranted smoothing techniques and parameters plays an important role in the development of a model. The misspecification of moving average lengths, linear or nonlinear trend, or ignorance of potentially important seasonal effects can limit the application of the calculated statistics. Algorithmic procedures can be useful if they result in a convergence at or about the true underlying value. Likelihood functions and maximum likelihood estimates are important techniques for determining optimal parameter values. They are explained in other chapters.

7
Spread Analysis

DEFINING THE PROCESS

Differentials are the epoxy of the marketplace. They define relationships not only within a market but among the various markets. By doing so, differentials infuse the cohesive value determination mechanism. Spreading—or swapping—is the adjustment process for this mechanism.

Spreads reflect the relationship between two or more prices. This relationship can be one of the basis, premium, discount, crush margin, crack margin, arbitrage, or simply the "spread." Unlike trading, which depends on anticipated movements in absolute prices, spread trading places positions to exploit an anticipated movement in the specified relationship, which can be varied and exotic. These positions can be: intracommodity such as a nearby Treasury bond futures versus a deferred Treasury bond futures; intermarket such as New York versus Chicago silver, or S&P 500 futures versus S&P 500 cash index (or surrogate); intercommodity such as platinum versus gold, or Treasury bills versus Eurodollars (the TED spread); or crop year such as July versus December cotton. These relational positions are extended to options as well. Table 7.1 lists the Treasury note over bond spread. Charts 7.1, 7.2, 7.3, 7.4, and 7.5 portray examples of various differential types.

Crush and reverse crush spreads occur within the soybean complex. Should margins prove profitable, then a crush spread may be warranted where the trader purchases the soybean futures and sells soybean products—the bean oil and meal—by the appropriate number of contracts. Or if soybeans are relatively uneconomical to "crush" given the value of its two main products, then a reverse crush can be undertaken where the products are purchased because they are comparatively cheap and the beans are sold since they are comparatively expensive. Chart 7.6 displays a crush relationship.

For the petroleum complex, the crack and reverse crack spreads reflect

TABLE 7.1. Treasury Note versus Treasury Bond Futures Spread

Date	September 1986		Notes over Bonds Spread
	T-Note	T-Bond	
July 29, 1986	$101\frac{3}{32}$	$96\frac{15}{32}$	$4\frac{20}{32}$
July 30, 1986	$101\frac{9}{32}$	$97\_$	$4\frac{9}{32}$
July 31, 1986	$101\frac{26}{32}$	$97\frac{26}{32}$	$4\_$
August 1, 1986	$102\frac{1}{32}$	$97\frac{13}{32}$	$4\frac{20}{32}$
August 4, 1986	$102\frac{2}{32}$	$97\frac{25}{32}$	$4\frac{9}{32}$
August 5, 1986	$101\frac{24}{32}$	$96\frac{18}{32}$	$5\frac{6}{32}$
August 6, 1986	$101\frac{7}{32}$	$96\frac{7}{32}$	5—
August 7, 1986	$101\frac{20}{32}$	$97\frac{5}{32}$	$4\frac{15}{32}$

Source: This table is based on Chicago Board of Trade data.

processing margins for the production of heating oil and gasoline products from the crude oil input. Positive margins encourage the purchase of crude and sale of products, while negative margins indicate the opposite positions.

The financial markets reflect differences in the yield curve and implied versus actual carrying rates. These spreads are known as repos or reverse repos. Also, traders in the currency and financial markets often refer to swaps which are in essence spread transactions as these specialized operations seek to exploit differences and establish new differentials. This is true even when swaps are done to switch assets or liabilities, convert currency denominations, extend or shorten maturities, and interchange fixed and floating rate obligations.

The important factor to remember is that spreads focus on relationships, be they relative (a/b) or the differences ($a - b$) between two or more time series.

In economic theory, spread trading would be the special applications case of General Equilibrium Economics. From that economic perspective, prices would not only seek out their equilibrium prices but do so within the entire framework given all other prices, applicable conditions, and constraints.

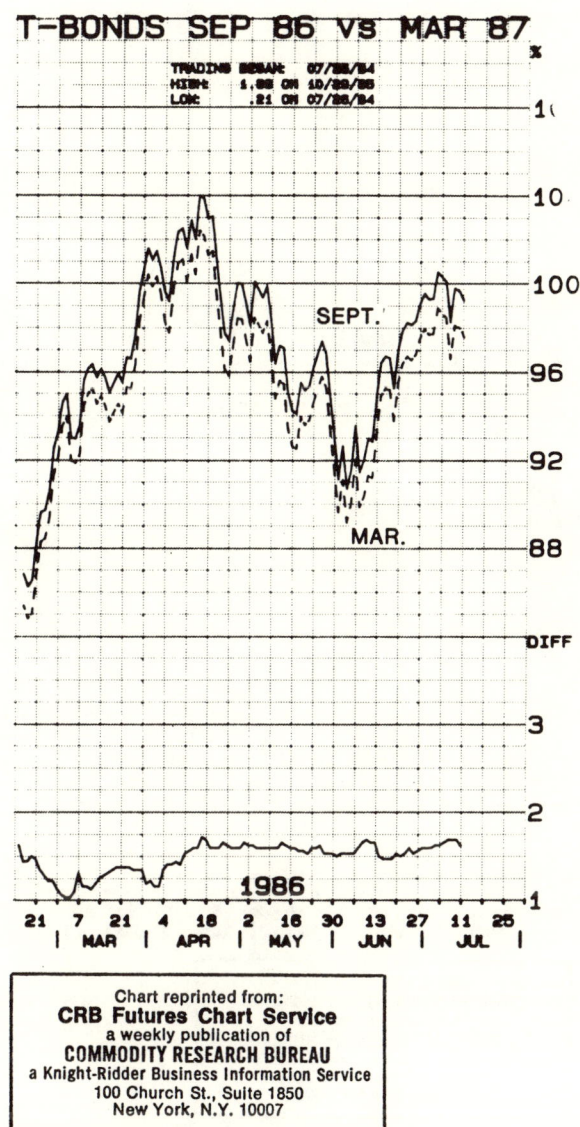

CHART 7.1 Intramarket spread

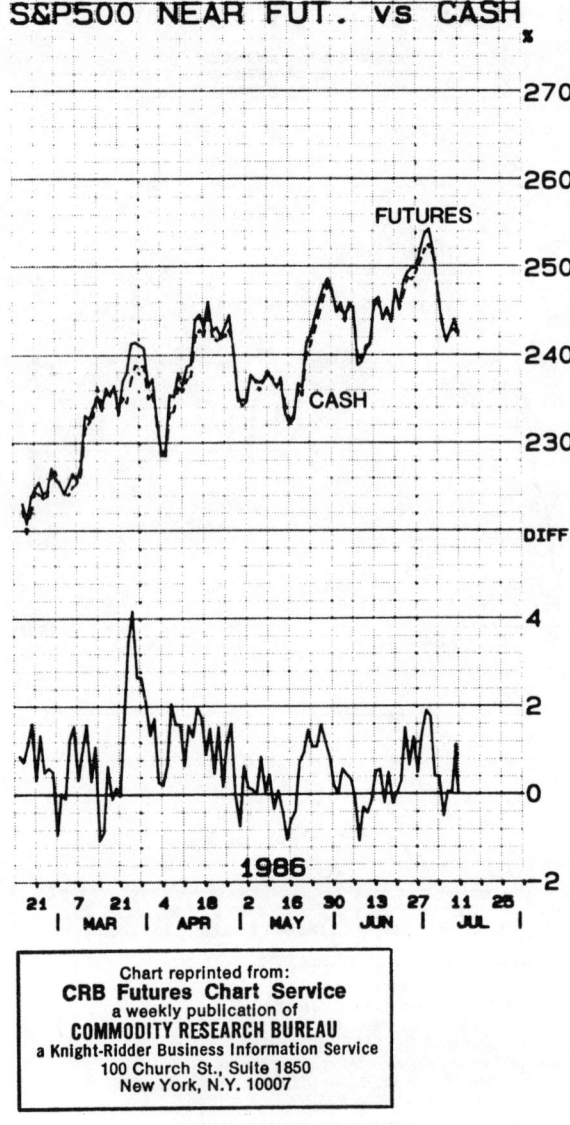

S&P500 NEAR FUT. vs CASH

FUTURES

CASH

1986

Chart reprinted from:
CRB Futures Chart Service
a weekly publication of
COMMODITY RESEARCH BUREAU
a Knight-Ridder Business Information Service
100 Church St., Suite 1850
New York, N.Y. 10007

CHART 7.2 Intermarket spread

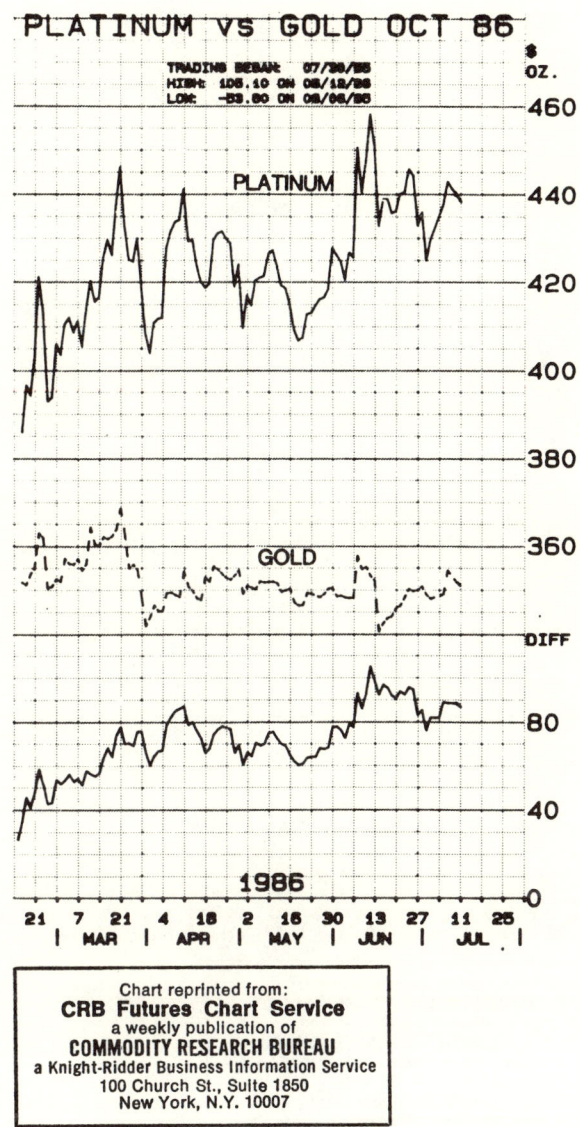

CHART 7.3 Intercommodity spread

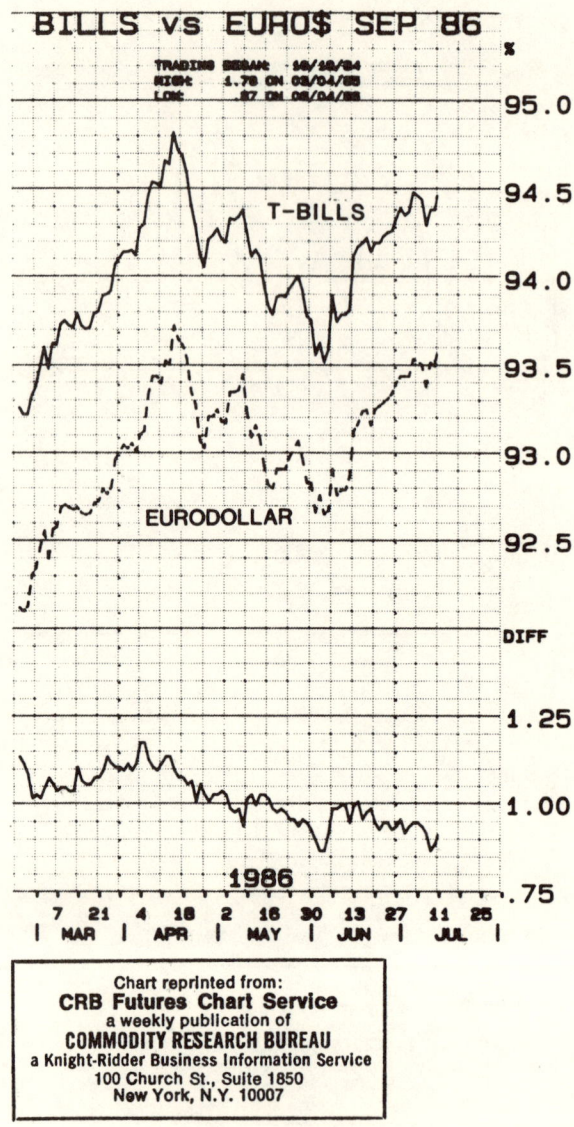

CHART 7.4 The TED spread

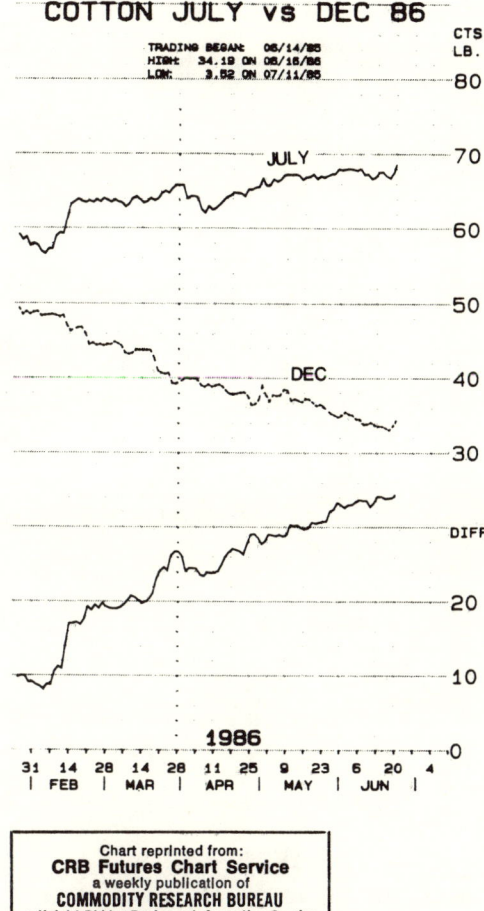

CHART 7.5 Crop year spread

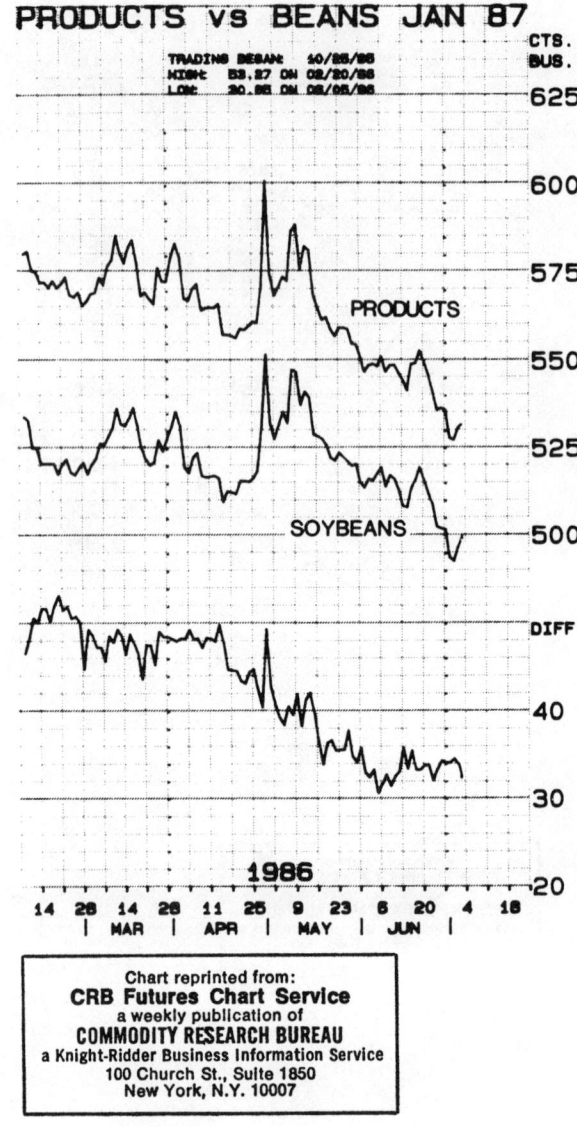

CHART 7.6 Products versus soybeans

THREE APPROACHES

There are three basic approaches to trading spreads:

1. Fundamental
2. Technical
3. Seasonal

Each approach has its own merits, and often two or more of the approaches can be blended together into a unified program.

COMPARABILITY

One of the more difficult tasks in evaluating spreads for trading purposes is to establish a basis for comparison. For most intracommodity spreads, this is straightforward. One need only buy x number of one month and sell x number of another month. For contracts which have different specifications, such as ounces, bushels, tonnage, maturity, yield, basis point response, or other value specification, the approach must be adjusted to arrive at comparability.

These weights essentially do one of two things. First, the weights can equate bushel-for-bushel type spreads such as wheat versus corn. Since both contracts specify 5,000 bushels for the trading unit, no adjustment is required. But pound-for-pound spreads in the livestock complex can require adjustments. To obtain poundage parity between live cattle and hogs, one must trade three contracts of live cattle versus four contracts of live hogs. Here, 3 × 40,000 pounds (or 120,000 pounds total) would compare to 4 × 30,000 pounds (or 120,000 pounds total). For a simple one-for-one contract spread between these two commodities, the trader would have 40,000 pounds of live cattle spread against 30,000 pounds of live hogs.

Similarly, the trader must not sell one contract of 3-month Treasury bill futures to offset a 6-month $1 million par value instrument. Instead, two futures contracts are probably more suitable to equate value changes due to basis point changes since the actual obligation has a maturity twice the specified futures contract; therefore its price response to yield swings would be greater.

This can be critical since spreads need not require the price of the long leg to go up and the price of the short leg to go down, but only that their differences act acceptably in a relative manner. Hence, the terms "narrowing" and "widening" become important considerations. Important expressions would be:

1. Discount has widened
2. Discount has narrowed
3. Premium has widened
4. Premium has narrowed

Second, the weights can compare values between the futures in question. Since prices and contract specifications are such for Japanese yen and Swiss francs, the trader need only match one contract of yen versus one contract of francs. The point value differences are such that the variations between contracts can be readily obtained.

However, doing a New York gold versus New York silver or platinum requires a weighted adjustment. Table 7.2 shows the importance of appropriately specifying the weights.

Although these spreads consisted of New York metals contracts, the gold/silver relationship was better described correlating total contract values—not ounces—while the gold/platinum relationship was better described, given the pricing features, by correlating the contracts on an ounce-for-ounce basis.

This comparability process becomes more complex when spreading various financial futures or option contracts. Sophisticated techniques are required for determining the appropriate initiating spread contract ratios since these can dramatically fluctuate due to the influence of par values, market values, coupons (discounts—premiums), call features, and maturities. Often these criteria must be evaluated on an adaptive basis.

RELATIVITY

This aspect of spread evaluation considers the relative values between commodities, either on an empiric or intrinsic valuation basis. The US Department of Agriculture (USDA) publishes tables of the nutritional values for various feeds. Typically, the loan values for feed grain closely approximate this relative value concept.

For example, if 1 pound of soybean meal has twice the nutritional value of 1 pound of corn, the economic minimum ratio value between the two commodities would be 2.00, or meal worth at least twice the price of corn on a per-pound basis. Of course, other factors influence a feed-livestock economy. Among these are: Meal is primarily a protein input while corn is a carbohydrate input; low relative values for meal to corn can generate greater substitution of meal into the feed mix. Conversely, relatively high meal to corn values will prompt a search for other satisfactory protein inputs in lieu of meal or a rationing for the meal input in the feed mix. From one perspective, the feed-livestock economy is a large-scale optimization model complete with feed requirements, feed constraints, and minimizing feed costs. One significant feature to this analytical approach is the determination of one set of relative value economic boundaries. In the case of feed grains, the consistency of lower economic value boundaries can provide critical information as to what constitutes cheap or relatively economical trading principles.

As far as upper boundaries for economic feeding relationships are concerned, the requirement of x percentage of protein, here soybean meal, can cause the relative values to climb dramatically. This is easily seen by exam-

TABLE 7.2. Importance of Weighting[a]

N.Y. Gold Price ($ per ounce)	N.Y. Silver Price ($ per ounce)	N.Y. Platinum Price ($ per ounce)	Gold Contract ($ Value)	Silver Contract ($ Value)	Platinum Contract ($ Value)
300.00	5.00	300.00	30,000	25,000 (1:1)	15,000 (1:2)
325.00	6.00	400.00	32,500	30,000 (1:1)	20,000 (3:5)
350.00	7.00	500.00	35,000	35,000 (1:1)	25,000 (5:7)
375.00	15.00	750.00	37,500	75,000 (2:1)	37,500 (1:1)

[a]The numbers in parentheses indicate the number of gold contracts to the other designated metal futures contracts in order to approximate contract value parity.

The weighting concept is related to the beta factor for securities and the delta factor for options. Adaptive adjustments in the spread mix arrangement may be warranted due to market conditions. Here, parity is sought relative to feasible contract integer size, though by implementing available futures options strategies, fractional shares can be accounted for on a surrogate basis.

ining the relative crop size of the two key crops and the potential for paying substantial premiums to input the required minimum of meal into a feed mix.

To illustrate this relativity concept, consider that in recent years U. S. corn production has approximated 8 billion bushels while soybean production has approximated 2 billion bushels. Casting aside other crops and carryovers, this indicates that soybeans are only 20 percent of total feed crop production (8 billion bushels corn + 2 billion bushels soybeans = 10 billion bushels crop size). From a marginal value perspective, a 100-million bushel variation in soybean availabilities is more potent than a 100-million bushel variation in corn availabilities. Numerically, the 100-million bushel variation for soybeans is $\pm 100/2,000$ or ± 5 percent, while for corn the 100 million bushel variation is only $\pm 100/8,000$ or ± 1.25 percent. This relationship between absolute availabilities partially explains the greater price volatility for soybeans as compared to corn. To put this corn/soybean situation in a different light, suppose the soybean crop gradually surpassed the size of the corn crop. In such a case, the opposite conclusion would tend to manifest itself, though there would still be intrinsic nutritional factors to be reckoned with.

This relativity analysis can be elaborated by aggregating livestock or feedgrain productivity and calculating the relative factors. Moreover, the relativity concept can be applied to other spreads such as foreign exchange, metals, or financial instruments.

Similarly, cross-hedge rates for currencies can provide temporary boundaries for relative currency movements; forecasts of yield curves can provide clues for financial relationships such as buying the short-term and selling the longer-term maturities; and predictions about economic activity can suggest whether platinum is relatively cheap compared to gold since the former is more responsive to industrial activity while the latter tends to attract buying or selling in greater part due to more monetary or politically motivated events. The important concept is the isolation of the principal factors influencing each commodity in the specified spread; then compare the impact of these factors to one another and obtain predictive models. The material presented in Chapter 4, Fundamental Analysis, provides statistical tools to analyze spreads on their relative economic basis. This section presented a focal point on considering factors for such analysis.

Fundamental Spreading

Consider that most of the grain produced in the United States is earmarked for the livestock industry (either domestic or foreign). Oats and corn are principal grains which have established futures markets. By going one more step we can include soybean meal.

Agricultural feed grains also offer valuable constraints or relative prices, though this phenomenon is primarily one-sided. Often, in surplus grain situations, the relative price values essentially establish minimum boundaries for various feed grain relationships.

Traders are aware that spread opportunities arise when wheat is relatively cheap to corn or meal is relatively cheap to oil, or oats to corn.

Technical Spreading

Spread opportunities can be evaluated technically. Some of the techniques are: moving averages, time intervals, chart analysis, and oscillators. The application of these techniques is similar to when they are applied to outright trading; however, rather than examining one futures price, they focus on the differences between two or more commodity prices or adjusted contract valuations. Table 7.3 lists moving averages for wheat, corn, and their differences. The signaling mechanism is similar for outright or spread trading. For example, if the short-term moving average is greater than the longer-term average, a buy condition is signaled; a lower valued short-term average when compared to the long-term average would indicate a sell condition.

Note that both commodities show concurrent uptrends, however, wheat is the long leg and corn the short leg for the spread. This was determined by the expansion of premium.

Additionally, the technical approach can be superimposed on a fundamentally oriented analysis as can also happen in outright trading programs.

Seasonal Spreading

Planting prospects, crop maturation developments, and harvest conditions all seasonally influence the behavior and trading strategies for agricul-

TABLE 7.3 Moving Averages for a Spread

Day	Wheat	Corn	Spread	3-Day Moving Average	5-Day Moving Average
1	$349\frac{1}{2}$	$246\frac{1}{4}$	$103\frac{1}{4}$		
2	$365\frac{1}{4}$	$245\frac{1}{4}$	111		
3	$360\frac{3}{4}$	$245\frac{1}{4}$	$115\frac{1}{2}$	109.92	
4	$361\frac{3}{4}$	$245\frac{3}{4}$	116	114.17	
5	$354\frac{1}{2}$	245	$109\frac{1}{2}$	113.67	111.05
6	$347\frac{1}{2}$	$241\frac{1}{4}$	$106\frac{1}{4}$	110.58	111.65
7	346	241	105	106.92	110.45
8	$346\frac{1}{2}$	239	$107\frac{1}{2}$	106.25	108.85
9	340	$236\frac{3}{4}$	$103\frac{1}{4}$	105.25	106.30
10	$338\frac{3}{4}$	$236\frac{1}{2}$	$102\frac{1}{4}$	104.33	104.85

Source: This table is based on Chicago Board of Trade data.

tural spreads. Livestock futures respond to farrowing, range, or seasonal slaughter factors. For instance, the different harvesting dates for oats and corn are a critical factor in the analysis of the corn/oats spread. Likewise, the variation between wheat and corn harvest dates affect those two commodities and their attendant spread series. One useful reference for this approach is the USDA's *Usual Planting and Harvesting Dates* publication. On a quantitative analysis basis, the methodology presented in Chapter 5, Seasonal Analysis, can be applied to spread differences or relative spread values instead of just the singular price or other economic movement. By quantitatively defining previous seasons' (or years') performances, the trader is prepared with information and not vague ideas. A word of caution is necessary: As in trading futures on an outright seasonal basis, the nonemergence or strong contrary-to-expected action of particular spreads generally implies that other powerful forces are prevailing. For example, a dramatic drought in corn producing areas one year can negate a prior expectation of a subsequent seasonal decline in corn prices during the subsequent harvest especially should supplies already be tight.

Thus a conditional analysis of spreads as to years when they behaved as expected and, more importantly, when they did not (the risk factor) is an important consideration which must be evaluated. By performing this two-fold analysis of spread behavior, the trader can define more clearly scenarios for usually recurring spread behavior and establish a second set of seasonal conditioning criteria for other situations.

8

Arbitrage and Short-Term Trading

TWO TRADING PERSPECTIVES

Short time frame trading strategies are examined in this chapter. There are two general approaches. The first is day trading, and the other is arbitraging. Arbitrage and some day-trade systems rely on the premise that prices are temporarily out-of-line. Day traders, who subscribe to this philosophy, are most concerned with overbought or oversold conditions. The appropriate procedure is to buy oversold markets and to sell overbought ones. In many senses, this activity is extremely sensitive to abrupt and greater-than-normal price swings.

A basic timing device for this style of trading is the oscillator. The time frame for such decision making is in minutes or perhaps hours, not days, weeks, or even months as is the case for longer-term position trading.

Similarly, arbitrageurs focus on relative position or price differentials. Should the basis or difference deviate from its normal value, then an arbitrage may be possible. Unlike the oscillatory type of day trading described, arbitraging is at least a two-dimensional task. There are two futures or markets to consider and, should an international market be involved such as New York versus London, a third dimension emerges—the foreign exchange consideration.

Arbitrages arise when the differences deviate from their normal expectations. Tumultuous or high activity days generate the greatest opportunities due to quotation lags, communication delays, or variance in quotes around the rings. These uncertainties are fewer or smaller for traders possessing superior communications and the resultant firm quotes.

A typical arbitrage occurs when a news event or series of events trigger volatile market action. At such frenzied times, market activity becomes erratic and the high volume places inordinately great demands on communi-

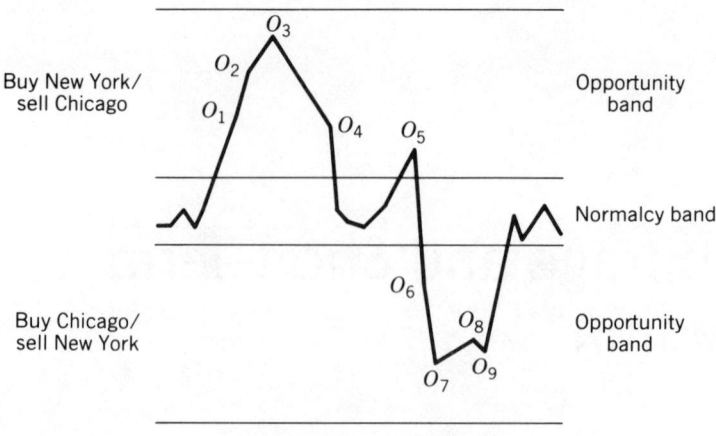

Buy New York/
sell Chicago

Opportunity
band

Normalcy band

Buy Chicago/
sell New York

Opportunity
band

$t \rightarrow$ elapsed time during trading day

FIGURE 8.1 Illustration of normalcy and opportunity bands for arbitrage

cations. Hence, one may encounter market replies which are 5, 10, or 15 minutes late.

Figure 8.1 illustrates the normalcy and opportunity bands for a hypothetical arbitrage between New York and Chicago silver. Departures from the middle initiate arbitrage positions, while returns to or within prompt the liquidation of the arbitrage position.

The subscripted Os in Figure 8.1 represent various arbitrage opportunities. In this particular example, O_1, O_2, O_3, O_4, and O_5 are buy New York/sell Chicago silver arbitrage opportunities; while O_6, O_7, O_8, and O_9 are buy Chicago/sell New York silver arbitrage opportunities. These opportunities have various profit potentials as measured by the actual value departure from the middle band. Even the middle band has a range of values as differences between exchange values fluctuate around their theoretical equilibrium, though then these fluctuations are not always sufficiently large to cover the variable costs to complete an arbitrage operation. These costs entail round-turn floor brokerage and fees. To more fully cost arbitrage transactions, communications, personnel, and other expenses must be determined.

The previous discussion focused on a two-dimensional arbitrage. Other opportunities can be multidimensional. These arise in the area of international markets. For example, a New York versus London silver arbitrage would entail three dimensions: the price of New York silver, the price of London silver, and the foreign exchange rates. A four-dimensional case would occur when a U.S. (or U.S.-dollar-denominated) trader sought to arbitrage London versus Zurich gold. The four dimensions would be: the Swiss franc exchange rate, the British pound exchange rate, the Zurich gold price, and the London gold price. Moreover, national or exchange regulations and restrictions compound the arbitrage task.

TABLE 8.1. HYPOTHETICAL SILVER ARBITRAGES[a]

New York Time[b]	New York Price[c]	Chicago Price	Differences	Impact	
				Net Cents	Net Dollars
11:15 A.M	815.00	816.00	−1.00	0	0
11:16 A.M.	817.00	817.00	0	0	0
11:17 A.M.	825.00	824.00	+1.00	0	0
11:18 A.M.	829.00 IA	835.00	−6.00	0	0
11:18 A.M.	837.00 LA	827.00	0	+4.00	+200.00
11:18 A.M.	827.00	836.00	+1.00	0	0
11:19 A.M.	832.00 IA	829.00	+3.00	0	0
11:19 A.M.	833.00 LA	833.00	0	+1.00	+50.00
11:20 A.M.	835.00	834.00	+1.00	0	0
11:21 A.M.	840.00	841.00	−1.00	0	0
11:22 A.M.	850.00 IA	845.00	+5.00	0	0
11:23 A.M.	845.00 LA	845.00	0	+3.00	+150.00

[a]Assume 2 cents covers total transactional expenses (brokerage is actually less) and all prices are quoted in U.S. cents per troy ounce.
[b]New York time represents transactional sequencing of trades during trading minutes.
[c]IA's initiate arbitrage; LA is liquidate arbitrage.

To reinforce the two-dimensional concept examine Table 8.1. It lists simultaneous, same-year December silver transactions. For simplicity, it is assumed that 2-cent or greater departures are necessary to make the arbitrage viable. The differences column lists the actual and per-ounce differences on simultaneous silver transactions on each exchange, while net impact in the cents column only lists values after subtracting the 2-cent variable expense once an arbitrage transaction is completed. Actual costs should be less. The net dollar impact column then transforms the costs-per-5,000-ounce requirements into net dollar amounts.

FAIR MARKET VALUE APPROACHES

Options and futures arbitrage trading frequently relies on a fair market valuation model. The premise is there is a mathematical relationship between the various options and their underlying futures markets. Should this relationship deviate from the postulated one, then the purchase of futures and sale of options or vice versa would be transacted. In theory the two markets strive for equilibrium values and practicably this is true. But transactional flows may be temporarily impeded or distorted due to the variety of other spreading and positioning transactions taking place. Additionally, not all the options trade simultaneously for every trade in the underlying futures. When a temporal lag occurs, values start to depart from the expectationally precise relationship. Once this departure becomes adequately feasible (it can still be slight) an arbitrage would be conducted. Not every variation is arbitraged but only those possessing satisfactory expectational characteristics.

OTHER SHORT-TERM TRADING STRATEGIES

Other short-term trading strategies are generally one-sided. That is, an outright long or short position is placed. There are two basic philosophies. The first, as in arbitraging, views abrupt price movements as those which knock prices out of equilibrium; hence prices should eventually return to their average or normal price range. Recalling material from Chapter 2, Technical Analysis, this perspective is best quantified by a contraswing or an oscillator-type approach since the trader views abrupt price movements on either overbought or oversold situations.

The second type of short-term trading is that of going with the underlying move. If the underlying trend is viewed as up, then the trader will try to scalp the market from the long side. If the dominant trend is viewed as down, then the trader will attempt to scalp the market from the short side.

Returning to the first strategy, opening gaps, particularly those which leave space between the opening and the prior session's trading range, provide opportunities for this type of trader. Aside from the dynamic gaps which reflect a structural change in the supply/demand outlook as presented in Chapter 3, Chart Analysis, most gaps, particularly intraday gaps, tend to get filled.

These styles of trading can easily be adapted to technical and chart analysis as well as subject to the rigors of statistical testing. Computerization can be implemented on a transactional basis that alerts the trader to potentially profitable price or basis deviations during the course of the trading day. Some traders have programmed themselves intuitively to recognize instantaneously these profitable conditions without any reliance on an electronic device. Likewise, scalping the market with an assumption of the underlying trend can also be analyzed and tested in accordance with procedures described throughout this text. The major difference between short- versus intermediate- and longer-term trading strategies is the relative time frame.

PROGRAM TRADING

One of the most notable arbitrage efforts is program trading. Here, an investment firm or professional trading group buys a representative basket of securities and sells the appropriate futures contracts or vice versa, depending on the calculated relationships. If computed differences are too wide relative to the organization's fair value formula then the actual securities are bought and the futures sold. Conversely, differences deemed too narrow spark the rapid sale of securities and the purchase of futures. The sudden appearance and attendant volume of these programs often make headlines as participants scramble to keep relative values within their expected fair value ranges. To more rapidly implement the necessary trades to effectuate the program trading arbitrage, predetermined instructions are often awaiting the signal to activate them into actual orders.

Other dimensions to these programs are the active consideration of futures and securities options relative to the actual stocks and underlying cash indexes as well as interest rates and dividend payment factors.

The unwinding of positions, particularly near option expiration dates, can cause quick price swings as individual market components adjust toward their theoretical or stipulated convergence prices. Any prevailing expectational values previously built into the carrying charge structure are now rapidly discounted.

Transactional Costs

An important success factor in short-term trading is the stringent control of transactional costs. On a per-trade basis, short-term trading strategies generally have lower expected average losses but commensurately lower expected average profits. To highlight this important concept, Table 8.2 compares two sets of hypothetical trading systems, one short term and the other long term.

It can be readily seen that relatively high transactional costs offset or even negate ordinary trading opportunities for the short-term approaches, while they tend to lessen but not completely offset the longer-term approaches. Also, these shorter-term approaches exhibit a greater dependence on better communications in order to expedite orders or to seize on mercurial opportunities. For the average trader, this dependence requires additional costs which must be evaluated before trading commences.

Superior Communications

A variation of the axiom "time waits for no man" would be "the markets wait for no one." Simply put, if the trader is unable to direct orders to particular exchanges in a timely manner, short-term trading opportunities may be missed. Besides ordinary cable transmissions for both telecommunications and quotation devices, many trading organizations have augmented their communications with equipment which relies on satellite-transmitted data.

Instant communication capability is necessary for arbitrage transactions. The potential for error or poor trading results when such trades are executed via direct dialing or even wire transmissions. It is important to possess the necessary equipment to pursue the desired trading strategy. As a final note, one must at least match other professionals in the field on communications and costs bases, or the trading program will be at a distinct disadvantage.

TABLE 8.2. TRANSACTIONAL COST IMPACT ON TRADING RESULTS (IN DOLLARS)[a]

	Short Term			Long Term			
Outcomes of Opportunities	Transacted 100 Trades	Net After $20 RT[b]	Net After $50 RT[b]	Outcomes of Opportunities	Transacted 20 Trades	Net After $20 RT[b]	Net After $50 RT[b]
−200	−20,000	−22,000	−25,000	−1,000	−20,000	−20,400	−21,000
−100	−10,000	−12,000	−15,000	−500	−10,000	−10,400	−11,000
0	0	−2,000	−5,000	0	0	−400	−1,000
(+40)	(+4,000)	(+2,000)	(−1,000)	(+200)	(+4,000)	(3,600)	(+3,000)
(+50)	(+5,000)	(+3,000)	(0)	(+250)	(+5,000)	(+4,600)	(+4,000)
+200	+20,000	+18,000	+15,000	+1,000	+20,000	+19,600	+19,000
+400	+40,000	+38,000	+35,000	+2,000	+40,000	+39,600	+39,000
Cumulative impact	+30,000	+20,000	+5,000		+30,000	+28,000	+25,000
(Cumulative impact)	(+39,000)	(+25,000)	(+4,000)		(+39,000)	(+36,200)	(+32,000)

[a]Table assumes:

1. Short term trader does 100 trades of each trading opportunity.
2. Long term trader does 20 trades of each trading opportunity and has a greater value for the outcomes which reflects longer-term approach.

Numbers in parentheses reflect marginal trades and parenthesized cumulative impacts reflect their inclusion in the analysis.
[b]RT means roundturn commission.

9
Hedging

THE MANAGEMENT OF RISK

Hedging is a management tool. When suitable for an organization, it reduces risk, improves working capital positions, and provides acquisition/marketing alternatives.

Its effectiveness can be evaluated quantitatively. Its ability to reduce price level risk serves as economic justification. In an analogy to insurance, a hedge need not be perfect or offer exact replacement; rather it should provide a mechanism to generate an acceptable degree of protection. Life, health, or property insurance policies do not provide for the return of life, the restoration of a previous health condition, or the identical replacement of property, but they do provide protection via a payment of insured value. So it is with a prudent hedge.

Hedges are established by four principal methods:

1. Contractual arrangements
2. Forward markets
3. Futures markets
4. Option markets

This text will focus on the last two methods; a synopsis of the first two methods will be given now. Concepts presented in this chapter are applicable to all four.

Contractual Arrangements

Contractual arrangements occur when two parties agree to a legally enforceable set of terms. A farmer may agree to sell grain to an elevator at a specified price for immediate or future shipment. Similarly, an underwriter can agree to arrange financing at a specific maturity and rate for a real estate developer or arrange venture capital for an entrepreneur.

Forward Markets

Forward markets can be of several varieties. They can be the foreign exchange markets where the designated units of currency will be transacted at a predetermined rate; or transactions in commodity markets whereby specific grades, quantities, and deliveries are to be satisfied at particular times in accordance with the other agreed-on stipulations. Sugar deliverable at a specified price 5 months hence is one example. Another would require the delivery of Swiss francs to a bank 78 days forward. Though there are futures contracts for these markets, it can be more advantageous to use the forward markets. More nearly exact quantities can be hedged or arranged through the cash-forward markets. Also, delivery terms can be more flexible and particularly satisfactory for the hedger.

Disadvantages for both these approaches are the lack of a premature off-set. In other words, most of these deals, with the exception of the foreign exchange forward markets, may severely penalize or even preclude a change in intention.

DEFINING THE RISKS

The first step in building a hedge program is to define what is at risk. A list of a few variables are:

Inventory values
Investment portfolios
Mineral reserves
Raw material costs
Foreign exchange rates
Potential changes in interest charges
Potential changes in interest receipts
Anticipated consumption or production

Once the major risks have been identified, the next step is to determine the scope of the hedging program. Is it better to hedge entire values, net values, or some other arrangement? Is yearly production, usage, or life-of-enterprise, particularly for mining, advisable? Analytical frameworks to solve these questions will be presented here and throughout the text.

TABLE 9.1. RISK TRANSFORMATION FOR LONG SPOT POSITION[a] (BRITISH POUND)

Time	Dollar per British Pound			Cumulative Change	
	Spot	Futures	Basis	Spot Value	Basis Value
t1	1.63	1.6200	.0100	—	—
t2	1.62	1.6150	.0050	−$250	−$125.00
t3	1.53	1.5225	.0075	−$2,500	−$62.50
t4	1.50	1.4950	.0050	−$3,250	−$125.00
t5	1.45	1.4400	.0100	−$4,500	0

[a]This table shows the spot market over or at a premium to the futures.
"Reproduced by permission of the Publishers, Charles Griffin and Company Ltd. of London, from Kendall, TIME-SERIES, 2nd Edn., 1976"

RISK TRANSFORMATIONS

Typically, hedging is the shifting of risk from hedgers to speculators or to the marketplace. More specifically, it is the process which transforms the potentially more hazardous price level risk into the more manageable basis risk. This transformation or reduction in risk is clearly demonstrated by Tables 9.1 and 9.2.

The hedge/not to hedge decision can be assessed by the likelihood of the basis to change in an unfavorable manner, as compared to the change in the outright position's price on a comparative value standard.

THE BASIS

The critical factor in any hedging program is the basis. By the basis, it is meant the relationship between the commodity to be hedged and the vehicle that will provide the hedge. Generally, the basis is derived by subtracting the price of the actual commodity to be hedged from the futures price. Moreover, this relationship should be acceptably stable. This does not mean that the

TABLE 9.2. RISK TRANSFORMATION FOR SHORT SPOT POSITION[a] (CRUDE OIL)

Time	Dollar per Barrel			Value Change	
	Spot	Futures	Basis	Spot	Basis
t1	9.75	10.50	.75	—	—
t2	10.50	11.40	.90	−$750	+$150
t3	12.25	12.95	.70	−$2,500	−$50
t4	14.00	14.60	.60	−$4,250	−$150
t5	16.00	16.80	.80	−$6,250	+$50

[a]This table shows the spot market under or at a discount to the futures.

basis cannot fluctuate but rather it should not do so in an erratically volatile manner. As will be demonstrated throughout this chapter, basis stability is probably the foremost feature for the hedges. At times, due to contract specifications such as grain delivery points, stipulated grades, or maturities, a hedge may seem unlikely. The only way to be reasonably sure is to run the numbers.

Graphs 9.1 and 9.2 portray cash-over and cash-under basis relationships. As the basis is a time series itself, it can be divided into four components:

1. Seasonality
2. Trend
3. Cyclic behavior
4. Random fluctuations

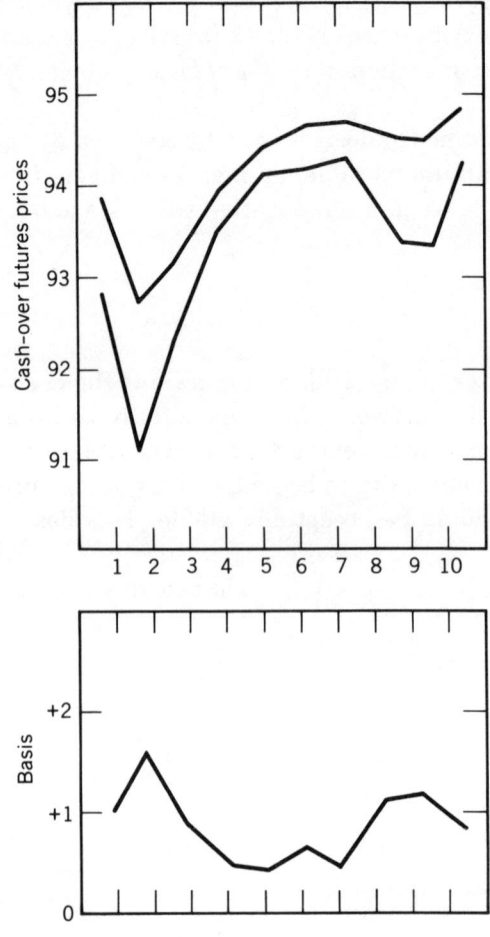

GRAPH 9.1 Cash-over basis for the municipal index

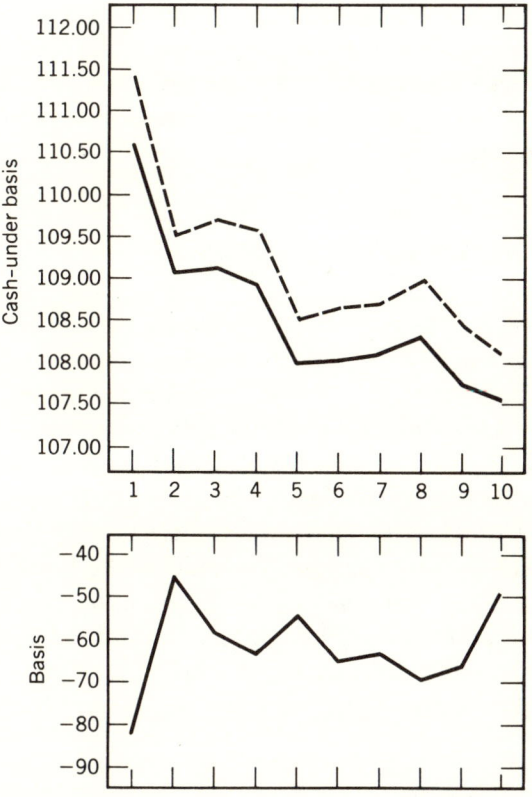

GRAPH 9.2 Cash-under basis for the U.S. index market

The seasonal and cyclical components are particularly evident in the agricultural and livestock markets. Planting uncertainties and harvesting pressures typically produce strong influences on the basis. Livestock placements, marketings, and herd numbers can generate dramatic swings for the meat futures. The trend element which can be present in any cash versus futures basis is a critical factor for most financial futures.

The time value of money and its attendant discounting or compounding properties is often responsible for most if not all the decay or appreciation as the futures and cash markets converge. This time value dissipation is complete for options.

TYPES OF HEDGES

There are two primary types of hedges: (1) short hedge, and (2) long hedge. In both cases, the protective element arises from offsetting value changes. For example, an unhedged silver producer is vulnerable to a fluctuating silver market. Day-to-day price changes can cause dramatic effects on profitability especially if the changes are negative. Silver ore profitably extractable at one price can be uneconomical at another. By hedging, the producer can establish favorable sales prices. Generally, the short hedge is used to protect production, inventories, or assets; while the long hedge is used to protect acquisition costs, supplies, and liabilities.

COMMON PROCESSING HEDGES

The crush spread reflects profitable processing margins for the crushing of soybeans. Here, the raw commodity—soybeans—is bought and the products—soyoil and meal—are sold. Similarly, the crack spread reflects refining margins whereby the crude oil is bought and its products—heating oil and gasoline—are sold. Finally, the feed spread requires the purchase of corn and feeder cattle and the sale of live cattle. All three spreads are done to lock in processing and profit margins. The opposite transactions are known as the reverse crush, crack, or feed spreads. The motivation for the reverse spreads is that prevailing board differences are unfavorable to continue to process profitably, and the products can be bought more cheaply than the primary input. Thus sell the input and buy the products. Foreign exchange considerations add other dimensions to the hedging program.

AN EXAMPLE OF BASIS BEHAVIOR

By examining Table 9.3, it can be seen that the cash price of copper plummeted from 60 cents to 50 cents between time periods $t1$ and $t7$. If there were no hedge, the loss in value per contract equivalent would have been $2,500 since each cent change is worth $250 per 25,000 pounds contract. If the posi-

TABLE 9.3. HYPOTHETICAL COPPER ILLUSTRATION (IN CENTS PER POUND)

Time	Cash	Futures	Basis	Cash Price Change	Futures Price Change	Basis Change
$t1$	60.00	65.00	5.00	.		
$t2$	58.00	62.90	4.90	−2.00	−2.10	−.10
$t3$	58.00	63.20	5.20	0.	+.30	+.30
$t4$	55.00	60.00	5.00	−3.00	−3.30	−.20
$t5$	54.50	58.00	3.50	−.50	−2.00	−.50
$t6$	52.00	57.40	5.40	−2.50	−.60	+.90
		A1 56.00	B1 6.00		−1.40	+.60
$t7$	50.00	A2 55.00	B2 5.00	−2.00	−2.40	−.40
		A3 54.00	B3 4.00		−2.40	−1.40

tion were hedged, then there would be three different outcomes due to three alternative futures prices: A1, A2, and A3. Additionally, these three different outcomes generated three different basis numbers: B1, B2, and B3. Depending on which futures price the hedge was lifted, the relative degree of protection varied.

Consider the first alternative, the short hedge was established at time period $t1$ at a 5-cent basis, futures over cash. Then at time period $t7$, it was lifted at a futures price of 56 cents, or more importantly at a 6-cent basis, futures over cash. It is evident that the 10-cent decline in the cash market was mostly offset by the increase in the value of the short position. Here, the 9-cent futures decline generated a compensatory value of $2,250 (9 × $250 per contract equivalent). The $250 difference between the $2,500 physical market decline and the compensatory increase of $2,250 is due to the variability of the basis. Nevertheless, the hedge was effective as it reduced a potential $2,500 risk to a significantly smaller $250 basis risk. To view it from another point, the hedge was 90 percent effective as it generated a 90 percent compensatory value versus the no-hedge situation.

The second alternative presents the perfect, or 100 percent effective, hedge. In this example, the 10-cent ($2,500) decline in the physical market is exactly offset by the $2,500 increase in compensatory value generated by the short hedge. Note that the hedge was established at a 5-cent futures over cash basis and lifted at the same 5-cent futures over cash basis.

The third alternative presents the case of a favorable move in the basis. In this example, not only was the $2,500 decline in physical copper offset by the $2,750 increase due to the hedge's compensatory value, but the hedge actually profited by a $250 gain due to the favorable move in the basis. In other words, the hedge basis was initiated at futures 5 cents over cash and lifted at futures 4 cents over cash. That favorable 1-cent basis improvement equaled $250, which is exactly equal to a 1-cent move in the futures.

To reinforce the merit of hedging, it should be recognized that only when the basis risk equals or exceeds the price level risk should the no-hedge action be taken.

A Hedging Paradox

The last paragraph in the preceding section offers an interesting paradox. It concerns hedge/no hedge decision-making criteria. As was mentioned, hedges should be undertaken so long as the basis risk is less than the price level risk. When these risks are equal, it is irrelevant whether one hedges or not; however, hedges cost money, or at the least commissions, so therefore they would not be pursued. Of course, for cases where the basis risk frequently and randomly exceeds the price level risk, hedging should be avoided since by doing so an organization would increase its risk relative to its expected return. So what does all this suggest? Could it mean that market behavior is such as to generate some paradoxical trading, particularly hedging strategies? The answer is yes. Some hedging programs may appear paradoxical, but they are not irrational.

The vast body of efficient market literature sustains this. For, given rational behavior by the firm, in this case a suitable hedge, the organization reduced its risk level for a given expected return. Or to put it somewhat differently it exchanged the possibility of extraordinarily large profits (or losses) for a reduction in risk.

This is particularly evident for financial futures trading where an unfavorable basis, or locking in a loss, may still be preferable to further exposure and potentially more severe losses.

Generally, an unfavorable basis is considered as the level where a hedge would lock in a loss, especially for mining or farming operations from mostly anticipatory perspectives; whereas favorable basis levels were those which locked in profits. This definition is more elusive in the financial markets: Even when a bond or stock portfolio is acquired at higher levels, protection is still workable through a hedging program—though at less than maximum levels.

Few would dispute that most insurance companies have prospered through good and bad times. Although insurance companies are considered conservative, a critical factor behind their historic success has been their recognition of the basis or expected value of their actuarial tables. They need not know in advance the exact date of death for every life policy holder or the date and extent of damage to each and every property and casualty policy holder. The insurers need only to know the probabilities. To go one step further, various risk classes are compiled such as: sex, age, smoker/nonsmoker, serious illness, occupation, and so on.

So too is the case with the prudent hedger. Certitude as to the outcome of each and every hedge is not necessary. Rather, it is satisfactory to have a reasonable approximation as to the expected value of hedging outcomes over time.

The recognition of the insurability concept of hedging has been partially responsible for the movement towards cash settlements. Another important reason for cash settlements is the intent to avoid unduly limited deliveries and basis fluctuations due to grade, quantity, location, or other factors.

CROSS HEDGING

Cross hedging is an extension of the hedging concept. When suitable, it permits management to adapt available futures to specific situations. For example, potential hedgers may balk at using futures since the available futures contracts do not exactly coincide with their delivery specifications, invest-

ment portfolios, or production grades. By statistically analyzing the basis behavior between actual positions versus various futures alternatives, it is conceivable that an acceptable hedging process can be developed using surrogate
contracts. This will be demonstrated in the next section.

CORRELATION AND CONVERGENCE

Hedging and cross hedging depend on both high correlation and convergence between cash and futures over time. The correlation between prices is
three-fold:

1. The degree of correlation between the absolute prices or yields
2. The degree of correlation between the first differences in absolute prices
   or yields
3. The degree of correlation between the dollar swings in the actual portfolio versus the hedge position

The important element for this triple correlative analysis is to ascertain not
only the associative behavior between the two time series, but also their behavior on a specified periodic basis—be it hourly, daily, weekly, or monthly.
The second correlative approach indicates whether the futures experience
changes similar to the cash markets for the prescribed periodic basis.

The third correlative aspect is the determination of the highest negative
or inverse relationship between dollar changes in the specified actual position
and the generated hedge offsetting values. The method presented later is applicable in all three cases.

Convergence is the property which relates the physical market or cash
index to the predicated futures. The futures contract's specifications stipulate
the underlying commodity, security, or index that is the delivery or settlement grade, while the numerical basis defines the mathematical relationship
between the cash and the board. At expiration, the convergence should be
complete as the spot futures market's prices approximate the underlying cash
market's prices given the premium-discount structure. For markets satisfied
by cash settlement and not a deliverable security or commodity, this convergence is complete. Therefore, futures gain parity by either losing their premium or discount to the cash. Graphs 9.3 and 9.4 illustrate convergence by
premium and discount dissipation.

One statistical technique for analyzing correlative properties is the rank
correlation test. By assigning rank values to actual values, one can readily
test the degree of statistical association between two time series. The municipal bond and several futures markets will be analyzed using this method.

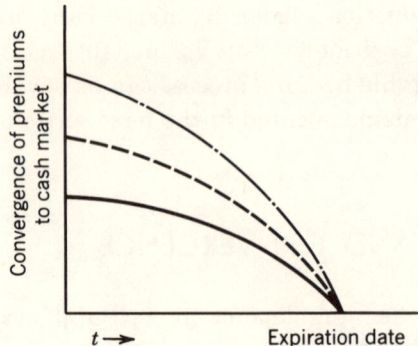

GRAPH 9.3 Convergence of premiums to cash market

Table 9.4 lists weekly data for the period of May 7, 1982 to September 3, 1982. At that time, the municipal bond futures contract was not in existence. Weekly data are used to present a generalized case with commonly acceptable benchmark series. Cross hedging may often be desirable even though a more nearly related futures market is developed due to liquidity considerations. The statistical test presented here is the Kendall rank test. Unlike some other correlation tests, this one is nonparametric, flexible, and reliable with small samples. This latter property is especially helpful when analyzing limited information such as brief time series. The evaluative expression for association is:

$$r = 1 - \frac{6\left(\sum d^2\right)}{n(n^2 - 1)}.$$

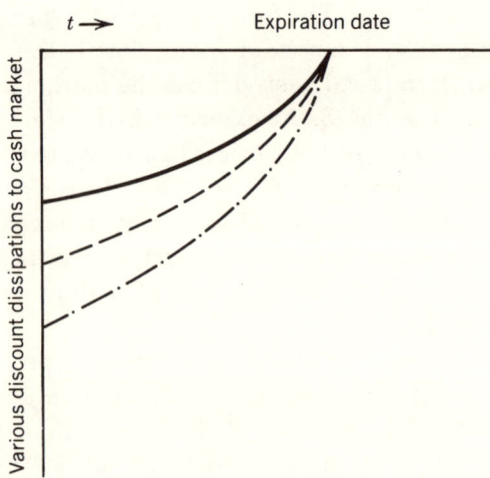

GRAPH 9.4 Various discount dissipations to cash market

TABLE 9.4. T-BOND FUTURES AND MUNICIPAL MARKET DATA (WEEKLY DATA FROM MAY 7, 1982 TO SEPTEMBER 3, 1982)

1982	Muni Rates Thursday		Muni Changes		T-Bond Futures Yields		Col. 6 − Col. 1	T-Bond Futures Yield Changes		$|d|$	$|d|^2$
	Rank	Yield	Rank	Yield	Rank	Yield	Basis	Rank	Yield	$[c_3 - c_8]$	$[c_{10}]^2$
05/07	8.5	12.04			15	13.01	+97				
05/14	8.5	12.04	6	0	12	13.14	+110	5.5	+13	.50	.25
05/21	13	11.96	11	−08	14	13.05	+109	10.5	−09	.50	.25
05/28	11	11.09	5	+03	9	13.30	+131	4	+25	1.00	1.00
06/04	7	12.13	4	+14	5	13.64	+151	1.5	+34	2.50	6.25
06/11	5	12.40	2	+27	4	13.69	+129	7.5	+05	5.50	30.25
06/18	1	12.63	3	+23	2	14.03	+140	1.5	+34	1.50	2.25
06/25	2	12.62	7.5	−01	1	14.16	+154	5.5	+13	2.00	4.00
07/02	3	12.58	9.5	−04	3	13.82	+124	15	−34	5.50	30.25
07/09	4	12.47	13.5	−11	6	13.62	+115	13	−20	.50	.25
07/16	6	12.36	13.5	−11	7	13.53	+117	10.5	−09	3.00	9.00
07/23	10	12.01	15	−35	11	13.16	+115	16	−37	1.00	1.00
07/30	12	11.97	9.5	−04	8	13.45	+148	3	+29	6.50	42.25
08/06	14	11.87	12	−10	10	13.21	+134	14	−24	2.00	4.00
08/13	15	11.86	7.5	−01	13	13.10	+124	12	−11	4.50	20.25
08/20	16	10.82	17	−104	18	12.31	+149	17	−79	0	0
08/27	18	10.38	16	−44	16	12.36	+198	7.5	+05	8.50	72.25
09/03	17	10.74	1	+36	17	12.35	+161	9	−01	8.00	64.00

Sources: U.S. Financial Data, Federal Reserve Bank of St. Louis; and the Chicago Board of Trade.

TABLE 9.5. T-NOTE FUTURES AND MUNICIPAL MARKET DATA (WEEKLY DATA FROM MAY 7, 1982 TO SEPTEMBER 3, 1982)

1982	Muni Rates Thursday		Muni Changes		T-Note Futures Yields		Col. 6 − Col. 1	T-Note Futures Yield Changes		$|d|$ $[c_3 - c_8]$	$|d|^2$ $[c_{10}]^2$
	Rank	Yield	Rank	Yield	Rank	Yield	Basis	Rank	Yield		
05/07	8.5	12.04		0	10	13.01	+97	9	−05	3	9
05/14	8.5	12.04	6	0	11	12.96	+92	10	−10	1	1
05/21	13	11.96	11	−08	14	12.86	+90	4	+19	1	1
05/28	11	11.09	5	+03	9	13.05	+106	5	+15	1	1
06/04	7	12.13	4	+14	7	13.20	+107	6	+09	4	16
06/11	5	12.40	2	+27	5	13.29	+89	1	+35	2	4
06/18	1	12.63	3	+23	2	13.64	+101	2	+30	5.5	30.25
06/25	2	12.62	7.5	−01	1	13.94	+132	15	−31	5.5	30.25
07/02	3	12.58	9.5	−04	3	13.63	+105	14	−21	.5	.25
07/09	4	12.47	13.5	−11	4	13.42	+95	12	−15	1.5	2.25
07/16	6	12.36	13.5	−11	6	13.27	+91	16	−34	1	1
07/23	10	12.01	15	−35	13	12.93	+92	3	+21	6.5	42.25
07/30	12	11.97	9.5	−04	8	13.14	+117	13	−19	1	1
08/06	14	11.87	12	−10	12	12.95	+108	11	−11	3.5	12.25
08/13	15	11.86	7.5	−01	15	12.84	+98	17	−87	0	0
08/20	16	10.82	17	−104	18	11.97	+115	7	+06	9	81
08/27	18	10.38	16	−44	16.5	12.03	+165	8	0	7	49
09/03	17	10.74	1	+36	16.5	12.03	+129				

Sources: *U.S. Financial Data*, Federal Reserve Bank of St. Louis; and the Chicago Board of Trade.

This r value is tested for significance, by applying:

$$\frac{\text{Prescribed significance level}}{\sqrt{n-1}}$$

where the prescribed values are 1.96, 2.55, and 2.58 for 95, 98, and 99 degrees of confidence, respectively. If the r value is greater than this calculated statistic, then the results are statistically significant for that level.

The comparative results are shown in Table 9.5. Although both the T-bond and T-note futures showed strong correlative tendencies versus the municipal market, the T-note futures had the edge. Its overall basis relationship to the municipal market as shown by Table 9.5 in column 7 was tighter than that in column 7 of Table 9.4, and the range was more compact indicating less dispersion about the central tendency value. Also the placement of the hedge would suitably relate the basis point values between the municipals and the selected financial futures.

Case 1. The Short Hedge

A silver producer has a mine which produces 5,000 ounces of .999 fineness silver per week. Moreover this production is consistent throughout the year and mining surveys indicate that the reserves are such that output will continue for eight more years. The previous year's range for spot silver varied between $8 to $15 per ounce and currently is $10 per ounce. It is estimated that variable production costs are $5.00 per ounce and the fixed cost is $3.50 per ounce at the given current production level of 260,000 ounces. Therefore, the breakeven price for this operation is $8.50 per ounce. Since current prices are $10, the producer is capable of making a profit of $1.50 per ounce. However, silver prices can be volatile; and assuming a selling price of at least $10 per ounce, can be costly, particularly if the market trends moderately lower over the next 52 weeks.

There are several alternatives which the producer can pursue:

1. No hedge
2. Partial hedge
3. Hedge via the nearbys
4. Hedge across time via rollovers
5. Hedge 3 months, 6 months, 12 months, and so forth

Matrix 9.1 presents a spectrum of no-hedge to fully hedged solutions. If the spot market remains constant, the producer improves its position since it can remain open despite lower prices—which could prompt competitors to withdraw from the market and shut down production.

MATRIX 9.1. EXPECTATIONAL REVENUE MATRIX FOR DECLINING PRICES[a] (IN DOLLARS)

	$10 IQ	$9 IIQ	$8 IIIQ	$7 IVQ	
No Hedge	650,000	585,000	520,000	455,000	2,210,000
25% Hedge	650,000	601,250	552,500	503,750	2,307,500
50% Hedge	650,000	617,500	585,000	552,500	2,405,000
75% Hedge	650,000	633,750	617,500	601,250	2,502,500
100% Hedge	650,000	650,000	650,000	650,000	2,600,000

[a]Matrix assumes: 1. Equal marketings of 65,000 ounces per quarter.
2. Hedges executed at $10 and no value added.

Additionally, the producer can secure a time value for its product by marketing silver effectively at not only the going spot price but by obtaining the adjusted time value for its production. Notice the dramatic impact in returns as illustrated in Matrix 9.2.

Case 2. The Long Hedge

An automotive parts manufacturer requires platinum for the production of catalytic convertors. He has several choices available to secure this commodity input. He can buy it at the contract price, use the futures market, or buy it on the spot market. On January 16, the contract price is $475 per ounce, the April futures is $370.40, and the free market is $365.50. (January futures were trading at $366.60.) The metal is needed for end-of-March production, so the manufacturer decides to use the April futures contract to price protect its 1,000-ounce requirement. This application is presented in Table 9.6.

If the manufacturer deferred its acquisition of platinum, it would have been confronted by a sharp $57,000 rise in material costs. However, through

MATRIX 9.2. EXPECTATIONAL REVENUE MATRIX FOR CONSTANT PRICES[a] (IN DOLLARS)

	IQ	IIQ	IIIQ	IVQ	Total Revenue
No Hedge	650,000	650,000	650,000	650,000	2,600,000
Full Hedge 8% Rate	663,000	676,000	689,000	702,000	2,730,000
Full Hedge 12% Rate	669,500	689,000	708,500	728,000	2,795,000

[a]Matrix assumes: Constant cash price of $10 throughout the year where the imputed carrying charge rates are 8 and 12 percent.

TABLE 9.6. LONG FUTURES HEDGE

Date	Cash	Futures
January 16	$365.50 per ounce or $365,500	Bought 20 contracts of April futures at $370.40 or $370,400
April 27	$422.50 per ounce or $422,500	Sold 20 contracts of April futures at $420.30 or $420,300
Change	$57,000 increase in spot market	$49,900 offsetting increase due to long hedge

hedging its cost protection was equal to $49,900 or 88 percent coverage. It also established the material's cost, enabling it to more accurately plan and price the finished products. If the manufacturer previously set finished good prices, it similarly limited the cost of one important input variable.

MULTIPLE BASIS DETERMINATIONS

The existence of multiple basis relationships broadens the application of hedging. Often, industrial production is not a one-time process but occurs throughout the year at various levels dictated by the fundamentals. Returning to our parts manufacturer, Table 9.7 lists some of these multiple basis relationships.

Observationally, several points can be established. First, column 3 indicates a swing from a positive futures-over-cash basis to a negative one. A singular and simplistic analysis would suggest an unfavorable movement in the basis for the long hedger. Yet the hedge achieved 88 percent protection despite this behavior. Second, columns 5 and 7 indicate further deterioration in these respectively positive futures-over-cash bases. The immediate implications are the movement toward convergence as the futures and cash markets progress along their time paths. It also demonstrates the relative firming of the spot market in regard to deferred deliveries. This flattening of time premiums can be beneficial for long hedgers, particularly when forward requirements are initiated at these more opportune levels. This is due to the convergence characteristic of the marketplace and the potential for a reestablishment of fuller carrying charges. If the premium becomes unduly negative, arbitrage activity will emerge and the time-forward costs can be secured at less-than-current market prices especially if the overall market structure moves into an inverted state. It would be more economical to fix those future requirements via the board than buying the metal at prevailing prices and incurring maintenance and financing charges. Finally, additional bases can

TABLE 9.7. MULTIPLE BASIS DETERMINATION

Date	C1 Cash Price	C2 April Futures	C3 C2 – C1 Basis	C4 July Futures	C5 C4 – C1 Basis	C6 October Futures	C7 C6 – C1 Basis
January 16	365.50	370.40	+4.90	373.20	+7.70	376.80	+11.30
February 10	360.25	361.70	+1.45	365.30	+5.05	368.50	+8.25
March 17	418.00	420.10	+2.10	423.60	+5.60	425.60	+7.60
March 27	422.50	420.30	−2.20	427.70	+5.20	430.00	+7.50

TABLE 9.8. COMPARATIVE VALUE ANALYSIS

Time	Percent		
	7	9	11
3 months	$6,396	$8,224	$10,051
6 months	$12,793	$16,448	$20,103
12 months	$25,585	$32,895	$40,205

$365,500 paid-in-full purchase

be established between the different futures months and commodity grades or security types.

For paid-in-full purchases, the resultant commitment of funds and imputed costs for lost opportunities would be staggering. Table 9.8 shows a comparative value analysis of this. This table assumes the platinum was paid-in-full, no borrowing to finance.

In the event of an overly optimistic forecast of production, the manufacturer would now be running the risk of unhedged actual material inventories (not requirements) as it paid for them in full and their values fluctuate with the underlying cash market. Also, any subsequent financing of these materials to generate working capital would be limited as lenders would not extend full market value for the metal but perhaps only 50 percent; whereas, a suitable hedge could elicit credit in the range of 80 to 90 percent of the market value. Finally, the manufacturer changed its specific risk from required input cost production to actual inventory price level exposure. Pursuing this latter state of affairs, the manufacturer's risk would be equal to the uncovered part. For example, should contracted sales require only 800 ounces, yet 1,000 ounces were purchased, the manufacturer's exposure would be 200 ounces from an inventory perspective.

ANTICIPATORY VERSUS ACTUAL POSITIONS

There are several distinctions between these two classes of hedging. For financial institutions, the precisely stated definition of regulatory bodies must be considered, as it isolates the size and approach for different hedging programs. Unfortunately, regulations vary among the states and even within corporate charters, so this text is unable to state the singularly definitive one. Nevertheless, the broad concepts will be examined.

Returning to our silver producer, its yearly production is anticipated. It may have previous sales to absorb the entire projected production. However, the silver has not been mined. Despite past experiences, there may be a production problem due to a strike, a collapsed shaft, or other adverse situation.

For this producer to hedge yearly production or even reserve content takes the hedge program mostly into the region of anticipation. Likewise, a farmer can only estimate forthcoming crop size according to expected growing conditions and planted acreage, favorable, average, or unfavorable; yet the farmer is not guaranteed a final production quantity when the crop is planted and the hedge established. This anticipatory process applies to money and pension fund managers, banking officers, and investment groups. Anticipatory hedging programs take into account the dynamic market environment.

For actual position hedging, the process is static. Given production, inventories, portfolio values, or other immediate concerns are the determining quantities. In this case, a farmer would only hedge when the crop is harvested, not when it is planted. The mining company would only hedge actual inventories and most recent production. Investment managers would only hedge that day's assets and liabilities with no consideration to future changes, no matter how well expected. The prevailing dollar amounts can be sizable, but managerial flexibility is compromised as well as operational planning.

Typically, an optimal hedge program combines elements of both. It takes into account the current production-input process and asset and liability components while simultaneously considering reasonably forecasted changes.

It is important to remember that hedging does not forecast future price levels—it establishes basis relationships.

ADAPTIVE HEDGING

The adaptive hedging process continuously reevaluates the hedging situation. It recognizes hedging as a dynamic, not static, process. Changes in conditions and expectations can prompt realignments and revisions in outstanding hedge positions. This is especially true for options delta hedging strategies.

For users, economic swings can improve or diminish estimated needs. For producers, such as farming and mining organizations, shifts in production estimates warrant revised hedging strategies. For example, cotton growers in high risk regions (those prone to erratic production due to weather) may on occasion have to revise the size of their hedges. In years of better-than-expected production, additional hedge contracts can be necessary to take into account a more sizable crop. Conversely, severe production problems can necessitate the reduction in hedge contracts as that cotton will not be harvested. This can be scientifically pursued, since crop condition statistics are reported from various sources as well as the farmer's own progressive assessment of the crop's condition. Was part of the planting washed out and not replaced? Did it germinate in a satisfactory manner? Is it maturing according to standard? These and other questions must be asked. In such cases, minimum-maximum boundaries can be laid out for the hedge program. For example, consider two growers: One has readily available irrigation supplies, the other does not. We shall assume that this one factor accounts for the variation in production. During drought years, Grower 2 can expect yields only equal to 50 percent of its planting expectations. For Grower 1, experience has been 85 percent of the planting expectation. In this scenario, Grower 1 can reasonably place an anticipatory hedge equal to 85 percent of expected crop around planting time or shortly thereafter. For Grower 2, in the absence of other information, the initial hedge should probably be approximately half of planting expectations as defined by production. But other information is available. Modifying our analysis, Grower 2's region only experiences drought conditions once every 4 years. Grower 2 can increase the initial hedge somewhat, but not too much. For Grower 1, this occurrence does not dramatically affect the final yield. Now suppose that Grower 2 still faces drought risk but it historically has occurred 1 year in 10. Then from an expected value perspective, the initial hedge can be substantially higher and adjustments can be made as the season's growing weather unfolds. A more complete evaluative framework is presented in Chapter 15, Conditional Analysis.

HEDGING FINANCIALS

Hedging financial instruments entails the following considerations:

1. Coupon rates
2. Par values
3. Maturities
4. Market values
5. Call dates
6. Other features attached to the instrument
7. Cheapest to deliver
8. Conversion factors

For asset and liability management programs, the accurate determination of gaps is required. Often there is a significant variation between maturities of not only outstanding deposits and loans but expected differences in asset and liability composition due to rollovers and shifts in the yield curve. For many financial institutions, the assets are often long term while the liabilities are short term. Subsequent examples will develop these concepts.

Case 3a. Financial Short Hedge

This example highlights the mechanics of a short hedge with the specific issue at a premium to its par value. A government security dealer hedged for its $4 million holdings of this particular issue since they were collateralized. Table 9.9 portrays the hedge. Here, the hedge generated an offset of $275,000 versus the gain of $427,500 for the inventoried position, resulting in a speculative profit of $152,500 for the firm. Although this outcome was favorable due to rising prices, the hedge offered only 64 percent coverage. If the market similarly declined rather than rallied, the overall impact would have been a net loss of $152,500. This example illustrates several points. A simplistic issue par value versus futures instrument par value hedge, though workable, can result in substantial slippage. Employing conversion factors will improve the quality of the hedge.

Case 3b. Conversion Adjusted Short Hedge

Adjusting the hedge by its appropriate conversion factor improves the relational offset. This is seen when the conversion factor of 1.6056 is applied to the information supplied in Case 3a. Conversion factors establish the invoicing values for the various deliverable securities given the arrays of coupons and maturities. Conversion factors adjust the delivery value invoice to reflect higher delivery values for higher coupon issues for a given maturity. They assign higher invoice values to longer maturities for a given coupon rate. Table 9.10 reflects the adjusted hedge.

Case 4a. Financial Long Hedge

This hedge is frequently employed on an anticipatory basis. For example, a money manager or corporation expects an inflow of cash on a particular

TABLE 9.9. FINANCIAL SHORT HEDGE

	Futures	Cash
Initiated hedge	Sold 40 contracts of June T-bond futures at $96\frac{12}{32}$	Has inventory of 4 MM Par Value 14s of Nov 2006 $154\frac{26}{32}$
Lifted hedge	Bought 40 contracts of June T-bond futures at $103\frac{8}{32}$	Sold inventory of 14s of Nov 2006 $165\frac{16}{32}$
Impact	Loss of $6\frac{28}{32}$ per contract, or $275,000	Gain of $10\frac{22}{32}$ per bond, or $427,500

TABLE 9.10. CONVERSION ADJUSTED SHORT HEDGE

	Futures	Cash
Initiated hedge	Sold 64 contracts of June T-bond futures at $96\frac{12}{32}$	Has inventory of 4 MM Par Value 14s of Nov 2006 $154\frac{26}{32}$
Lifted hedge	Bought 64 contracts of June T-bond futures at $103\frac{8}{32}$	Sold inventory of 14s of Nov 2006 $165\frac{16}{32}$
Impact	Loss of $6\frac{28}{32}$ per contract, or $440,000	Gain of $10\frac{22}{32}$ per bond, or $427,500

date. This inflow can be a periodic infusion of investment funds, rentals, or insurance premiums to name a few. For example, an insurance company is entitled to receive $12 million two months hence while its treasurer expects interest rates to decline substantially over that time. According to forecasts, delays in investing those funds will be costly due to the potential for sharply lower interest income. The treasurer determines to lock in current rates by using the board. Table 9.11 indicates the steps involved. The treasurer's outlook was correct and it was fortunate the hedge was placed. Its coverage was excessive since it was established on a nonadjusted basis.

Case 4b. Adjusted Long Hedge

Had the treasurer pursued this approach, coverage would have been closer by $51,250. Table 9.12 represents this situation.

TABLE 9.11. FINANCIAL LONG HEDGE

	Futures	Cash
Initiated hedge	Bought 120 contracts of Sept T-note futures $95\frac{20}{32}$	Intend to purchase the $6\frac{3}{4}$s of Feb 1993 trading at $93\frac{16}{32}$
Three weeks later hedge lifted	Sold 120 contracts of Sept T-note futures at $102\frac{1}{32}$	Bought the $6\frac{3}{4}$s of Feb 1993 at $98\frac{25}{32}$
Impact	Gain of $6\frac{16}{32}$ per bond, or $768,750	Net increase per bond of $5\frac{9}{32}$, or $633,750

TABLE 9.12. ADJUSTED LONG HEDGE

	Futures	Cash
Initiated hedge	Bought 112 contracts of Sept T-note futures	Intend to purchase the $6\frac{3}{4}$s of Feb 1993
	$95\frac{20}{32}$	trading of $93\frac{16}{32}$
Three weeks later hedge lifted	Sold 112 contracts of Sept T-note futures at	Bought the $6\frac{3}{4}$s of Feb 1993 at
	$102\frac{1}{32}$	$98\frac{25}{32}$
Impact	Gain of $6\frac{13}{32}$ per bond, or	Net increase per bond of $5\frac{9}{32}$, or
	$717,500	$633,750

Case 5a. Stock Short Hedge

An investor's portfolio of utility stocks is valued at $2,185,319. She decides to hedge it with S&P futures since she is apprehensive about a pullback and seeks to protect current values. This decision to maintain the utility holdings rather than liquidate all or a portion of them is partially due to the portfolio's components soon becoming eligible for preferential long-term capital gains treatment. On March 20, the June S&P futures was trading at 239.50; she decides that the hedge was to be placed. As each full point is worth $500, she quickly calculated the number of contracts as being:

$$\frac{2,185,319}{500 \times 239.50} = 18.25$$

or 18 contracts. Subsequently, the S&P futures advanced to 246.00 on April 22, while the holdings were valued at $2,233,766. Table 9.13 represents this situation.

The hedge worked, but on a net value basis the $58,500 increase in S&P futures was greater than the actual portfolio advance by $11,053. If fewer contracts were sold, the offsetting relationship would have been tighter. The straightforward selling of market values ignored the beta relationship between the portfolio and its hedging instrument.

Case 5b. Beta Adjusted Short Hedge

The utility investor had a brother with similar investments who was aware of the beta factor. This second investor determined the beta factor for

TABLE 9.13. STOCK SHORT HEDGE

	Futures Hedge	Utility Portfolio
March 20	Sold 18 contracts of June S&P futures @ 239.50	$2,185,319
April 22	Bought 18 contracts of June S&P futures @ 246.00	$2,232,766
Net change	−$58,500	+$47,447

his portfolio to be .80 as related to the S&P market. Beta reflects the degree of response between the given security, portfolio, or index to a benchmark index. Here, it related the expected change in the portfolio to the S&P market. Generally, the beta factor is determined by regressing the particular security or portfolio to the designated benchmark index. The beta is the coefficient of regression (the b) of the ordinary expression $a + bx = y$. Thus a beta of .80 would mean that the portfolio would be expected to change by 8 percent for every 10 percent change in the underlying index. Beta can also be negative, thereby indicating an inverse relationship. Table 9.14 applies this knowledge.

The beta-weighted hedge is determined by weighting the unadjusted number of contracts (here it was 18.25) by the beta factor, or $18.25 \times .80 = 14.60$. Again a fractional number of contracts is indicated; and to reflect the integer amounts about this number, Table 9.14 presents Alternative 1 where the hedge consists of 14 contracts and Alternative 2 where the hedge consists of 15 contracts. As expected, the alternative hedges straddled the portfolio value change. In Alternative 1, the investor experienced a slight net gain of $1,947 while Alternative 2 produced a slight net loss of $1,303. Clearly, both alternatives in Table 9.14 generated tighter hedging bases than the one in Table 9.13.

Case 6a. Stock Long Hedge

A money manager anticipates a scheduled inflow of $35 million 1 month forward. Forecasts indicate improving equity values over that time. Moreover, this manager trades high technology issues. The straightforward application of:

$$\frac{\text{Market value}}{\text{Hedging instrument value}} = \text{number of hedge contracts}$$

indicates the anticipatory hedge purchase of 307.62 contracts. After rounding up, this situation is represented by Table 9.15. This table shows that the lack

TABLE 9.14. BETA ADJUSTED STOCK SHORT HEDGE

Futures Hedge Alternative 1	Futures Hedge Alternative 2	Utility Portfolio
Sold 14 contracts of June S&P futures @ 239.50	Sold 15 contracts of June S&P futures @ 239.50	$2,185,319
Bought 14 contracts of June S&P futures @ 246.00	Bought 15 contracts of June S&P futures @ 246.00	$2,232,766
−$45,500	−$48,750	+$47,447

of a hedge would have required an additional $2,896,671 for the previously desired share purchase or the subsequent purchase of 8.3 percent fewer shares. The anticipatory buy hedge provided coverage equal to $2,148,300 but it still fell short of the market's rise by $748,371. This shortfall was attributable to the relative responsiveness of the high technology issues versus the S&P index.

Case 6b. Beta Adjusted Long Stock Hedge

Had the portfolio manager applied the beta weight to the anticipatory hedge, the dollar differential would have been significantly narrower indicating a tighter basis. Here, the adjustment is:

$$\frac{\text{Expected funds inflow}}{\text{Current contract value}} \times \text{beta factor} = \text{\# of contracts}$$

$$\text{or} \quad \frac{35,000,000}{113,775} \times 1.35 = 415.29.$$

The adjustment is presented in Table 9.16.

A comparison between columns 1 and 3 indicates a very tight fit. The

TABLE 9.15. STOCK LONG HEDGE

	Futures Hedge	Security Values
February 26	Buys 308 contracts of June S&P futures @ 227.55	Preferred purchase of anticipated $35,000,000 inflow
March 26	Sells 308 contracts of June S&P futures @ 241.50	Subsequent value of high technology securities $37,896,671
Net dollar change	$2,148,300	$2,896,671

TABLE 9.16. BETA ADJUSTED LONG STOCK HEDGE

Futures Hedge Based on 1.35 Beta	Outcome 1 Hedge Protection	Outcome 2 Intended Security Purchase
Bought 415 contracts of June S&P futures @ 227.55	Preferred purchase of anticipated inflow of $35,000,000	Preferred purchase of anticipated inflow of $35,000,000
Sold 415 contracts of June S&P futures @ 241.50	$37,145,682	Subsequent value of preferred investment $37,896,671
$2,894,625	$2,145,682	$2,896,671

hedge provided $2,894,625 of insurance against higher values. The difference came to a shortfall of only $2,046, and this was due to the fact that fractional contracts are not traded. What if the actual beta action were different from the expected one? Columns 1 and 2 give one alternative. For this outcome, the hedge generated $2,894,625 (the same as before) but the intended securities advanced by one $2,145,682, which implies that the position was over-hedged by $748,943. The initiating procedure was correct; but subsequent market behavior for the intended securities for that time frame behaved with a beta of 1.25, not the estimated 1.35 factor.

This departure between expected and actual values is one weakness of beta and conversion factor adjustments. These adjustments to the factors may not be statistically precise for every time interval over extensive periods. As mentioned throughout this text, parameters can and will shift over time. Nevertheless, various adaptive and conditional techniques can be employed, which, on-balance, should dampen the aberrant effects of these nonstationary characteristics.

HEDGING WITH OPTIONS

Options add enormous flexibility to a hedging program. They can preclude margin calls, generate additional income in the form of premiums, offer various degrees of immunization, and complement futures hedging strategies. Options on futures are exactly that: They represent a particular option for a specified futures position. The exercise of an option creates the underlying futures position at the stipulated strike price. The following three cases illustrate the usefulness of options within hedge programs.

Case 1. Long Call Option Hedge

An emerging manufacturer requires silver for its production. It is a growing company, and maintaining adequate cash balances is critical to its wel-

fare. Although business prospects are optimistic, the competitiveness of the
marketplace for the company's particular products is such that they cannot
easily pass on raw material price increases. It has been determined that, by
hedging the silver requirement, they can comfortably bid on large-scale orders. Their third quarter requirement is 100,000 ounces. Table 9.17 portrays
the situation. Columns 1, 2, and 3 indicate: Option 1 is the near-the-money
approach, Option 2 is the nearest out-of-the-money alternative, and column 3
is the cash market activity. Had the manufacturer pursued Option 1, it would
have experienced a $16,500 loss on its option hedge position, but was able to
buy physical silver 38.90 cents per ounce cheaper or $38,900. The net benefit
was cash market improvement − net futures premium = net hedge benefit,
or $38,900 − $16,500 = $22,400. This is true since, at the time of the physical
transaction, the hedge would be lifted. Although the total initial options premium was $25,500, the manufacturer managed to recover $9,000 of it.

Similarly, Option 2 enabled the company to purchase silver at a better
price despite adverse premium movement. Here, the net benefit was $25,600.

Had the company pursued the futures purchase route, it would have effectively locked in a price of $5.8980 to be subsequently adjusted by the im-
provement, from the company's perspective, in the silver cash market. It was
able to buy physical silver for $36,500 cheaper on April 16 than on March 17,
but this was mostly offset by the $38,900 futures hedge loss. Had the market
advanced, the futures hedge would have outperformed the other two options;
though, depending on degree of advance, they still would have contributed
offseting hedge values. In an advancing situation, Option 1 would have provided more protection than Option 2 due to their relative strike prices.

Case 2. Long Put Option Hedge

A subsidiary of a multinational trading company periodically accumu-
lates deutschemark balances due to its sales in West Germany. Rather than
converting those receipts into U.S. dollars, the company prefers to be in marks
but are wary of volatile swings in the foreign exchange markets. Management

TABLE 9.17. ALTERNATIVE LONG CALL OPTION HEDGES

Date	Option 1 $6.00 Strike	Option 2 $6.25 Strike	Cash Market	July Futures
March 17	25.5 per ounce or premium of $25,500	18.5 per ounce or premium of $18,500	$5.77 per ounce ($577,000 value)	$589,80
April 16	9.0 per ounce or $9,000	5.2 per ounce or $5,200	$5.405 per ounce ($540,500 value)	$550.90
	−16.5 per ounce or −$16,500	−13.3 per ounce or −$13,300	−$36,500 decline for cash equivalent	$38,90 −$38,900

TABLE 9.18. ALTERNATIVE LONG PUT OPTION HEDGES

Date	June Strike Price $.43/DM Option 1	June Strike Price $.44/DM Option 2	Cash Market	June Futures Market
February 26	55 points or premium of $68,750	87 points or premium of $108,750	12,500,000 DM .4450/DM $5,562,500 spot value	.4506 $5,632,500 contract value
April 7	159 points or premium of $198,750	230 points or premium of $287,500	12,500,000 DM .4178/DM $5,222,500 spot value	.4208 $5,260,000 contract value
Net Change	104 points $130,000	143 points $178,750	.0272/DM $340,000 change in value	.0298 $372,500

expects the dollar to depreciate over the intermediate-to-longer term, but in an erratic manner. They seek to limit the risk attributable to large-scale currency intervention that could abruptly bolster the dollar and adversely impact the profitability of the enterprise. Also, they want to keep their alternatives open should they decide at a later date to convert their deutschemark balances. Table 9.18 illustrates this situation.

The purchase of the out-of-the-money put (Option 1) produced protection of $130,000, which trimmed the cash market loss to $210,000. Greater protection was provided by Option 2, which was nearer-to-the-money. The adjusted loss was only $161,250. It should be noted that the increased protection of $48,750 exceeded the initial premium differential of $40,000. Finally, had the firm placed a futures hedge, the compensatory offset was $372,500, or $32,500 greater than the spot market loss. This apparent overage was due to the capture of the time value differential.

Case 3. Call Option Writes

A bullion trading company seeks to enhance the returns on a portion of its 10,000 ounce inventory. It is prepared to write calls against 15 percent of the position or the equivalent of 15 futures contracts. As it expects the market to remain relatively stable near term, the company seeks to capture larger premiums. Table 9.19 illustrates this. The progressive decline in option values is beneficial to the writer here. Although June futures were slightly higher a month (March 24) after the write, Option 1 position was ahead by $2,850 while the Option 2 position was $3,000 ahead. At the close of business on the subsequent day, Option 1 was ahead by $7,500 and Option 2 was ahead by $6,900. If the futures did not mount a subsequent rally, the writer would eventually claim $22,500 for the Option 1 write or $16,200 for the Option 2 write. There would be no incentive for the purchaser to exercise under these conditions as the strike price of the call was higher than the underlying futures.

TABLE 9.19. CALL OPTION WRITES

Date	$350.00 Strike Price Option 1	$360.00 Strike Price Option 2	June Futures
February 24	$15.00 per ounce or $22,500	$10.80 per ounce or $16,200	$354.90
March 24	$13.10 per ounce or $19,650	$8.80 per ounce or $13,200	$355.10
March 25	$10.00 per ounce or $15,000	$6.20 per ounce or $9,300	$347.70

RATIO WRITES

This technique considers the delta relationship between the futures and the specified option. It relates the responsiveness of the option to changes in the underlying futures price. For example, if the delta was .50, then a completely covered ratio write would require the sale of 2 calls, not 1, for the futures equivalent position. Similarly, a delta of .33 would indicate the sale of 3 calls to obtain the necessary compensatory value. The reciprocal of the delta provides the number of contracts necessary for the ratio write per unit of futures equivalent. Ratio hedging is adaptive, as underlying futures market price changes can cause substantial swings in delta values. This requires a dynamic trading strategy to adjust to shifts in the delta values.

SCALING

Though applications of hedging strategies vary among organizations, the placement of scale orders is a useful tool. It does not require the execution of the hedge futures or options positions to be conducted at only one price or difference. Rather it affords flexibility to accommodate various market conditions and expectations. By placing scale orders, an organization establishes quantitative boundaries as to preferred levels and subsequent basis relationships.

Using the data in Table 9.19, the firm could have specified the scale of Option 1 contracts on February 24 as follows: Sell 5 at 16.00, 5 at 15.00, and 5 at 14.00. If there was a subsequent buyback, it could have been specified as: Buy 15 contracts starting at 10.50—one every 10 points down. Of course, these specifications may not always be actualized. Sometimes, only partials are accomplished. Nevertheless, when trading against a level or specified basis, scaling layers the execution of orders and can optimize performance. Scaling can take on the shape of a certain percentage of orders to be executed at the market and the remainder at the other acceptable limits. The scaling process need not be done in neat units, but it should approximate the firm's requirements by presenting a probabilistic-expected value framework in the placement of orders.

ASSET AND LIABILITY MANAGEMENT

One of the more complex areas facing financial hedgers is that of asset and liability management. The matching of current assets and liabilities and the taking into account of potentially rapid changes in their future composi-

TABLE 9.20. MACRO GAP ANALYSIS

	≤ 3 Months	> 3 Months	Total
Liabilities + equity	150MM	65MM	215MM
Assets	20MM	195MM	215MM
Gaps (over, under)	130MM over	130MM under	

tion can have a dramatic impact on profitability and liquidity. Interest-rate-sensitive assets and liabilities can quickly change their maturity and rate composition due to yield curve and expectational changes. Swings in business, mortgage, and personal loan demands can alter an institution's portfolio without notice. Flights to quality or at least liquidity can just as quickly affect the liability format. Typically, lending institutions are confronted with funding relatively longer-term income-producing assets with short-term maturity liabilities. There are two basic approaches to analyze these variables. They are macro gap analysis and micro gap analysis. A gap refers to the differential between the assets and liabilities for a specified maturity class.

Macro Analysis

Though arbitrary, it should readily partition the problem into a few major groups, such as: 3-, 6-, or 12-month maturities. For example, a particular institution's funding is primarily derived from liabilities with maturities not exceeding three months, such as passbook savings and certificates of deposit. Its assets are mostly fixed-rate mortgages with indicated maturities of at least 15 years.

One example of this is shown in Table 9.20 and another (Table 9.21) is slightly more partitioned.

In both cases the funding was overwhelmingly short term while the predominant asset maturity was very long term. If this composition were underhedged, the institution could experience severe problems—particularly in an advancing interest rate scenario—since they would be forced to pay progressively higher rates which would, when permitted, escalate on a very short-term horizon. Exacerbating the problem would be the reduction in market

TABLE 9.21. PARTITIONED MACRO GAP ANALYSIS

	≤ 3 Months	> 3 Months but ≤ 15 Years	≥ 15 Years
Liabilities + equity	150MM	55MM	10MM
Assets	20MM	50MM	145MM
Gaps (over, under)	130MM over	5MM over	135MM under

values for the existing portfolio. If funds were needed, they could only be generated by realizing a substantial loss in the held investments as their market values would have deteriorated.

Micro Analysis

This is a calibrated extension of the macro analysis. Instead of a coarse short-term versus long-term presentation, the analyst refines the objective by specifying multiple time frames to more nearly identify important gaps. There can be many parts to the solution as gaps can occur in different ways for the various maturities. The following table applies this microscopic approach to the previous example. It has been determined that there are five important maturity classes that sufficiently categorize the institution's position. Though the arrangement of rows can be placed in any consistent manner, they were purposely arranged in Table 9.22 to emphasize the magnitude of the gaps.

This micro analysis demonstrates an overwhelming majority of $197 million in liabilities that have maturities of 6 months or less. Simultaneously, it can be seen $177 million of the assets have maturities greater than 6 months. The distribution of assets and liabilities appear in Graph 9.5. The two primary gaps occur at the tails of the maturity distribution. There is a $90 million liability gap in the 1-month-or-less maturity, while the greater-than-or-equal-to-15-year maturity poses a $135 million asset-over-liability gap. In the event of rapidly rising rates, the institution would find its interest expense climbing while the interest income would be basically stagnant if the terms of the investments were mostly fixed and not variable.

Assets and liabilities have three major valuation components:

1. Maturity
2. Interest (income or expense)
3. Value

Maturity is a variable that for the moment will be considered a constant. If the hedge were designed to protect against liability interest expense, then

TABLE 9.22. MICRO GAP ANALYSIS[a] (IN MILLIONS OF DOLLARS)

	$t < 1$ Month	$1 < t <$ 3 Months	$3 < t <$ 6 Months	6 Months $< t$ < 15 Years	$t > 15$ Years	Total
Liabilities and equity	98	52	47	8	10	215
Assets	8	12	18	32	145	215
$ gaps	90	40	29	−24	−135	0

[a]t is the time to maturity

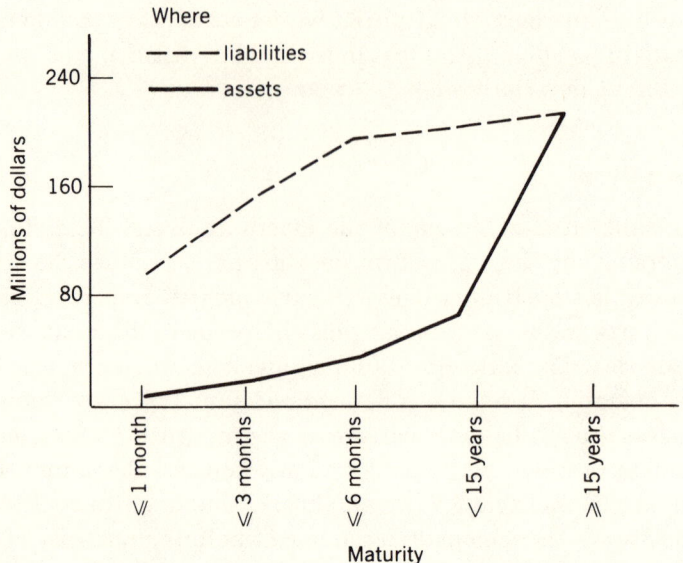

GRAPH 9.5 Distribution of assets and liabilities

a sell hedge would be initiated. If the value of the outstanding liability were to be preserved, then a buy hedge would be initiated. To protect asset values, a sell hedge is required; whereas, a buy hedge would be necessary to protect the income stream.

In all cases it is important to determine the dominant risk concerns for an organization. In the example, the institution would be most sensitive to escalating interest expenses while being vulnerable to reductions in portfolio values. Thus one or two sell hedges would be necessary. If it were decided that interest expense was the most important risk, then a sale of T-bill or Euro-dollar futures would be conducted to protect the institution from potentially higher interest charges on its liabilities that fund the asset base. This is seen by the following:

Liabilities Per $ million			Assets Per $ million		
1%	2%	3%	1%	2%	3%
$10,000	$20,000	$30,000	0	0	0

Here, the interest expense rose by $10,000 to $30,000 for the liabilities over a year while asset income did not change. One reason for this is many of these fixed asset commitments were previously placed and little or no effective turn-over was experienced. But the maturities of the liabilities do change and frequently so do their interest rates.

FLOW OF FUNDS ANALYSIS

This topic concerns the flow of assets and liabilities. It is this transitional analysis that enables an organization not only to reflect static needs but to account for dynamic requirements. By forecasting its expected movements of capital in regard to changes in distributions and deposits, the firm is in a better posture to determine likely position requirements. These changes can be induced by yield curve shifts, additional fundings, withdrawals, changes in portfolio composition or investment policies, and the imposition or removal of services.

DURATION ANALYSIS

Duration analysis refines the estimation of expected maturity lives versus their stated maturities. It is more than the simple averaging of outstanding terms since it considers the impact of rate changes and the subsequent response to asset financing or liability preference. Specifically, it considers the net present values of the entire funds stream over the remainder of the stipulated maturity, subject to call provisions. Discounted instruments, such as T-bills and zero coupons have no adjusted durational lives. Their expected lives are their stipulated terms. This topic is particularly important for mortgage and bond-trading organizations. Significant declines in interest rates can induce fairly quick swings toward refinancing whereby previously high-yielding paper is supplanted by lower-yielding paper, reducing an institution's gross income stream. The analysis highlights how instruments tend to have shorter expected lives than their stipulated ones. By having this additional information, more accurate flow-of-funds analyses are possible. This concept is akin to that of elasticity as it relates percent yield changes to price changes.

PREMIUMS AND DISCOUNTS

The rule of thumb is to buy the discount and sell the premium when feasible. This allows a more favorable basis as it capitalizes on time values. However, it cannot be blindly applied. For agricultural-related commodities, differences between crop years can be dramatic due to substantial variations in production, usage, and carryover estimates. For financial futures, these differences are best exemplified by gyrations in the yield curve. For example, the pricing structure for some commodities can be inverted in the old crop and flat or nearly so in the new crop. Moreover, the old crop can be at a substantial premium relative to the new crop. As far as rollovers that seek to protect inventory values between these years, substantial differences can occur. Although prices strive toward continuity, the expectations can be so radical between years that favorably hedged inventories may not be so when it is time to roll over for hedge maintenance. For such times, it can produce a buyer's market for the forwards and a seller's market for the nearbys. Supplies can be so severely limited in the old crop that further substantial price rises occur, generating the need for cash to maintain hedge-short positions.

Financial futures pose similar problems. In an environment of a positively sloped yield curve, the rolling forward of short hedges to maintain portfolio values can only be done by selling a discounted month. This is particularly the case for debt instruments. As time works against these short hedges, on the rollover additional contracts may have to be initiated in order to maintain the basis point integrity of the hedge. Perceptions of forthcoming changes in the character of the yield curve must be appraised in order to select the optimal delivery months. For short hedges in a rapidly flattening situation of a positive yield curve while rates are falling, the nearby months can offer the best alternatives. Conversely, for long hedgers, the better months would be the more deferred ones.

MONTH SELECTIONS

Premiums and discounts are two variables that influence the hedging month selection process. Other considerations are the matching of needs and expectations, any contractual commitments, and the underlying fundamentals. For agricultural commodities, this would mean trading the appropriate crop year deliveries. A cotton grower could not very well establish a reliable production hedge by selling July cotton against a crop to be harvested in October of the same calender year. There can be two substantially different sets of economic fundamentals. Besides, the grower could be shorting a delivery month in a tight year versus expected production to be forthcoming in a bumper crop year.

Conceivably, near-term maturities can be used to hedge longer-term maturities via elaborate basis point hedges, but any slight departure from prevailing yield curve structure could generate sizable equity swings and subsequent hedge realignments. This phenomenon is prevalent in the area of adjustable rate mortgage financing. Typically, the adjustments are made on a short-term such as a 6- or 12-month schedule, while the commitment can be for 20, 25, or 30 years.

One direct solution to this dichotomy is to dissect the instrument and determine its characteristics. Aside from prevailing practices of offering "below market" first-year rates, the problem becomes one of establishing the suitable basis. For this it must be determined whether the commitment is a 1-year instrument to be renewed 29 times (30 year mortgage); or a 30-year instrument to be renewed once a year. Renewal here is not a renewal of commitment, but a revision of rate terms to be conducted on a periodic schedule. Concurrently, the underlying stipulated basis must be established. Do rates fluctuate in accordance to swings for a specific Treasury bill maturity, Eurodollar maturity, federal home loan rate, or whatever stipulated standard? By isolating this variable the hedge program can be analyzed. If the dominant number of adjustments are predicated on a short maturity instrument or index, then the solution lies in the realm of T-bill, Eurodollar, or certificate of deposit futures. If the adjustments are predicated on subsequent levels in the various fixed mortgage instruments, Treasury note or Treasury bond levels, then the character of the hedge more nearly approximates these longer-maturity instruments. It is important to realize that a basis is established such as: 2 points above the then prevailing federal home loan rate or 3 points over the 6-month Treasury bill rate. In effect, the mechanism of against actuals (AAs) and exchange-for-physicals (EFPs) has been invoked; except here the borrower pays the appropriate interest and principal amounts while the lender delivers the contractually designated mortgage funds. Refinements to this approach entail the historic and expected basis relationship analyses and then the implementing of the suitable hedge vehicles in an acceptable basis point adjustment program.

HEDGING CONSTRAINTS

A hedging program is subject to constraints. Among these are:

1. Funds available for initial and variation margins
2. Position sizes—internal and external conditions
3. Industry or state regulations; for example, banks, pension funds, savings and loans and insurance companies are all subject to various constraints
4. Total assets and/or total liabilities
5. Net assets
6. Interest charges
7. Interest receipts
8. Production—actual or anticipated
9. Usage—actual or anticipated
10. Time horizon

OFFSETS, SETTLEMENTS, AND DELIVERIES

The offset of a hedge can be accomplished several ways. For a sell hedge, the appropriate buy back or covering is done. If the original position was a buy hedge, then the futures are sold or liquidated. This lifting of the futures or options is conducted when the attendant cash position is altered or transactionally completed. Deliveries are another way of completing the hedge. A farmer may issue a delivery notice and then physically deliver the grain to the delivery notice holder pursuant to the provisions of the futures contract. A gold trader may want to take the delivery of bullion. In each case, the trading parties may find it to their advantage to make or take delivery of the underlying commodity. These deliveries are often predicated on the prevailing basis versus the initiated one; or they can be related to marketing and acquisition requirements.

Since the Eurodollar contract, the number of futures contracts which are now settled by cash has grown. The mechanism is simple; during the course of the hedge, the variating equity is drawn away or reestablished. Then on the expiration day a long does not receive any commodity, security, or portfolio; rather the final reconciliation is conducted. Also, the short does not make any physical delivery, but rather is subject to a final reconciliation to be made by cash.

Other Physical Offsets

Five other physical offsets are:

1. AAs (Against Actuals)
2. Against cash
3. EFPs (Exchange-for-Physicals)
4. Ex-pit
5. On-call

Though they vary in name according to the particular exchange, they are very similar in approach. Typically, AAs are executed in tropical products, against cash in the grain industry, while EFPs are executed for metals and resources and on-call for the textile business.

Each represents the exchange of a futures position for a predetermined cash transaction at a previously established basis. For example, an exporting firm may exchange the appropriate futures contracts to a grain company in exchange for physical wheat to be shipped overseas. The established basis will reflect premiums or discounts for grade as well as any shipping and handling costs.

These transactions are of great commercial importance as they are equally valid for hedging and cross-hedging purposes. They impart exactness to deliverable grades, destinations, and timetables. Once the basis is established, its variability is transformed into a constant. Not all the risk is eliminated, as performance remains to be seen; however, that area of risk is aside from the hedge per se.

These transactions are culminated outside the ring or pit, unlike other trades. The exchanges make provisions for these bona fide hedging transactions involving an actual cash position to be conveyed for a futures position to be conducted outside the outcry process so that the quantities are not altered, they go to the appropriate parties, and the pricing is established. The final stipulated price need not even be the most recent market one but any one within the exchange's regulations and contractual commitments.

The buyer's call indicates that the buyer, at his or her option, sets the price within the proscribed time period, while the seller's call enables the seller to establish the price within the proscribed time period. In each instance, the basis had been previously established.

TRADING THE BASIS

This expression encompasses several concepts. It can refer to cash and futures positioning. For example, a firm contracts to purchase a certain grade of vegetable oil at a stipulated basis, be it over/under the specified futures contract. One way to lock in the price is to purchase the appropriate amount of contracts of soybean oil thereby fixing the cost. The firm can wait to buy the futures at a later time, but it is subject to subsequent prevailing futures price levels. In this situation it is looking for lower board prices with the intent of securing a lower effective price as it already knows what the stipulated basis is. It is important to remember that the basis does not change here, but the firm may not even buy the futures as a price-protective instrument. Again, the basis did not change, only the effective price did (if there was any change in the underlying futures contract).

Trading the basis can also refer to arbitraging approaches. Whenever possible, previous arrangements may be canceled with little or no penalty and new positions established at a more favorable basis. Or, given subsequent differences in the markets, readjustments in the cash and futures positions can be prompted. Events can alter a trading desk's posture. On balance, they may be net short cash securities satisfying retail and/or institutional demand with the intent of covering at more favorable levels. This can occur at any time, but it is easier to visualize during a major auction. During this state of affairs, a brief appearance of implied rates versus actual repo rate difference occurs. The firm can buy cash securities, finance, and hedge them; then collect the slight favorable differential between the market's implied financing rate and the firm's own actual rate. This latter example highlights the two-sided view of the marketplace: levels and the basis.

The basis is what makes a hedge viable. Sometimes the terms or the market's conditions are such that the basis levels are unfavorable for placing the appropriate futures/options positions. These are commonly referred to buyer's or seller's markets. The criterion then becomes one of whether the locked-in loss is still preferable to further erosion in the protective element. It is a strategic decision that evaluates the expected further price (value) risks relative to unfavorable but nevertheless still helpful transformation to expectedly lower basis risks.

FUTURES OR OPTIONS

The selection of hedge vehicles is an important decision. For firms or subsidiaries that have limited funding resources, options often are the better choice. Though somewhat more expensive than outright futures hedging, they afford variable degrees of protection. The higher cost is due to the inherent time value of the option when purchased; and even though the option moves into the money or more deeply so, this property continues to depreciate over time and at expiration the time value is zero. Moreover, the underlying futures can have imputed time value due to carrying charge structure and this complete costing can be doubly expensive. Nevertheless, hedging by the purchase of options can be satisfactory as there will be no variation margin calls requiring the infusion of cash.

More complex hedging arrangements either through the writing of options or as a hybrid program consisting of both options and futures strategies can offer flexible hedges and even augment an organization's profitability. An evaluative technique is presented in Chapter 15.

MARGINING POSITIONS

The available financing approaches can significantly affect the overall performance and profitability of the enterprise. Although variation margin calls must be satisfied by cash, initial margins can be established by cash, actual Treasury bills, warrants, or receipts. For users and producers alike, the last techniques require only the deposit of acceptable receipts of underlying actual positions to establish the hedge. For corporate treasurers, the deposit of T-bills can be attractive. Rather than holding them in-house or at another financial depository, they can be journaled to a brokerage firm to hold them for initial margin. Thus the interest can still be collected, which maintains overall profitability, and here, enhances that of the hedge. Returns of 5, 6, 7 or more percent per annum can quickly affect results, and there is no change in the composition of the balance sheet assets except where these securities are held. Suitable metal inventories can be financing vehicles, requiring no interest charges, and still remain a part of the firm's assets. Since by themselves they produce no interest income, they can be transformed into vehicles precluding real financial opportunity costs by being available for original margins, or, when borrowed against, particularly when hedged, a source of working capital and a reservoir for potential variation calls. The purchase of options can eliminate the hazard of margin calls, but a time value must be paid. For writers, a source of potential income due to premiums is unveiled.

10

Foreign Exchange

THE INTERNATIONAL INFLUENCE

Multinational corporations, importers/exporters, and other parties that have interests in securities or commodities denominated in currencies other than their own can discover those investments and business transactions may be subject to great risk if not properly protected. An excellent example of this was the placement of funds in Mexican banks. If, allured by interest rates as high as 25 percent payable per annum by Mexican banks, one converted U.S. dollars into Mexican pesos, financial disaster could have resulted if the investment were not hedged. By looking at Chart 10.1, you see the futures market collapse reflects the dramatic devaluation that occurred during the first week of August 1982. It would have been devastating for those who maintained unhedged peso balances.

Similarly dramatic situations are portrayed by Charts 10.2, 10.3, and 10.4, which reflect abrupt changes in currency values when agreement to influence the U.S. dollar through interest rates was established.

Assuming U.S. dollars were converted into pesos at .0165 cents per peso, the subsequent peso decline resulted in an approximately 67 percent (non-annualized) value decline. To reinforce the catastrophic impact of this, consider that if the pesos stabilized at .0055 cents per peso, at the end of a year the financial loss would appear to be 42 percent. This is simply calculated by the nominal rate + currency movement + financial return. Since the apparent nominal rate was +25 percent and the currency movement was −67 percent, the expression approximately would be: +25 − 67 = −42. But in actuality it was worse. The following analyses to account for hedging considerations will demonstrate this. Consider these definitions:

Nominal return (forex factor) + principal (forex factor) = forex adjusted return

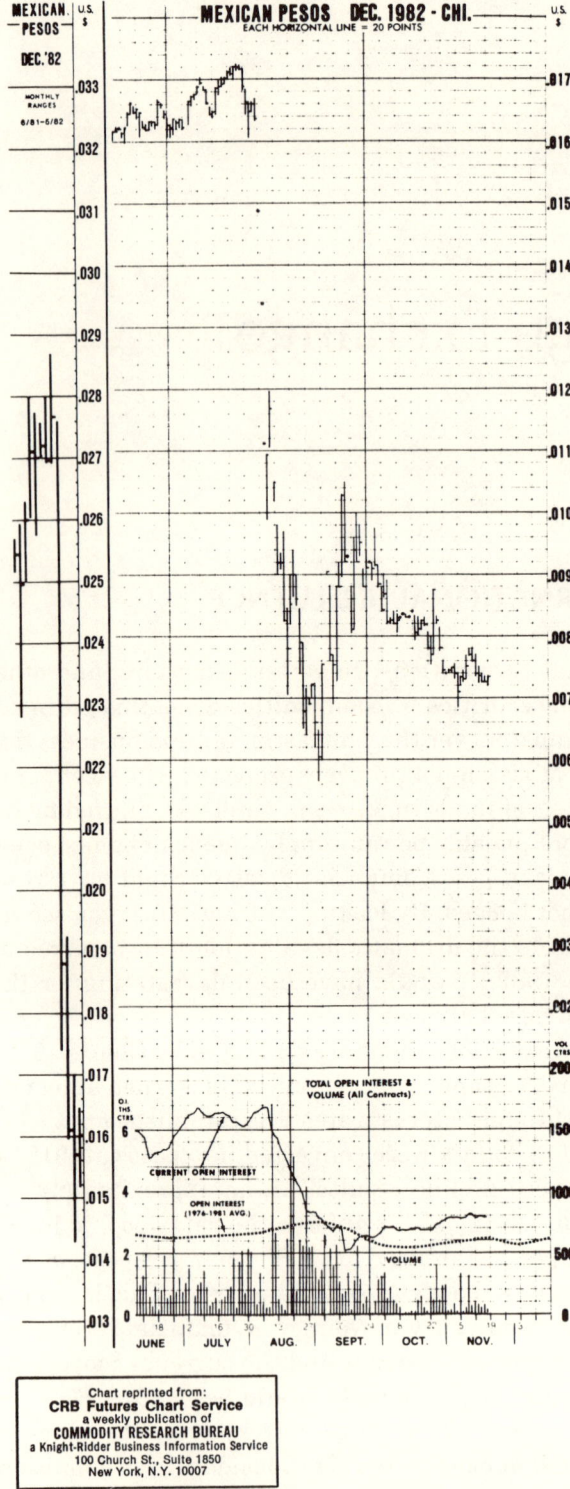

CHART 10.1 Peso devaluation

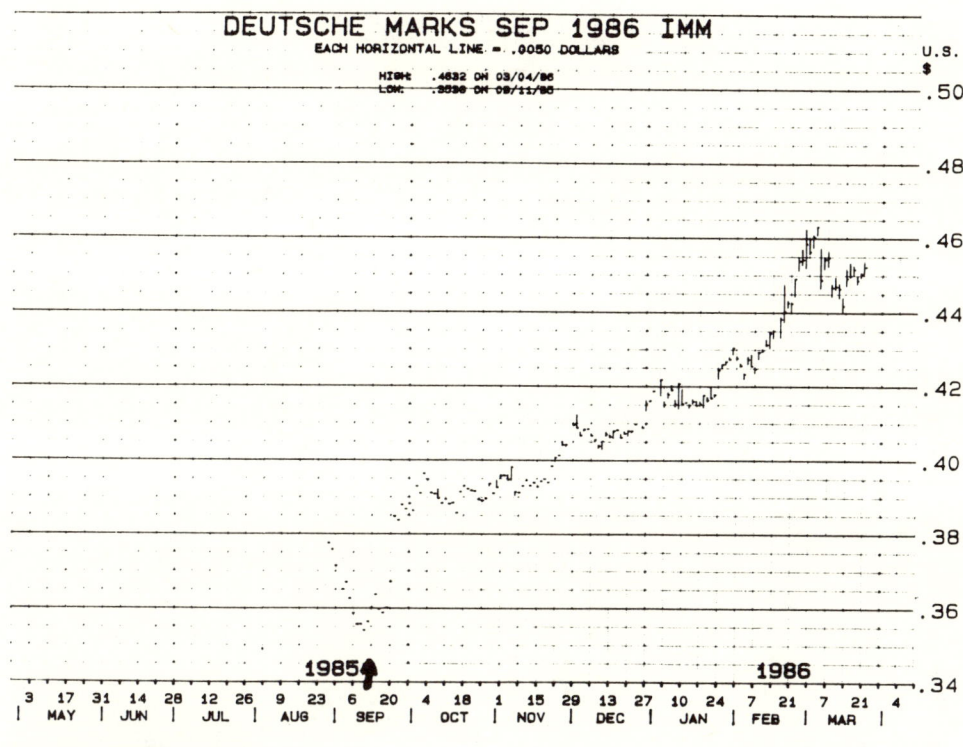

CHART 10.2 Response to G-5 meeting

where:

forex factor = [(1 + currency value change) + (value of hedge)]

Definitions:

Nominal return: return provided by interest

Principal: the amount of the investment, transaction, book value, outstanding liabilities, plant equipment, inventories, real estate, and other outstanding assets.

Currency value change: the percentage change in a currency value expressed in decimals. For example, 50 percent would be .50, 27 percent would be .27 and so on.

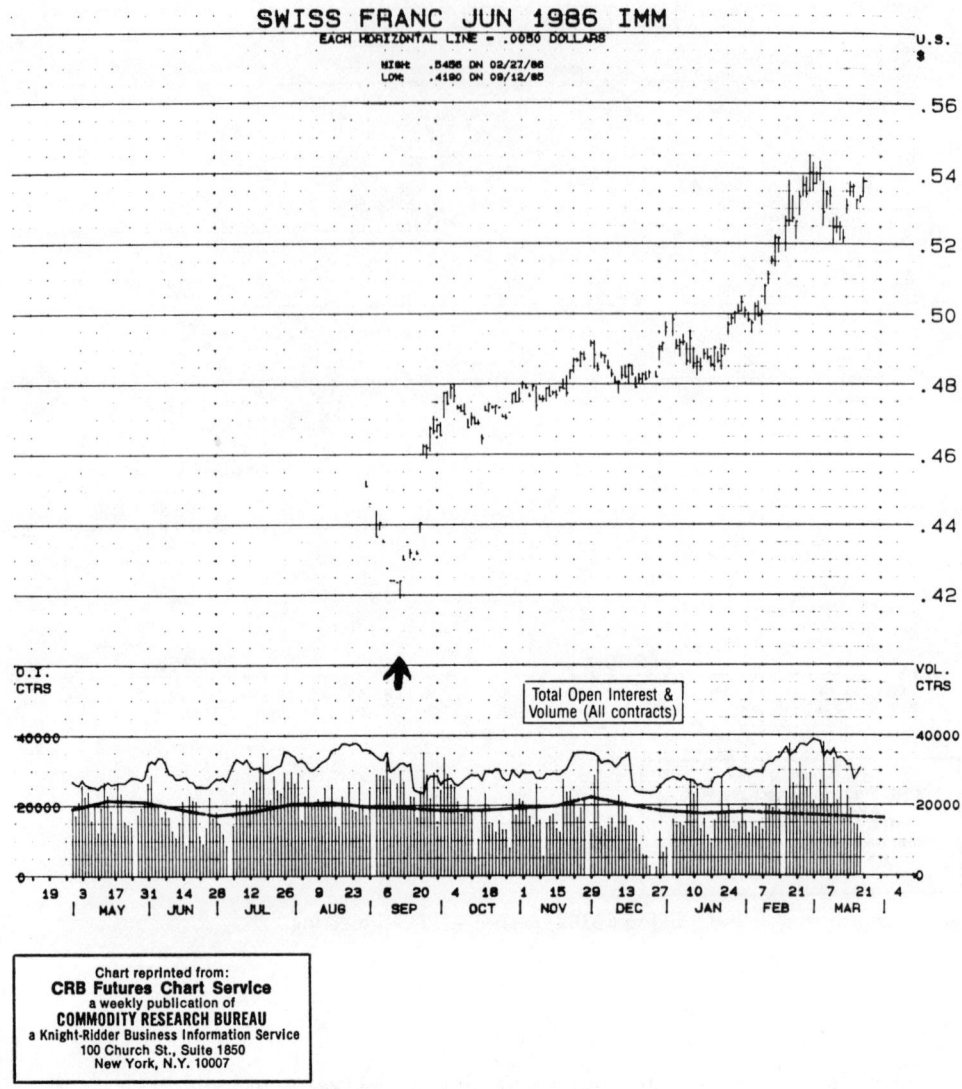

CHART 10.3 Response to G-5 meeting

Forex adjusted return: the unified financial return, taking into account the nominal transactional return, the foreign exchange impact, and the value of the hedge.

The analysis can be further refined by considering the time value of money aspects per each factor, therefore having an even more accurate assessment of the transaction's return.

The following three examples demonstrate the situation of: no hedge, limited to principal hedge, and full interest and principal hedge. By using a hedge

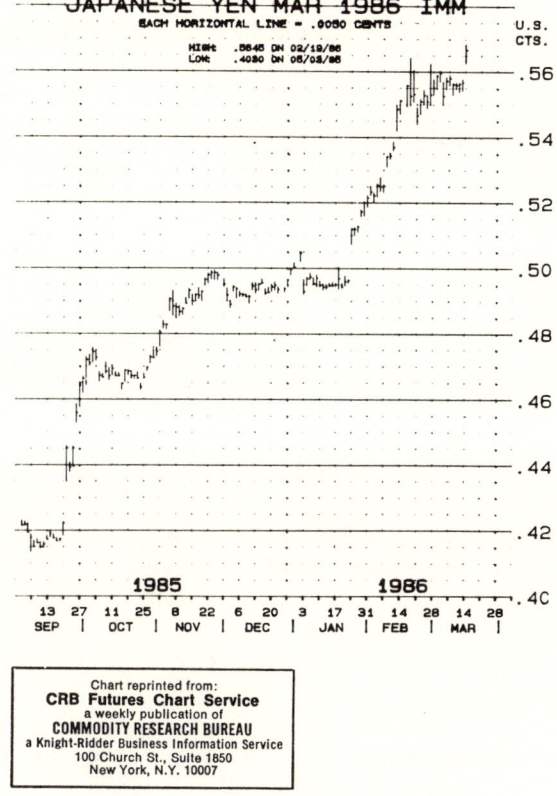

CHART 10.4 Response to G-5 meeting

perspective, the financial argument becomes more lucid and compelling as it isolates the impact of foreign exchange movements.

Example 10.1. No Hedge

This example assumes a $1 million capital commitment and an initially apparent return of $250,000, or 25 percent. Returning to the peso situation provided earlier, a more accurate result would be:

Nominal return (forex factor) + principal (forex factor) = forex adjusted amount

$250,000 [(1 − .67) + 0] + $1,000,000 [(1 − .67) + 0] =

$250,000 (.33)   + $1,000,000 (.33)   =

$82,500   + $333,333   =

$415,833 or approximately a 58.5% loss

and not a 25 percent gain or even the aforementioned 42 percent loss. The $415,833 would be the funds available after 1 year where the pesos were reconverted into U.S. dollars.

Example 10.2. Limited Hedge

Nominal return (forex factor) + principal (forex factor) = forex adjusted amount

$250,000 [(1 − .67) + 0] + $1,000,000 [(1 − .67) + .67] =

$250,000 (.33)   + $1,000,000 (1.00)   =

$82,500   + $1,000,000   =

$1,082,500 or approximately an 8.25% real gain.

In this case, the investor protected the principal portion of his or her funds but not the return (interest payments). As is readily seen, the principal portion was intact and there was a market currency adjusted real return of $82,500 or 8.25 percent per annum.

Example 10.3. Full Hedge

Nominal return (forex factor) + principal (forex factor) = forex adjusted amount

$250,000 [(1 − .67) + .67] + $1,000,000 [(1 − .67) + .67] =

$250,000 (1.00)   + $1,000,000 (1.00)   =

$250,000   + $1,000,000   =

$1,250,000 or the 25% expected gain.

This third example demonstrates the value of full currency protection as the investor not only preserved the principal, but also maintained protection on the nominal return. In this case, he realized nominal return adjusted for currency changes was $250,000, or 25 percent per annum.

INTERNATIONAL SECURITY TRADING

Portfolio strategies in the global securities markets must include foreign exchange factors. A correct market posture without the appropriate currency action can produce illusory profits and real losses. See Alternative 1 in Table 10.1.

TABLE 10.1. ALTERNATIVE INTERNATIONAL PORTFOLIO VALUATIONS

	U.S. Dollar Value of Portfolio[a]	U.S. Portfolio	West Germany Portfolio	United Kingdom Portfolio	
Initial capitalization less cash reserve	$45,000,000	$15,000,000	37,500,000 DM	10,000,000 BP	DM/BP Value
			$15,000,000	$15,000,000	Initial Rate
			($.40 per DM)	($1.50 per £)	
Alternative 1	$43,500,000	$18,000,000	45,000,000 DM	10,000,000 BP	DM/BP Value
	$40,500,000	$15,000,000	$13,500,000	$12,000,000	Alternative 1 rate
	$37,500,000	$12,000,000	($.30 per DM)	($1.20 per £)	
Alternative 2	$50,350,000	$18,000,000	37,500,000 DM	8,000,000 BP	DM/BP Value
	$47,350,000	$15,000,000	$18,750,000	$13,600,000	Alternative 2 rate
	$44,350,000	$12,000,000	($.50 per DM)	($1.70 per £)	
Alternative 3	$36,600,000	$18,000,000	30,000,000 DM	8,000,000 BP	DM/BP Value
	$33,600,000	$15,000,000	$9,000,000	$9,600,000	Alternative 3 rate
	$30,600,000	$12,000,000	($.30 per DM)	($1.20 per £)	
Alternative 4	$50,000,000	$18,000,000	30,000,000 DM	10,000,000 BP	DM/BP Value
	$47,000,000	$15,000,000	$15,000,000	$17,000,000	Alternative 4 rate
	$44,000,000	$12,000,000	($.50 per DM)	($1.70 per £)	
Alternative 5	$48,000,000	$18,000,000	30,000,000 DM	12,000,000 BP	DM/BP Value
	$45,000,000	$15,000,000	$12,000,000	$18,000,000	Alternative 5 rate
	$42,000,000	$12,000,000	($.40 per DM)	($1.50 per £)	

[a]U.S. portfolio column displays three alternative market valuations: $18,000,000; $15,000,000; and $12,000,000.

TABLE 10.2. HEDGED ALTERNATIVE INTERNATIONAL PORTFOLIO VALUATIONS

	U.S. Dollar Value of Portfolio[a]	U.S. Portfolio	West Germany Portfolio[b]	United Kingdom Portfolio[c]	DM/BP Value
Initial capitalization less cash reserve	$45,000,000	$15,000,000	37,500,000 DM	10,000,000 BP	DM/BP Value
			$15,000,000	$15,000,000	Initial Rate
			($.40 per DM)	($1.50 per £)	
Alternative 1	$51,000,000	$18,000,000	45,000,000 DM	10,000,000 BP	DM/BP Value
	$48,000,000	$15,000,000	$18,000,000	$15,000,000	
	$45,000,000	$12,000,000	($.40 per DM)	($1.50 per £)	Alternative 1 rate
Alternative 2	$45,000,000	$18,000,000	37,500,000 DM	8,000,000 BP	DM/BP Value
	$42,000,000	$15,000,000	$15,000,000	$12,000,000	
	$39,000,000	$12,000,000	($.40 per DM)	($1.50 per £)	Alternative 2 rate
Alternative 3	$42,000,000	$18,000,000	30,000,000 DM	8,000,000 BP	DM/BP Value
	$39,000,000	$15,000,000	$12,000,000	$12,000,000	
	$36,000,000	$12,000,000	($.40 per DM)	($1.50 per £)	Alternative 3 rate
Alternative 4	$45,000,000	$18,000,000	30,000,000 DM	10,000,000 BP	DM/BP Value
	$42,000,000	$15,000,000	$12,000,000	$15,000,000	
	$39,000,000	$12,000,000	($.40 per DM)	($1.50 per £)	Alternative 4 rate
Alternative 5	$48,000,000	$18,000,000	30,000,000 DM	12,000,000 BP	DM/BP Value
	$45,000,000	$15,000,000	$12,000,000	$18,000,000	
	$42,000,000	$12,000,000	($.40 per DM)	($1.50 per £)	Alternative 5 rate

[a] U.S. portfolio column displays three alternative market valuations, which are: $18,000,000; $15,000,000; and $12,000,000.
[b] DM hedged at $.40.
[c] £ hedged at $1.50.

Consider the situation of a stock fund which begins operations with an initial funding of U.S. $50 million. The manager seeks to maintain a cash balance of $5 million, or 10 percent, and equal commitments in American, British, and West German securities. In the event the manager does not like the particular level of securities at the outset but is satisfied with the currency rates, a buy hedge of the currencies is warranted to lock in those values pending the purchase of actual securities. As the actual securities are acquired, the pro rata liquidation of the currency buy hedge is to be conducted. Conversely, the purchase of securities would necessitate the application of sell hedges to protect currency values.

Table 10.1 highlights several portfolio alternatives that consider advancing and declining security values in the denominated currency units, adjusted by fluctuations in the underlying currency exchange rates. Due to the multiplicative nature of currency value adjustments, unhedged portfolio values are doubly vulnerable to adverse security and currency swings. On the reward side, the gains are potentially magnified as well.

Table 10.2 lists the currency hedged adjusted portfolio values. Notice the tempering effect on market value fluctuations.

IMPORT PERSPECTIVE

The interrelationships and movements among currencies can offer important advantages when recognized or poor management results when ignored. Consider the situation of a U.S. importer of European specialty chocolates. Her requirements and constraints are: try to secure 200,000 pounds of chocolate goods with a budget of $1 million. In the past, the importer's experience suggested that each pound of chocolate costs 12.5 Swiss francs or deutschemarks per pound or the equivalent of $5.00 per pound based on Table 10.3 exchange rates. However, in a world of rapidly changing and importantly trending movements in currencies, her purchasing strategy can produce a significant impact on her firm's profitability.

Table 10.3 indicates that when the Swiss franc and deutschemark are both 40 cents to a U.S. dollar, there is no financial advantage in securing chocolate supplies from producers in either nation. Moreover, the importer can satisfy the requirement of 200,000 pounds of chocolate within the $1 million budget. But currencies do fluctuate in value. Table 10.4 highlights the case whereby the deutschemark fell in value both to the U.S. dollar and Swiss franc.

As can be seen in Table 10.4, given the change in currency rates the importer could only satisfy 177,778 pounds of chocolate by a purchase from the Swiss company, leaving the importer 22,222 pounds under her requirement, while she could purchase 228,571 pounds from the West German company,

TABLE 10.3. IMPORT PERSPECTIVES[a] ($1 MILLION BUDGET)

	Currency U.S. $/Unit	Currency Units/$	Currency Total Units	Pounds of Chocolate	Overage/ Underage	Savings/ Additional Costs
West German	.40	2.50	2,500,000	200,000	0	0
Swiss	.40	2.50	2,500,000	200,000	0	0

[a] One pound of chocolate costs 12.5 francs, marks.

providing an extra 28,571 pounds of chocolate for the same $1 million budget. If the primary objective were not so much to stay within the budget but rather secure the 200,000 pounds of chocolate to satisfy sales commitments, then the importer would have saved $125,000 by buying from the West German company or spent an additional $125,000 by purchasing from the Swiss company.

The following illustrates how this is determined:

West German Situation

12.5 deutschemarks per pound of chocolate (unit cost)

35 cents or 2.86 deutschemarks to the dollar (currency price)

$1 million budget

200,000 pounds of chocolate required

To determine the number of marks available for purchase:

$$\frac{\text{Dollar budget}}{\text{Currency unit value}} = \frac{\$1,000,000}{.35} = 2,857,143 \text{ Deutschemarks}/\$1,000,000$$

To determine the pounds of chocolate available for $1,000,000:

$$\frac{\text{Currency available}}{\text{Currency unit price}} = \frac{2,857,143}{12.5} = 228,571 \text{ pounds of chocolate}$$

TABLE 10.4. ALTERNATIVE IMPORT PERSPECTIVES ($1 MILLION BUDGET)

	Currency U.S. $/Unit	Currency Units/$	Currency Total Units	Pounds of Chocolate	Overage/ Underage	Savings/ Additional Costs
West German	.35	2.86	2,857,143	228,571	+28,571	+125,000
Swiss	.45	2.22	2,222,222	177,778	−22,222	−125,000

If only 200,000 pounds were required, then to determine savings (additional cost), the procedure is:

$$\text{Requirement} \times \text{unit cost foreign price} = \text{foreign currency required}$$

$$200,000 \times 12.5 \text{ Deutschemarks} = 2,500,000 \text{ Deutschemarks}$$

$$\text{Dollar cost} = \text{currency units required} \times \text{currency unit price}$$

$$\$875,000 = 2,500,000 \times .35$$

The savings (additional cost) is determined as follows:

$$\text{Budget} - \text{financial requirement} = \text{savings (additional cost)}$$

For the West German example, it is:

$$\$1,000,000 - \$875,000 = +\$125,000$$

In this case it is a savings. The mechanics are similar for the Swiss franc situation.

EXPORT PERSPECTIVE

This section will analyze the relative attractiveness of United States versus Canadian wheat to an overseas buyer. To emphasize the situation, the perspective will take into account the conversion of gold for the necessary purchase. All gold prices will be denominated in U.S. dollars. The situation requires the purchase of 10 million bushels of wheat with a budget of 70,000 ounces of gold allocated to make the purchase. Table 10.5 depicts the U.S. and Canadian dollar freely exchangeable at one for one.

As can be seen, only when the price of gold was at $500 per ounce or more could both the grain requirement and budgeting constraint be satisfied. If gold fell below $500 per ounce, the grain requirement could not be satisfied unless additional funding were forthcoming. Table 10.6 illustrates what happens if the U.S. dollar strengthened relative to the Canadian dollar.

Here, a weaker Canadian dollar in U.S. terms could satisfy overseas buying when gold is $400 per ounce, to the extent it is within the budgeting allotment and provides the exact grain requirement. For the other cases, Canadian wheat was also financially attractive relative to U.S. wheat due to foreign exchange considerations. The importance of this is to quantify the relative attractiveness of similar products given a fluctuating exchange rate.

TABLE 10.5. EXPORT PERSPECTIVES: U.S. AND CANADIAN DOLLAR PARITY

			Currency Units Available	Purchasaeble Bushels of Wheat	Bushels +Overage/ −Underage	Ounces of Gold +Savings/ −Additional	Price of Gold per Ounce
United States	3.50	1:1	28,000,000	8,000,000	−2,000,000	−17,500	$400
Canada	3.50	1:1	28,000,000	8,000,000	−2,000,000	−17,500	
United States	3.50	1:1	35,000,000	10,000,000	0	0	$500
Canada	3.50	1:1	35,000,000	10,000,000	0	0	
United States	3.50	1:1	42,000,000	12,000,000	+2,000,000	+11,666.7	$600
Canada	3.50	1:1	42,000,000	12,000,000	+2,000,000	+11,666.7	

TABLE 10.6. EXPORT PERSPECTIVES: CHANGES BETWEEN U.S. AND CANADIAN DOLLAR RATES

			Currency Units Available	Purchaseable Bushels of Wheat	Bushels +Overage/ −Underage	Ounces of Gold +Savings/ −Additional	Price of Gold per Ounce
United States	3.50	1:1.25	28,000,000	8,000,000	−2,000,000	−17,500	$400
Canada	3.50	1.25:1	35,000,000	10,000,000	0	0	
United States	3.50	1:1.25	35,000,000	10,000,000	0	0	$500
Canada	3.50	1.25:1	43,750,000	12,500,000	+2,500,000	+14,000	
United States	3.50	1:1.25	42,000,000	12,000,000	+2,000,000	+11,666.7	$600
Canada	3.50	1.25:1	52,500,000	15,000,000	+5,000,000	+23,333.3	

The U.S. dollar strengthened from parity with the Canadian dollar as shown in Table 10.5 to a rate where 80 U.S. cents could purchase one Canadian dollar, or 125 Canadian cents would be necessary to purchase one American dollar.

Depending on the relative strength or weakness of considered currencies, a country could experience diminished exports in the event its currency strengthened—or greater exports if its currency weakened on a purely relative value basis. Conversely, the previous section demonstrated a stronger currency could command greater value for goods imported while its weakening would dampen the financial incentives to import from stronger value countries.

INTEREST RATE DIFFERENTIALS

Principle factors which influence the flow of capital and currency valuations are the interest rate differentials. If interest rates are higher in country A relative to country B, then one would expect flows of funds to enter country A in order to capitalize on a more advantageous rate. This inflow should lower the then-prevailing interest rate differential while bolstering country A's currency in the interim. Opposing forces would affect country B's status.

The straightforward calculation of interest rate differentials only presents a partial result, as it more often than not only computes the nominal differential and not the real differential. One must take into account the inflationary or deflationary variables which are affecting prevailing interest rates. Additionally, as ordinary rates have a default or riskiness premium built into the rate structure, so do interest rates on an international level. The defaults here can be: relaxation or tightening of capital flow regulations; tiered market rates; threats of currency devaluation or revaluation; the replacement of the current monetary unit by another denomination; and the existing yield curves.

By carefully refining the variables and introducing them into the decision-making process, a more accurate assessment of real interest rate differentials can be accomplished. Recall the Mexican peso example presented earlier and the recurring financing problems of many South American nations. There, high interest rates are the rule, but these are substantially modified by exceptionally high, monetarily induced inflation conditions.

Other Factors

Other variables influencing import-export analysis and policies which can encourage exports are: special credit arrangements, grants, trading partner status, subsidy, and taxation policies. On an import basis the imposition of quotas or tariffs can reduce the attractiveness of various imports as well as reserves available for international transactions. Embargoes, tiered currency conversion rates, or national policies also influence the international trade situation.

A QUANTITATIVE CONSIDERATION

The myriad of international trade provisions, financial futures, and import-export requirements warrants the use of optimization programming procedures. By utilizing these techniques, one can ascertain the more efficient supply or favorable export markets. Additionally, fundamental analysis introduces requirements and commitments which quantify the analytical task.

A FINAL NOTE

From a speculative perspective, foreign exchange fluctuations can provide rewarding opportunities. For these to arrive, it is generally better to have liabilities (borrowed funds) denominated in a country with a depreciating currency and assets in a country with an appreciating currency. Since, in the former case, after currencies have been appropriately converted, fewer funds are required to pay off debts; while in the latter, after appropriate conversions, assets can be valued or redeemed for higher values. By pursuing a hedging plan, the speculative element in foreign transactions can be reduced.

11
Financial Factors

PERSPECTIVES

In recent years, the volatility in the money/credit markets has high-lighted the impact of financial factors on commodity movements and relation-ships. On a monetary basis, changes in money supply have put inflationary or deflationary pressures on commodity prices. Similarly, changes in interest rates have dominated intramarket differences (spreads) as well as currency valuations. Relatively high real interest rates have discouraged inventory building while inflationary pressures prompt a shift out of intangible assets into tangible ones such as: gold, silver, land, or other commodities. Sudden shifts in inflationary expectations can produce dramatic declines in the prices of staple commodities that generate substantial infusions of funds into the security and credit markets.

CARRYING CHARGES

There are two basic components of carrying charges:

1. Financing costs
2. Storage and insurance costs

The easiest way to visualize changes in carrying charges is the variation in interest rates. It is important whether storables are carried at 6, 12, or 18 percent. In addition to initial price, carrying costs must be covered in order to achieve a profit. Table 11.1 covers the finance charges concept.

As is readily seen, the cost of maintaining inventoried positions rises ever so dramatically, particularly given higher interest rates and lengthened du-

195

TABLE 11.1. FINANCIAL IMPACT OF $10.00 SPOT SILVER[a] (DOLLARS PER OUNCE)

Rates	3-Year Simple Finance	3-Year SF EP	3-Year CF Charges	3-Year Compound EP	12-Year Simple Finance	12-Year SF EP	12-Year CF Charges	12-Year Compound EP
6	1.80	11.80	1.91	11.91	7.20	17.20	10.12	20.12
12	3.60	13.60	4.05	14.05	14.40	24.40	28.96	38.96
18	5.40	15.40	6.43	16.43	21.60	31.60	62.88	72.88
24	7.20	17.20	9.07	19.07	28.80	38.80	122.15	132.15

[a] SF = simple finance cost
CF = compound finance cost
EF = effective price

rations in lieu of paying off interest charges on an annual basis. In the latter case, the amount to be financed compounds since there is no payoff until the position is liquidated.

Three expressions are useful in determining the value of compounding. They are:

$$EP_1 = P(1 + r)^t \qquad \text{(Expression 1)}$$

$$EP_2 = P(1 + r)^{tn} \qquad \text{(Expression 2)}$$

$$EP_3 = Pe^{rt} \qquad \text{(Expression 3)}$$

Since $(1 + 1/n) = e$ or 2.718 as $n \to \infty$, Expression 3 reflects the continuous compounding situation.

where: EP = the effective price or amount

P = the initial price, amount or principal

r = interest rate on annual basis

t = term

n = subdivision units of the term

These expressions establish the foundations for the CPI-W futures contract, enabling traders to capture real rate of returns. By hedging with this contract, inflationary/deflationary impacted nominal rates of interest are adjusted more nearly to approximate the real rate of interest. The formula which generates the CPI-W futures prices is:

$$CPI_{t+m} = CPI_t(1 + I)$$

where: I = annual inflation rate, decimally expressed

   t = base month

   m = months between CPI values.

Returning to the data in Table 11.1, the effective price of silver, accounting for its financing for 3 years at 12 percent per annum, would be:

$$EP_1 = 10.00 \, (1 + .12)^3$$

$$EP_1 = 10.00 \, (1.404928)$$

$$EP_1 = 14.05$$

If the interest charge were compounded monthly, then the effective price would have been:

$$EP_2 = 10.00 \, (1 + .12)^{3 \times 12}$$

$$EP_2 = 10.00 \, (1.01)^{36}$$

$$EP_2 = 10.00 \, (1.4307)$$

$$EP_2 = 14.31$$

If the interest charge were compounded continuously, then the effective price would have been:

$$EP_3 = 10.00 \, (e^{.12 \times 3})$$

$$EP_3 = 10.00 \, (1.4333)$$

$$EP_3 = 14.33$$

To determine the finance charges, simply subtract the initial price from the effective price. The result would be: $14.05 - $10.00 = $4.05 in finance charges for 3 years at 12 percent per annum, $4.31 for 3 years compounded monthly, and $4.33 for 3 years compounded continuously.

INFLATIONARY ADJUSTMENTS

As in the case of finance charges, an inflationary expectations model can be formulated from Expressions 1 and 2. Instead of i for interest rate, substitute e for inflationary expectations. The mathematics remain the same. Returning to Table 11.1, assume the rates are now inflationary ones. If silver were trading at $10.00 an ounce now and inflation was expected to be 18 percent for the next 3 years, then the inflation expectational price for silver would be $16.43 per ounce 3 years hence.

It should be remembered that generally the market's nominal rate of interest (r) consists of two components: (1) a growth rate factor and (2) a price level rate (inflationary/deflationary) factor. This would be $r = i + e$.

STORAGE AND INSURANCE CONSIDERATIONS

There is another cost factor for carrying charges and that is the storage and insurance component. Many firms can minimize these charges since the cost per unit varies due to volume; and it is, so to speak, not necessarily priced for outside sale to secure a profit. Since these costs rapidly diminish on a per-unit basis, the carrying charge spreads would tend to reflect the most efficient carriers; and that partly explains why carrying charges seldom reflect full costs, since they are more closely approximated by financing costs. To understand this, assume a financial institution maintained facilities for its own bullion trading purposes. The storage capacity was 240,000 ounces. Moreover, it offered its services as a depository to others. For the moment, what it charges outside parties for its depository activities has little impact on its own carrying charge/spreading activity. If it costs $12,000 per year to maintain such facilities, regardless of the actual amount stored, it is easy to see that carrying 1 ounce of silver there would cost $12,000 a year apart from financing costs. Two ounces would reduce this to $6,000 per ounce, 10,000 ounces would drop it to $1.20 per ounce, and 100,000 ounces would further reduce the storage component to 12 cents per ounce, or 1 cent per month per ounce. Chart 11.1 graphically depicts the rapid decline in per-unit storage charges.

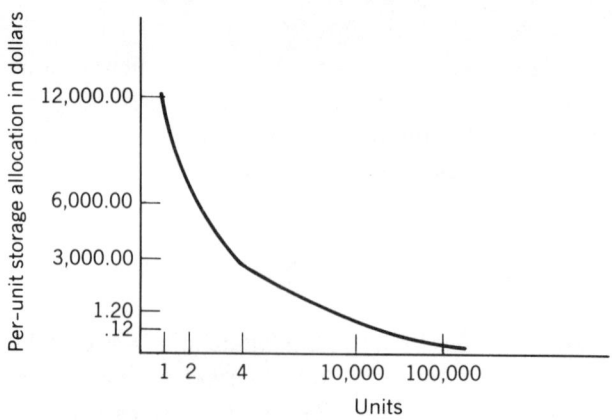

CHART 11.1 Decline in per unit storage charge.

This chart is predicated on a storage attribution function where the cost factor attributable to each unit is equal to storage costs divided by inventory size. Thus, if there were only one unit, the whole cost would be attributed to that one unit. Or, in the case of 100,000 units, the amount attributed to each unit would be .00001 of the storage cost per unit. Knowing that it costs $12,000 per annum regardless of amounts traded, the cost per unit for 100,000 would be: total storage cost × attribution factor; or $.12 per unit.

Interestingly, if the firm only required space for 120,000 ounces (its estimated annual sales) for its trading program, it could lease the other space—here another 120,000 units capacity. In the event the firm priced the storage at its internal cost and fully leased the remaining space, it effectively received its storage space for zero storage cost, thereby requiring only a coverage of its financing costs, and conceivably making it one of the more efficient carrying charge spreaders in the marketplace.

Additionally, the presentation of warrants can be used for initial margining purposes. Since part, if not all, of the inventory maintained consists of deliverable futures, the warehouse receipts could be used for margining purposes. Moreover, though policies vary among commission merchants, 90 percent of the market value of the receipt is permissible for the establishment of hedge positions; otherwise the marginable value varies between 50 to 75 percent depending on market conditions.

INVENTORY MODELING

Inventory modeling improves the quantification of required storage, leaseable storage, and financing costs. Looking back at the bullion operation, the 120,000 ounces is to be marketed over a year. The firm is not willing to incur a negative inventory position; that is, temporarily be out (short) of bullion for delivery thereby precluding the technique of borrowing silver to satisfy sales. Given historical experiences, the marketing is fairly constant throughout the year so, on average, they sell 333.33 ounces per day per 360-day year. Table 11.2 will compare optimal inventory and restocking amounts for 5, 10, and 20 percent financing. The examples consider stocking set-up

TABLE 11.2. INVENTORY ANALYSIS[a]

Interest rate	5%	10%	20%
Inventory in ounces	15,430.25	10,910.84	7,715.13
Days between restocking	46.29	32.73	23.14

[a] Based on sales assumption of 333.33 ounces per day.

TABLE 11.3. INVENTORY ANALYSIS FOR
INCREASED SALES[a]

Interest rate	5%	10%	20%
+50% or 500 ounces per day	18,898.22	13,363.06	9,449.11
+100% or 667 ounces per day	21,827.24	15,434.19	10,913.62

[a]Based on sales assumption of 333.33 ounces per day.

costs at $500 per delivery due to armored car, personnel, and other related expenses.

As can be seen, the doubling of finance charges from 5 to 10 percent does not reduce required inventories by 50 percent, it only reduces them by 29 percent. It is only when the financing charges went up from 5 to 20 percent that the required inventory fell by 50 percent; but the days between restocking also fell by 50 percent. The rationale behind this is the functional relationship of the ordering cost relative to the inventory's financing.

Equally important is the functional relationship of changes in estimated sales to optimal inventory levels. Table 11.3 demonstrates that optimal inventories do not vary proportionally with changes in sales.

A 50 percent increase in daily sales indicates only a 22.5 percent increase in required inventory for the representative financing rates. Additionally, only a 41.5 percent increase in required inventories was necessary when sales doubled for the representative financing categories. This suggests that inventory response to sales is functionally square-root related to sales, and not a directly proportional response.

For the bullion trader, required inventories can be pared down or made available for hedging strategies, such as cash and carry (when sufficiently attractive) or option writes.

This analysis can be applied to other commodities, both raw and finished, their attendant inventories, and firm or country carryover responses to changes in sales and interest rates.

LOAN-ADJUSTED VALUE THEORY

This presentation is applicable to all commodities and other financial alternatives; however, only the specialized case of commodities that have established futures markets will be examined. In certain respects, it is the reciprocal case of carrying charges.

One example of this theory was the corn market of 1982. There were three basic pricing alternatives available: the cash market, the futures market, and the loan program. Although complex interrelationships existed among these pricing alternatives, important distinctions also existed.

To better understand the theory, it is easier to explain in an example its converse. For example, if a farmer chooses the best effective price available and the cash corn price were $4.00 per bushel, the loan price $2.50 per bushel, and the futures market at $3.00, it is obvious that the best market to sell corn would be the cash market since the price is the highest.

It would not be advantageous to place corn in the loan program. Similarly, a cash corn price of $3.00 per bushel, a futures price of $4.00 per bushel and a loan price of $2.50 per bushel would imply that sales would be made in the futures market, since once again the loan program is least attractive and the cash market would encourage arbitraging actions that would pressure the prevailing differences to narrow their absolute variations. Moreover, loan programs are suitable in years of abundant available supplies to help farmers cushion reductions in their incomes. Loan program sales or placements are not ordinary outlets during bull markets.

The bearish scenario will now be explained. So long as effective cash or futures prices are higher than the loan program's prices, sales will not be made in the latter. Once cash or futures go under the loan program's price, farmers that are able to participate in the loan will tend to use that marketing outlet according to their individual limitations and requirements. Thus the overall market starts to fragment into three distinctly different parts or marketing outlets. Under such conditions, farmers with access to the loan program would tend to use it since it would provide the highest effective price. As cash and futures prices move lower, a discounting factor emerges that provides indications as to an effective minimum economic value for futures, which can be substantially different from cash and loan prices. Essentially, there are two factors that underpin futures during loan markets and that can keep futures significantly above cash though below loan. They are interest rates and available storage capacity for futures deliveries.

Examining the interest rates, consider the following expressions:

$$EP_4 = \frac{P}{(1 + r)^t} \qquad \text{(Expression 4)}$$

$$EP_5 = \frac{P}{(1 + r)^{tn}} \qquad \text{(Expression 5)}$$

$$EP_6 = \frac{P}{e^{rt}} \qquad \text{(Expression 6)}$$

These expressions are familiar, since they are the reciprocal forms of Expressions 1, 2, and 3, respectively. Here, instead of compounding amounts

TABLE 11.4. LOAN-ADJUSTED CORN PRICES (IN DOLLARS PER BUSHEL)

Financing Rates	$2.50/bushel loan				$2.55/bushel loan			
	3-Month	6-Month	9-Month	12-Month	3-Month	6-Month	9-Month	12-Month
10	2.44	2.38	2.33	2.27	2.49	2.43	2.37	2.32
12	2.43	2.36	2.29	2.23	2.48	2.41	2.34	2.28
14	2.42	2.34	2.26	2.19	2.46	2.38	2.31	2.24
16	2.40	2.31	2.23	2.16	2.45	2.36	2.28	2.20

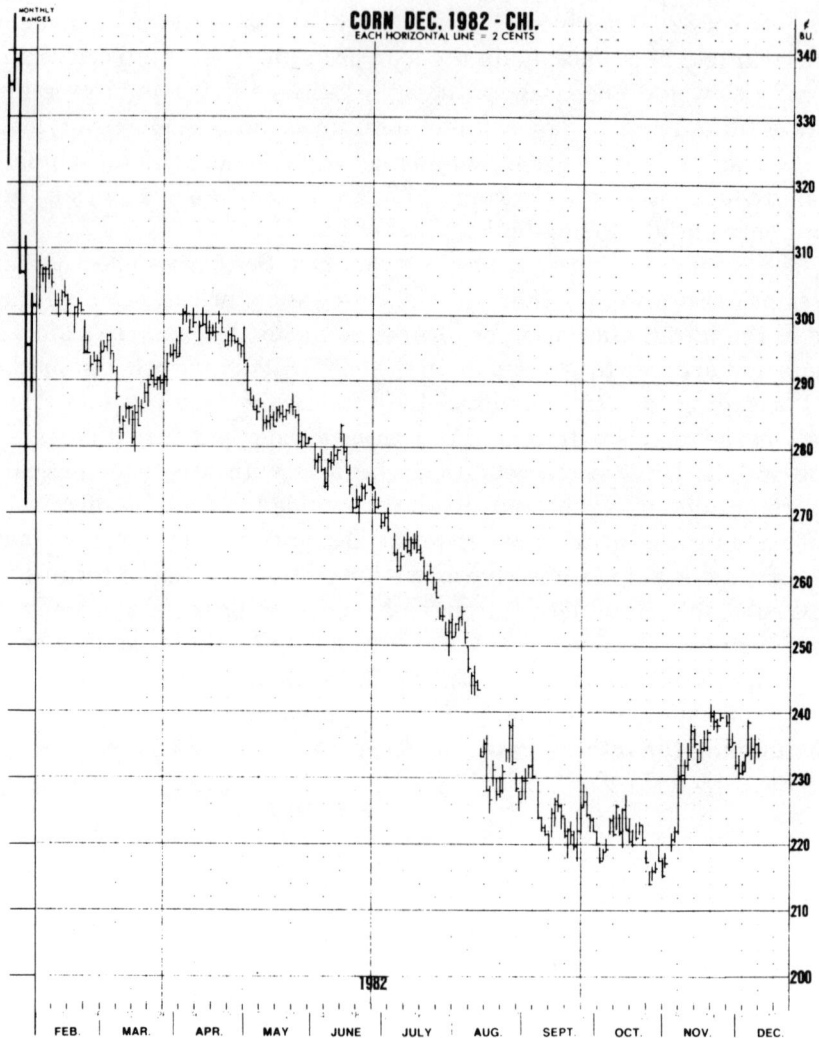

CHART 11.2 Loan-adjusted value and PIK response

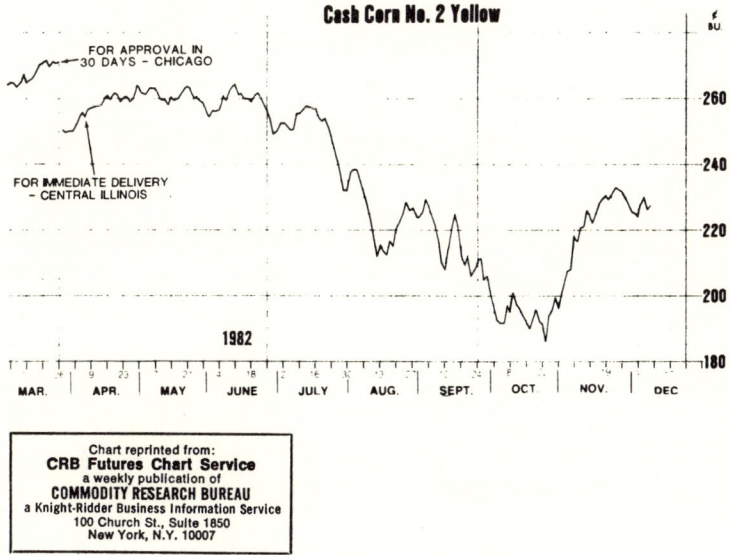

CHART 11.3 Cash Corn Market

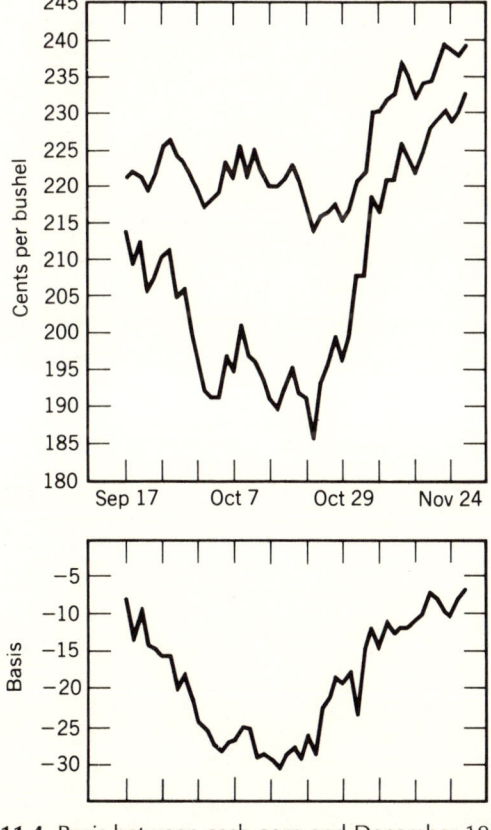

CHART 11.4 Basis between cash corn and December 1982 futures

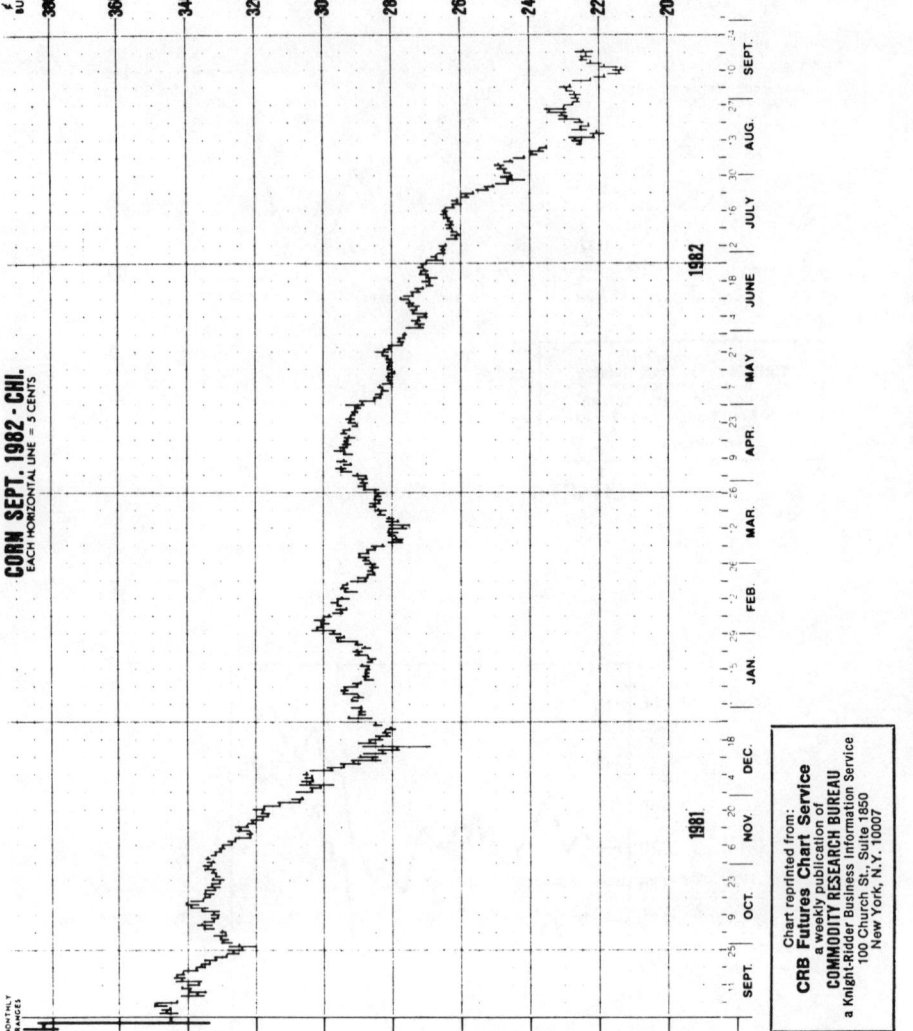

CHART 11.5 Loan-adjusted value and PIK influence

or prices, they discount amounts or prices. Table 11.4 lists associative loan adjustable values for nearby corn futures for two loan prices, four rates of interest, and four time horizons. Notice how the loan adjusted value for corn declines with progressively higher financing rates or progressively longer time horizons. This is how it should respond, for it would be the same for borrowing money. Just because the loan price is $2.50, $2.55, or whatever the prevailing level is, the farmer does not effectively reap that level as the effective price since there are attendant financing and storage charges. The longer the corn is in the program, the lower the effective value for the farmer. Charts 11.2, 11.3, and 11.4 represent December 1982 corn futures, cash No. 2 corn, and a basis chart between cash corn and December 1982 corn futures.

Note how all three markets progressively weakened until the end of October 1982. Moreover, the weakness in the cash was more pronounced than that displayed by the futures. In fact, the latter exhibited impressive stability around the $2.18 to $2.20 area. Since the corn seasonal year is October through September, the implication for the above analysis would be the presence of a 1-year discounting consideration at work. On a historical note, a reluctance of farmers to move corn near the end of October 1982 sparked the sharp rally in cash prices. Additionally, the implementation of the payment-in-kind (PIK) program reinforced the rise in prices at that time. Nevertheless, the establishment of a lower effective economic boundary for nearby corn futures developed. This behavior prevailed for the September 1982 corn futures contract. Despite the brief departure between the $2.18 to $2.20 area, prices did stage a comeback above that level before the contract's expiration (see Chart 11.5.).

AVAILABLE DELIVERABLE STORAGE CAPACITY

The other principal factor present in price activity for futures and cash is the availability of storage capacity. For financial futures this concept would be available position carrying constraints. The lack of acceptable storage capacity, the greater the impetus to move the harvested commodities. From a future perspective, deliverable storage is much more limited than farm and commercial storage capacity. Additionally, corn or other deliverable commodities must be acceptably graded and in an acceptably stipulated facility to make "good" delivery. Transportation problems, inclement weather, and other factors can affect the amount of these commodities available for delivery. This relatively small amount of deliverable capacity relative to overall storage capacity, and available corn (or whatever commodity is being analyzed), accounts for a potential premium situation for delivered product relative to national average prices.

During loan-type markets (bearish conditions), just because cash prices are very low relative to nearby futures prices, it still may not be possible to

TABLE 11.5. CRUDE OIL INITIALLY $34 PER BARREL
DEFLATIONARY EXPECTATIONAL PRICES (IN
DOLLARS PER BARREL)

Deflation Rate	1-Year Price	5-Year Price	10-Year Price
3	33.01	29.33	25.30
6	32.08	25.41	18.99
9	31.19	22.10	14.36

take full advantage of the situation. For example, cash prices can be $1.80 per bushel and attendant delivery costs—including transportation, financing and storage—may be 25 cents per bushel; but this does not necessarily mean that one can buy corn in the cash market and deliver it against the board even if prevailing prices are $2.25, thus obtaining an arbitrage profit of 20 cents per bushel. It may well be that all deliverable capacity is accounted for at that particular time period. Any decrease of movement of grain into "accounted-for" storage would only cause the maintenance (or probable increase) of premium value for actual deliverable futures relative to its cash market.

DEFLATIONARY ADJUSTMENTS

Since the compounding model was used for inflationary adjustments, the discounting model is used for deflationary adjustments. Table 11.5 presents a case of deflationary expectations as applied to the crude oil market. Expression 3 provided the model for the tabular contents. Table 11.5 indicates that if deflationary expectations were 3 percent for 5 years, the price of oil would be $29.33/barrel; while deflationary expectations of 9 percent per year for 10 years would indicate an oil price of $14.36, all other things being equal.

SUMMARY

Fluctuations in interest rates and variable storage capacity or positioning ability directly influence intra- and intermarket differentials. Changes in carrying charges impact prices and storage costs which can generate structural shifts in the participant's desires to maintain various inventory levels.

12
Testing

WHAT IS INFORMATION?

Information is money, but information costs. In the past, decision makers intuitively assessed the value of information versus its cost. Now, with the growth of computer usage the ability to collect and analyze data has increased at a phenomenal rate.

Testing is an integral part of the information process. Here too, the procedure requires time and money; and the more detailed or complex the analysis, the greater its cost. Once testing commences, the results yielded in the earlier studies may be reactivated or modified. To put it differently, every time testing is undertaken, the operator's knowledge—information—should grow in a building block fashion. Study *A* is one building block and Study *B* is another block.

This chapter examines several testing procedures which are amenable to either broadstroke or fine-tuning analysis.

IMPORTANCE OF TESTING

The possession of ideas, concepts, and data in and of themselves are valueless. They must be considered or acted on to be of use. The quality of ideas, concepts, and data is critical to determine, and the best method is testing. Testing yields other benefits as well. It forces the manager to specifically define concepts, hypotheses, and parameters. In return for this effort, the manager receives quantifiable results.

MATRICES

A highly informative arrangement of data is the matrix. In its simplest form, it is a construction of rows and columns. For example, a two-by-two (2

× 2) matrix would appear as a square divided into four arrangements or groups: *A*, *B*, *C*, and *D* (see Example 12.1). Similarly, a three-by-three (3 × 3) matrix would appear as a square divided into nine arrangements or groups: *A* through *I* (see Example 12.2). Thus the number of components or groups of the size *r* × *c* (rows by columns) is equal to the number of rows times the number of columns. Although in Examples 12.1 and 12.2 the number of rows equaled the number of columns, this need not be the case. Mathematically, Examples 12.1 and 12.2 represent square matrices.

As the testing logic is expanded, the power of a matrix becomes awesome—though it can be expensive and cumbersome to analyze.

For example, suppose simple moving averages for March, June, September, and December Swiss franc futures were to be evaluated for the period of 1977 to 1986 as to average trade profitability for given combinations of moving averages. One solution would be to test a horizon of short-term moving averages of lengths of 1 to 10 days. Likewise, the long-term averages would equal size 10 and the column would be size 10. Then the number of groups would be 100. Clearly this is not exhaustive, but it is illustrative. (See Example 12.3.) Here, an inclusive series was examined. Size equals the number of observations, not necessarily the largest number for the rows and columns. This will be highlighted in a subsequent example.

For simple moving average arrangements, not all of the groups are useful, as can be seen in Example 12.3, they "X" out. The reason for this is that in 45 groups the short-term averages would have had more days than the long-term averages, while in 10 groups the short-term averages would have been equal to the long-term averages. They are also X-ed out.

At this point, we shall explore three basic matrices which will be referred to as:

1. Project matrix
2. Scanning matrix
3. Detail matrix

Although the three possess the same mathematical properties, their applications are different.

	1	2
1	A	B
2	C	D

EXAMPLE 12.1 Two-by-two (2 × 2) matrix

	1	2	3
1	A	B	C
2	D	E	F
3	G	H	I

EXAMPLE 12.2 Three-by-three (3 × 3) matrix

	1	2	3	4	5	6	7	8	9	10			
1	X										9	45	
2	X	X									8	36	
3	X	X	X								7	23	
4	X	X	X	X							6	21	
5	X	X	X	X	X						5	15	
6	X	X	X	X	X	X					4	10	
7	X	X	X	X	X	X	X				3	6	
8	X	X	X	X	X	X	X	X			2	3	
9	X	X	X	X	X	X	X	X	X		1		
10	X	X	X	X	X	X	X	X	X	X			

Short-term moving average average length (left axis); Long-term moving average average length (right axis)

EXAMPLE 12.3 Hypothetical average profit per trade for Swiss francs

Project Matrix

The project matrix represents the complete size and detail of a given testing task. It may refer to the number of transactions, average profitability per trade, worst negative trading sequence, or whatever aspect of a trading program the manager is evaluating. As will be demonstrated soon, it may be a Herculean task to analyze this matrix in its entirety.

Scanning Matrix

The scanning matrix is derived from the project matrix. Its purpose is to scan expeditiously the vast scope of data posed by the project matrix while minimizing the detail.

Detail Matrix

The detail matrix carefully focuses on the small areas of the project and scanning matrices. It is usually used after a scanning matrix indicated potentially promising regions.

The interaction among the three matrices can be described as a microscope. For a given instrument, the lower power lenses permit viewing a broader area of the slide's subject. By increasing the lens power to gain greater detail, field area is reduced. Finally, the highest power lens yields the best detail, but the field area has once again been substantially reduced. By judiciously specifying the parameters for the matrices, the manager can examine market data in an analogous fashion. To visualize the impact of more comprehensive testing, the manager can consider the case of a 100×100 matrix, shown by Example 12.4. Remember it contains 10,000 groups.

Not only is this very expensive to test in its present state, but may be unnecessary. Rather, the manager can initially scan the considered 100×100 matrix by constructing a matrix where the values of the rows or columns increase by steps or increments. Then, if a group appears promising, he or she can focus on that group with greater detail.

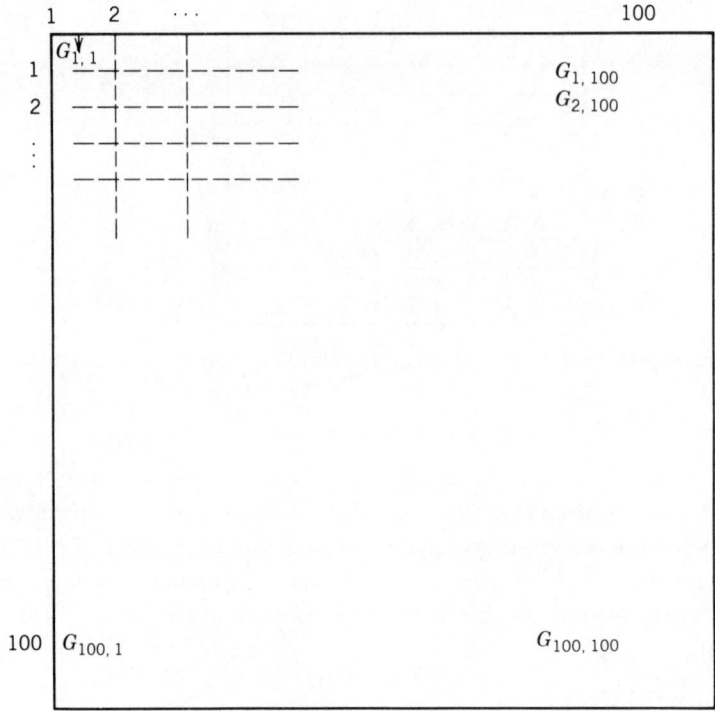

Where: $G_{1,1}$ represents the group defined by row 1, column 1.
         $G_{1,100}$ represents the group defined by row 1, column 100.
         $G_{100,99}$ represents the group defined by row 100, column 99.

EXAMPLE 12.4 100 × 100 Project Matrix

Example 12.5 is one representation of reducing the problem to a more manageable size. Here, a 10 × 10 matrix selectively represents the 100 × 100 matrix. The major difference between the two besides the actual size is the assignment of increments of 10 and not of 1. Then the rows gain valuewise as: 1, 11, 21, 31, 41, 51, 61, 71, 81, 91, for a total of 10 (row) observations. Similarly, the columns grow valuewise as: 11, 21, 31, 41, 51, 61, 71, 81, 91, 101. Again we have 10 (column) observations.

This scanning matrix contains only 100 groups as opposed to the more formidable 10,000 groups. Although in this special simple moving average situation there are realistically fewer than 100 (or 10,000) usable groups, for other parameters a 10 × 10 matrix may represent 100 potentially usable groups. Likewise, the 100 × 100 matrix could contain 10,000 potentially usable groups.

Moreover, it effectively covers the same territory of the project matrix, but in a more cost-and time-effective manner. It is amenable to an increase of focus or detail, but with only 1 percent of the effort. The prospective groups on which to focus are the detail matrices indicated by the + groups within

Long-term moving average

		1	2	3	4	5	6	7	8	9	10
		11	21	31	41	51	61	71	81	91	101
1	1	−	−	−	−	−	−	−	−	−	−
	11	X	−	−	−	−	−	−	−	−	−
3	21	X	X	+	−	+	+	−	−	−	−
4	31	X	X	X	−	−	+	−	+	−	−
5	41	X	X	X	X	−	−	+	+	−	−
6	51	X	X	X	X	X	−	−	−	−	−
7	61	X	X	X	X	X	X	−	−	−	−
8	71	X	X	X	X	X	X	X	−	−	−
9	81	X	X	X	X	X	X	X	X	−	−
10	91	X	X	X	X	X	X	X	X	X	−

Short-term moving average (row axis label, rows 3–10)

7 of 55 are profitable groups, 48 are not

− losses
+ profits
X not applicable

EXAMPLE 12.5 Scanning Matrix

the scanning matrix. In the hypothetical project, there were seven + groups that warrant further examination, since they exhibit profitable tendencies. The groups are: G 21,31; G 21,51; G 21,61; G 31,61; G 31,81; G 41,71; and G 41,81.

Starting with G 21,31, the manager will construct an appropriate detail matrix. Here, the detail matrix will examine combinations of short-term moving averages starting with the 21st day and ending in the 30th day, against long-term moving averages of lengths starting with the 31st day and ending on the 40th day. Example 12.6 portrays this detail matrix.

Once again a 10 × 10 matrix emerges which contains 100 groups. To reiterate, it has 10 row observations and 10 column observations. The values of the row observations start at 21 and end at 30, while the values of the column observations start at 31 and end at 40. Unlike the previous matrices, Example 12.6 consists of 100 potentially usable groups since in every case the comparative short-term average length is less than the comparative long-term average length.

The flexibility of a matrix is highlighted in the analysis. Matrices can be partitioned into submatrices. In Example 12.6, four submatrices have been bounded which are called I, II, III, and IV. Since the merit of the moving average arrangements is now determined, one must know the likelihoods of the test results.

Submatrix I possesses 19 profitable arrangements out of a possible 25. Submatrix II possesses 21 profitable arrangements out of 25. Submatrix III possesses 14 out of 25, and submatrix IV possesses 13 out of 25. This occurrence suggests the best results are clustered in II. Also submatrices I and II

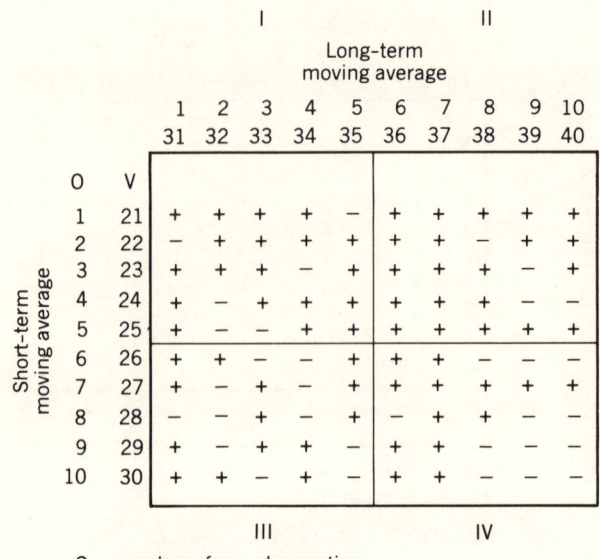

O = number of row observations.
V = row values

EXAMPLE 12.6 Detail Matrix

contain 40 winners out of 50 arrangements, whereas III and IV contain 27 winners out of 50 arrangements. Graphically, this is shown in Example 12.7.

It also indicates the number of winners by rows, columns, and grand totals. The importance of the clustering effect is that it shows the concentration of potential winning arrangements—extremely vital since the markets are dynamic. In other words, as time passes, previously profitable moving average parameters may cease to be so, and other parameter arrangements may become profitable. Thus parameter selection within a cluster tends to be more reliable, since the decision maker can operate with a knowledge and confidence that the pattern for potential profits is concentrated and not isolated.

If the maximum parameter arrangement is within a profitable cluster, the dynamics of the marketplace are not as suddenly ruinous since the best pa-

		Row winners/totals
I 19	II 21	40W/50
III 14	IV 13	27W/50
Column winners/totals 33W/50	34W/50	67W/100

Total of 67 winners out of 100 arrangements as depicted in Example 12.6.

EXAMPLE 12.7 Quadrant winner totals

	51	52	53	54	55	56	57	58	59	60	
21	−	−	−	+	+	−	+	−	+	−	4
22	+	+	−	+	−	+28	+44	+27	+	+	8
23	−	−	+	−	+51	+41	+33	+51	+32	−	6
24	−	+	−	−	+39	+40	B +90	+40	+29	+	7
25	−	−	+	−	+	+42	+36	+37	−	+	6
26	−	−	−	+	−	+15	+22	+31	−	−	5
27	−33	−49	−51	−25	−	+	−	+	+	+	3
28	−81	−72	−63	−29	−	−	−	−	−	−	0
29	−70	A +200	−65	−34	−	+	−	+	−	−	3
30	−80	−79	−55	−40	−	−	−	+	−	+	2
											44

EXAMPLE 12.8 Profitable cluster

rameter arrangement may still fall within a profitable cluster. Example 12.8 portrays these concepts given a dynamic shift in parameter arrangements.

The numbers in the matrix represent significant percent changes in committed equity for specific arrangements; whereas the +s and the −s represent slight positive or negative changes. In an actual test matrix, all the usable arrangements will contain both positive and negative numerical results. As subsequent examples will show, a variety of concepts, items, and data can be assessed in the matrix. Some practitioners call these arrangements contingency tables, depending on the nature of the data and the problem. Thus arrangements A 24,57; A 29,52; and A 28,52 respectively represent +10, +200, and −72 percent changes in committed equity for a series of trades over a specified period.

As time passes, the underlying structure of the market shifts. Graphically, point B replaces one of the points in the dark gray area. If the manager were using an arrangement in this gray area, he or she probably still would be using a profitable arrangement, and possibly a better one.

This is not the case for a movement of point A as it drifts into the light gray area. There is still a 200 percent return arrangement, but its parameters have changed. Since the operator was using one specific arrangement (A 29,52) he or she probably is no longer profitable–and in this case definitely is not. In truth, drifting arrangements probably do not actually replace one another. Rather, the drifter represents a change not only of the parameters but also of the values attributed to the arrangements. This concept is akin to nonstationarity of estimates and time-series observations.

After isolating the performing arrangements in terms of one aspect—raw profitability—the operator must assess other factors. Just because one moving average (or a cluster of moving averages) exhibits an acceptably high rate of return (its reward) the trader must also consider its variability (risk). In other words, a particular moving average Ar,c^{12} exhibits the best profitability, say,

200 percent over time; but it may require a risk of 50, 75, 100 percent, or more. The designation Ar,c refers to arrangements of a specified row value r, and specified column value c. Sometimes, the expected payoff percent may actually be less than the expected risk. Gaming enthusiasts refer to this relationship as the odds. Not only do they want to know the payoff if they win, but what is required on their part to play (their wager). Also, they must know if it is a dollar bet—a dollar bet potentially equals more than, or less than a dollar won. The same applies here. The greater the likelihood of occurrence, generally the smaller the reward. There can be high probabilistic situations whereby the entry capital commitment is so high as to preclude the participation of most interested, but undercapitalized, parties. Moreover, there is no guarantee for success, only a high expected value. Actuaries are especially aware of this concept: The older the policy holder, the higher the premium, since the older policy holder is more likely to be approaching death.

IMPORTANT TRADING ASPECTS

Depending on the nature of the project, the following commentary provides guidelines for commonly investigated aspects. It is not exhaustive since each manager and client must determine which factors are necessary for each project in terms of its priorities. These guidelines can apply to various trading techniques, such as simple moving averages, other weighted averages, daily rules, weekly rules, oscillators, or fundamental forecasts.

1. *Average Trade Expectation.* This is the average profit (loss) generated by a given technique and parameters, given all historical trades.
2. *Average Profitable Trade.* The average size of all profitable trades. This factor considers only winning trades.
3. *Average Losing Trade.* The average size of all losing trades. This factor considers only losing trades.
4. *Ratio of Winners to Losers.* Relates the number of winning trades to losing trades.
5. *Ratio of Win Size to Loss Size.* Relates average dollar gain to average dollar loss.
6. *Average Time of Winning Trades.* Analyzes the duration of the average winning trade.
7. *Average Time of Losing Trades.* Analyzes the duration of the average losing trade.
8. *Average Time per Trade.* Analyzes the duration of the average trade considering both winners and losers.
9. *Maximum Gain for Best Trade.* The computation of the maximum dollar gain for best trade.

10. *Maximum Gain for a Sequence of Trades.* Computes the maximum dollar gain for a consecutive run of winners.

11. *Maximum Loss for Worst Trade.* Computation of the maximum dollar loss for worst trade.

12. *Maximum Loss for a Sequence of Trades.* Computation of the maximum dollar loss for a consecutive run of losers.

13. *Average Transaction Cost.* An amount selected by the trader/researcher to be assessed against all trades to determine the impact of commissions and fees on the trading program.

14. *Maximum Portfolio Loss.* The dollar amount lost during a losing streak for all observed positions.

15. *Maximum Portfolio Gain.* The dollar amount gained during the best winning streak for all observed positions.

16. *Average Portfolio Gain.* The average dollar gain for all winning streaks on a portfolio basis.

17. *Average Portfolio Loss.* The average dollar drawdown for all losing streaks on a portfolio basis.

18. *Determination of Required Capital.* This factor needs to be considered since not all traders have the necessary funding to take many or all desired positions. High margin requirements on the occurrence of a major losing streak can force equities below the margin requirements or even beyond the resources of the trader.

19. *Slippage Factor.* Many traders determine the in and out prices based on the opening, closing, or average of these two prices. However, an alternate technique would be the application of a slippage factor which would assess the impact of less favorable fills under adverse market conditions. Essentially, this technique provides a more conservative estimate of trading results.

20. *Historical Slippage Factor.* This is the historical analysis of actual trading slippage costs. This is useful in the ongoing evaluation of trade executions. It can also be compared to number 19 to determine if the actual costs are less than or greater than imputed ones.

TREND TEST

One statistical test which can be applied for the determination of a trend appears in Table 12.1. It had been proposed and developed independently by H. B. Mann and M. G. Kendall. Table 12.1 supplies data on 5-year U.S. Treasury securities yields. This test can be applied to yield differences as well.

The test is constructed to determine the statistical array or disarray in a series of numbers. By assigning the rank value 1 to the smallest number, the

TABLE 12.1. FIVE-YEAR TREASURY SECURITIES
YIELDS

1986	Yield	Rank	Positive Score
4–11	7.04	2	8
4–18	6.80	1	8
4–25	7.10	3	7
5–2	7.21	5	5
5–9	7.19	4	5
6–16	7.58	6	4
5–23	7.78	8	2
5–30	7.70	7	2
6–6	8.02	10	0
6–13	7.93	9	0
			41

Source: U.S. Financial Data, Federal Reserve Bank of St.
Louis.

rank value 2 to the next smallest number, and so on until the value n is assigned to the last observation, the series is thus ordinally ranked. Next, a positive score is calculated for each observation. In the example, the June 6 yield of 8.02 is the largest value and it has the highest rank—10. Since there is no greater number following it in the series, its positive score is 0. The April 18 yield of 6.80 was the lowest value and it is ranked 1. At that point there were 8 greater values in the series, so its positive score was 8.

Now a summation of the positive scores is computed. Here, $P = 8 + 8 + 7 + 5 + 5 + 4 + 2 + 2 + 0 + 0 = 41$. Substituting this P value into a total score equation, the result is:

$$S = 2P - (\tfrac{1}{2})(N)(N - 1) \quad \text{(Total score equation)}$$

$$S = 2(41) - \tfrac{1}{2}(10)(9)$$

$$S = 82 - 45$$

$$S = +37$$

Finally, the calculation of Kendall's tau value τ is performed. The equation for it is:

$$\tau = \frac{2S}{N(N - 1)}$$

and by substitution, the numerical value is:

$$\tau = \frac{2(+37)}{(10)\,(9)}$$

$$= \frac{+74}{90}$$

$$+.82$$

This τ value of $+.82$ suggests a positive relationship over time; in other words an uptrend, since there is a plus sign attached to the τ value. Had the sign been negative, it would have suggested a negative relationship or downtrend. The significance of this relationship is determined by consulting statistical tables that show this occurrence to have a probability of less than 1 percent, or it is to be considered significant at the 99 percent level. The appropriate statistical table is for the "S" values for Kendall's correlation coefficient which is listed in various statistical texts.

OTHER TESTS

The application of other statistical techniques can assist in the determination of market conditions and their expected values. Psychometric testing tools are particularly suitable as they can assign numeric structure to situations which are usually described in a qualitative manner, such as bullish, bearish, or neutral; and where cardinally based evaluative statistics can be difficult and potentially misleading to apply.

13
Options

A RELATIONSHIP TO FUTURES

A futures option is an option on a futures position and not the underlying security or tangible itself. Only by exercising the option and then sustaining the underlying futures position until a delivery is completed do the actuals become the primary factor. Exceptions to this are those futures whose settlement is consummated by cash and not a specific security, portfolio, or commodity. However, the relationship between the actuals and the futures is an important consideration as well as the relationship between the option and its underlying futures market.

DESCRIPTION

An option refers to the right, not obligations, of a purchaser to exercise an agreement according to its stipulations. A writer of an option is obligated in the event of an exercise to satisfy the terms of the option. The option purchaser's risk is limited to the premium plus transactional costs incurred for the purchase. Choosing to exercise an option and maintain the underlying futures position can result in exposure to the risks prevailing on that particular futures market until that futures position is offset.

The writer of an option can be partially immunized against risk by writing a covered option. For example, a government security dealer may write covered calls against a portion or all of his or her inventory of Treasury bonds acceptable for futures delivery. By writing such calls, the government security dealer may obtain higher returns by the receipt of premiums. This partial immunization of market risk arises if the Treasury bond market does not advance particularly much, or if bond prices fall to a level where the amount of premium received offsets the amount of dollar inventory lost. If bonds continue to drop below that covered position, actual inventory losses begin to occur. Should the bond market advance beyond the effective strike price area, a bond futures position could be called away and the government securities dealer would have essentially profited from the received premium and not necessarily the advance in the underlying inventoried position.

In this advancing market scenario, a writer of an uncovered call would have fared even more poorly, since that writer is vulnerable to the vagaries of the marketplace without a suitably hedged position.

There are two basic types of options: calls and puts. Various arrangements of these can be: combinations, straddles, and spreads.

CALLS

Upon payment of premium, calls confer on the purchaser the right to secure an underlying futures position at a stipulated strike price during a specified time period. Typically, the purchase of a call implies that the purchaser is looking for rising prices. For example: suppose that during the month of December 1985, April 1986 futures gold is trading at $350 per ounce. Moreover, the purchaser expects the price to advance sharply to $450 or more during the life of the call option. Although there is a choice of strike prices for various premiums, assume a purchase of an April 1986 call with an exercise price of $360 for a $22-per-ounce premium. In this hypothetical case, the buyer of the call would pay $22 × 100 (ounces) = $2,200 premium. Assuming the buyer's judgment is correct and gold sharply rallied soon thereafter to $460 an ounce, there would be a paper profit of:

$460 per ounce − $360 strike price = $100 profit per ounce, or $10,000

However, the premium cost was $2,200 so the net profit would be $7,800 ($10,000 − $2,200), using this strategy without considering other transactional costs. Of course, had the futures been purchased outright, the profit would have been:

$460 per ounce

   − $350 (prevailing April 1986 price—not the strike price of $360)

   = $110 profit per ounce, or $11,000

before transactional costs. Obviously, the buyer would have maximized his gain by going long the futures directly instead of buying a call. But in the event the buyer made a wrong assessment of the market outlook, he could have reduced his risk by buying the call because of the limited risk aspect of trading options. To understand this, suppose that after the call was purchased, the gold market sharply declined from $350 to $240 per ounce. Compare the two strategies:

Outright Long Futures Position	Bought a Call Option
$240 subsequent market price	$240 subsequent market price
−$350 initial purchase price	−$360 strike price
−$110 loss per ounce, or	$0 since call was not exercised, however, the option premium was $2,200, therefore a $2,200 loss was realized.
−$11,000 per contract	

It is seen that the loss would have been $11,000 on the outright long futures position but only $2,200 for the unexercised call. Thus the trader would have fared better by $8,800 by buying the call in this particular case.

PUTS

Puts are purchased when the buyer has a bearish outlook on a given market. The purchaser of a put has the right to place a position with the writer at a specified strike price within the specified time period. Expectationally, the purchaser of a put is looking for the opportunity where the eventual market price falls considerably lower than the strike price. In the event of an exercise the purchaser acquires a short position at the strike price whereas the writer acquires the offsetting long position at the strike price. To see how this strategy compares to an outright short position, again assume the April 1986 gold futures market is trading at $350 per ounce. The hypothetical purchaser of a put expects that during the forthcoming months gold will trade at $275 or lower. If the prevailing premium for this put was $30 per ounce, the premium would be $3,000. Assuming the trader's forecast was correct, we see:

Outright Short Futures Position	Purchase of Put Option
$350 short sale price	$360 strike price
−$250 market price	−$250 subsequent market price
$100 profit/ounce, or	$110 profit/ounce, $11,000 for put; from this, subtract the premium of $3,000, yielding an $8,000 profit for the position
$10,000/contract	

Again, both strategies were profitable, with the outright futures the most profitable. But the subsequent comparison will highlight the limited risk feature inherent in the purchase of options. Here, the purchaser of the put still had the same market outlook, but an adverse event occurred. Gold prices meteorically climbed soon after the purchase of the put. Comparatively:

Outright Short Futures Position	Purchase of Put Option
$350 short sale price	$360 strike price
−$500 subsequent market price	−$500 subsequent market price
−$150 loss/ounce or	$0 since put would not be
−$15,000/contract	meaningful to exercise; however, as the put cost $3,000, the loss would be $3,000

The outright short position would have incurred a $15,000 loss, but the put would have limited the exposure to a loss of only $3,000, thus precluding an additional $12,000 loss. Why wouldn't the put be exercised? For the simple reason that, by doing so, the purchaser would incur the loss of $140 per ounce or $14,000 per contract ($500 − $360 = $140, or $14,000 per contract) in addition to the $3,000 premium, or a $17,000 loss. Clearly, such an exercise would not be in the purchaser's interests.

Premiums

Initially, the premium is the sum paid by the purchaser of an option (put or call) to the writer of the option. Strictly speaking, this payment of premium is a one-time occurrence. For subsequent transactions on the prevailing option position, the premium refers to the dollar amount at which the previously created option, exchanges hands until its exercise, liquidation, or expiration. Although the terms, such as strike price and expiration date, remain the same, subsequent transactions can be conducted at various premium levels, which are dependent on a wide range of then-prevailing market factors. Also, the maintenance of an option position by the purchaser is assessed by its market value; or, in other words, at what premium it could change hands in the marketplace. Currently, long positions in options are not marked-to-market for equity purposes. However, writers of options are subject to margin calls as well as to exercise risk.

In the following section, the primary factors which influence the amount of premium or the valuation of an option will be analyzed. Among these are: the strike price, the time duration before expiration, and the expected volatility and trend in the underlying futures market, interest rates, and other market factors.

Generally, options with a low likelihood of exercise have low premiums, while options with high probabilities of being exercised have correspondingly high premium values.

Strike Price

The level where an option will be priced on its exercise is the strike price. For a call option, it is the exact level where the underlying futures long position can be obtained; while for a put, it is the stipulated level whereby a short position can be placed. For example: If during the month of December 1986, a February 1987 gold call option was listed with a $460 strike price, the purchaser of the call would have the right to secure the underlying long February 1987 gold futures position at $460 if the call were to be exercised, regardless of where the underlying futures markets were trading.

Similarly, a purchaser of a put with a stipulated strike price of $460 per ounce would have the right to claim a short position, which would be placed at $460 per ounce, regardless where the underlying gold futures market was trading.

Time Duration

The time duration refers to the temporal trading horizon where an option expires if not exercised. Each option has a stipulated exercise expiration date. For example, Comex gold options can currently expire at February, April, August, October, and December. However, not all months are traded concurrently. Moreover, each exchange has its own timetable for the actual expiration of the option, predicated on the underlying futures. For Comex options, the designated months refer to the specific underlying futures expiration and not the option itself. For example, February 1986 gold options expired in January 1986. Likewise, March 1986 Comex silver options expired in February 1986. As the expression "time is money" asserts, so too with options. Generally, the greater the time horizon granted for an option, the greater the inherent value will be. From a premium perspective, it generally costs more to buy an option with a longer life. For example, if two options were analyzed during the month of December 1987, and both had identical strike prices, the option which had longer to go before its expiration would be worth more and thus have a higher premium value attributed to it. To visualize this, examine Chart 13.1, which uses the corresponding formula presented in Chapter 11, Financial Factors. As can be seen, a premium of $1,000 or $2,000 today (0) is worth progressively more at the 2-month interval, 4-month interval, and 6-month interval. Table 13.1 provides the data.

Conversely, the longer an option remains out of the money, the less value it will have. This is due to the progressively shorter time horizon and its di-

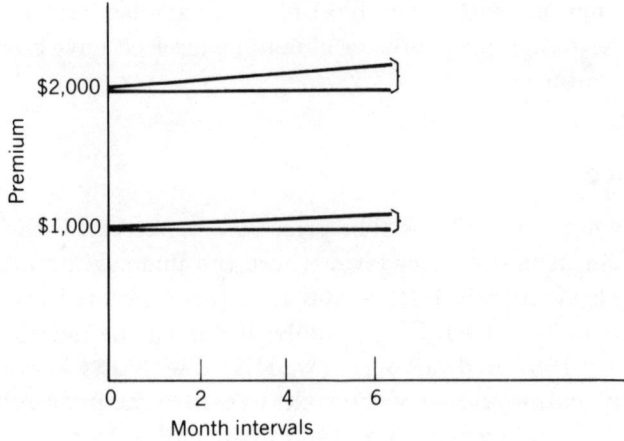

CHART 13.1 Imputed Premium Values

minished potential for being exercised. This concept is graphically depicted by Chart 13.2.

Notice how in each case (1, 2, and 3) the option lost value over the passage of time. This is to be expected, since there was a declining likelihood of either a profitable exercise or offsetting liquidation of the purchased option. As is always the case in the absence of an exercise or offsetting liquidation, an option becomes worthless at its expiration.

Expected Volatility and Trend

The marketplace's evaluation of an underlying trend and expected volatility factor also influences options premiums. For example, if the sugar market were generally assumed to be in a major bull market, and past history suggested wide volatility, the premiums for options, especially calls, would tend to be relatively higher priced than puts with comparable strike prices and expiration dates. In this case, the likelihood of exercise for a call would be greater than the likelihood of exercise for a put. Similarly, if the outlook were for interest rates to move erratically higher (i.e., bond prices were to work lower) then the relative price of a Treasury bond put premium would be greater than the comparable call premium.

TABLE 13.1. IMPUTED PREMIUM VALUES[a]

Premium	2-Month Interval	4-Month Interval	6-Month Interval
$1,000	$1,016.81	$1,033.90	$1,051.27
$2,000	$2,033.62	$2,067.80	$2,102.54

[a]Imputed at 10 percent interest rate where $\text{Value}_{rt} = \text{Premium} \times e^{rt}$

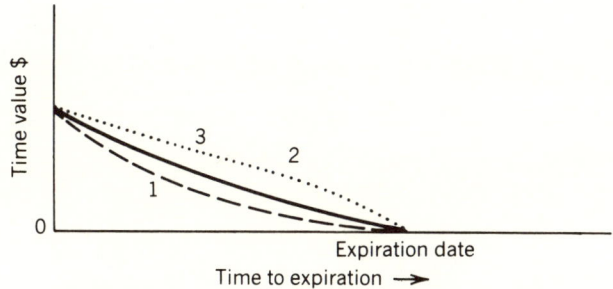

CHART 13.2 Three declining valuation models

Interest Rates

The market's rate of interest influences premiums as well. During periods of high interest rates the various alternatives for either writing or purchasing options can offer differing rates of return. The only way to improve the competitive price for a writer in such a case is to demand more premium dollars to make it economically attractive to grant an option. Additionally, as was shown in Chapter 11, Financial Factors, interest rate movements can generate a profound influence in the pricing of futures themselves.

Typically, the interest rate is the short-term rate, which can be the 3-month T-bill rate. Other choices could be the rates which reflect T-bills, CDs and Eurodollars for the time to expiration, such as: 9 days, 7 weeks, or 5 months. Also, the trader's opportunity cost can be substituted into the evaluative models to ascertain whether it is satisfactory to commit funds to such endeavors.

Other Market Factors

The level of potential and actual transaction costs also influences the decisions to write, purchase, or exercise options. Moreover, the supply and demand characteristics of the options themselves must be analyzed.

Chart 13.3 illustrates several important concepts when trading options. They are:

1. At the money
2. In the money
3. Out of the money
4. Deep out of the money
5. Intrinsic value

1. In the rigorous sense, at the money means that an option's underlying

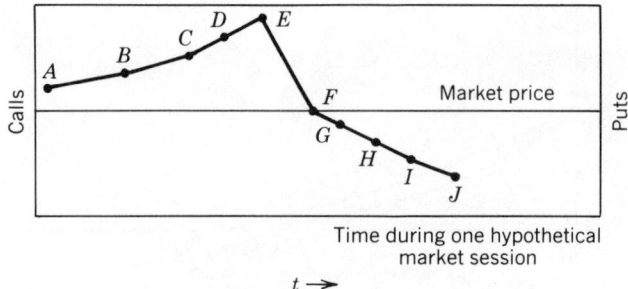

Note: Points *A* through *J* refer to various strike prices

CHART 13.3 Five other option concepts

futures market price is equal to the options stipulated strike price. In Chart 13.3, only point *F* satisfies this condition. However, conventionally speaking, the situation of at the money could also entail those options that have strike prices nearest to the market price. This wider definition would enable points *A* and *G* for both puts and calls to be considered at-the-money options.

2. In the money refers to an option's price being favorably related to the prevailing market price. "Favorably related" means an exercise of the option at its strike price would provide a better and profitable price than that prevailing price in the underlying futures market. For purchased calls, this means that strike prices are below the market price—or points *G*, *H*, *I*, and *J*: and for puts the in-the-money points would be *A*, *B*, *C*, *D*, and *E*.

3. Out of the money refers to the situation where the strike price for the specified option is not favorably priced relative to its underlying futures price. Simply stated, a call option with a $480 strike in a market with a prevailing $450 price would be out of the money by $30. Similarly, a put option with a $400 strike price in a $450 marketplace would be $50 out of the money. Returning to Chart 13.3, the out-of-the-money points for calls would be *A*, *B*, *C*, *D*, and *E*. Whereas, the out-of-the-money points for puts would be *G*, *H*, *I*, and *J*.

4. Deep out of the money refers to the situation where an option's strike price is very far, and unfavorably so, from the prevailing market price. For calls, these points would be *D* and *E*. Generally, options which are deep out of the money tend to have premiums which primarily approximate the time value characteristics.

5. Intrinsic value refers to options which have favorable strike prices relative to the market price. Only options which are in the money possess intrinsic value. It is determined by the difference between the strike price and the market price. All other options have no intrinsic value, though they may have market value.

TABLE 13.2. HIERARCHY OF RISKS FOR OPTION TRADING

Risk Potential	Strategy	Rationale
Greatest protection limited risk	Purchase of put or call	Only premium plus transaction costs can be lost
Moderate protection greater risk	Writing covered options trading combinations	Receipt of premium will somewhat reduce loss as well existence of covered position Dampens losses
No protection risk	Writing uncovered options	Although premiums received, they may not offset entire loss; uncovered call theoretically more risk than uncovered put

VARIATIONS

Although puts and calls are the two basic option types, they can be arranged in a wide variety of ways. For example, a purchase of a put and a call is considered a combination (long straddle). Likewise, the sale of a put and a call is another combination (short straddle). A purchase and sale of two different calls on the same market is a spread, as is a purchase and sale of two different puts. These differences among puts and calls arise from different expiration dates, strike prices, or both. For example, an April 1986 call with a $360 strike price is different from an April 1986 call with a $400 strike price.

Summary

The purchase or writing of options depends on the trader's needs and outlooks. Generally, the purchase of a call or the writing of a put (particularly an uncovered one) indicates a bullish posture in the marketplace. Since the purchase of an option was examined earlier, only its sale will be addressed here. By selling a put, the writer receives the premium and expects the underlying futures market to remain relatively stable or advance, thereby precluding an exercise of the option. Conversely, the writing of a call or the purchase of a put implies that the trader looks for a bearish movement in price. As the purchase of a put was examined earlier, only the writing of a call (covered or uncovered) will be analyzed here. The writer of a call receives the premium and generally expects prices to remain somewhat stable, or decline, thereby precluding the exercise of the call. In the case of a covered call, the trader has the commodity or underlying futures to present if the option is exercised. By writing such a call against inventories, the trader may receive a higher-than-ordinary return due to the receipt of premium. But if the market rallied, the trader's price protection could be limited as the covered inventory could be effectively called away. In the case of a written uncovered call, there is no inventory position which covers the call; and the writer would be much more out of the pocket in order to satisfy the obligation to meet the exercised call.

The hierarchy of risk protection for trading options is presented in Table 13.2.

STRATEGIES

This section describes the more common strategies, as most others are hybrids of these basic approaches. In this commentary, commissions, monitoring, and other costs are omitted. Currently, each exchange has its own requirements regarding option position maintenance, and this lack of uniformity can affect the performance of a given strategy for different futures.

1. *Buy a Call.* Bullish or protective strategy. There are three basic possibilities. They are the purchase of a near-, in-, and out-of-the-money option. Loss in all cases is limited to the premium, while the gains are potentially unlimited. The decision is in determining which option offers the suitable reward risk characteristics. As each strike has a different delta, the responsiveness to favorable/unfavorable influences will produce considerable variations in price movements. Can be used to offset short positions.

2. *Buy a Put.* Bearish or protective strategy. Three basic possibilities: the purchase of a near-, in-, and out-of-the-money option. Loss in all cases is limited to the premium, while the gains are potentially unlimited. The decision is to determine which option offers the suitable reward/risk characteristics. As each strike has a different delta, the responsiveness to favorable/unfavorable influences will produce considerable variations in price movements. Can be used to offset long positions.

3. *Sell a Call.* Bearish or protective strategy. Three basic possibilities: in-, near-, and out-of-the-money. Potentially unlimited loss while gain is limited to premium received. Can require variation margin due to adverse movements. The seller of deep-in-the-money options runs the risk of exercise, which may offset prevailing long positions or establish a short futures position. Can be used as a covered call write against inventory with the intention of securing higher returns via the receipt of premium. Particularly the case for an expected stable or declining market environment.

4. *Sell a Put.* Bullish or protective strategy. Three basic possibilities: in-, near-, and out-of-the-money. Potentially unlimited loss versus gain limited to premium received. Can require variation margin due to adverse movements. The seller of deep-in-the-money puts runs the risk of exercise, which may offset prevailing short positions or establish a long futures position at the strike price. Can be used as an offset against short actuals positions or enhancer of returns if futures market stabilizes or goes higher.

5. *Buy a Call. Sell a Call.* This can be achieved by buying a lower strike and selling a higher strike price for a given option month. This would generate a net transactional debit. Moderately bullish. If the purchase was of the higher strike and the sale was of the lower strike, then the position would generate a net transactional credit. This strategy is moderately bearish. See horizontal and vertical spreads.

6. *Buy a Put. Sell a Put.* This can be achieved by buying a higher strike price and selling a lower strike price for a given option month. This would generate a net debit. Moderately bearish. If the purchase were of the lower strike and the sale of the higher strike, a net credit would be generated. Moderately bullish. See horizontal and vertical spreads.

7. *Buy a Call. Sell a Put.* Bullish strategy. Creates a synthetic futures

long position. Gain potentially unlimited when adjusted by net premium component. Loss is unlimited. Variation margin may be necessary to satisfy the put write leg should adverse movement occur. Depending on strikes, can generate net transactional credits or debits.

8. *Buy a Put. Sell a Call.* Bearish strategy. Creates a synthetic futures short position. Gain potentially unlimited less net transactional premium cost. Loss is potentially unlimited. Variation margin may be necessary to satisfy the call write leg should adverse movement occur. Depending on strikes, can generate transactional credits or debits.

9. *Long Futures. Buy a Put.* Moderately bullish. Purchase of put option diminishes potential gain but offers a degree of protection depending on quantity and strike prices of put position.

10. *Long Futures. Sell a Call.* Moderately bullish. Maximum risk limitation equal to amount of premium received. Writer exposed to potential exercise which may draw away long position.

11. *Short Futures. Buy a Call.* Moderately bearish. Purchase of option diminishes potential gain but offers a degree of protection depending on quantity and strike prices of call position. Lower strike prices offer higher degree of protection but commensurately reduce potential gains.

12. *Short Futures. Sell a Put.* Moderately bearish. Maximum risk limitation equal to premium received. Writer exposed to potential exercise which may offset short futures position.

13. *Ratio Hedge.* Dependent on prevailing deltas for specified options relative to underlying futures. For example, a trader long one futures contract of copper can sell two at-the-money calls, hence the ratio of two options to one future. Or, the trader can sell four copper options which have individual deltas of .25. Here, the ratio would be four options to one future. Moreover, the trader could sell one option with a .50 delta and two options with .25 deltas. In these examples, the trader initially achieved a delta neutral hedge, since the price variation of the underlying futures is offset by the price variation of the option position. These ratios can require considerable adjustments, since the delta values themselves fluctuate according to prevailing market conditions. Ratio hedges need not be delta neutral. They can be greater or less than 1.00 depending on outlook. When the ratio is greater than 1.00, an over-write strategy is being pursued.

14. *Vertical Option Spread.* This spread is established by the purchase and sale of a call (put) for the same expiration month at different strike prices. These positions can generate either net transactional debits or credits. There are two bullish postures: the purchase of a low strike call and the sale of a higher strike call; or the purchase of a low exercise put and the sale of a higher exercise put. The two bearish strategies are: the purchase of a high exercise put and the sale of a lower exercise put; or buying a high exercise

call and selling a lower exercise call. There are several caveats. The wider the range between the strikes, particularly if the sold option is deep-in-the-money, can potentially collapse the spread strategy due to a higher likelihood of exercise by the purchaser of that option. Also, the purchase of deep-in-the-money options can imply negative leverage by requiring excessively high capital commitments.

15. *Horizontal Spread.* Also known as calender or time spreads. Can be moderately bullish or bearish strategies. However, pronounced movements in yield curve slopes, inversion, or return to carrying charges can generate substantial moves. This spread is established by purchasing and selling a call (put) for the same strike price but for different expiration months. For example, the purchase of a September bond option at 98 and the sale of the June bond option at 98 is one horizontal spread. This strategy is dependent on the variation of the relative time value decay of premiums. Typically, near-the-money options exhibit the most rapid time value decay. Moreover, this comparative decline in time value is greater for the nearer month than for the longer duration options. Thus the trader would look to sell the nearby and purchase the deferred option to potentially exploit the variation in time value decay. If the trader expects the deferred month to strengthen relative to the nearby, a calendar call spread is positioned; whereas, expectations of relatively greater declines for the forward months warrant a calendar put spread position. These strategies will generate either transactional credits or debits.

16. *Long Strangle. Buy a Call. Buy a Put.* Trader expects dramatically extensive move in market but uncertain as to the direction. The purchase of near- or out-of-the-money options is the rule here. For relatively modest capital commitments, the trader can achieve potentially limitless gains for limited risk. No chance of unfavorable exercise by an outside party. Potential gain reduced by the payment of two premiums.

17. *Short Strangle. Sell a Call. Sell a Put.* Trader expects comparative market stability. Gain limited to premiums received. Loss unlimited. Greater protection afforded by going further out of the money, but premiums significantly reduced. Risk of option exercise, and this adversity can be two-sided in whipsawing markets.

18. *Synthetics.* The construction of a quasifutures position. Risk and reward characteristics can be calibrated to more or less nearly approximate the underlying futures. This is produced by the various combinatorial arrangements of option types, expirations, and strike prices.

19. *Butterflies.* A strategy where the more common arrangements are (1) the purchase of one call, the sale of two calls, and the purchase of another call; (2) the purchase of a put, the sale of two puts, and the purchase of another put; (3) the sale of a call, the purchase of two calls, and the sale of another call; and (4) and the sale of a put, the purchase of two puts, and the sale of a put.

20. *Credit Spread.* A strategy by which the write leg or legs generate premiums greater than those paid out to establish complementary purchase legs.

21. *Debit Spread.* A strategy by which the purchase leg or legs incur premium costs greater than those secured by the complementary write legs.

22. *Time Spread.* Those which are predicated on the relative variations in time value decay rates among different expiration months. (See horizontal spread.)

OTHER CONSIDERATIONS

In-the-money options, particularly those deeply so, are less attrative than those trading about the money. The substantial capital commitment for these purchases can entail important higher opportunity costs, as any further appreciation cannot be converted to other uses due to prevailing margining requirements. The purchaser is not only paying one imputed carrying charge for the underlying instrument, but another one due to the higher implied interest element of the richer priced premium. This condition is referred to as negative leverage. For example, this starts to occur when the premium for a T-note option exceeds the margin to initiate the underlying futures position. This situation is even more pronounced when the option is two or more strikes within the money.

Liquidity of trading centers on the strikes at and near the money. Substantial departures from these strike price norms can result in a lack of active trading interest.

As a rule of thumb, the at-the-money or immediate in-the-money options typically have premiums just under or over the original margin to initiate the underlying futures position. Since at-the-money options have deltas approximating .50, the potentially rapid movement into an in-the-money condition will produce subsequent appreciation at a tick-for-tick basis. From a purchase perspective, the potential to secure effectively the underlying futures position for risk limited to the initial premium is an attractive feature. For grantors of options, any favorable departure from an in-the-money or at-the-money condition means a rapid shift in margin requirements and the increased potential to eventually claim the premium.

VOLATILITY MEASUREMENTS

Option evaluation models depend on volatility. More specifically, they consider the standard deviation of annualized returns. For evaluation purposes, the greater the standard deviation (volatility), the higher the premium. The reason being that the option has a higher likelihood of moving into profitable ranges or crossing over into exercisable regions. For the moment, we will put aside the issue of an option being at the money or in the money. A shift towards higher volatility makes an option more valuable; and in fact, this factor becomes the critical pricing influence. Models which calculate theoretical fair values are reliant on it. Additionally, these models are used to determine the implied volatility of an option. Departures from theoretical fair values can be exploited for arbitrage purposes.

AN OPTION MODEL

Fisher Black and Myron Scholes are commonly recognized as the postulators of option valuation models. Black applied the stock option valuation mechanism to the commodity markets. The following is a presentation of that model as listed by John W. Labuszewski; and Jeanne Cairns Sinquefield in "Inside the Commodity Option Markets."

$$C = e^{-rt}[FN(d1) - SN(d2)]$$

$$d1 = \frac{[\ln(F/S) + ts^2/2]}{s\sqrt{t}}$$

$$d2 = d1 - s\sqrt{t}$$

where:
  C = theoretical call premium or its fair market value
  F = the futures price
  S = the strike price
  r = interest rate
  t = time until expiration expressed in years
  s = standard deviation
  N = a normal cumulative probability distribution

and for puts the expression is:

$$P = -e^{-rt}[FN(-d1) - SN(-d2)]$$

where P = the theoretical put premium

The use of natural logarithmic notation states a continuous pricing mechanism. Also, a relative pricing arrangement is used. As demonstrated in Chapter 11, Financial Factors, the continuous compounding-discounting of an economic time series gives rise to the e factor. The use of ln relative pricing transforms a time series into a log-normal one which dispenses with the probability of negative prices, though not returns.

EVALUATIVE PROCESS

The process for evaluating the fair market value becomes one of specifying strike and underlying futures prices, the time to expiration for the option, the short-term rate of interest, and a volatility factor. Once these data are supplied, the theoretical fair value can be computed, particularly as there is a variety of software available for this purpose. Going one step further, many of these programs can also solve for the implied volatility attributable to an option. Here, the inputs are the strike and underlying futures prices, short-term rate of interest, and the market price of the option. The critical point in either of these solutions is that these models do not predict where the option is necessarily going but rather what its fair price should be; or, what value the market is attributing to the volatility variable. In the first case, the assignment of the volatility factor is generally made by a historic analysis of its variation, whereas for the latter the trader is attempting to discern whether the market price of the option is predicated on a comparatively large or small variability influence vis-à-vis the trader's own. Should the solution indicate a rather rich premium for the option due to a high implied volatility factor, the trader would be inclined to sell that option since its value is relatively high compared to the trader's estimated volatility criterion. Conversely, should the implied volatility be relatively low, the trader would favor the option's purchase. These departures from theoretical or expected values provide the opportunities for arbitraging or spreading.

Refining the option evaluative process introduces the concept of expectational volatility. Though historic and implied volatilities can be useful in estimating this parameter, particularly by applying the Bayesian Analysis procedure, the traders' perceptions of the expected value of volatility should be the primary reason why an option is purchased or sold.

This factor more fully explains the incidence of prima facie solutions suggesting a bias in the pricing of options. Although options are traded for hedging, speculative, and arbitrage motivations, it is the expected value for these trading programs which is the focal point and not what its fair value should be per se. Consider the case of outright trading. A trader does not buy a Ginnie Mae contract because of what its current fair price is, but rather what it should be, given the trader's outlook. Although historic information can be employed in the decision-making process, the trader's rationale for this simple purchase is that Ginnie Mae rates are expected to fall thereby profiting from the attendant rise in Ginnie Mae futures prices. This confluence of the various expectations of the market participants is what propels prices. As most research indicates, current market prices reflect the known or given information for assets; but this pricing also entails expectations for future events. These continuous evaluative and reevaluative processes account for the fluctuating price paths of assets. For example, in strongly trending markets, the appearance of a bullish or bearish bias manifests itself. For up markets, calls appear to have an important premium bias relative to puts. This is due not so much to the simplistically quantified increase of volatility, but rather the increase in bullish expectations. In other words, the probability distribution then takes on the skewed shape, suggesting higher expectations of positive price movement, as opposed to a uniform expectation of equally likely higher or lower prices.

Returning to the common evaluative models, the assignment of volatility via the standard deviation assumes that returns or changes in prices will occur about the mean value plus or minus one standard deviation approximately 67 percent of the time, and 95 percent of the time for two standard deviations.

As has been indicated in other chapters, this assumed normality of returns and their variations is not constant over time, or even representative of actual generating processes. In fact, stationary processes are essentially those which are trendless or at least transformed time series whereby trending influences are removed. Nonstationary time series reflect not only significantly shifting mean values, but also produce radically different mean and variance values for different segments. The changes can be so substantial that increasing the number of observations (data points) does not improve the reliability of estimates and their true parameter values. Particularly, variance estimates will not converge towards their underlying values; and, for such cases, the variance is considered infinite, even though ordinary statistical analysis methods will produce a calculated variance estimate. Surrogate methods for ascertaining volatility estimates are required. Among these are the interquartile and interfractile ranges. It is during remarkable markets that extraordinary profits or losses are incurred, and this implies departures from common-normal expectations. On a comparative basis, the returns produced within an options time series are greater than for the underlying futures. This magnification of movement is partially attributable to the greater leverage inherent in options trading. Its unique pricing process and the potentially wide swings in the delta characteristic are other important parts.

The ability to rapidly assimilate new information and revise prior estimates is afforded by Bayesian Analysis. (See Chapter 15, Conditional Analysis.) For the moment, it is sufficient to say that the introduction of likelihood values from given recent observations can quickly modify the probability distributions and assist in calculating better approximations of expected values for the option. Thus, should the market appear to reflect a strong bias due to skewedness or heightened volatility due to increased occurrences of outliers, the evaluative process can now take these important departures quickly into consideration.

IMPUTING A PROBABILISTIC STRUCTURE

By assigning a schedule of outcome probabilities, a trader can compute the expected value for an option given current data and expected conditions. This procedure redefines the trader's probabilitistic structure for determining the potential worth and disparity (for arbitrage purposes) for trading options.

Figures 13.1, 13.2, 13.3, 13.4, and 13.5 display this concept for two different perceptions of the possible attainments of 98, 100, 102, 104, and 106 market levels for Treasury note futures, given two different probability assignments of 20, 25, 40, 10, and 5 percent. Figures 13.1 and 13.3 represent the outright probability assignments; Figures 13.2 and 13.4 represent the cumulative assignments; and Figure 13.5 represents the disparity between Figures 13.2 and 13.4.

There is a $900 disparity between expected mean values for the evaluation of this option between the two participants. Such differences can arise not only due to the expected probabilities but interest rate factors and volatility as well.

One method of calculating these expectational premium values is by mod-

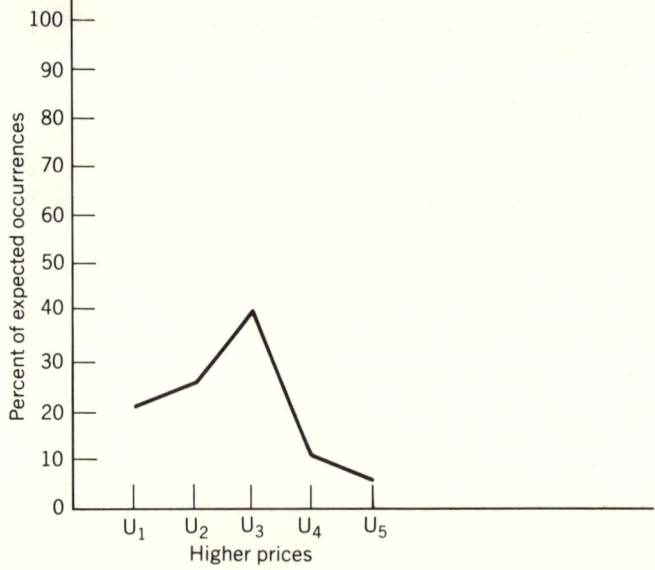

FIGURE 13.1 Perception 1 of various market level attainments

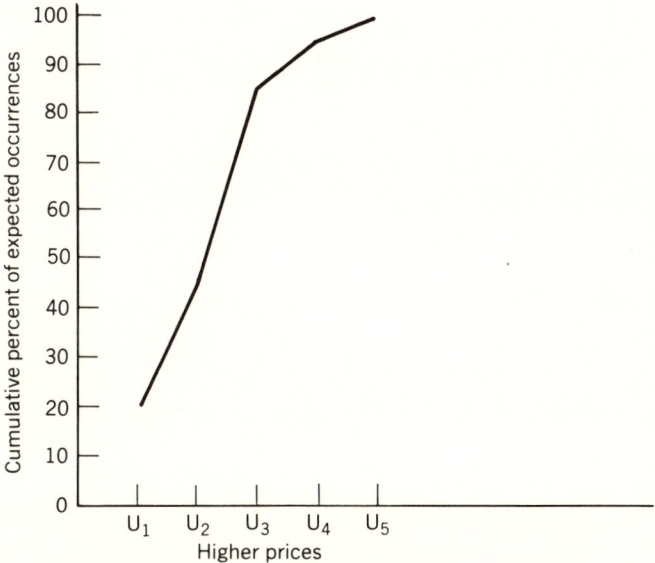

FIGURE 13.2 Perception 1 on cumulative basis

ifying the preferred fair value formula to accommodate anticipated conditional states and their likely outcomes.

For calls, these revisions, when applied to the earlier expressions become:

$$E(C_i) = W_i\{e^{-rt}[F_iN(d1) - SN(d2)]\}$$

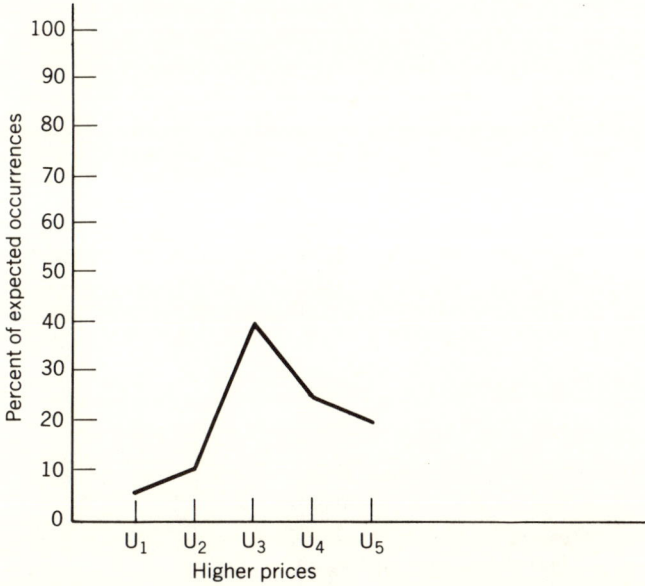

FIGURE 13.3 Perception 2 of various market level attainments

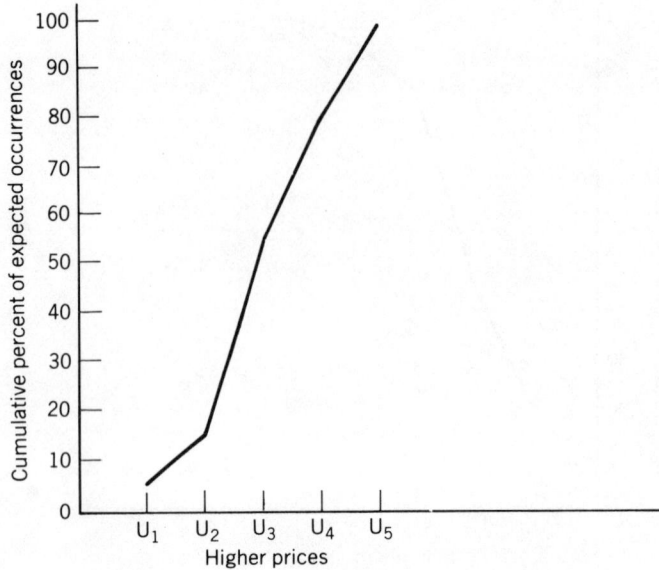

FIGURE 13.4 Perception 2 on cumulative basis

and $d1 = [\ln (F_i/S) + ts^2/2]/s\sqrt{t}$

where:

$E(C_i)$ refers to the expected call premium value over i conditional states

F_i refers to the imputed market values for corresponding market states

W_i refers to the probabilistic weights assigned to the i conditional states

and where $\Sigma_i = 1.00$

Prices in Points	P_1	V_1	P_2	V_2
5	.20	1.00	.50	.25
4	.25	1.00	.10	.40
3	.40	1.20	.40	1.20
2	.10	.20	.25	.50
1	.50	.05	.20	.20
Expected values		3.45		2.55

Expected value disparity .90 or $900 per option.

P_1 is perception one probability
V_1 is perception one valuation
P_2 is perception two probability
V_2 is perception two valuation

FIGURE 13.5. Evaluation disparity between the two perceptions

Similarly, the revised expression for expectational put values become:

$$E(P_i) = W_i\{-e^{-rt}[F_i N(-d1) - SN(-d2)]\}$$

and $d1 = [\ln (F_i/S) + ts^2/2]/s\sqrt{t}$

where $E(P_i)$ is the expected put premium value over i conditional states.

In both cases, $d2$ is determined as before.

The importance of this approach is that it quantifies the trader's estimates for option valuation given a limited number of conditional states. This approach is particularly helpful when comparing outright versus option trading and hedging strategies under serious time limitation constraints. The results generated indicate the expected dollar outlooks without the added costs of continuous, and occasionally excessive, delta-related trading adjustments for options programs. Ignoring this feature can increase the expenses for many portfolio insurance programs, thereby reducing returns. Also, it presents funding guidelines to a program's equity paths for adverse, neutral, and favorable conditions. Finally, it shifts a trading program from being exclusively response-oriented to being sensitive to changes in expectations.

SUMMARY OF EVALUATIVE MODELS

The weaknesses of most models are the assumptions of:

1. (Log)normally generated returns
2. Constant or slightly drifting variance (standard deviation)
3. Implied symmetry of the probability distribution for the specified time segment
4. Lack of predictive ability
5. Assumption of constant interest rate

The strengths of these models include:

1. Excellent framework, which allows quantification of important pricing influences
2. Initial assumption of normality is a good starting point, since it can be modified quickly by acceptable statistical techniques.
3. Amenable to many analytical techniques with modest transformations

4. Presents the common expectation of value though not necessarily the market's

5. Assumption of constant interest rate not particularly troublesome for short duration options, especially in a relatively stable interest rate environment.

14

Portfolio Considerations

IMPORTANT CONCEPTS

Portfolio theory conceptualizes efficient diversification and dominant investment alternatives. Efficient diversification means that a certain combination of assets exhibits less covariability than other considered combinations. Assets in this discussion are commodities or futures with designated trading approaches, parameters, and rules. For example, December Treasury notes traded by a 5- and 10-day simple moving average are considered an asset. December Treasury notes traded by a 7- and 20-day simple moving average are another. Since each trading variation imparts its own risk and reward characteristics, the variety of assets is limitless; however, recall that Chapter 12, Testing, points out methods to limit and define suitable assets in order to construct acceptable portfolios and trading programs.

By reducing covariability among returns, a smoother and more consistent trading program and portfolio emerge. For the moment, consider covariability on an intuitive level. Portfolio 1 (P1) (Table 14.1) consists of one contract of soybeans, soymeal, and soyoil. Portfolio 2 (P2) (Table 14.1) consists of one contract of soybeans, copper, and sugar. Casting aside margin requirements, daily and longer-term volatility, and other such factors, it is obvious the assets in P1 are highly related to one another; in fact, assets 2 and 3 are products of soybeans. Hence the success or failure of this portfolio is very dependent on factors relevant to the soybean market. Moreover, even if the trading approaches and parameters were adequately chosen for each soy asset, the covariability between the assets will be rather high. One tactic to reduce the high level of covariability is to trade soybeans with a short-term approach, soymeal with an intermediate approach, and soyoil with a longer-term approach. If market activity becomes increasingly volatile on a daily or weekly basis, the longer-term approaches will offer some degree of immunity to whipsawing.

TABLE 14.1. PORTFOLIOS 1 AND 2

Portfolio 1			Portfolio 2		
Asset	E (return)	E (risk)	Asset	E (return)	E (risk)
Soybeans	2,000	1,000	Soybeans	2,000	1,000
Soymeal	1,500	750	Copper	1,500	750
Soyoil	1,000	500	Sugar	1,000	500
Summation for portfolio	4,500	2,250		4,500	2,250

Another tactic is to track some of the assets in the old crop months and the remainder in the new crop months. Although once again P1 is susceptible to events in the soybean market, the risks are, so to speak, spread over time.

As demonstrated in Chapter 7, Spread Analysis, old/new crop months can offer interesting spreading possibilities due to the existence of very different fundamental arguments. Similarly, financial instruments exhibit yield curve differentials due to distinctions among various maturities and other economic factors.

Examining P2, we note three rather different assets. One is a member of the soybean complex (soybeans), another is an industrial metal (copper), the third is a tropical foodstuff (sugar). Thus the primary factors influencing each of these assets are not universal to all three. For example, soybeans may be in tight supply, the demand for copper may be weak due to softening economic activity, and sugar may be erratic due to conflicting research findings pertaining to its dietary usefulness, questionable European beet crop conditions, and rapid substitution of high fructose corn sweeteners. To complete the analysis, a few assumptions are necessary. Previous testing indicates all the comparative assets offer identical expected returns with given levels of risk. Second, it is assumed the assets in P2 were tested and they displayed less covariability than those in P1.

Since the expected returns for the assets in P1 are highly dependent on influences pertaining to the soybean market, the manager of such a portfolio encounters numerous conditional risks.

TABLE 14.2. PORTFOLIOS 3 AND 4

Portfolio 3			Portfolio 4		
Asset	E (return)	E (risk)	Asset	E (return)	E (risk)
Soybeans	2,000	1,000	Soybeans	2,000	1,000
Soymeal	1,500	750	Copper	1,500	750
Soyoil	1,000	700	Sugar	1,000	500
Summation for portfolio	4,500	2,450		4,500	2,250

TABLE 14.3. PORTFOLIOS 5 AND 6

	Portfolio 5			Portfolio 6	
Asset	E (return)	E (risk)	Asset	E (return)	E (risk)
Soybeans	2,000	1,000	Soybeans	2,000	1,000
Soymeal	1,500	750	Copper	1,800	750
Soyoil	1,000	700	Sugar	1,000	500
Summation for portfolio	4,500	2,450		4,800	2,250

Condition 1: Specific Commodity Risk. The soybean assets experience an abrupt change in trend direction opposite to given positions. On a comparative basis, such a financial shock would tend to only affect one asset in P2, while affecting all assets in P1.

Condition 2: Sector Risk. Even if a major shock does not occur in the soybean complex, the assets in P1 are extremely dependent on influences in the agricultural markets.

Condition 3: Other Risks. A force majeure is declared at a large copper mine, a dramatic impact on the copper asset in P2, but negligible impact on other P2 and P1 assets.

As can be seen from conditions 1 and 2, the occurrence of an important influence can disrupt not only a commodity but an entire portfolio. Thus the emphasis is on realistic diversification.

The previous example highlighted dominance. Dominance means that if two or more investments offer the same expected yield but one requires less risk, then it is the dominant investment. To further emphasize this concept, examine Table 14.2. Again there are two portfolios, P3 and P4. Note that P3 varies from P1 by its E (risk), or expected risk. P2 is equal to P4. Since P3 and P4 offer the same expected returns but P4 does it with less expected risk, then P4 is dominant and preferred to P3.

Put another way, if the considered investments exhibit the same expected risk factors, but one offers a greater expected yield, then it is dominant and preferred to its alternatives. Table 14.3 illustrates this. Here, P6 is preferred to P5.

Using the same logic in a broader sense, a group of portfolios can be dominant relative to other alternative portfolios.

AN OVERVIEW OF THE THEORIES

The vast majority of portfolio theories depends on what is known as normal distributions. This means that the expected returns and their variations

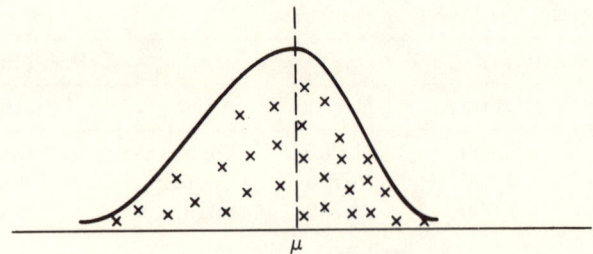

FIGURE 14.1 Bell-shaped curve where characteristic exponent equals 2

are generated by a function, the expected values of which when plotted provide the commonly known bell-shaped curve. (See Figure 14.1.)

This is very helpful since it affords the opportunity to use parametric testing procedures such as ordinary regression analysis, mean values, standard deviations, and variance. However, if the underlying generating function is not normal and cannot be transformed adequately into such, a host of problems can arise, many of which can create havoc with ordinary statistical testing procedures and applications. For instance, the assumption of a normal function provides a premise for portfolio diversification. Since it is given that the expected values behave normally, a broadly based portfolio may reduce risk by minimizing covariability among the portfolio assets. If the characteristic exponent of the generating function is less than 2, then the bell-shaped curve flattens at its center with a commensurate thickening of its tails. (See Figure 14.2.) This poses potential hazards as greater likelihoods of expected values will occur in the tails and correspondingly fewer at and about the mean (μ). For approximations of standardized Cauchy distributions, the incidence can be nearly twice as likely in the tails than would be normally expected. This creates situations of potentially greater performance or risk. On a portfolio basis, depending how much the characteristic exponent is less than 2, it is conceivable and statistically probable that diversification may actually increase risk, and the best portfolio may probably be a single asset one.

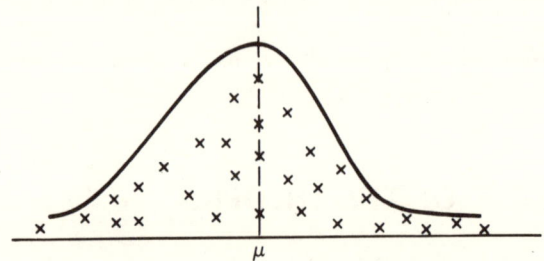

FIGURE 14.2 Bell-shaped curve where characteristic exponent is less than 2

The higher probabilities of outliers indicate higher joint probabilities for outliers of the portfolio. This means that the multiple (jointly) likelihoods of adverse swings are substantially greater than normally expected.

Consider the situation of a two-asset portfolio. Initially it is estimated that the occurrence of an extremely adverse event is 1 percent for each of the assets. This does not mean that the joint probability is 2 percent, but rather $.01 \times .01 = .0001$ or 1 of 10,000 likely occurrences. For three assets, the arithmetic would produce $.01 \times .01 \times .01 = .000001$, or the likelihood of all three assets to experience concurrent adverse events would be 1 of 1 million likely occurrences. This reduction in risk essentially requires independence among the observations or returns. The emergence of dependence, particularly a strong dependence, alters the portfolio's risk reduction attributes. There has been some quantitative research that suggests that dependence among asset returns occurs during extraordinary market conditions. This implies that one cannot expect to generate the rapid risk reduction properties of the simple multiplicative joint probabilities; but rather the risks seem to be constant (though larger than normally expected) when the returns shift away from normalcy conditions. To document this, the analyst must analyze those conditional states where extraordinarily large returns (positive and negative) occur and assess the correlative properties among the specified assets.

Much empirical research indicates that stock asset returns possess a characteristic exponent of approximately 1.7, though other assets such as Treasury issues and futures behave as if their characteristic exponents were considerably less than 2. For the former class of investments, the use of parametric statistical techniques is acceptable provided the tester/trader is aware of the limitations of this research. For other classes it may be necessary to analyze on a nonparametric basis.

One can develop tests to attempt to ascertain the underlying mechanisms that generate expected returns for given trading techniques for each asset. Several nonparametric testing techniques are presented in this text. The statistical elegance of nonparametric techniques is that they are indifferent to the underlying generating functions.

EQUITY CLASSES

This term refers to the spectrum of portfolios, whose primary characteristic is the quantity of available trading funds. For example, there are three trading portfolios, the values of which are $5,000, $50,000, and $5 million, respectively. Then there are three distinct equity classes. Actually, there are as many equity classes as there are different size portfolios. However, managed accounts, futures funds, and trading programs require certain initial contributions with specified deposit and withdrawal features.

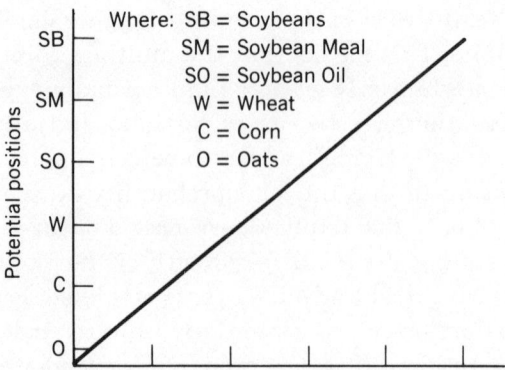

FIGURE 14.3 Increasing investment opportunities due to increasing available equity

For a futures manager, equity class imposes a stringent constraint on the program. The trading is to be limited to x number of dollars and that is all. For a managed portfolio advisor, the difference in equity classes indicates that various trades or size of positions may vary from one portfolio to another, from one client to another. This variation can become very large when comparing a larger managed account, say, $500,000 with a relatively smaller one of $25,000.

Graphically, Figure 14.3 demonstrates the effect of available equity on potential grain market positions. As can be seen, the greater the available equity from the minimum required equity, the greater the grain market position opportunities. In other words, not only can the larger accounts trade soyoil, soymeal, and soybeans; but they are potentially capable of doing all three plus oats, wheat, and corn. This equity attribute is applicable to other markets such as the energy, currency, and financial sectors. A dramatic example of the importance of equity class was the culminating top of the metals markets during the first quarter of 1980. At that time silver margins were approximately $90,000 per contract, well up from year earlier levels of $1,000 to $2,000. The imposition of retroactive margin requirements provided additional influences on the marketplace. For accounts to qualify for one contract of silver they required a minimum of $90,000 of equity, thus disqualifying a vast number of less capitalized accounts.

RISK CLASSES

Here the primary characteristic is risk. Though several portfolios may be identical in their equity characteristics, they may vary widely in risk tolerance. For example, a money manager handles three $150,000 accounts. Generally speaking, these can assume identical market positions. However, Ac-

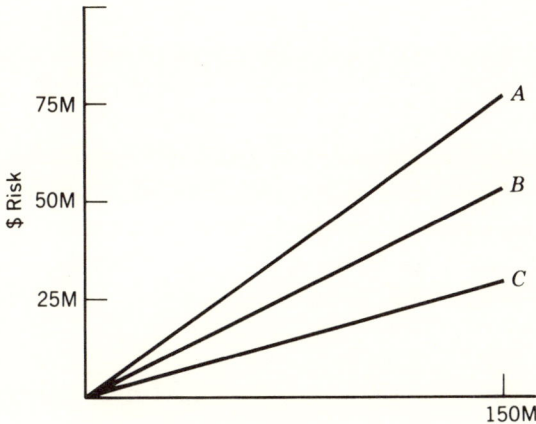

FIGURE 14.4 Alternative capitalization

count *A* seeks aggressive positions, Account *C* seeks a conservative posture, and Account *B* is somewhere in between. How can the risk tolerance of an account be determined? A straightforward way is to ask: One good question is, "How much of the available equity is actual risk capital?"

Although many brokerage firms require minimum account size whether for speculation, hedging, or management, it does not necessarily mean that the entire amount is at risk or, once committed, will be exhausted.

Returning to the example of the three $150,000 portfolios: Account *A* states that it is prepared to risk $75,000 of the $150,000 capitalization; Account *B* states that it is prepared to risk $50,000 of its $150,000 capitalization; and Account *C* states that it is prepared to risk $25,000 of its $150,000 capitalization. This quantitative measurement of risk tolerance is very helpful since it places a numerical boundary on the trading strategy. It also dispenses

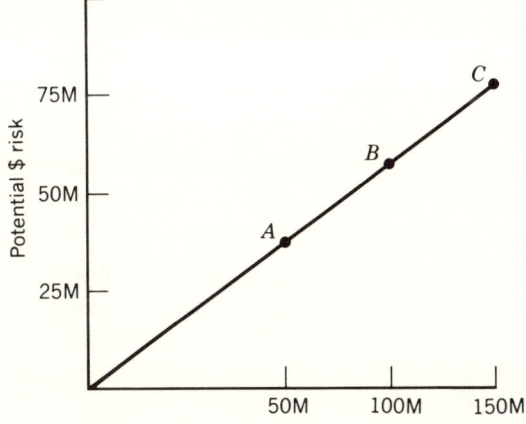

FIGURE 14.5 Expected profit assuming a reward/risk ratio of 2:1

with the situations where an account states that it is very aggressive, is prepared to open with $150,000, but is only prepared to risk $5,000. Even on an intuitive level, it can be recognized that this account is not suited for aggressive management.

Moreover, the account prepared to risk more should be potentially in a position to capture higher rewards—otherwise why risk more capital? This concept is graphically represented by Figures 14.4 and 14.5.

Why is there a difference between available capitalization and dollar risk tolerance? It is as basic as the underlying goals and constraints of each market participant.

COMPATIBILITY

As in sports, marriage, or business combinations, a good team is more than a collection of the seemingly best athletes, people, or firms. Ability, demonstrated and potential, is important; but it is also crucial for each component to act harmoniously with the others. The same is true in constructing portfolios. As in an earlier example, it can turn out that the best approaches for trading soybeans, meal, and oil are excellent on their own merits; but when placed together they produce erratic and potentially poor combined results. To determine compatibility for a given portfolio, testing procedures are employed which quantify the combined expected returns and risks.

GROUPING

By grouping, a money manager carefully congregates accounts into groups or sections. As previously seen, portfolios can consist of infinite variations in size, risk tolerance, profit objectives, and other factors. However, there are elements of commonality among these portfolios. For example, Figure 14.6 depicts one grouping arrangement.

This shows 100 various managed accounts, selectively grouped into conservative, moderate, and aggressive risk classes while providing the manager with those account totals. By arranging account data in this fashion, the manager now has more "manageable" information at his or her disposal. Effectively, the manager has reduced the problem from managing 100 accounts to managing 15 groups. Of course, the equity, risk classes, or other specifications can influence the number or shape of the groups. Additionally, there can be grouping arrangements for computerized, fundamental, technical, spread, arbitrage, or chart programs. But once again, given the increase in variables, the manager is in an excellent position to reduce the management task to

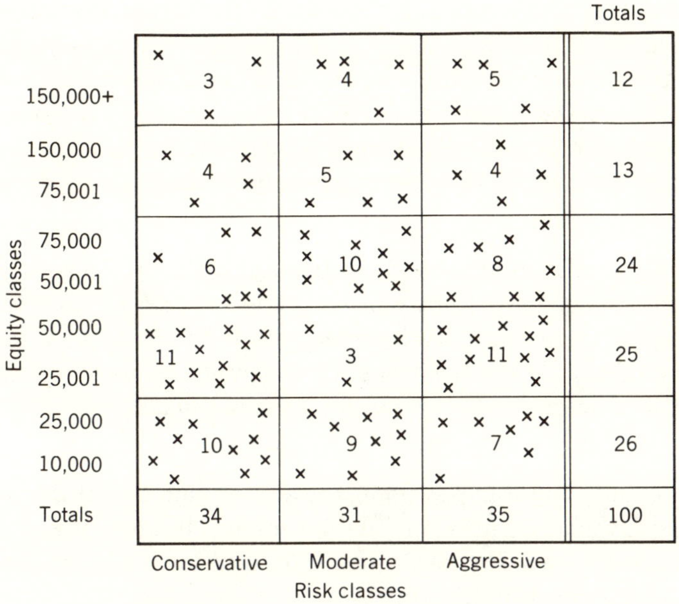

	Conservative	Moderate	Aggressive	Totals
150,000+	3	4	5	12
150,000 / 75,001	4	5	4	13
75,000 / 50,001	6	10	8	24
50,000 / 25,001	11	3	11	25
25,000 / 10,000	10	9	7	26
Totals	34	31	35	100

Equity classes — Risk classes

FIGURE 14.6 Account groupings

that of trading several groups and not a plethora of accounts. It should be noted that this approach recognizes and responds to situations where various accounts can and should be traded differently due to their significantly different characteristics.

CASH FLOW PRINCIPLES

One of the more difficult problems for money managers is the timing of a new trading program. Success or failure is very often linked to the time of implementation. In the futures markets, the old expression "What a difference a day makes!" is particularly true.

When a new account opens, does it actively enter into the program for the given groups?

Optional courses of action for the new account (program) include:

1. Take only new signals or new positions
2. Take existing positions
3. Take only winning positions
4. Take losing positions within the stop-out parameters
5. Partially commit funds and increase positions over time

Point 1. Take only new signals. By following this tactic, a manager can miss some of the most dramatic moves; for, if a major trend is underway, a fresh signal will tend to occur during a consolidation or congestion phase and not at the ultimate trend reversal point. Hence, the signal may be actually against the major move. Moreover, a move may be so powerful that any new accounts not present at the time of the initial signal may miss a very sizable portion of it.

Point 2. Take existing positions. By following this point, an account will participate in the major moves but will be prone to some whipsawing, particularly if the systems generate trades which are in the midst of a losing streak. However, by taking all the positions, the account assumes immediate diversification, which is generally preferable to experiencing the risk of a single position, particularly a new signal. (See Point 1.)

Point 3. Take only winning positions; the assumption is that the winners will keep moving favorably. However, the optimum risk point may tend periodically to drift away from any new midstream positions. Also, this can present a situation of only partial diversification or no position.

Point 4. Take losing positions within stop-out parameters; the assumption is that the trade was good when initiated and will remain so until it is stopped out or reversed. Given the adverse price movement, a new entry may actually be better off given the generally reduced dollar risk—the market can be closer to its stop-out point. Also, as in Point 3, this can produce a case of partial diversification.

Point 5. Partial fund commitment. This point is so very important, it will be addressed as a concept in the next section.

FUND COMMITMENT OVER TIME

For smaller accounts, up to $50,000, it is difficult to disburse funds over time and still achieve the benefits of diversification due to insufficient funds. The greater the sum involved, the greater the need to allocate funds over time. The rationale for this is that the account will stabilize its performance over the specified time span and increase its likelihood of longevity. These allocations can be weekly, monthly, or quarterly. They can be equal parts, declining fractional commitments, or increasing fractional commitments. Whatever the specified arrangement, it generally is advantageous to allocate the committed funds over time. Another variation is the spreading of new accounts over time. Money managers can optimize results by receiving 10 new accounts per month for a year rather than 120 new accounts in just one week,

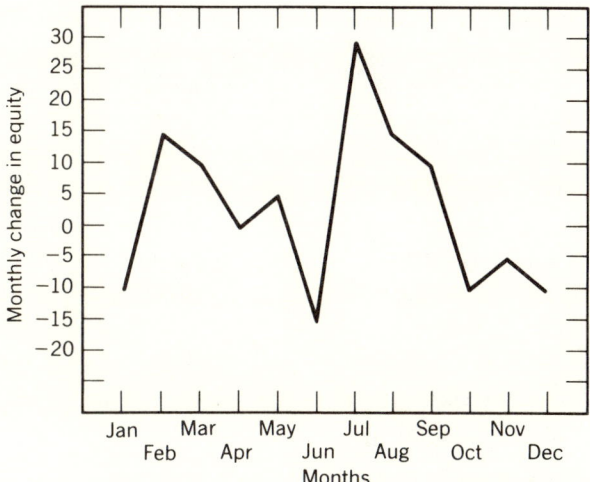

FIGURE 14.7 Monthly change in equity

month, or quarter. The reason is simple: Overall fund commitment approximates the situation of the large account disbursing funds over time. Moreover, individual account results acquire a continuity effect in terms of long-term performance.

Figure 14.7 shows the monthly percentage change in equity (monthly performance). Figure 14.8 graphs the cumulative result of the percentage changes in monthly equity. The best case would be to open the account at point *C* and close it at point *D*. But as in other businesses, anticipating the best opening time and closing time is extremely difficult—if not futile. If Detroit could do it, it would be a mixed blessing, because of start-up costs, continuity of prod-

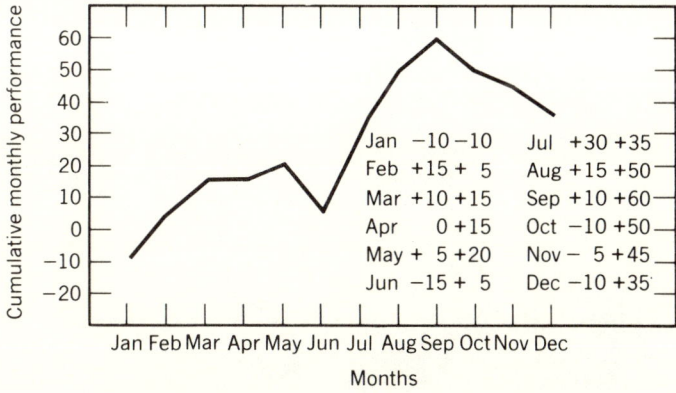

Jan	−10	−10	Jul	+30	+35
Feb	+15	+ 5	Aug	+15	+50
Mar	+10	+15	Sep	+10	+60
Apr	0	+15	Oct	−10	+50
May	+ 5	+20	Nov	− 5	+45
Jun	−15	+ 5	Dec	−10	+35

FIGURE 14.8 Cumulative monthly performance

uct, and servicing to consider. Besides, their goal is to remain in business over the long-run, not in brief, periodic business sessions. So too in the case of futures trading. The objective is to approach and operate it as a business.

INDIVIDUAL FUTURES SYSTEMS

There are as many individual systems as there are individuals. To construct an individual commodity system, a checklist must be established and compiled. One example is:

1. Amount of available capital
2. Amount of at-risk capital
3. Time commitment
4. Profit objective (reward/risk ratio)
5. Risk toleration (hedging, conservative, moderate, aggressive)
6. Type of approaches (computerized, fundamental, technical spread, arbitrage, or a combination of these four or other approaches)
7. Degree of diversification (or prohibition of certain futures)
8. Size of positions
9. Testing procedures
10. Assessment criteria (benchmarks to determine whether the program was successful)

Once the checklist is established, the process is straightforward. Items 1 to 8 are relatively simple to comply with. However, items 9 and 10 require greater effort. The important concept is to construct a system which will satisfy most, if not all, the established checkpoints.

15
Conditional Analysis

QUANTIFYING EXPECTATIONS

Conditional analysis is invaluable for improving the quality and the quantification of decision making. It enhances the performance of trading programs by forcing the probabilistic assignment of outcomes and their expected values. Unlike many gaming situations, whereby the participants have the knowledge of the game's parameters and underlying random processes available to them, the marketplace poses exceptional problems.

Research has shown that the generating functions for returns are not Gaussian. Moreover, they may be unique for the different futures, options, securities, and debt markets. The importance of this is that the random process is not known and the estimation of parameters requires specialized techniques. The accuracy of estimates given by ordinary regression analysis or other tools dependent on independent and normally distributed variables can be costly due to inaccurate expected values. To cope with this, nonparametric techniques are required.

One method to improve the estimation of expected values is Bayesian analysis. This method does not depend on a particular random generating process. Moreover, it absorbs observed data (information) into the evaluation model. Various statisticians have referred to this method as the theory of inverse probability or subjective probability.

There is an important amount of overlapping when analyzing market behavior and random processes. For example, the probability of a specific number appearing on a roulette wheel or die has been determined. Similarly, card games and lotteries can be evaluated on an expected value basis both from monetary and utility perspectives. Some casinos permit the playing of blackjack on a conditional basis though they will continue to pay on an adjusted unconditional one. Expressed differently, the house will permit card counting participants even though this approach improves the odds for the card-count-ing player relative to the expectations of the house. However, most casinos do not permit the activity; and, moreover, to confound exceptional card counters, the size of the playing deck is increased so that the distribution of playing cards occurs on a more nearly unconditional basis versus a conditional one. Similarly, the better bridge and pinochle players remember what cards were shown, played, and probably in the hands of the different players for each stage of the game. Even bidding techniques give astute players clues as to possible card holdings, particularly as the cards start to be displayed during the course of the game.

Likewise, business decisions are generally conditioned by the numbers, gut feelings, or past experiences. Sometimes these past experiences are suffi-cient to inform management as to the expected profitability of their various decisions. The best case of this is the insurance industry. By compiling data bases of the critical factors influencing payments, payouts, and the expected profit, they can determine whether or not specific policy underwritings are advisable for specific premium levels. The actuaries can compute the life ex-pectancy of various classes of individuals and then present premium-payout schedules. Although the actuaries may not know exactly who is going to die and at what precise moment, they have an excellent grasp of how many and by when. This same type of an approach is amenable to market analysis.

The quality of information and its correct applications should improve the decision-making process so as to enhance the expected rewards or reduce the expected risks. Although considerable academic research has postulated that expected returns equal the market returns, this is stated for the population and not necessarily for each sample. It has been shown that a firm cannot continue indefinitely to grow at a rate greater than that of the market, though certain organizations can and do for limited time periods. As a corollary, not all firms can exceed the market's return. It is understood that some decision makers are better at their positions than others and hence are more efficient. So too is the case with trading.

This chapter will now present several examples to define the concepts, and then delve into the more complex decision-making strategies.

For comparative analysis we will examine the attitudes and actions of two traders, designated TR1 and TR2. Although both have access to identical in-formation, they approach their trading decisions differently. TR1 assumes that the Eurodollar market is as likely to go up as to go down. For the moment, his empirical research indicates that the market's usual net daily change is equal to $500, or 20 points. TR2 agrees with the net daily change analysis but he initially perceives the market to be in an uptrend.

TR1's expected outcome is equal to zero because, as Figure 15.1 demon-strates, the up path is assigned a 50 percent chance of occurring, which is exactly equal to the 50 percent assignment for the down path.

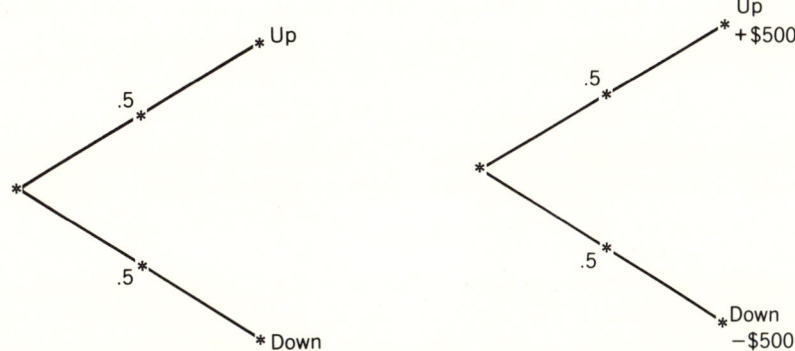

FIGURE 15.1 TR1 Bayesian path assignment   **FIGURE 15.2** TR1 Bayesian expected value

Figure 15.2 further develops this concept. Note the monetary expectation assigned to each path. Since each path is equally likely to achieve a $500 change in value, the simple mathematical evaluation becomes:

$$(.5)(+\$500) + (.5)(-\$500) = \text{TR1 expected value}$$

$$(+\$250) + (-\$250) \quad = 0$$

$$0 = \text{TR1 expected value}$$

TR2 has a different expectation. She looks for the market to work higher. Her subjective perception is that the market will go up 60 percent of the time and down 40 percent of the time. Moreover, she concurs with the empirical $500 net daily change parameter. TR2's 60 percent up and 40 percent down assignment is represented by Figure 15.3.

Proceeding with the analysis, note how Figure 15.4 portrays the direc-

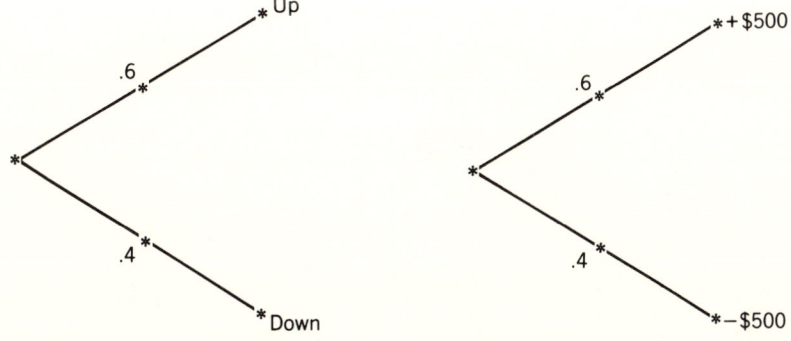

FIGURE 15.3 TR2 Bayesian path assignment   **FIGURE 15.4** TR2 Bayesian expected value

tional assignment and the different monetary assignment. Mathematically, Figure 15.4 has an expected value of +$100. This result is arrived by:

$$(.6) (+\$500) + (.4) (-\$500) = \text{TR2 expected value}$$
$$(+\$300) + (-\$200) \quad = +\$100$$
$$+\$100 \quad = \text{TR2 expected value}$$

Of course, both can be wrong not only in terms of the true net daily change estimates but in terms of the market's directional expectations. For example, TR1 views an uptrend as being a 50 percent prospect, while TR2 views the uptrend prospects as being 60 percent. Subsequent data reveal that the actual trend for the next 20 trading days was down. The relative frequency of up days was only 7 out of 20, or 35 percent, while the down days occurred 13 out of 20 times, or 65 percent of the time. Moreover, the daily net change worked out to be $400. This state of affairs appears as Figure 15.5.

The expected value of a long position works out to be:

$$(.35) (+\$400) + (.65) (-\$400) =$$
$$(+\$140) + (-\$260) \quad = -\$120$$

per day or −$2,400 over the period of 20 days. The latter loss is calculated by:

$$(7) (+\$400) + (13) (-\$400) = \text{expected value for long position}$$
$$(+2,800) + (-\$5,200) \quad = -\$2,400$$
$$-\$2,400 \quad = \text{for 20-day period}$$

By analyzing each decision and its subsequent path, a trader can continuously revise or maintain an outlook. The Bayesian approach accommodates

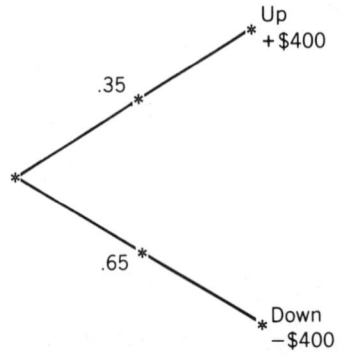

FIGURE 15.5 Subsequent evaluation

this updating capability and, in fact, is an integral part of the adaptive methodology.

To initiate the Bayesian approach, the decision maker surmises the probabilities of the occurrence of the events, such as up market and down market. Here there are two states; conditions or possible events. However, the probability assignment need not be limited to two paths. They can be three, four, or as many as practicable. For example, the traders now consider three possible outcomes:

1. Up market direction
2. Neutral—consolidating market direction
3. Down market direction

Once again TR1 thinks that all directional conditions are identical in probabilistic occurrence. Thus he assigns each potential outcome path a one-third or .333 + probability of occurring. TR2 now evaluates the problem as a 60 percent chance of an up market, a 10 percent chance of a consolidating market and a 30 percent chance of being a down market. Notice that in all cases the assignment of the prior probabilities totaled 1.00 or 100 percent. For cases where it is certain an event will occur, then a probability of 1.00 would seem to be in order; but then this expectational approach would not be necessary. Conversely, conditions that certainly would not occur would be assigned 0 or no chance of happening. Again this assignment is not necessary or acceptable.

Figure 15.6 presents TR1's expectations in diagram form.

Notice the one-third chance of occurrence for each directional outcome. Additionally, to simplify the valuation, up or down swings are expected to be of a magnitude of $600, while a consolidating market entails a negative out-

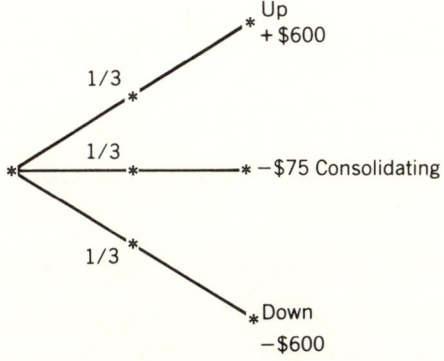

FIGURE 15.6 TR1's expectations

come of \$75 due to transaction and monitoring costs. The expected value is then:

$$(\tfrac{1}{3})\,(+\$600) + (\tfrac{1}{3})\,(-\$75) + (\tfrac{1}{3})\,(-\$600) = \text{TR1 expected value}$$

$$(+\$200) + (-\$25) \quad + (-\$200) \quad\quad = -\$25$$

$$-\$25 \quad\quad\quad = \text{TR1 expected value}$$

TR2's new expectation is represented by Figure 15.7.
Her evaluation now becomes:

$$(.60)\,(+\$600) + (.10)\,(-\$75) + (.30)\,(-\$600) = \text{TR2 expected value}$$

$$(+\$360) + (-\$7.50) \quad + (-\$180) \quad\quad = +\$172.50$$

$$+\$172.50 \quad\quad = \text{TR2 expected value}$$

Once again, TR2 has a positive expected value, but this time TR1 actually would have had a negative one had he decided to participate.

This expectational approach can be applied easily to hedging decisions. In addition to ascertaining price level directional moves, the hedger would evaluate the directional basis moves. The logic is the same, only the variables are different.

Take the example of a pension fund manager who seeks to protect an inventory of corporate bonds. For the moment, we will not consider the "appropriate" hedge ratio; but rather, for simplicity, we will assume a unit approach. That is one futures contract per \$100,000 par value. For actual hedging the optimal hedge ratio should be considered since it does make a difference as to the goodness-of-fit for the overall hedge.

Table 15.1 lists the expected paths with the attendant probabilities and dollar outcomes.

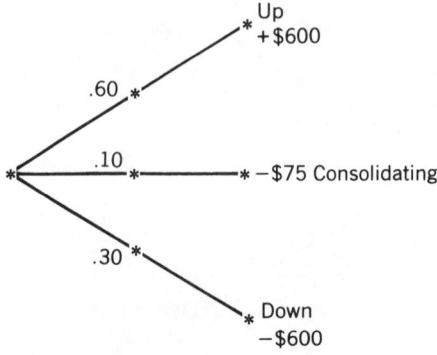

FIGURE 15.7 TR2's expectations

TABLE 15.1. EXPECTATIONS OF BOND BASIS BEHAVIOR

Behavior	Prior Probability of Occurrence	Basis Point Change	Basis Point Dollar Impact	Expected Dollar Impact
Most favorable	.05	+10	+312.50	+15.62
Favorable	.55	+8	+250.00	+137.50
Neutral	.15	0	0	0
Negative	.15	−4	−125.00	−18.75
Most negative	.10	−8	−312.50	−31.25
	1.00			$103.12

Graphically, the contents of Table 15.1 appear in Figure 15.8. Notice that by summing the values in column 2 the total probability of 1.00 is achieved, while the summing of the expected values for each path is identical to summing the values in column 5 of Table 15.1.

The information provided by Table 15.1 and Figure 15.8 complement the hedging process. The most immediate task is to define the evaluated risks and then to determine an optimal hedging strategy. This problem has two separate parts: overall expected value risks and the expected basis risks. As was demonstrated earlier, even unfavorable basis behavior can reduce the overall risk level for a firm by transforming a substantial portion of the value or price level risk to the more manageable basis risk. By more clearly identifying the major influences on the trading decision process, a trader can operate more efficiently with reduced levels of risk.

TEMPORAL ANALYSIS

By extending the time horizon for the present format, we will arrive at a temporal approach to decision making. Here, the temporal ordering of events generates new possible outcomes for our two traders.

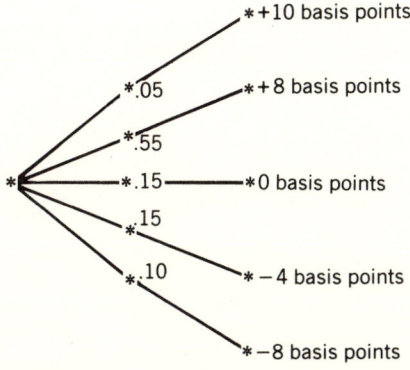

FIGURE 15.8 Pension manager's expectations

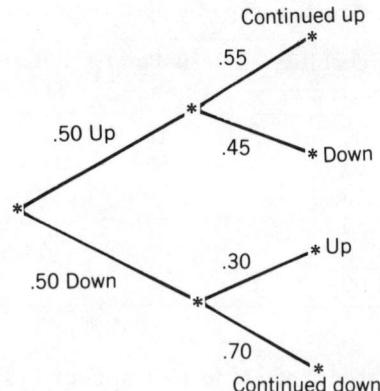

FIGURE 15.9 TR1's temporal analysis example

Let's examine TR1 again. Although he initially believes one directional outcome is as likely as another, he also thinks that the first observed directional change—be it daily, weekly, monthly, or whatever time frame, filter or other indicator—is a harbinger of things to come. If the first change is up, he modifies his expectations, leading him to think that subsequent up movements will occur 55 percent of the time and the down moves only 45 percent of the time. Additionally, should the first change be down, he thinks the subsequent changes will have a downward bias of 70 percent and an upward bias of 30 percent. Graphically, this appears as Figure 15.9.

It is important to note that the assignment of probabilities for all paths departing from a decision event denoted by asterisk equal 1.00, or 100 percent. Subsequent paths, like the initial departure paths, need not be limited to only two possible occurrences. Furthermore, the decision tree need not be symmetrical. It is the province of the trader/analyst to ascertain the alternative outcomes and the attendant probabilities.

Given the assigned probabilities, TR1 now wants to evaluate the probability of an up market. The evaluative process becomes:

$$P(UU)_1 = P(U)P(U\ U) \quad \text{(Part 1)}$$
$$= (.50)\ (.55)$$
$$= .275$$

$$P(UD)_1 = P(U)P(D\ U) \quad \text{(Part 2)}$$
$$= (.50)\ (.45)$$
$$= .225$$

$$P(DU)_1 = P(D)P(U\ D) \quad \text{(Part 3)}$$
$$= (.50)\ (.30)$$
$$= .15$$

$$P(DD)_1 = P(D)P(D \ D) \quad \text{(Part 4)}$$

$$= (.50)(.70)$$

$$= .35$$

Part 1 represents the probability of an up market given the sequences of two upward changes. Part 2 represents the probability of a down market given an initial upward change. Part 3 represents the probability of an initial downward change. Part 4 represents the probability of a down market given an initial downward change and a subsequent downward confirmation.

Thus TR1's probabilities perception of an upward market becomes:

$$P(\text{Up})_1 = \text{Part 1} + \text{Part 3}$$

$$P(\text{Up})_1 = (.275) + (.15)$$

$$P(\text{Up})_1 = .425$$

and his probability perception of a downward market becomes:

$$P(\text{Down})_1 = \text{Part 2} + \text{Part 4}$$

$$P(\text{Down})_1 = (.225) + (.35)$$

$$P(\text{Down})_1 = .575$$

Again the unitary overall probability of 1.00 is established when one adds the probability of the upward and downward markets.

For TR2, the upward probabilistic expectation is that, given an initial upward change, the market is now expected to follow through 70 percent and to fail or go down 30 percent of the time. Additionally, if the initial change

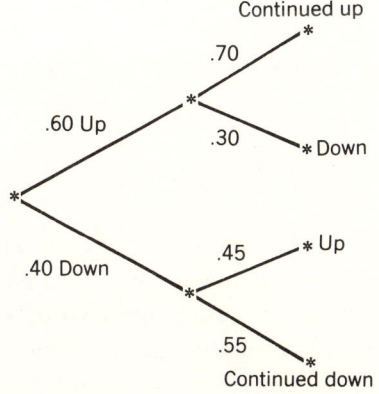

FIGURE 15.10 TR2's temporal analysis example

was down, then she expects the subsequent chance of an up market to be 45 percent and the chance of a subsequent downward move to be 55 percent. Graphically, this appears as Figure 15.10.

TR2's evaluation of the constituent up and down market probabilities becomes:

$$P(UU)_2 = P(U)P(UU) \quad \text{(Part 1)}$$
$$= (.60)(.70)$$
$$= .42$$
$$P(UD)_2 = P(U)P(DU) \quad \text{(Part 2)}$$
$$= (.60)(.30)$$
$$= .18$$
$$P(DU)_2 = P(D)P(UD) \quad \text{(Part 3)}$$
$$= (.40)(.45)$$
$$= (.18)$$
$$P(DD)_2 = P(D)P(DD) \quad \text{(Part 4)}$$
$$= (.40)(.55)$$
$$= (.22)$$

Therefore TR2's overall up market expectation on a temporal basis is:

$$P(Up)_2 = \text{Part 1} + \text{Part 3}$$
$$P(Up)_2 = (.42) + (.18)$$
$$P(Up)_2 = .60$$

and her overall downward market expectation is:

$$P(Down)_2 = \text{Part 2} + \text{Part 4}$$
$$P(Down)_2 = (.18) + (.22)$$
$$P(Down)_2 = .40$$

It is evident that, given the temporal horizon, TR1 now has an overall negative bias; whereas, TR2 continues to exhibit a positive bias towards the market. A simple comparison of their respective upward—P(UP)—probabilities and downward—P(Down)—probabilities confirms this.

INTERVENING EVENTS

Intervening events means that, when a recognizable event occurs, its associated probabilities are immediately interjected into the decision making process. Examples of these events could be:

1. Freezes
2. Limit moves
3. Specified point or dollar swing for the given futures
4. Cumulative adverse behavior in the basis
5. Key reversal day
6. Discount rate change
7. Attractive arbitrage differential
8. Other designated important event

These intervening events can be ranked ordinally, with the event with the greatest perceived impact implemented first. Or, depending on how complex the decision-making process is, all designated events can be absorbed, thereby conditionalizing the overall expectation.

To visualize this, consider Figures 15.11a and 15.11b.

Figure 15.11a represents a pre-intervening event decision tree, whereas Figure 15.11b represents a post-intervening event decision tree. What initially appeared favorable for continued stock price appreciation now signals

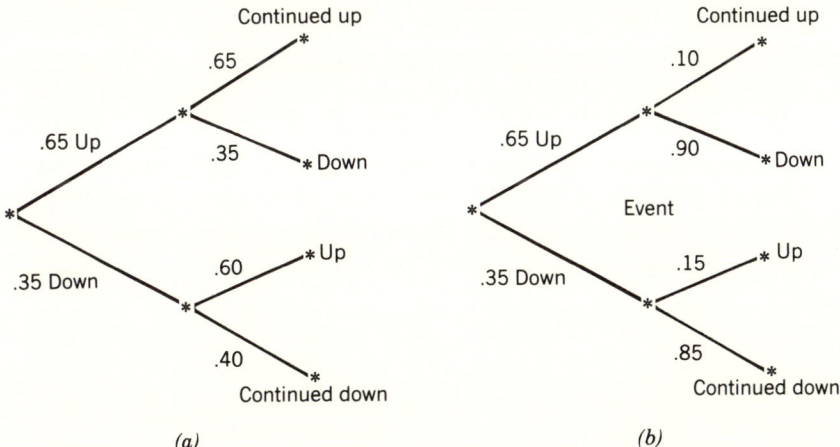

(a)   *(b)*

FIGURE 15.11 (a) Preintervening event decision tree and (b) postintervening event decision tree

at the very least extreme caution and, probabilistically, a strong downward bias.

By evaluating the probability for both figures it is seen that the overall 63 percent prospect of an upward market abruptly changed to a conditionalized 86 percent chance for a downward move. It is interesting to note that should the trader not have participated in the upward move but only made a decision at the time after the intervening event his or her probabilistic expectation would be significantly better since there was no weighting by the previous probabilities. Expressed differently, this trader only took a position after an important event and his or her temporal exposure in the marketplace was more limited. This trader's behavior shows he or she does not think it necessary to be in the market at all—or even most of the time. However, various financial institutions or other enterprises may find it impossible to stop positioning, underwriting, or investing. They may have a host of regulatory and internal restrictions as to placement and divestitures, and thus must maintain a position. Similarly, the bullion environment may be such that sales are expected to be weak. This does not imply a complete termination of business until a more optimistic climate exists, but it can imply a reduction in production and inventory levels.

The ramifications of this during times of greater expected risk for traders are that hedge coverage may be expected to increase during times of greater expected risk and to diminish during expectations of more favorable times.

PRIOR PROBABILITIES

The assignment of prior probabilities is the first step in constructing a decision tree and implementing the Bayesian framework. The beauty of the Bayesian procedure is that it is operable even though prior information may be sparse or nonexistent. For the latter case, assignment of prior probabilities can be completely subjective and still be statistically acceptable. If some information exists, this can be introduced into the decision making process. When data become available their absorption into the evaluative model refines the overall expected probability distribution. Significant attributes of this are:

1. A little information can go a long way
2. Better defined distributions, better expected values
3. The probabilistic updating generally results in a near approximation of the underlying distribution function

TABLE 15.2. SMALL SAMPLE MODIFYING
PRIOR INFORMATION

Observation Number	Observations Y_i
1	0.699
2	0.320
3	−0.799
4	−0.927
5	0.373
6	−0.648
7	1.572
8	−0.319
9	2.049
10	−3.077

Where the sample mean is $\frac{1}{10} y_i = -.0757$

Source: Arnold Zellner, *An Introduction to Bayesian Inference in Econometrics,* Wiley, New York, 1971.

To see the importance of this, consider Table 15.2. The observations easily could be rates of return or change. They could also be estimates of other data.

Graphically, Figure 15.12 portrays the rapid compression of revised expectations given a likelihood-modified prior probability distribution.

RELATIVE FREQUENCIES

Relative frequencies are empirically derived. They are the actual occurrence of observations related to sample size. Symbolically this would be:

$$rf_i = \sum o_i/n.$$

This means that a given observation of a specified class would be weighted relative to the size of the sample. For example, consider the following changes in price for the June S&P futures as presented in Table 15.3.

Although probabilities are the theoretical values for a particular distribution, relative frequencies can be used as a surrogate to help define the shape and structure of an unknown and, preferably, stable distribution. In fact, as sample size increases, the relative frequencies take on the shape of the underlying distribution and therefore more nearly approximate its true nature. This is indicated by $f(x_i) \rightarrow P(x_i)$ as i approaches infinity.

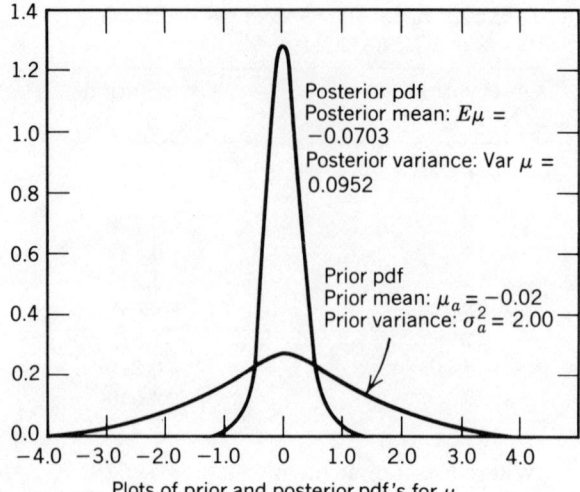

Plots of prior and posterior pdf's for μ.

FIGURE 15.12 Rapid compression of revised expectations given likelihood-modified prior probability (*Source:* Arnold Zellner, *An Introduction to Bayesian Inference in Econometrics,* Wiley, New York, 1971)

LIKELIHOODS

Likelihoods refer to the probability of an event conditional to the sample's observations. The likelihood function refines the prior probabilities in a multiplicative manner. The result is referred to as the posterior probability. The importance of the likelihood function is that it "conditions" the model by applying observed data to the initially conceived framework. It is a crucial com-

TABLE 15.3. RELATIVE CLASS FREQUENCIES FOR S&P FUTURES (HYPOTHETICAL CHANGES)

Change in Points	Occurrences	Relative Frequency	Percent
−400 or more	5	$\frac{5}{100}$	5
−395 to −300	4	$\frac{4}{100}$	4
−295 to −200	11	$\frac{11}{100}$	11
−195 to −100	12	$\frac{12}{100}$	12
−95 to 0	27	$\frac{27}{100}$	27
+5 to +100	22	$\frac{22}{100}$	22
+105 to +200	11	$\frac{11}{100}$	11
+205 to +300	5	$\frac{5}{100}$	5
+305 or more	3	$\frac{3}{100}$	3
Totals	100	$\frac{100}{100}$	100

ponent to the Bayesian approach as it revises the early prior estimates which could have been extremely vague and quickly improves the state of knowledge about the underlying forces prevailing upon the evaluation model.

It should be noted that for distributions which have definable parameters, maximum likelihood functions can be established and solved for parameter estimates. (This concept is more fully explained in most advanced statistical texts and need not be pursued any further here. It should only be understood that there is substantial theoretical work and proofs that validate this concept, enabling the analyst/trader to construct models more comfortably.)

Portfolio Considerations

The portfolio considerations of this are several. First, should the underlying distributions be similar among each other as far as the various portfolio elements are concerned, then there is greater confidence in analyzing common statistical approaches to evaluating the portfolio in its entirety. However, should the processes vary in a statistically significant sense, then the common terms of covariation and covariance matrices take on a dubious meaning and are suspect. The problem need not be insurmountable if nonparametric methods are applied to analyze specified situations.

DECISION THEORY APPROACHES

There is voluminous material on decision theory, the classic being, *The Theory of Games and Economic Behavior*, by John Von Neumann and Oskar Morgenstern. The literature provides frameworks that demonstrate the maximization of expected returns is not always pursued; and, in fact, can be detrimental to an organization since often the maximum profit can only be attained with an inordinate amount of risk.

The previously analyzed Bayesian approach is appropriate with this more generalized approach. Taking the example of coffee, consider a payoff matrix which reflects freeze and nonfreeze conditions. Again TR1 and TR2 will assess the situation. TR1 thinks that a freeze in Brazilian coffee growing regions is as likely as not. Thus he assigns a 50 percent chance to both weather conditions. For him the problem appears as Table 15.4.

TABLE 15.4. FREEZE PAYOFF MATRIX

Prediction	Freeze	No Freeze
Freeze	+$18,750	−$3,750
No freeze	+$22,500	−$750

The value for trading freeze scares is:

$(.50) (+\$18,750) + (.50) (-\$3,750) =$ expected value of freeze for Trader 1

$(+\$9,375)$ $+ (-\$1,875)$

$+\$7,500$

TR2, a subscriber to a private weather service, learns that there is only a 20 percent chance of a hard freeze and an 80 percent chance of no freeze. Thus her informed expected value assessment becomes:

$(.20) (+\$18,750) + (.80) (-\$3,750) =$ expected value of freeze for Trader 2

$(+\$3,750)$ $+ (-\$3,000)$

$+\$750$

Although TR2 has a position expected value as does TR1, TR1 thinks that the trade is worth substantially more than TR2 does.

Curiously though rationally, the second part of each matrix has the highest expected payoff. Since markets tend to discount the prevailing sentiment, the reasonable chance of a freeze builds a premium into the price; but, should the weather prove otherwise (no freeze), then the crop price is adjusted not only by the recently acquired preevent freeze premium but also there is now one day less of potential freeze damage. Weather sensitive commodities often have critical calendar periods. Should weather conditions not be severe, these markets quickly adjust in the earlier part of the weather sensitive period, since then the prices for the crops or supplies are not subject to sharp adjustments in availabilities. As each day passes without actual incident, the prior demand has either been satisfied or the quality and crop size have been partially guaranteed due to harvest, thus reducing the overall exposure on daily and cumulative bases.

Additionally, the unexpected occurrence of a freeze causes a more dramatic movement in prices and expected values since a preevent premium is not particularly built into the prices. Additionally, the lack of a freeze only causes an ordinary attrition in prices.

Here, the expected value for TR1 of a no-freeze strategy would be:

$(.50) (+\$22,500) + (.50) (-\$750) =$

$(+\$11,250)$ $+ (-\$375)$ $=$

$+\$10,875$

while TR2's expectation would be:

$$(.20)\,(+\$22{,}500) + (.80)\,(-\$750) =$$
$$(+\$4{,}500) \qquad + (-\$600) \qquad =$$
$$+\$3{,}900$$

In Table 15.5, the raw range is the initial range value for freeze/no freeze occurrences. The adjusted value is the .50 weighting adjustment for both events for TR1. The adjusted informed outlook reflects the value of the weather forecast's conditioning on TR2's expectations. If she had no weather expectation, her valuation would have been equal to TR1's outlook. Notice the reduction in TR2's expected range variability to the value of information.

These two traders have demonstrated that unexpected payoffs can be higher than commonly "expected" ones. The value of information dramatically alters the expected value for each while potentially reducing its variability. The early assignment of values can be grossly inaccurate, impairing the entire evaluative process and of course presenting a seriously distorted outlook of both the expected and actual realities of the marketplace. These distortions can usually be reduced with subsequent information, thereby validating this method.

DETERMINING THE INDIFFERENCE PROBABILITY

After examining Table 15.6, at what point is a trader indifferent as to whether to buy bonds or S&P futures? One approach considers the probability of an event's occurrence. For our example, depending how high or low the probability of an oil price cut is, the trader's expected value for each position varies in that, given a probability of an oil price cut of greater than 50 percent, the trader should buy the S&P since the expected value is then greater than that of the bonds. Otherwise, the better choice is the other position. At a probability of exactly 50 percent, the trader here is indifferent.

TABLE 15.5. EXPECTED VALUES OF RANGES

	Raw	Adjusted
Uninformed outlook (TR1)	$23,250	$11,625
Informed outlook (TR2)	$23,250	$5,100

TABLE 15.6. BOND VERSUS S&P FUTURES

	Oil Price Change		
	Yes	No	
Buy bonds	+$4,000	+$1,000	$5,000/2 = +$2,500
Buy S&P futures	+$3,500	+$1,500	$5,000/2 − +$2,500

The evaluative mechanism for the expected value of a T-bond futures purchase is:

$$4,000p + 1,000 (1 - p) \quad =$$
$$4,000p + 1,000 - 1,000p =$$
$$3,000p + 1,000$$

While the mechanism for the expected value of the S&P futures is:

$$3,500p + 1,500 (1 - p) \quad =$$
$$3,500p + 1,500 - 1,500p =$$
$$2,000p + 1,500$$

And by equating the two evaluative expressions, the indifference probability is:

$$3,000p + 1,000 = 2,000p + 1,500$$
$$1,000p = 500$$
$$p = 500/1,000$$
$$p = .50$$

Therefore if the trader assumes a price cut is equally likely to happen as not, then he or she can statistically (in a Bayesian sense) be equally as comfortable buying either the bonds or stock futures; but if there is an economi-

TABLE 15.7. BOND VERSUS S&P FUTURES: OIL PRICE CHANGE

	.70 Yes	.30 No	
Buy bonds	$2,800	$300	$3100/2 = $1,550
Buy S&P futures	$2,250	$450	$2700/2 = $1,350

TABLE 15.8. BOND VERSUS S&P FUTURES: OIL PRICE CHANGE

	.51 Yes	.49 No	
Buy bonds	$2,040	$490	$2530/2 = $1,765
Buy S&P futures	$1,785	$735	$2520/2 = $1,760

TABLE 15.9. BOND VERSUS S&P FUTURES: OIL PRICE CHANGE

	.49 Yes	.51 No	
Buy bonds	$1,960	$510	$2,470/2 = $1,235
Buy S&P futures	$1,715	$765	$2,480/2 = $1,240

TABLE 15.10. BOND VERSUS S&P FUTURES: OIL PRICE CHANGE

	.30 Yes	.70 No	
Buy bonds	$1,200	$700	$1,900/2 = $ 950
Buy S&P futures	$1,050	$1,050	$2,100/2 = $1,050

cally feasible way to determine that probability of a price cut/no price cut then the trader should assign the respective probabilities and isolate the better trade. Tables 15.7, 15.8, 15.9, and 15.10 present four different probabilistic evaluations.

OPTIONS VERSUS OUTRIGHT POSITIONING

This example evaluates whether to trade options or futures within a probabilistic framework. The trader is faced with a situation of central bank intervention versus no intervention. Table 15.11 represents the alternatives of trading Japanese yen futures or options.

The evaluative mechanism is:

Probability for Futures Probability for Options

$$3,000p - 1,000 (1 - p) \quad = 2,000p - 500 (1 - p)$$
$$3,000p - 1,000 + 1,000p \quad = 2,000p - 500 + 500p$$
$$4,000p - 1,000 \quad = 2,500p - 500$$
$$+1,500p \quad = +500$$
$$p \quad = 500/1,500$$
$$p \quad = 1/3$$

TABLE 15.11. FUTURES VERSUS OPTIONS EVALUATIVE FRAMEWORK: IMPLICIT 50–50 OCCURRENCES

	Intervention	No Intervention	Expected Value
Futures	+$3,000	−$1,000	+$1,000
Options	+$2,000	−$500	+$750

TABLE 15.12. OPTIONS PREFERRED ALTERNATIVE

	25% Intervention	75% No Intervention	Conditional Expected Value
Futures	+$750	−$750	0
Options	+$500	−$375	+$125

TABLE 15.13. FUTURES PREFERRED ALTERNATIVE

	75% Intervention	25% No Intervention	Conditionalized Expected Value
Futures	−$2,250	−$250	+$2,000
Options	+$1,500	−$125	+$1,375

Therefore if the probability of intervention is greater than $\frac{1}{3}$ or .333+ percent, the rule would be to trade the futures versus the options. If the probability is less than $\frac{1}{3}$ or .333+ percent, then options would be preferred to futures. Tables 15.12 and 15.13 present two such cases.

OBSERVATIONS

The previous examples indicate that equal prior expected values do not imply indifference to the selection of a trade. Recalling the oil price cut situation, the trader was confronted between choosing T-bonds or S&P futures. Only by applying conditional analysis was a criterion established and the appropriate trade selected.

The simple application of expected values or return risk criteria do not necessarily provide acceptable decision making rules in and of themselves. The futures versus options case demonstrated that the futures had the higher raw expected value and a 3-to-1 profit-to-risk ratio, while options had a lower expected value but a higher reward to risk (4-to-1) ratio. When a probabilistic assignment was applied, the trading rule was established indicating that options were preferable for some conditions and futures for the remainder.

NONPARAMETRIC ANALYSIS

The interdependence among observed data for many economic time series adversely affects the straightforward application of standard parametric statistical techniques. Two important reasons for this are that these series often exhibit nonrandomness tendencies and they are not generated by a simple normal distribution process.

There are several methods of coping with these facts. They are:

1. Define the underlying distribution process
2. Transform the data so that its transformation acceptably approximates normally distributed characteristics or those for other readily definable distributions
3. Apply nonparametric techniques

The first method entails a high level of statistical proficiency. The data can be so unstationary or unstable that two separate and distinct time intervals for the same series can produce significantly different parameter estimates, such as mean, variance, and skewness. This method is the most time consuming of the three. Its primary advantage is that the potential isolation and definitive specification of the underlying random process can yield superior estimates for subsequent expected value analysis.

The transformation of data is reasonably easy and statistically supportable. Often a simple transformation can change a problematical series into a neatly behaving one. Additionally, simple transformations often eliminate nonlinearity, observational interdependence, or impart suitable, normally distributed properties. By transforming the salient series, the application of regression and other similarly based analytical techniques becomes justifiable. The analyst can assume a fairly comfortable level of confidence in the reliability of the statistical analyses and forecasts.

The third method is the most straightforward. It makes very few assumptions about the nature of the time series. For example, it does not presuppose normality, independence among the observations and, depending on technique, can work with the three basic classifications of data. These are: nominal, ordinal, and cardinal listings. Of the three methodologies, applying nonparametric techniques is the most versatile, but it has a major disadvantage. It loses specificity. This drawback arises since the approach eventually ignores the specific numerical information in a given time series and typically supplants that numerical content with an ordering arrangement or assignment of + or − runs.

This drawback can be a temporary one as the analysis can produce results which are incorporable for subsequent analyses. Also, for many purposes a violation of a distributive continuity assumption is a minor one and does not materially affect the conclusions.

Earlier in the text, nonparametric cyclical and trend analysis techniques were presented (see Chapters 6, Cyclical Analysis, and 12, Testing). This chapter's earlier material offered a framework for establishing departure points and enhancing modeling efforts. We will now survey other related topics.

FRACTILES

Fractiles represent specified fragments of a distribution. The three most common cases are: percentiles, deciles, and quartiles. Typically, they are used to locate a median value or, when differenced, to establish a dispersion statistic. Their importance is to reflect data intervals in a satisfactory manner. For large numbers of observations whereby small fractiles are most suitable, the percentile approach is best. If data are limited, then the decile or quartile approaches may be better. Essentially, they can be used to establish a framework to test probability distributions or classified data against theoretical versus expected values, or one group against another. Standard techniques are chi-square and Kolmogorov-Smirnov tests.

PERCENTILES

There are 99 percentiles. Percentile 1 reflects 1 percent of the observed or theoretical data. At percentile 2, 2 percent of the data is contained. This progression continues until the 99th percentile above which 1 percent of the data is contained. The 50th percentile is equal to the median. As far as dispersion is concerned the differences between any two percentiles represents a percentage of data. For example, percentile 7 minus percentile 2 reflects that 5 percent of the observations.

DECILES

There are 9 deciles. At decile 1, 10 percent of the data is contained; at decile 3, 30 percent of the data is contained; and at decile 9, 90 percent of the data is below it and 10 percent of the data is above it. Decile 5 is the median since half the values fall below it and half above it. As with percentiles, any differencing between decile values accounts for a dispersion statistic.

QUARTILES

There are three quartiles. At quartile 1, 25 percent of the data is contained; at quartile 2, 50 percent of the data is contained. It is also the median value. At quartile 3, 75 percent of the data is accounted for and above quartile 3 the remaining 25 percent occurs. The frequently used interquartile dispersion statistic is simply quartile 3 minus quartile 1; or in other words, 50 percent of the data is dispersed within one quartile about the median. For distributions which have nonsymmetrical attributes, this dispersion statistic is very useful. For symmetrical distributions, the median and the mean are identical; for others, the median can be more representative of the central location parameter.

For unstable distribution processes, the median and some statistically satisfactory dispersion statistic, such as, the interquartile range, can be more relevant than the commonly applied mean variance approach. This is due to the fact that the median can exhibit greater stability than the mean statistic; while fluctuations about the central value area can be better described by a more general dispersion standard.

16
Trading Programs

OPTIMAL TRADING SYSTEMS

The multitude of trading programs requires a selection process to identify the one program, or combination of programs, most suitable. One analogy to this is a baseball team. The manager tries to select the optimum combination of long ball, consistent hitting, and pitching to field a winning team. The material presented in Chapter 12, Testing, provided a framework to assist in this determination. The quantitative procedure is the same, but the focus is different. When the testing of techniques and parameters is satisfactorily completed, then the manager goes about simulating the expectational profitability-risk of specific techniques, parameters, and trading rules and implementing them into an unified system. He or she already has the quantitative results on a technique-by-technique basis. Likewise, the manager knows the past expectational outcomes for various parameters and rules for each technique. However, the overall unified impact or results are still in doubt. The case of maximum individual technique and parameter arrangement selections does not necessarily mean that on an unified system's basis the results will also be maximized. In fact, a collection of maximum individual performers can produce a highly erratic, unstable system. Excellent results for Treasury bills, notes, and bonds trading do not necessarily have very favorable reward-risk characteristics when combined into a three-commodity trading program. More often than not, the favorable operating conditions coincide for each; but equally important, would unfavorable conditions be evident concurrently. Thus it is important to test various combinations of individually satisfactory techniques, parameters, rules, and futures as a unified portfolio to establish historical reward-risk characteristics as a unified portfolio.

SINGULAR APPROACHES

In the simple case, this is the use of one technique and parameter arrangement for one future. It can be generalized to the application of a single technique with identical parameters and rules for more than one futures market. The major assumption here is that a technique and similar parameters and rules operate as well if not better for all futures during all phases of market behavior than more conditionalized specifications. In other words, the singular specification assumes that it works equally well in bull markets, bear markets, or protracted trading phases.

COMPOSITE APPROACHES

This perspective assumes that a trading program is constructed by using different techniques, parameters, and rules not only for various futures but even for one specific future itself. One instance of this is the layering tactic of trading or building positions. This is conceptually distinct from the scaling placement of orders. Different techniques and different parameters can give widely varying timing signals for the initiation or liquidation of positions. An example of this is the use of one technique but varying parameters. The variety of parameters can in effect make the approach short-, intermediate-, and long-term in timing. The operator using a weekly interval technique may buy one unit on a close above the 2-week highs, a second unit on a close above the 5-week highs, and the third unit on a close above the 12-week highs. The main point is that all the trading activity is not governed by the occurrence of just one timing event. Hence the entire position is less likely to be subject to sporadic whipsawing. Another aspect of composite trading approaches is the use of different rules, parameters, or techniques for the various phases, such as uptrend, downtrend, and consolidating markets.

Of course, the definition of the different phases requires a framework, preferably a quantitative one. One mathematical tool that offers promise of this identification of bullish, bearish, or indeterminate markets is discriminant analysis and its nonparametric complement, neighbor analysis. These procedures attempt to distinguish the principal quantitative factors prevalent during the phases in question. They have been very useful in establishing criteria for credit worthiness, the likelihood of bankruptcy, and classification of groups.

Composite trading approaches recognize there is no one best way to trade a spectrum of funds especially for many clients and organizations. Equity, risk, and opportunity characteristics can be substantially different among traders, thus warranting the application of uniting several approaches.

CONTRACT SPECIFICATION

This is not as simple as it initially appears. The choice of contract month in agricultural/livestock futures can cause a trader to be in the old or the new crop. For other types of futures, such as the financials and the currencies, the importance of the slope and potential change in the slope of the yield curve can have important bearing on which month to choose. Additionally, the trader must pick an acceptable delivery month that has adequate value or open interest to comfortably initiate and liquidate his or her positions. Some futures, such as livestock and currencies, have an overwhelming proportion of the open interest in the nearby or two nearest delivery months. For other futures, the proportion of open interest is still favored towards the nearby, but a somewhat higher proportion occurs in the more deferred months.

Hedgers need to match their requirements against available delivery months, or to comply with contractual stipulations for subsequent cash transactions predicated on the futures market.

Premiums and discounts can also have a bearing as to which month to trade. Generally speaking, it is usually better to buy discounted months and sell the premium months. In a simplistic trading approach, this can be operationally difficult. If there were an assumption about the underlying major trend, this problematic condition can be minimized. Moreover, if the manager were correct in his or her judgment, the losses from losing trades could be minimized since the occurrence of shifts between ordinary carrying charge markets and inverted markets are usually dictated by greater swings in the price of the spot or nearby months as opposed to concurrent but smaller swings in the more deferred months. This would be the case since bullish markets generally become inverted ones while a change in underlying trend causes a return to an ordinary carrying charge situation.

There is a word of caution. The precious metals, currencies, and potato futures markets have actually responded in reverse fashion. However, for the first two, the maximum, feasible departure in intermonth differences has been restrained primarily by interest rate differentials, or economically full carrying charges. Movements beyond the economic boundaries established for these futures prompts arbitraging forces forward to restrain effectively the extent of magnitude of growth in intermonth differences, going from the nearest to the most distant available month.

Rollovers, or switching the position from one delivery month to another, require analysis. It can happen that the manager correctly determined and positioned himself in a market move. Assuming the manager bought a future in a month which initially was at a discount to others, that with the passage of time not only did the market advance but also its structure shifted from that of carrying charges to one of inversion. If he determined that the trend

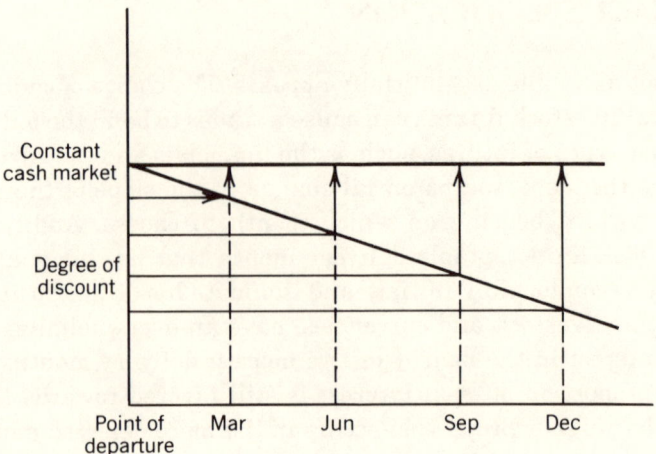

FIGURE 16.1 Constant cash market and degree of discount

was still up, but for various reasons had to liquidate his holdings in which probably became a nearby month, he would likely be better off rolling over his position into a similar, though discounted, delivery. One economic rationale for this is that if nothing changed fundamentally, the more deferred, discounted month would approach the level of the cash market with the passage of time. Figure 16.1 shows this. As can be seen from this figure, each progressive month rose to the cash market level as the delivery month became spot. Particularly note that the deferred months were at greater discounts as shown by their early discounts or distances from the constant cash market line. It is important to recognize that the greater the initial discount, the greater potential appreciation. To further understand this, examine Figure 16.2.

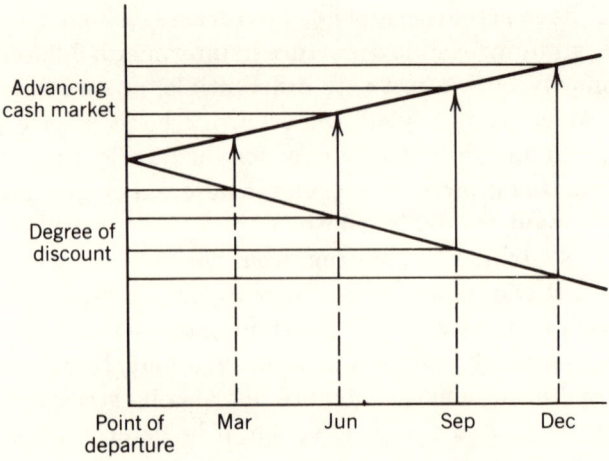

FIGURE 16.2 Advancing cash market and degree of discount

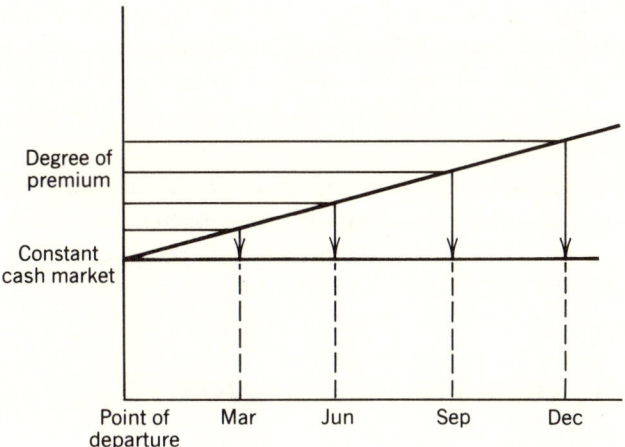

FIGURE 16.3 Constant cash market and degree of premium

Again notice how each deferred month rises to the prevailing cash market level, and equals it at expiration time. Although the slopes govern how quickly money could have been made in these cases, the absolute differences (distances) dictated how much could have been made. Before examining a bearish scenario, it is important to remember that transactional costs also influence this delivery contract selection process. Generally, if the differences are greater that the transactional costs of chosing one month over another, then the appropriately differenced (discount/premium) delivery month should be considered. If this were not the case, substantial arbitrage profits would have been available though not reaped. Conversely, in bearishly perceived conditions, the approach would have been the opposite. Figure 16.3 shows this.

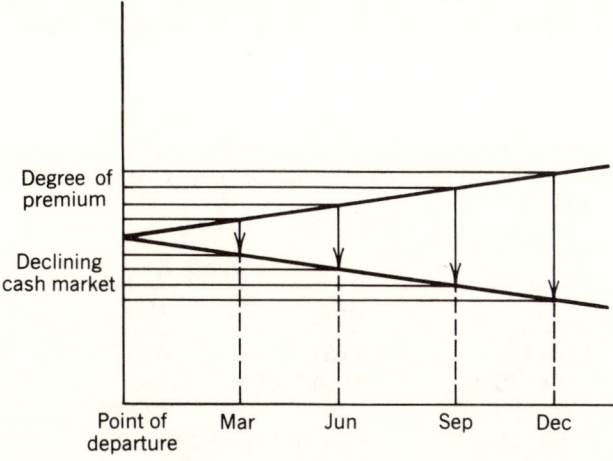

FIGURE 16.4 Declining cash market and degree of premium

Notice the ensuing decline in each delivery month as it approached the contract cash market level. Simplifying the analysis, the richer premium months that were sold resulted in greater profits on a per-trade basis. To conclude this study, a declining cash market situation is presented by Figure 16.4.

In Figure 16.4, the profit potential of selling a premium month in a declining market is dramatized. It can offer the highest per-trade profit potential as its difference is the greatest distance from the point of departure to the expiration date.

THE MYTH OF SUPER PERFORMANCE

There can be and are periods of superior performance for trading programs, but the clockwork maintenance of super performance is a myth. As seen in Table 16.1, it does not take very long for the higher rates of return to generate enormous wealth.

This rapid growth was accomplished without subsequent deposits, only the compounding of initial capital. There are several critical factors to consider. In a probabilistic sense, it is better to achieve earlier successes, for then the trading program acquires a degree of stability and funding and does not have to await anxiously the occurrence of favorable events.

For example, if only 3 out of 20 wells prove economically feasible, and this is sufficient to perform profitably, it is better that they happen early in the drilling program since there is no guarantee that for any 20 attempts exactly 3 wells will come in. From another perspective, an organization can have funds limited for only 17 tries and, as chance would have it, the first 17 were dry for that particular driller on that specific leasehold. Of course, the next three attempts by another party on that parcel were successful but the fact remains that it is a probabilistic venture. To improve the chances of success, mineral surveys were conducted for the former, and for futures trading, research is pursued.

TABLE 16.1. $10,000 INITIAL INVESTMENT END-OF-YEAR CUMULATIVE ACCOUNT SIZE IN TERMS OF DOLLARS

Percentage Rates of Growth	Years			
	5	10	15	20
10	16,105	25,937	41,772	67,275
20	24,883	61,917	154,070	383,376
30	37,129	137,858	511,859	1,900,496
40	53,782	289,255	1,555,681	8,366,825
50	75,938	576,650	4,378,959	33,252,567
100	320,000	10,240,000	32,768,001	10,485,759,990

The above indicates that a sufficiently adverse event, though limited to a small time frame, can still have a substantial influence not only on that year's profitability but the overall performance as well. This is highlighted by the application of the ruin statistics.

EVALUATING TRADING PROGRAMS

The evaluation of trading programs is a delicate though necessary task. A strictly "bottom line" orientation ignores risk and focuses only on maximum profits.

Surely, different strategies must be implemented to account for capitalization, risk aversion, hedging requirements, speculative outlooks, or other considerations. Only by compiling performance and its achievement path against previously established criteria can a trading program be assessed. Statistical guidelines, such as, sequential testing, which was presented earlier, are useful techniques.

Comparative Approaches

The application of rates of return (change) and average return (change) can be seriously misleading. Performance for one program can be measured by some variation of simple averaging, while another program considers the time value of money and therefore uses a geometrically averaged approach. Comparatively, the latter approach would have a conservative bias but a better reflection of performance. It would more accurately weigh the flow-of-funds (both deposits and withdrawals) and their influence on returns. Unless one is aware of the magnitude of performance bias for the applied arbitrary deposit/withdrawal adjustment rules, the interpretation of the overall program's performance is subject to question.

Performance Is More Than Returns

The trading programs must be evaluated not only in terms of their returns and their variability, but against other objectives. For hedging programs, the imputed basis relationship must be acceptably consistent to be useful. For speculative programs, the rewards must be better than those offered by lower-risk alternatives, and occur in a reasonably acceptable manner. Constancy of returns here is not the rule, but there must be a framework to capture the better opportunities as they emerge and develop. An extremely attractive advantage of futures trading is that it complements a financial portfolio by presenting a spectrum of exploitable situations and a mechanism for reducing risks. The implementation of a reasonably grounded program makes the difference for trading results.

17
Updating

MONITORING THE PROGRAM

This is the third interacting factor of a program. Once the initial testing has been completed and trading commenced, the actual results may appear to differ from those expected. One way to determine if material change has occurred is to retest or update.

The need for updating arises when the operator is aware of new approaches, concepts, or structural changes in the marketplace. Or, it can be a periodic feature of the program.

Fundamentally there may be new patterns in livestock feeding, metallurgical substitution in manufacturing, changes in the dietary habits of consumers, or revisions in foreign exchange, monetary, or fiscal policies.

From a technical perspective, this can mean a change in moving average parameters, the inconsistency of ordinary reversal days, or the emergence of a Big Day theory.

THE BIG DAY THEORY

The Big Day theory focuses on large, particularly historic, price changes that strongly suggest the direction of the next major price trend. Often this price change is among the largest price increases or decreases in many years or even the entire history of a given exchange's records. Downside examples of this would be the historic collapse of coffee, sugar, and silver prices. (See Charts 17.1, 17.2, and 17.3.)

Upside evidence of this would be the relatively large jumps in Treasury bill, Treasury bond, stock indexes, and stock futures. (See Charts 17.4, 17.5, 17.6, and 17.7, respectively.)

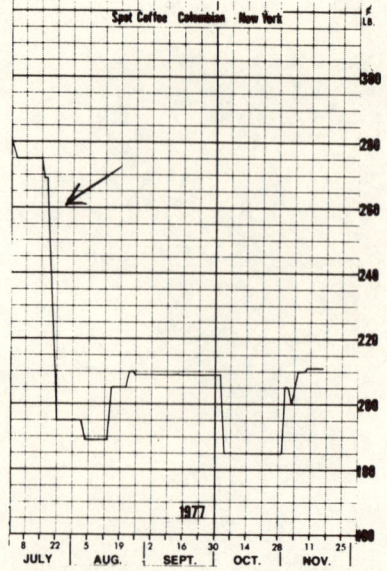

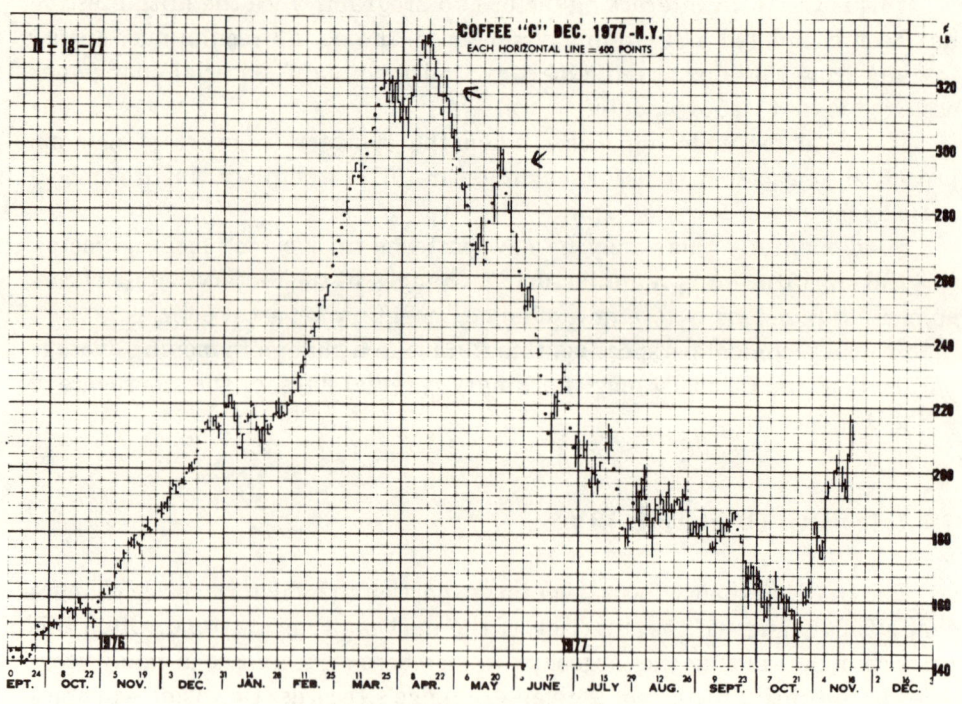

CHART 17.1 Downside Big Day

286

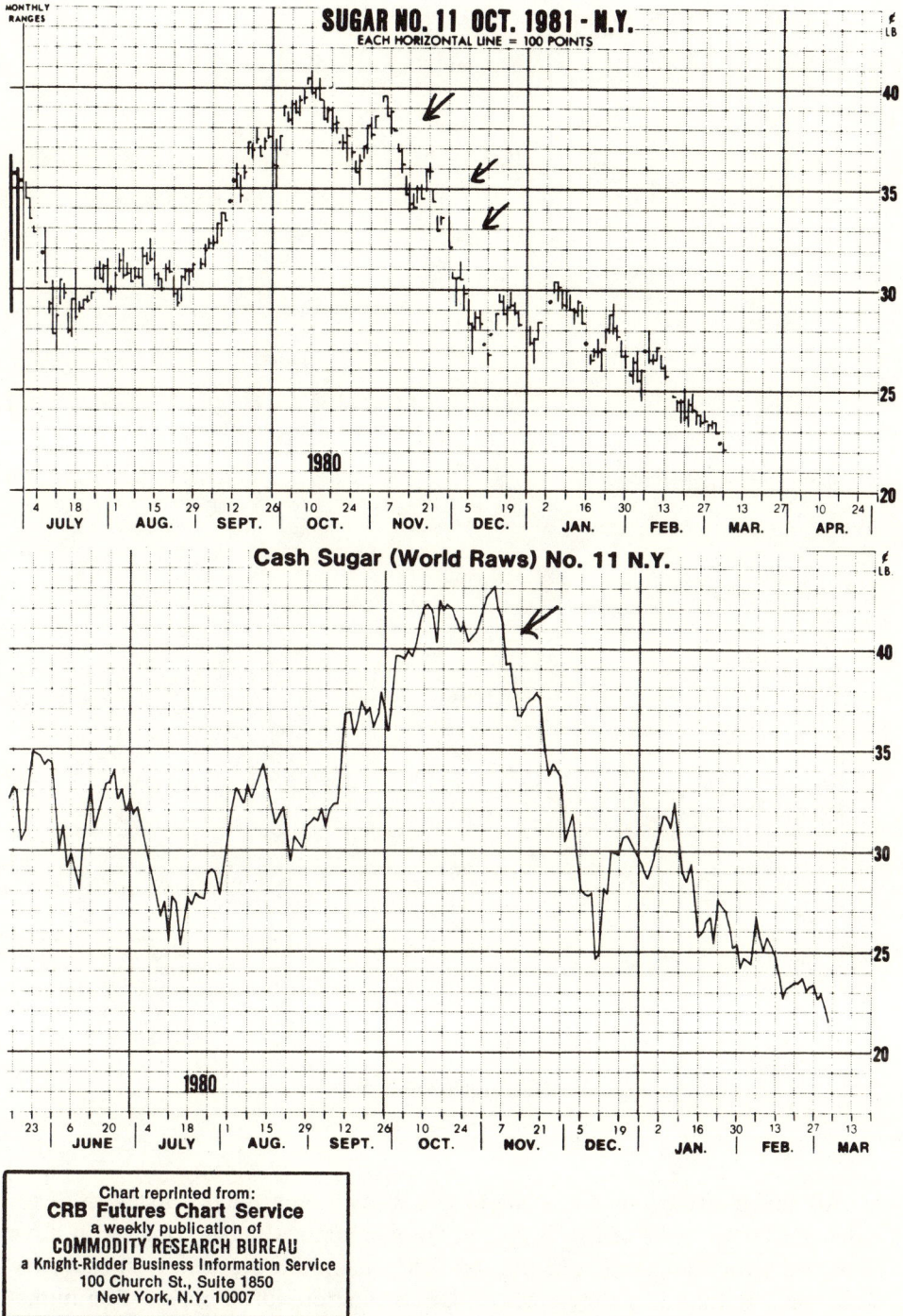

CHART 17.2 Downside Big Day

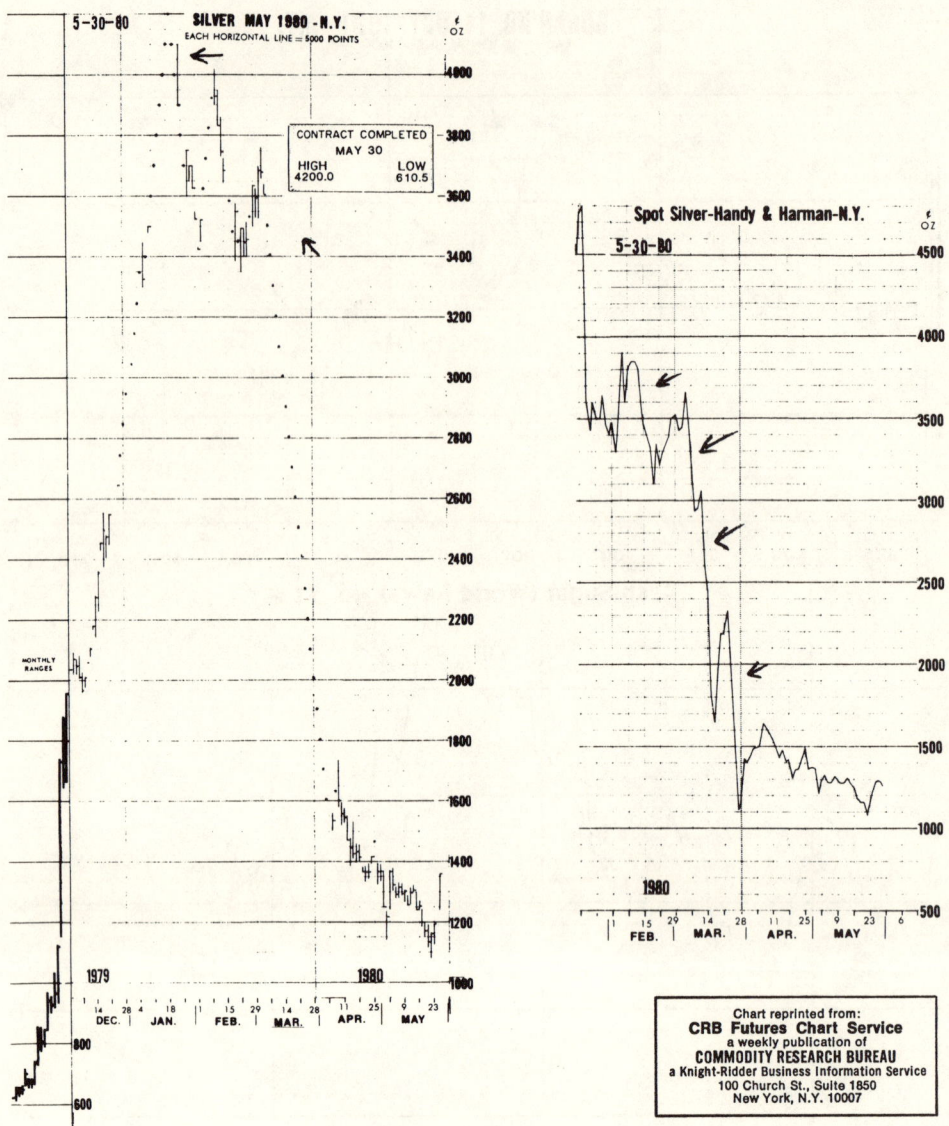

CHART 17.3 Downside Big Day

All seven situations were precursors of awesome major moves in directions similar to those of the Big Day. On a structural basis, this could have coincided with exchange rule changes, the onset of a seemingly speculative panic, or a change in policy posture. Often concrete news may not be immediately available; however, as trading days continue, the motivating mechanism becomes more visible.

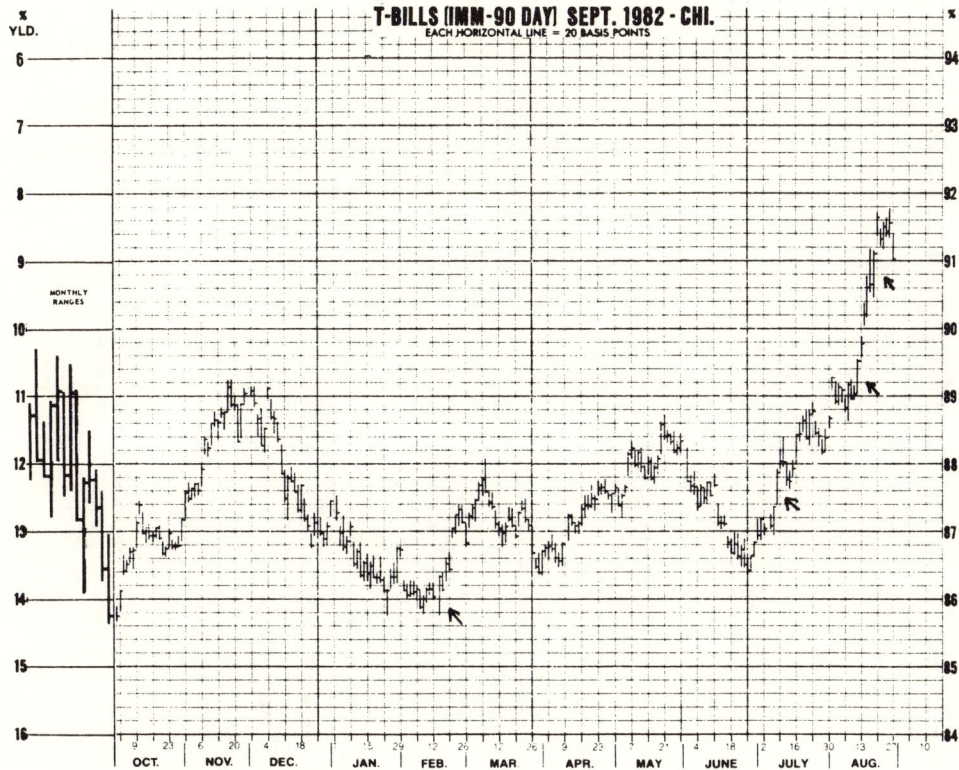

CHART 17.4 Upside Big Day

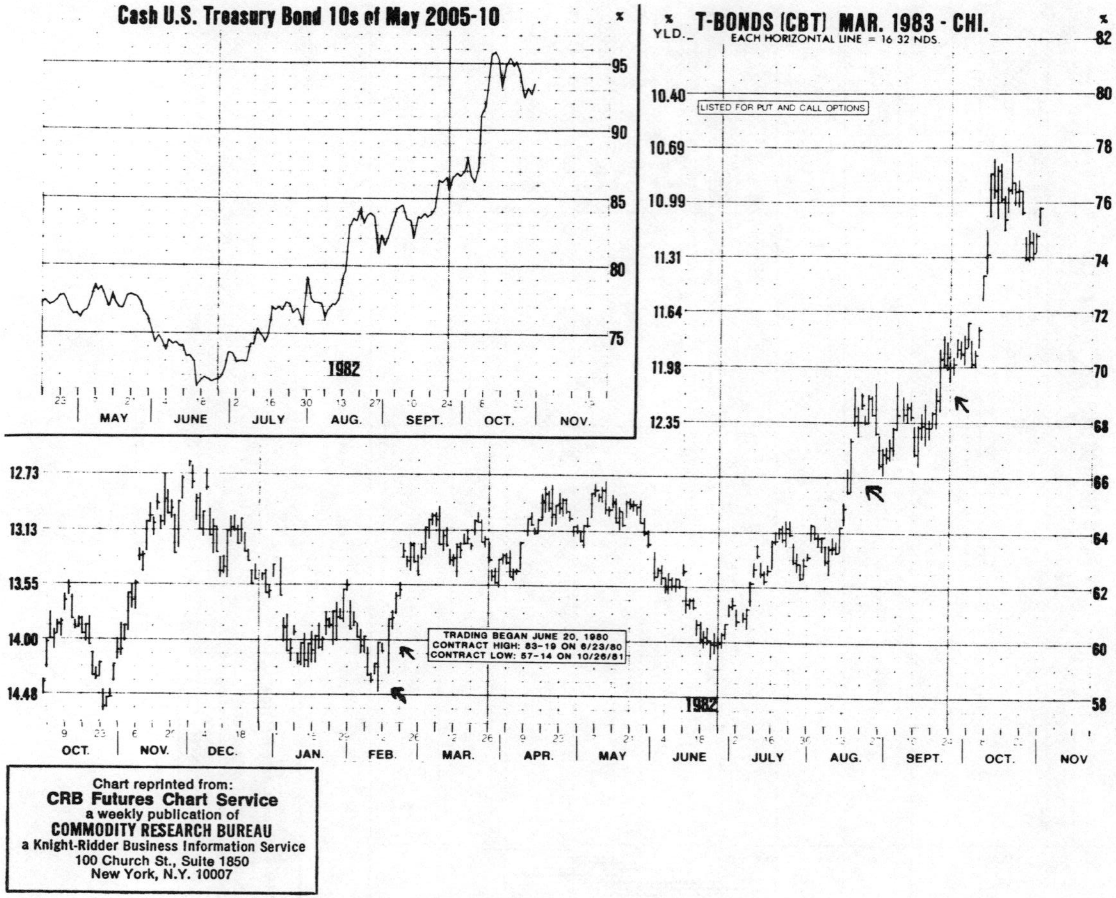

CHART 17.5 Upside Big Day

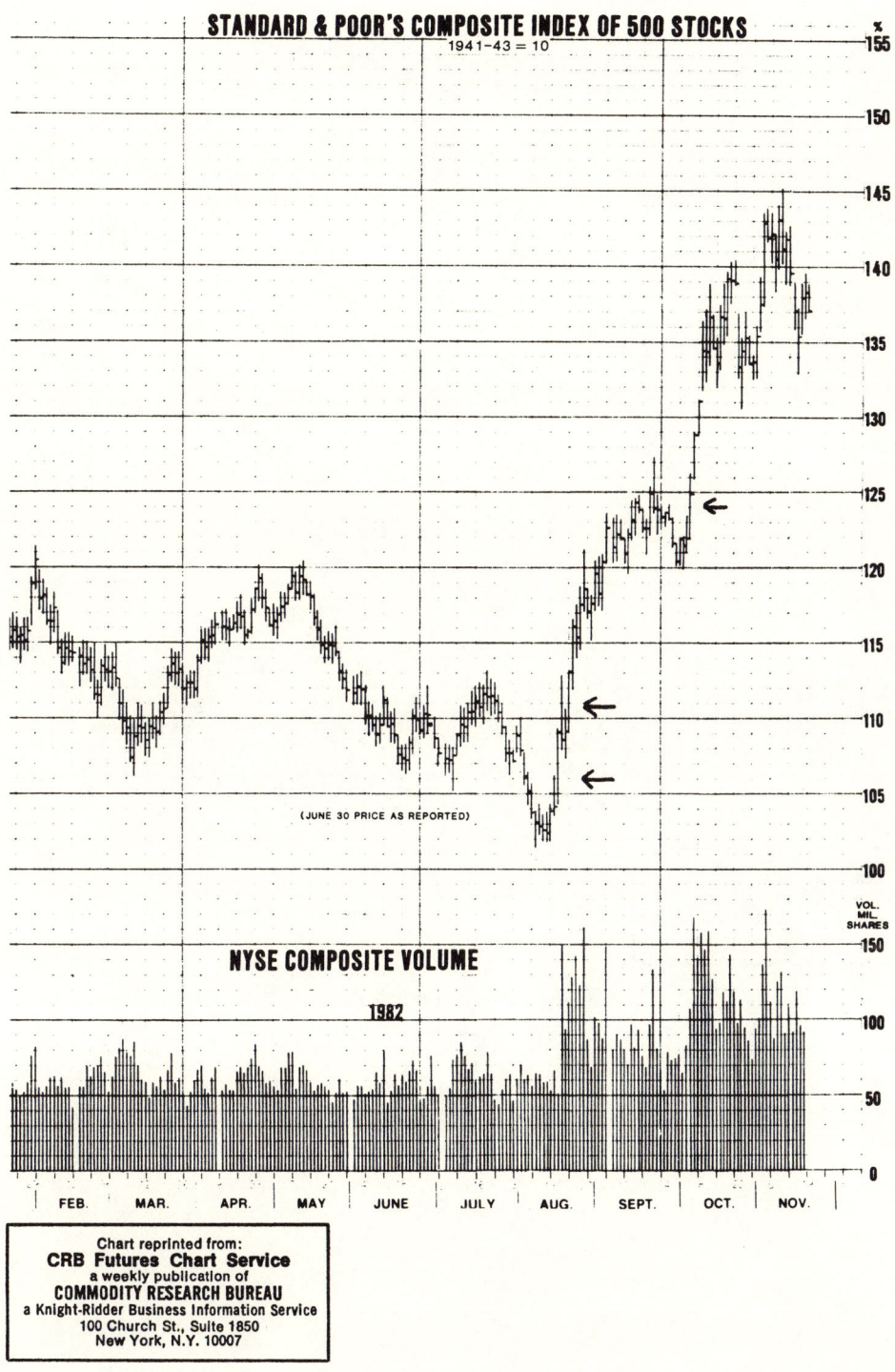

CHART 17.6 Upside Big Day

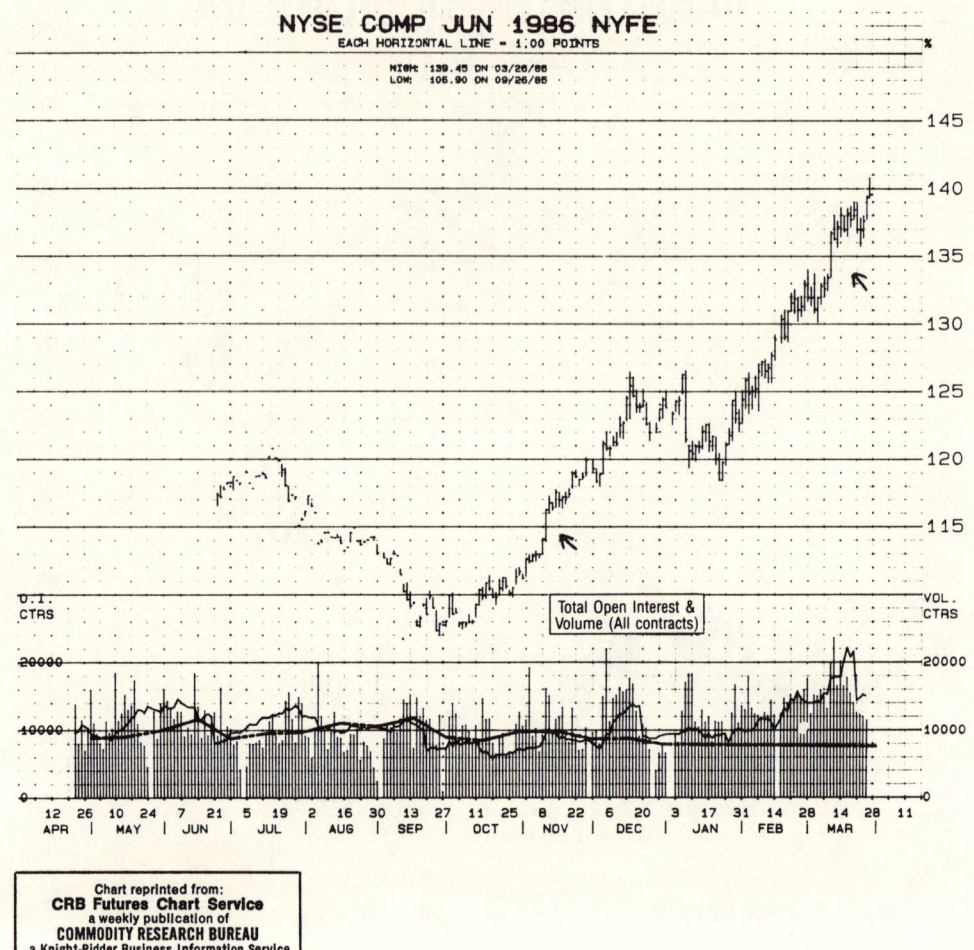

NYSE COMP JUN 1986 NYFE
EACH HORIZONTAL LINE = 1.00 POINTS
HIGH: 139.45 ON 03/26/86
LOW: 106.90 ON 09/26/85

Total Open Interest & Volume (All contracts)

CHART 17.7 Upside Big Day

CONDITIONAL STATES RECOGNITION

As seen, these extraordinarily large price change periods assist in the identification of important conditional states for interpreting the market's subsequent behavior. Equally important, these large change dates have statistical characteristics that demonstrate considerable interdependence among observations and not the general research-and-applications assumption of independence. This finding cannot be overstressed. Notice the similarity between T-bill, T-bond, and stock index futures as shown in Charts 17.4, 17.5, 17.6, and 17.7. Another situation was the impact of the G-5 meeting on rates, which is dramatically shown by Charts 17.8, 17.9, 17.10, and 17.11.

These occurrences do not suggest statistical independence. In fact, going on this assumption, the probability of these events simultaneously occurring for the various futures markets should be very remote. Instead, they tend to be more commonplace. The importance of this is twofold. First, a trading program must be prepared to take advantage of extremely favorable performance conditions. Second, the program must be constructed in such a manner as to make it more responsive to adverse outlier conditions.

Refining the Concept

Refining this concept somewhat more, it can be applied to relatively recent large price moves. The resultant price move is not as historic as those posed earlier. This situation generally occurs when a price series shows consistently small daily price movements and then suddenly a relatively large price change. Live cattle and live hog contracts are good examples of this. (See Charts 17.12 and 17.13.)

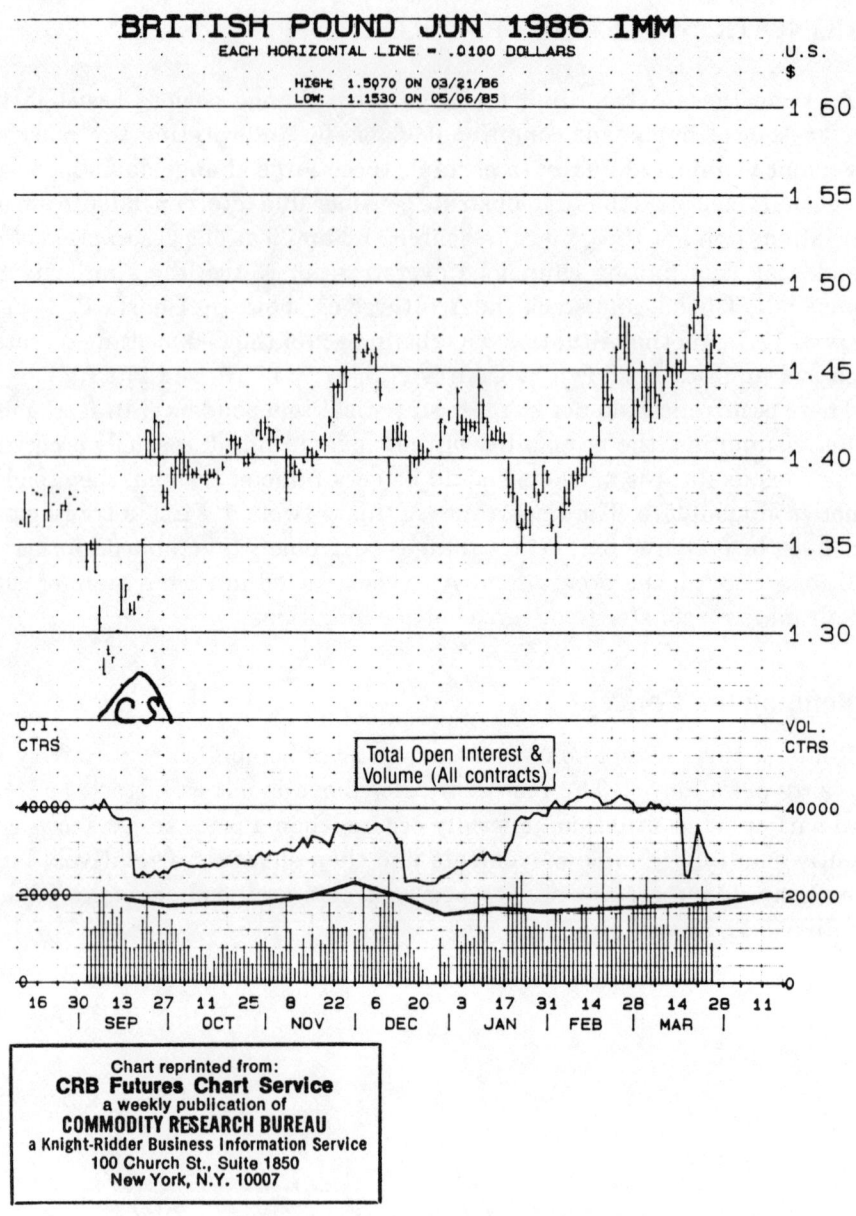

CHART 17.8 Conditional states recognition

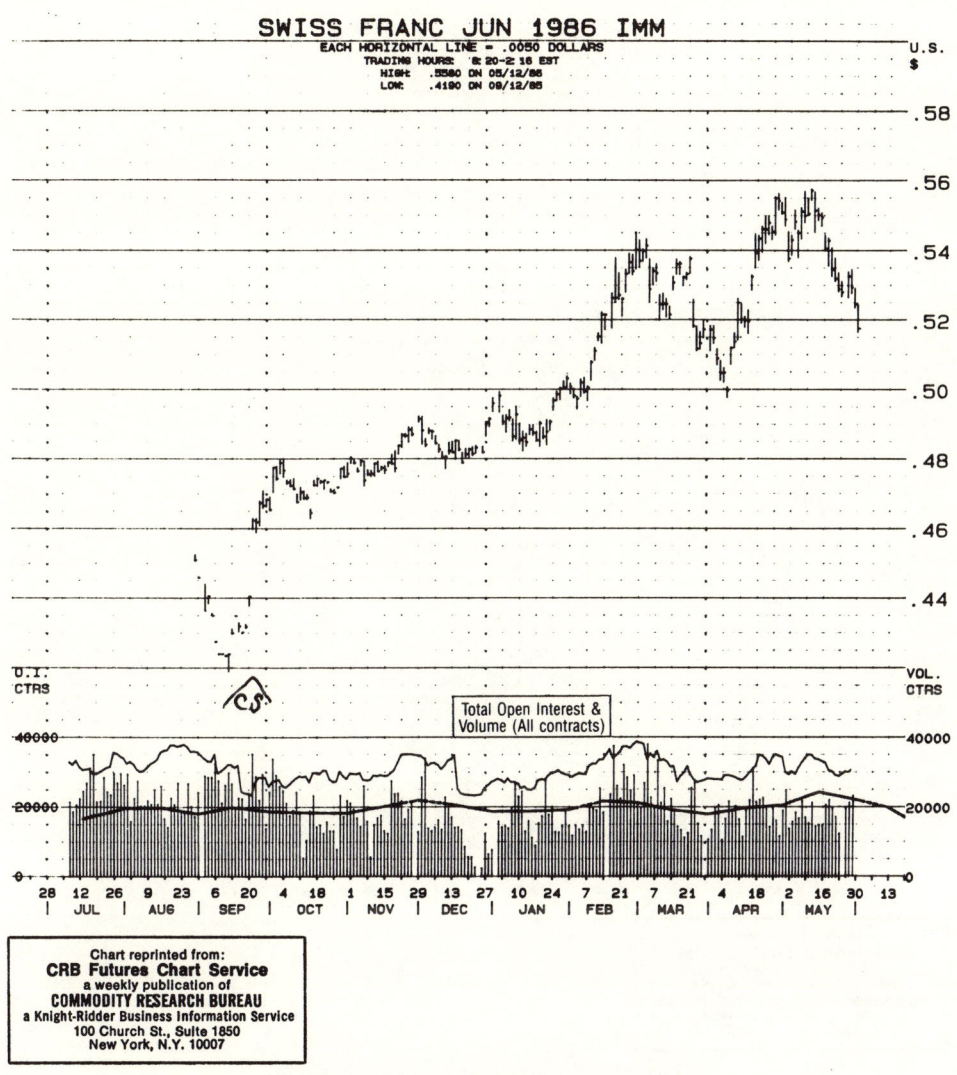

CHART 17.9 Conditional states recognition

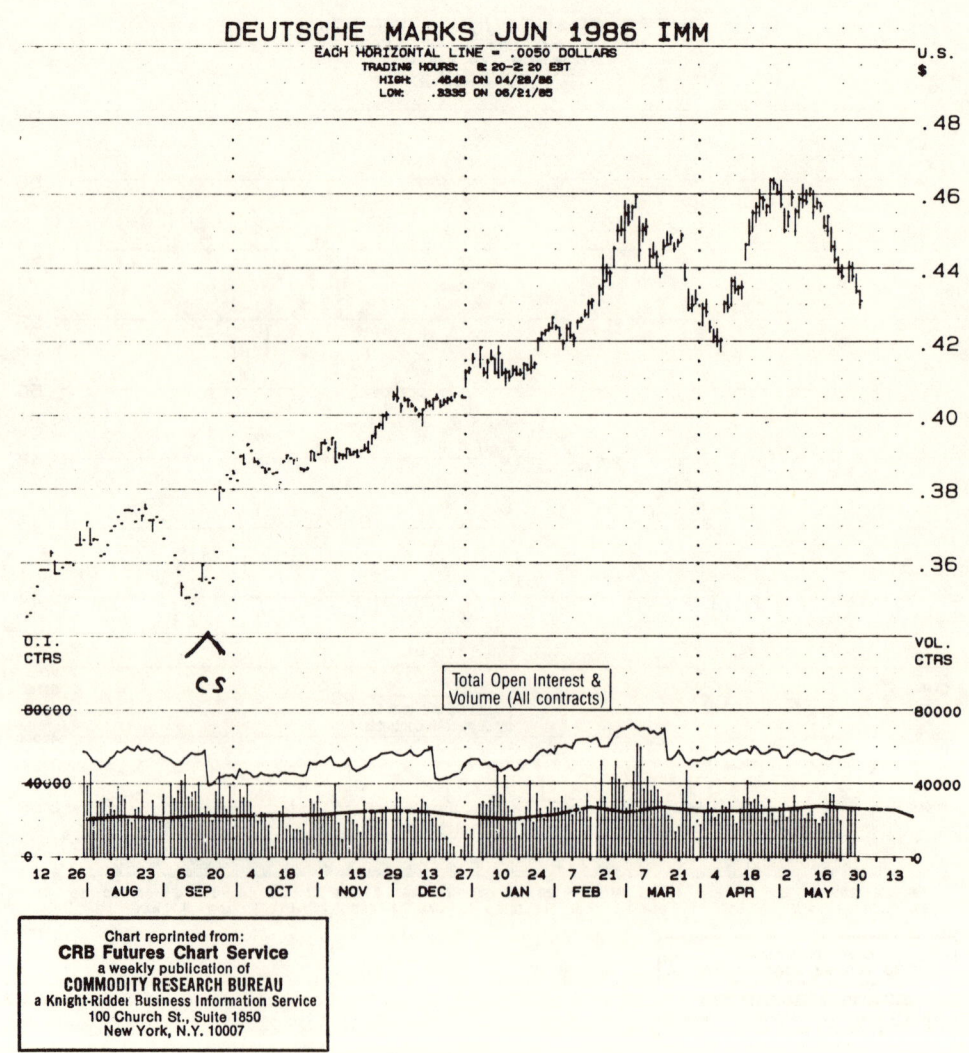

DEUTSCHE MARKS JUN 1986 IMM

EACH HORIZONTAL LINE = .0050 DOLLARS
TRADING HOURS: 8: 20–2 20 EST
HIGH: .4646 ON 04/28/86
LOW: .3335 ON 06/21/85

U.S.
$

Total Open Interest &
Volume (All contracts)

O.I.
CTRS

VOL.
CTRS

C S

CHART 17.10 Conditional states recognition

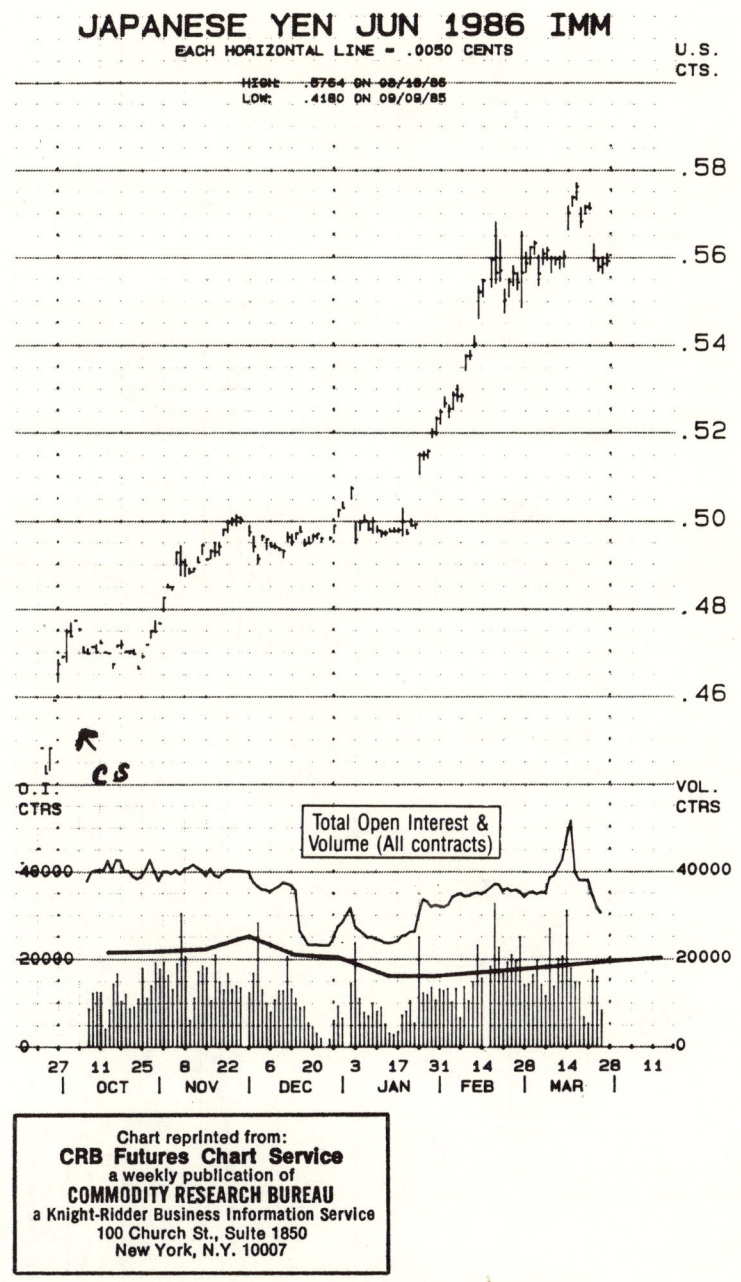

JAPANESE YEN JUN 1986 IMM

EACH HORIZONTAL LINE = .0050 CENTS

HIGH: .5764 ON 03/18/86
LOW: .4180 ON 09/09/85

U.S. CTS.

.58
.56
.54
.52
.50
.48
.46

O.I. CTRS

Total Open Interest & Volume (All contracts)

VOL. CTRS

40000

20000

0

27 11 25 8 22 6 20 3 17 31 14 28 14 28 11
| OCT | NOV | DEC | JAN | FEB | MAR |

CHART 17.11 Conditional states recognition

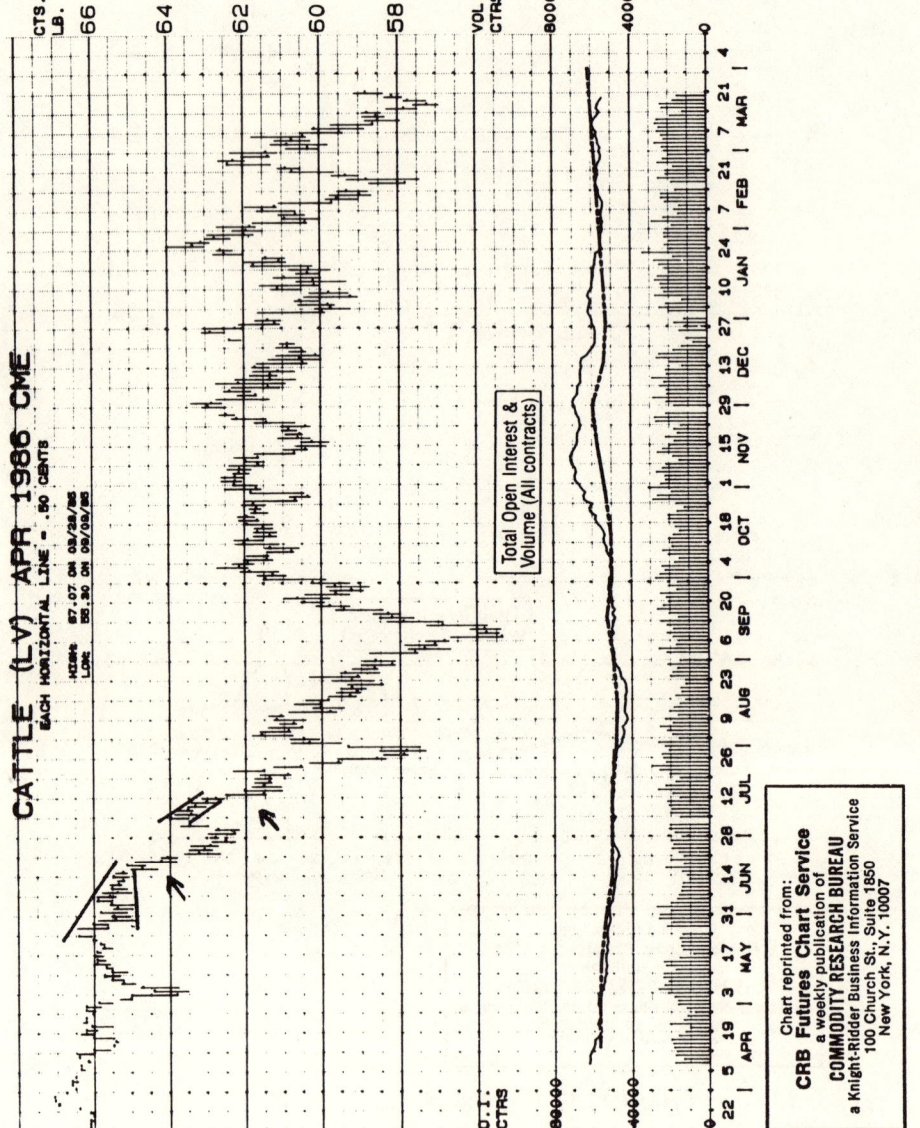

CHART 17.12 Refining the concept

298

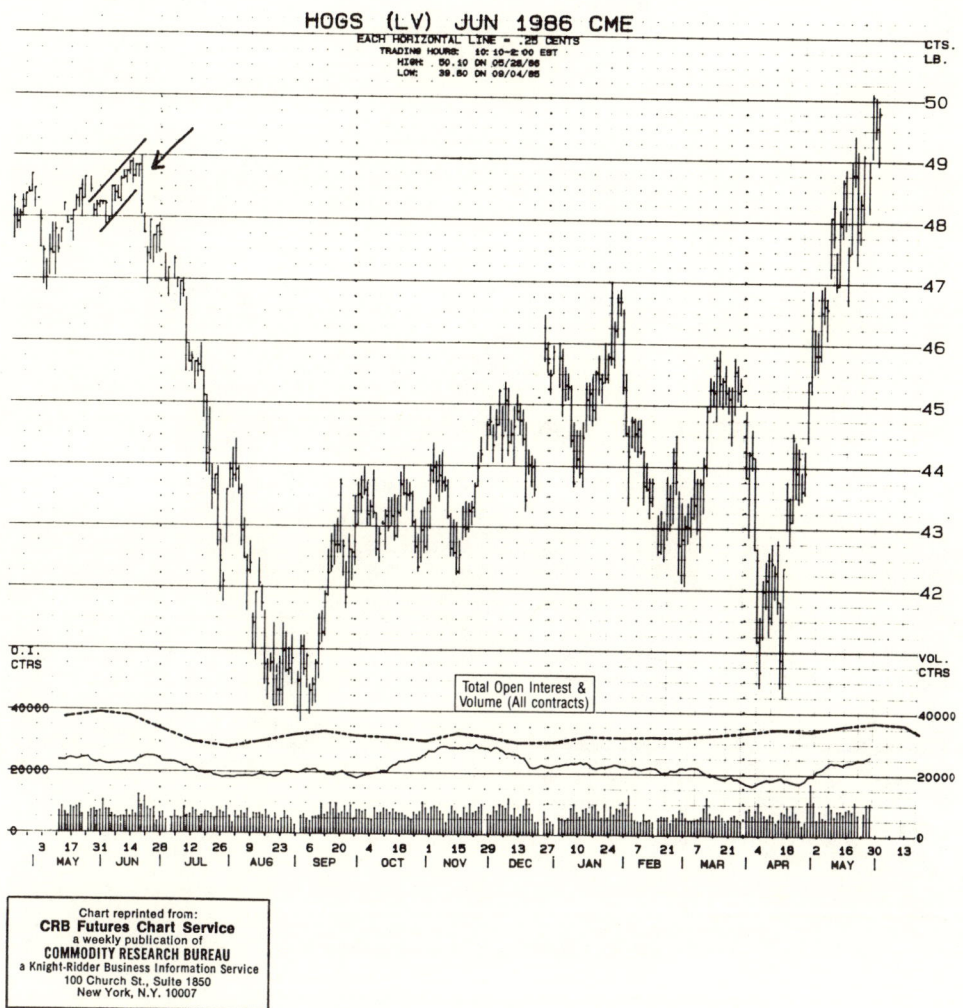

CHART 17.13 Refining the concept

AN ARROW DAY

Another consequence of a dynamic marketplace and the proliferation of computerized or technical trading programs is the Arrow Day, or price spike. Usually this anomaly occurs around a congestion area. Depending on the exact timing and parameters of the multitudinous technical/mechanical programs, an Arrow Day emerges. Typically, this results in a false breakout, as values are apparently forced out of an equilibrium (congestion) area temporarily and then fundamentally oriented buying (selling) pressures drive the market back into balance. Moreover, the direction of the Arrow Day, as for the Big Day, provides guidance for the next trend. Charts 17.14, 17.15, and 17.16

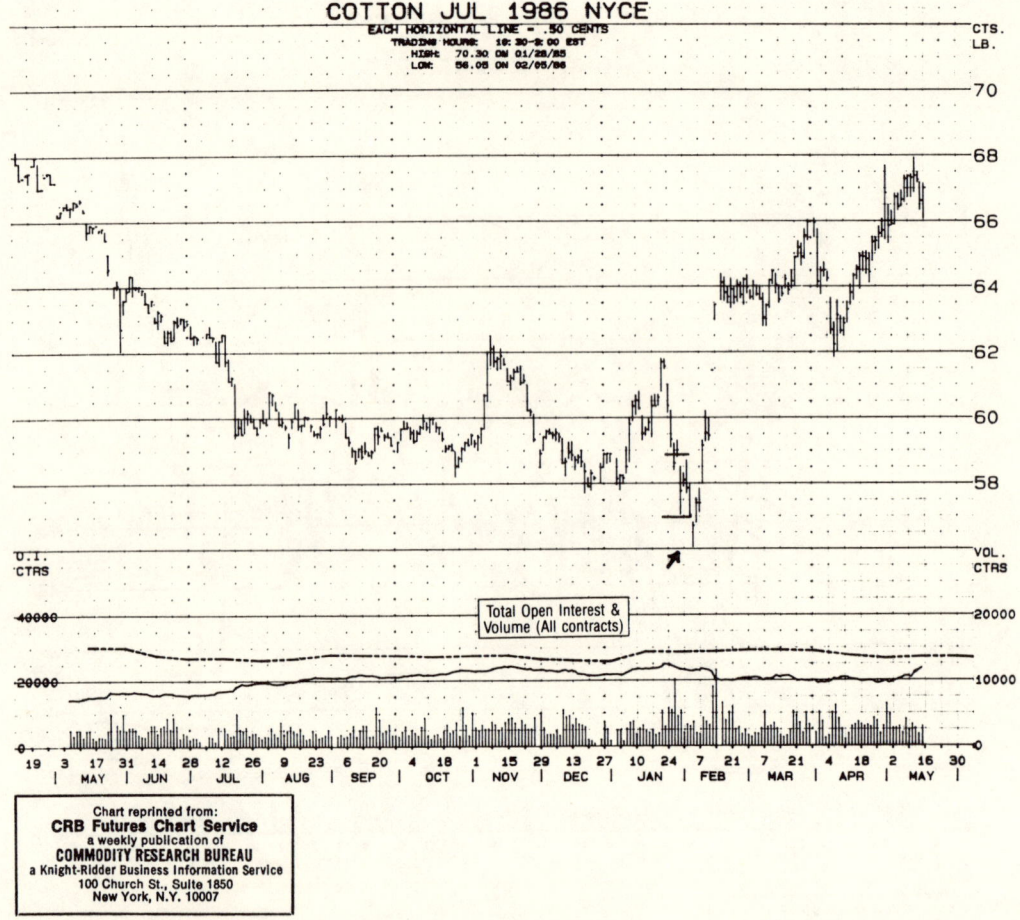

CHART 17.14 Arrow Day

illustrate three cases, each of which indicated an imminent change in price trend. The recognition of these important events can improve a program's performance by conditionalizing its perspectives.

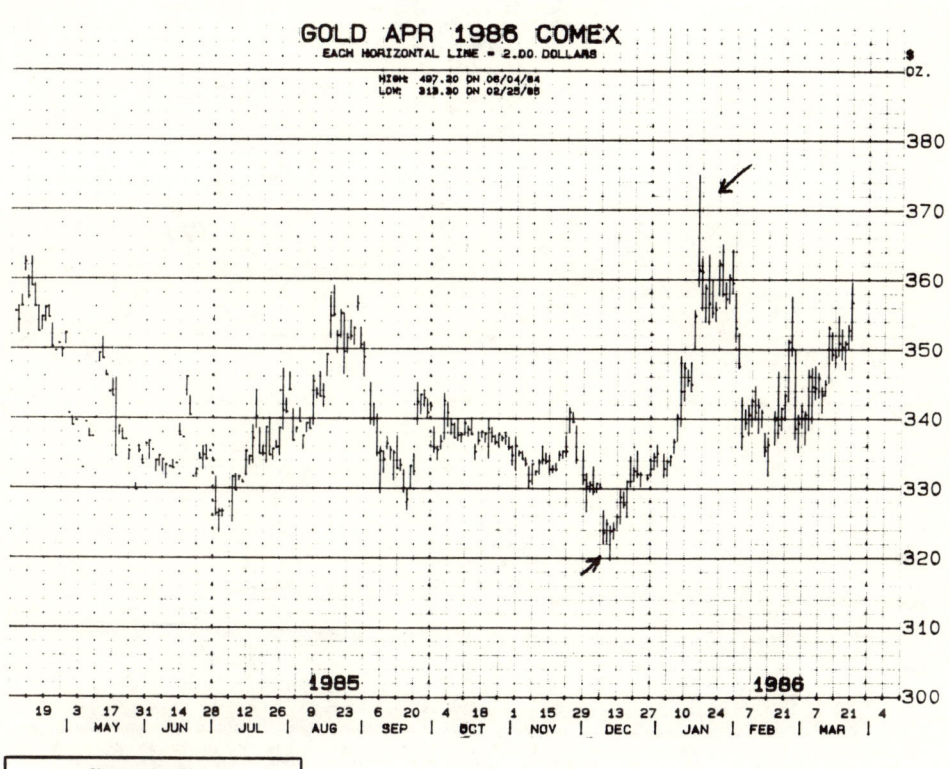

GOLD APR 1986 COMEX

. EACH HORIZONTAL LINE = 2.00 DOLLARS .

HIGH: 497.20 ON 08/04/84
LOW: 313.30 ON 02/25/85

CHART 17.15 Arrow Day

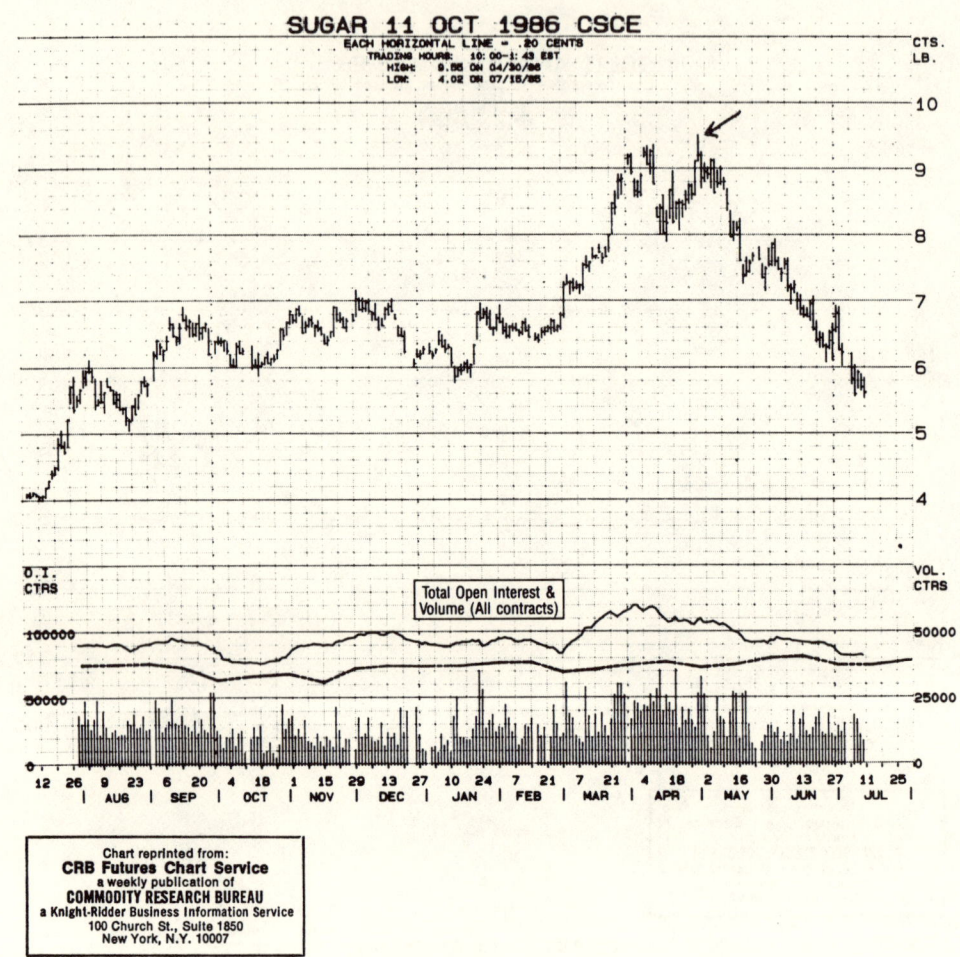

SUGAR 11 OCT 1986 CSCE

EACH HORIZONTAL LINE = .20 CENTS
TRADING HOURS: 10:00-1:43 EST
HIGH: 9.58 ON 04/30/86
LOW: 4.02 ON 07/18/85

Total Open Interest & Volume (All contracts)

Chart reprinted from:
CRB Futures Chart Service
a weekly publication of
COMMODITY RESEARCH BUREAU
a Knight-Ridder Business Information Service
100 Church St., Suite 1850
New York, N.Y. 10007

CHART 17.16 Arrow Day

SHIFTING PARAMETERS

As mentioned in Chapter 12, Testing, parameters tend to change over time. Because of this, it is preferable to select parameter arrangements within acceptable profitability clusters so as to maintain a degree of consistency. Otherwise, even subtle shifts in parameter arrangements can quickly push a program into a losing situation.

The quantitative updating techniques are similar to those used in the initial testing phase. Depending on how much time has lapsed between the initial testing and the updating phases, relatively little effort may be required to revise a program.

Essentially, one should focus on those parameters used in the initial trading program and the areas contiguous to that initially profitable area. Matrices 17.1 and 17.2 illustrate this procedure. As you may recall these matrices correspond to the initial project and detail matrices. Since the initial detail matrix provided parameter values for the trading program, the operator in his updating phase would probably be better off by reexamining those values and moves around the detail matrix first. Referring to another conceptual matrix presented in the Chapter 12, Testing, the operator would also use the scanning matrix. This particular matrix helps make the transition from the detail matrix values to those surrounding the detail matrix. (See Matrix 17.3.)

Again, the time and financial savings can be substantial. Instead of retesting an entire project matrix, the operator can focus on smaller areas within the matrices. Comparatively, the operator can avoid retesting a 100×100 matrix (potentially 10,000 arrangements) and focus on a 10×10 matrix (100 arrangements) or even a 20×20 matrix (400 arrangements). To emphasize the importance of this, a 10×10 matrix update would require only 1 percent of the time necessary to similarly compute and appraise a 100×100 matrix.

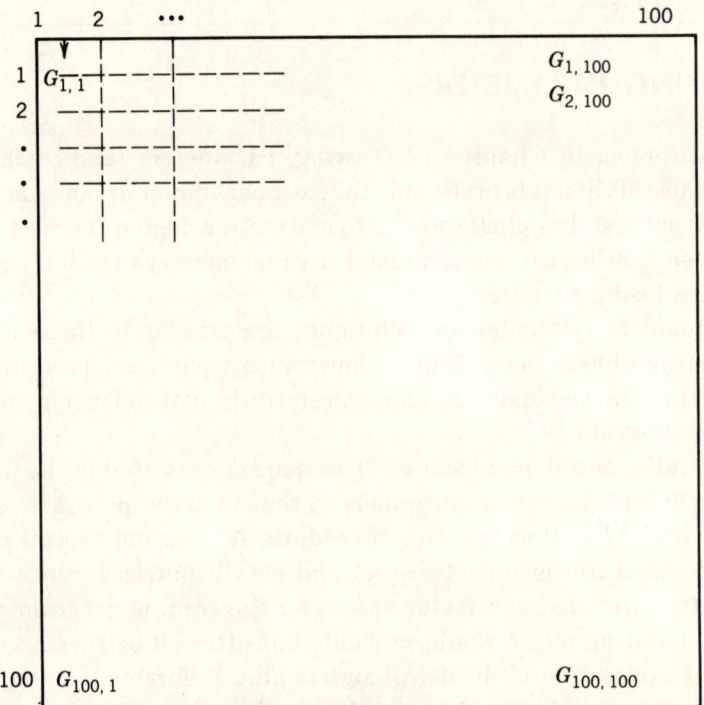

Where: $G_{1,1}$ represents the group defined by row 1, column 1.
$G_{1,100}$ represents the group defined by row 1, column 100
$G_{100,99}$ represents the group defined by row 100, column 99.

MATRIX 17.1 Initial project matrix 100×100 matrix

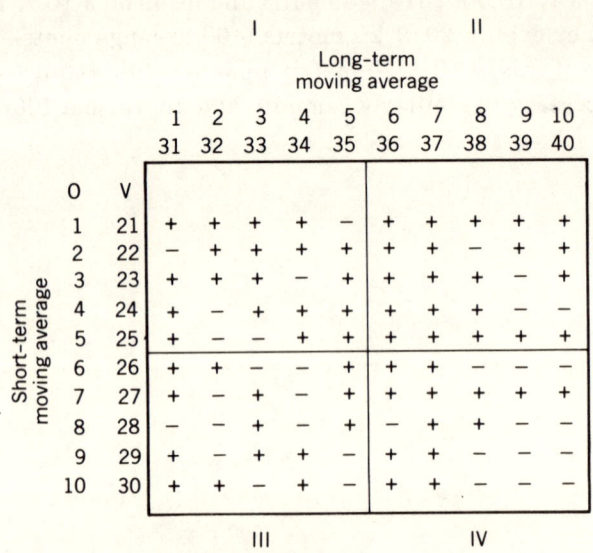

		I					II				
		Long-term moving average									
		1	2	3	4	5	6	7	8	9	10
		31	32	33	34	35	36	37	38	39	40
O	V										
1	21	+	+	+	+	−	+	+	+	+	+
2	22	−	+	+	+	+	+	+	−	+	+
3	23	+	+	+	−	+	+	+	+	−	+
4	24	+	−	+	+	+	+	+	+	−	−
5	25	+	−	−	+	+	+	+	+	+	+
6	26	+	+	−	−	+	+	+	−	−	−
7	27	+	−	+	−	+	+	+	+	+	+
8	28	−	−	+	−	+	−	+	+	−	−
9	29	+	−	+	+	−	+	+	−	−	−
10	30	+	+	−	+	−	+	+	−	−	−

III   IV

O = number of row observations.
V = row values

MATRIX 17.2 Detail matrix

		Long-term moving average									
		1	2	3	4	5	6	7	8	9	10
		11	21	31	41	51	61	71	81	91	101
	1	–	–	–	–	–	–	–	–	–	–
	11	X	–	–	–	–	–	–	–	–	–
3	21	X	X	+	–	+	+	–	–	–	–
4	31	X	X	X	–	–	+	–	+	–	–
5	41	X	X	X	X	–	–	+	+	–	–
6	51	X	X	X	X	X	–	–	–	–	–
7	61	X	X	X	X	X	X	–	–	–	–
8	71	X	X	X	X	X	X	X	–	–	–
9	81	X	X	X	X	X	X	X	X	–	–
10	91	X	X	X	X	X	X	X	X	X	–

(Short-term moving average)

7 of 55 are profitable groups, 48 are not

–   losses
+   profits
X   not applicable

MATRIX 17.3 Scanning matrix

EXPEDIENCY

Trading problems often require expediency of action and cannot be postponed pending additional exhaustive analysis. Upon segmenting the problems and assessing the most likely decision criteria regions, modifications can be implemented to maintain program continuity. Many of the techniques presented throughout this text are statistically functional with small sample sizes and adaptable to quantitative real time updating. Should these selective efforts prove unsatisfactory, then more extensive research and reliability testing must be pursued.

CONCLUSION

The proper application of statistical techniques improves the performance of hedging and trading programs. It does so by rigorously defining risks, identifying opportunities, and quantifying the relationships between these two key factors. The techniques presented in this text are amenable to rapid revisions that are fundamentally sound but not time consuming. This is especially crucial for on-line trading operations. The probabilistic nature of trading and economic activity must be recognized in order to achieve successful performance.

BIBLIOGRAPHY

Aacker, David A., Ed., *Multivariate Analysis in Marketing: Theory and Application*, Wadsworth, Belmont, CA, 1971.

Adams, F. Gerard, and Jere R. Behrman, *Econometric Models of World Agricultural Markets*, Ballinger, Cambridge, MA, 1976.

Altman, Edward I., Ed., *Financial Handbook*, 5th ed., Wiley, New York, 1981.

Anderson, T. W., *The Statistical Analysis of Time Series*, Wiley, New York, 1971.

Archer, Stephen H., and J. C. Francis, *Portfolio Analysis*, Prentice-Hall, Englewood Cliffs, NJ, 1971.

Arrow, Kenneth J., *Essays in the Theory of Risk Bearing*, Markham, Chicago, 1971.

Arthur, Henry B., *Commodity Futures as a Business Management Tool*, The President and Fellows of Harvard College, Boston, MA, 1971.

Ash, Robert B., *Basic Probability Theory*, Wiley, New York, 1970.

Awad, Elias M., and Data Processing Management Association, *Automatic Data Processing: Principles and Procedures*, Prentice-Hall, Englewood Cliffs, NJ, 1966.

Bach, George Leland, *Economics: An Introduction to Analysis and Policy*, 5th ed., Prentice-Hall, Englewood Cliffs, NJ, 1966.

Barnes, Robert M., *Taming the Pits: A Technical Approach to Commodity Trading*, Wiley, New York, 1979.

Baratz, Morton S., Ed., *Commodity Money Management Yearbook*, vol. 3, Ronald, New York, 1982.

Baumol, William J., *Economic Theory and Operations Analysis*, 3rd ed., Prentice-Hall, Englewood Cliffs, NJ, 1961.

Beckhard, Richard, *Organization Development: Strategies and Models*, Addision-Wesley, Reading, MA, 1969.

Bernstein, Jacob, *The Handbook of Commodity Cycles: A Window on Time*, Wiley, New York, 1982.

Bernstein, Jacob, *The Investor's Quotient*, Wiley, New York, 1980.

Beyer, William H., *Handbook of Tables for Probability and Statistics*, 2nd ed., Chemical Rubber Co., Cleveland, OH, 1968.

Blackwell, David, and M. A. Girshick, *Theory of Games and Statistical Decisions*, Dover, NY, 1954.

Board of Trade of the City of Chicago, *Commodity Trading Manual*, 5th rev. ed., Board of Trade of the City of Chicago, 1971.

Bogen, Jules I., Ed., *Financial Handbook*, 4th ed., Ronald, NY, 1968.

Box, George E. P., and Gwilym M. Jenkins, *Time Series Analysis Forecasting and Control*, Holden-Day, San Francisco, CA, 1970.

Brigham, Eugene F., and Fred J. Weston, *Essentials of Managerial Finance*, Holt, Rinehart & Winston, New York, 1972.

Burkhead, C. E., R. C. Max, R. B. Karnes, and E. Reid, *Usual Planting and Harvesting Dates*, rev. ed., USDA, SRS, Agriculture Handbook No. 283, Washington, DC, March 1972.

Campbell, Donald T., and Julian C. Stanley, *Experimental and Quasi-Experimental Designs for Research*, Rand McNally, Chicago, 1963.

Carleton, William T., and Eugene M. Lerner, *A Theory of Financial Analysis*, Harcourt, Brace & World, New York, 1966.

Chiang, Alpha C., *Fundamental Methods of Mathematical Economics*, McGraw-Hill, New York, 1967.

Chicago Board of Trade, *Commodity Futures Trading: Bibliography Cumulative through 1976*, Chicago Board of Trade, Chicago.

Chicago Board of Trade, *Grains*, Chicago Board of Trade, 1973.

Chicago Board of Trade, *Selected Writings of Holbrook Working*, Board of Trade of the City of Chicago, 1977.

Chicago Board of Trade, *Sources of Financial Futures Information: A Bibliography*, Chicago Board of Trade, 1980.

Chicago Board of Trade, *Sources of Financial Futures Information: A Bibliography, 1981 Supplement*, Chicago Board of Trade, 1981.

Chicago Mercantile Exchange, *Bibliography and Information Source List*, Chicago Mercantile Exchange, 1980.

Chou, Ya-lun, *Statistical Analysis with Business and Financial Applications*, Holt, Rinehart & Winston, New York, 1969.

Chow, Gregory C., *Analysis and Control of Dynamic Economic Systems*, Wiley, New York, 1975.

Cohen, James B., and Sidney M. Robbins, *The Financial Manager*, Harper & Row, New York, 1966.

Cootner, Paul, H., Ed., *The Random Character of Stock Market Prices*, rev. ed., MIT Press, Cambridge, MA, 1964.

Darst, David M., *The Handbook of the Bond and Money Markets*, McGraw-Hill, New York, 1981.

Davis, James A., *Elementary Survey Analysis*, Prentice-Hall, Englewood Cliffs, NJ, 1971.

Dewey, Edward R., with Og Mandino, *Cycles: The Mysterious Forces That Trigger Events*, Hawthorn Books, New York, 1971.

Dippel, Gene, and William C. House, *Information Systems: Data Processing and Evaluation*, Scott, Foresman, 1969.

Doob, J. L., *Stochastic Processes*, Wiley, New York, 1953.

Dougall, Herbert E., *Capital Markets and Institutions*, 2nd ed., Prentice-Hall, Englewood Cliffs, NJ, 1970.

Dougall, Herbert E., and Harry G. Guthman, *Corporate Financial Policy*, Prentice-Hall, Englewood Cliffs, NJ, 1962.

Drucker, Peter F., *Men, Ideas, and Politics*, Harper & Row, New York, 1971.

Edwards, Robert D., and John Magee, *Technical Analysis of Stock Trends*, Springfield, MA, 1966.

Ellsworth, P. T., *The International Economy*, 4th ed., Macmillan, New York, 1969.

Elton, Edwin J., and Martin J. Gruber, eds., *Security Evaluation and Portfolio Analysis*, Prentice-Hall, Englewood Cliffs, NJ, 1972.

Engel, Louis, *How to Buy Stocks*, 4th rev. ed., Bantam, New York, 1967.

Fox, Karl A., and William C. Merrill, *An Introduction to Economic Statistics*, Wiley, New York, 1970.

Freund, John E., *College Mathematics with Business Applications*, Prentice-Hall, Englewood Cliffs, NJ, 1969.

Freund, John E., and Frank J. Williams, *Elementary Business Statistics: The Modern Approach*, Prentice-Hall, Englewood Cliffs, NJ, 1964.

Friedman, Milton, *A Program for Monetary Stability*, Fordham University Press, New York, 1969.

Friedman, Milton, *A Theory of the Consumption Function*, Princeton University Press, Princeton, NJ, 1971.

Friedman, Milton, *Dollars and Deficits*, Prentice-Hall, Englewood Cliffs, NJ, 1968.

Friedman, Milton, *Essays in Positive Economics*, University of Chicago Press, Chicago, 1966.

Friedman, Milton, Ed., *Studies in the Quantity Theory of Money*, University of Chicago Press, Chicago, 1965.

Frost, Alfred John, and Robert R. Prechter, Jr., *Elliott Wave Principle: Key to Stock Market Profits*, New Classics Library, Chappaqua, NY, 1978.

Fuller, Leonard E., *Basic Matrix Theory*, Prentice-Hall, Englewood Cliffs, NJ, 1962.

Gann, W. D., *How to Make Profits Trading in Commodities*, Lambert-Gann, Pomeroy, WA, 1976.

Gann, William D., *Truth of the Stock Tape*, Lambert-Gann, Pomeroy, WA, 1976.

Gann, William D., *45 Years in Wall Street*, Lambert-Gann, Pomeroy, WA, 1976.

Gnugnoli, Giuliano, and Herbert Maisel, *Simulation of Discrete Stochastic Systems*, Simulation Science Research Associates, Chicago, 1972.

Gold, Gerald, *Modern Commodity Futures Trading*, Commodity Research Bureau, New York, 1959.

Goldberg, Ray A., *Agribusiness Coordination*, President and Fellows of Harvard College, Boston, MA, 1968.

Gordon, Robert A., *Business Fluctuations*, 2nd ed., Harper & Row, New York, 1961.

Gould, Bruce G., *How to Make Money in Commodities*, Bruce Gould Publications, Seattle, WA, 1980.

Granville, Joseph E., *A Strategy of Daily Stock Market Timing for Maximum Profit*, Prentice-Hall, Englewood Cliffs, NJ, 1960.

Granville, Joseph E., *Granville's New Key to Stock Market Profits*, Prentice-Hall, Englewood Cliffs, NJ, 1969.

Gross, Alan E., Barry E. Collins, and James M. Bryan, *An Introduction to Research in Social Psychology*, Wiley, New York, 1972.

Grushcow, Jack, and Courtney Smith, *Profits Through Seasonal Trading*, Ronald, New York, 1980.

Haimann, Theo, and William G. Scott, *Management in the Modern Organization*, Houghton Mifflin, Boston, 1970.

Hare, Jr., Van Court, *Systems Analysis: A Diagnostic Approach*, Harcourt Brace & World, New York, 1967.

Harlow, Charles V., Herbert L. Stone, and Richard J. Teweles, *The Commodity Futures Game*, McGraw-Hill, New York, 1974.

Hieronymus, Thomas A., *Economics of Futures Trading*, Commodity Research Bureau, New York, 1971.

Hester, Donald D., and James Tobin, Eds., *Financial Markets and Economic Activity*, Wiley, New York, 1971.

Hoel, Paul G., *An Introduction to Mathematical Statistics*, Wiley, New York, 1971.

Hogg, Robert V., and Allen T. Craig, *Introduction to Mathematical Statistics*, 3rd ed., Macmillan, New York, 1970.

Hurst, J. M., *The Profit Magic of Stock Transaction Timing*, Prentice-Hall, Englewood Cliffs, NJ, 1970.

Jaedicke, Robert K., and Robert T. Sprouse, *Accounting Flows: Income, Funds, and Cash*, Prentice-Hall, Englewood Cliffs, NJ, 1965.

Jensen, Michael C., Ed., *Studies in the Theory of Capital Markets*, Praeger, New York, 1972.

Jiler, Harry, Ed., *Guide to Commodity Price Forecasting*, Commodity Research Bureau, New York, 1971.

Johnson, Lynwood A., and Douglas C. Montgomery, *Forecasting and Time Series Analysis*, McGraw-Hill, New York, 1976.

Johnson, Norman I., and Samuel Kotz, *Continuous Univariate Distributions, Volume 1*, Houghton Mifflin, Boston, 1970.

Kaufman, P. J., *Commodity Trading Systems and Methods*, Wiley, New York, 1978.

Kaufman, Perry J., *Handbook of Futures Markets: Commodity, Financial, Stock Index, and Options*, Wiley, New York, 1984.

Kendall, Sir Maurice, *Time Series*, 2nd ed., Hafner, New York, 1976.

Kerekes, Gabriel T., and Frank H. Zarb, Eds., *The Stock Market Handbook*, Dow Jones–Irwin, Homewood, IL, 1970.

Labuszewski, John, and Jeanne Cairns Sinquefield, *Inside the Commodity Option Markets*, Wiley, New York, 1984.

Labys, Walter C., *Quantitative Models of Commodity Markets*, Ballinger, Cambridge, MA, 1975.

Labys, Walter C., and C. W. J. Granger, *Speculation, Hedging and Commodity Price Forecasts*, Heath Lexington, Lexington, MA, 1970.

Lancaster, Kelvin, *Mathematical Economics*, Macmillian, New York, 1970.

Levin, Richard I., and Rudolph P. Lamone, *Quantitative Disciplines in Management Decisions*, Dickenson, Belmont, CA, 1969.

Levy, Robert A., *The Relative Strength Concept of Common Stock Forecasting*, Investors Intelligence, New York, 1968.

Lietaer, Bernard A., *Financial Management of Foreign Exchange*, The MIT Press, Cambridge, MA, 1971.

Lindow, Wesley, *Inside the Money Market*, Random House, New York, 1972.

Loosigian, Allan M., *Interest Rate Futures*, Dow Jones, Princeton, NJ, 1980.

Mao, James C. T., *Quantitative Analysis of Financial Decisions*, Macmillan, New York, 1969.

Markowitz, Harry M., *Portfolio Selection*, Yale University Press, New Haven, CT, 1969.

Mass, Nathaniel J., *Economic Cycles: An Analysis of Underlying Causes*, Wright-Allen, Cambridge, MA, 1975.

Mitchell, Wesley Clair, *Business Cycles and Their Causes*, University of California Press, Berkeley and Los Angeles, 1963.

Morganstern, Oskar, and John Von Neumann, *Theory of Games and Economic Behavior*, Wiley, New York, 1976.

Orgler, Yair E., *Cash Management: Methods and Models*, Wadsworth, Belmont, CA, 1970.

Patel, Charles, *Technical Trading Systems for Commodities and Stocks*, Trading Systems Research, Walnut Creek, CA, 1980.

Patinkin, Don, *Money, Interest and Prices*, 2nd ed., Harper & Row, New York, 1965.

Peck, A. E., Ed., *Selected Writings on Futures Markets*, Board of Trade of the City of Chicago, 1977.

Peck, A. E., Ed., *View from the Trade*, Book 3, Board of Trade of the City of Chicago, 1978.

Prechter, Jr., Robert R., Ed., *The Major Works of R. N. Elliott*, New Classics Library, Chappaqua, New York, 1980.

Pring, Martin J., *Technical Analysis Explained: An Illustrative Guide for the Investor*, McGraw-Hill, New York, 1980.

Riehl, Heinz, and Rita M., Rodriguez, *Foreign Exchange Markets*, McGraw-Hill, New York, 1977.

Ritter, Lawrence S., and William L. Silber, *Money*, Basic Books, New York, 1970.

Rivett, Patrick, *Model Building for Decision Analysis*, Wiley, Chichester, England, 1980.

Robbins, Sidney, *The Securities Market*, Free Press, New York, 1966.

Robichek, Alexander A., and Stewart C. Myers, *Optimal Financing Decisions*, Prentice-Hall, Englewood Cliffs, NJ, 1965.

Roll, Richard, *The Behavior of Interest Rates*, Basic Books, New York, 1970.

Rose, Joy, and Leon Rose, Eds., *Commodity Money Management Yearbooks*, L. J. R. Inc., Columbia, MD, 1980.

Rosen, Lawrence R., *The Dow Jones–Irwin Guide to Interest*, Dow Jones–Irwin, Inc., Homewood, IL, 1974.

Schein, Edgar H., *Process Consultation: Its Role in Organization Development*, Addison-Wesley, Reading, MA, 1969.

Schlaifer, Robert, *Probability and Statistics for Business Decisions*, McGraw-Hill, New York, 1959.

Schwartz, Edward W., *How to Use Interest Rate Futures Contacts*, Dow Jones–Irwin, Inc., Homewood, IL, 1979.

Selby, Samuel M., Ed., *Standard Mathematical Tables*, 21st ed., Chemical Rubber Co., Cleveland, OH, 1973.

Shell, Karl, and Giorgio P. Szego, Eds., *Mathematical Methods in Investment and Finance*, North Holland, Amsterdam, Netherlands, 1972.

Siegel, Sidney, *Nonparametric Statistics*, McGraw-Hill, New York, 1956.

Silvey, S. D., *Statistical Inference*, Penguin, Baltimore, MD, 1970.

Sklarew, Arthur, *Techniques of a Professional Commodity Chart Analyst*, Commodity Research Bureau Inc., New York, 1980.

Sloan, Harold S., and Arnold J. Zurcher, *A Dictionary of Economics*, 4th ed. rev., Barnes & Noble, New York, 1968.

Solomon, Ezra, *The Theory of Financial Management*, Columbia University Press, New York, 1963.

Spencer, Milton H., *Managerial Economics*, 3rd ed., Richard D. Irwin, Homewood, IL, 1968.

Sprinkel, Beryl W., *Money and Markets*, Richard D. Irwin, Homewood, IL, 1971.

Sprinkel, Beryl W., *Money and Stock Prices*, Richard D. Irwin, Homewood, IL, 1974.

Stalnaker, Ashford W., and Bevan K. Youse, *Calculus*, International Textbook Company, Scranton, PA, 1969.

Stapleton, R. C., *The Theory of Corporate Finance*, George G. Harrap, London, 1970.

Starr, Martin K., *Management: A Modern Approach*, Harcourt Brace Jovanovich, New York, 1971.

Statistical Reporting Service, USDA, *Scope and Methods of the Statistical Reporting Service*, Miscellaneous Publication No. 1308, U. S. Government Printing Office, Washington, DC, July, 1975.

Stigler, George J., *The Theory of Price*, 3rd ed., Macmillian, New York, 1966.

Sveshnikov, A. A., *Problems in Probability Theory: Mathematical Statistics and Theory of Random Functions*, Dover, New York, 1978.

Teichroew, Daniel, *An Introduction to Management Science*, Wiley, New York, 1964.

Teweles, Richard J., Charles V. Harlow, and Herbert L. Stone, *The Commodity Futures Game. Who Wins? Who Loses? Why?*, McGraw-Hill, New York, 1974.

Theodore, Chris A., *Applied Mathematics: An Introduction*, Richard D. Irwin, Homewood, IL, 1965.

Tintner, Gerhard, *Econometrics*, Wiley, New York, 1967.

United States Department of Agriculture, *Agriculture Handbook*, No. 23, Statistical Reporting, rev. U. S. Government Printing Office, March 1972.

Vancil, Richard F., Ed., *Financial Executive's Handbook*, Dow Jones–Irwin, Homewood, IL, 1970.

Van Horne, James C., *Function and Analysis of Capital Market Rates*, Prentice-Hall, Englewood Cliffs, NJ, 1970.

Wagner, Harvey M., *Principles of Operations Research*, Prentice-Hall, Englewood Cliffs, NJ, 1969.

Wald, Abraham, *Sequential Analysis*, Dover, New York, 1973.

Wallis, W. Allen, and Geoffrey H. Moore, *A Significance Test for Time Series and Other Ordered Observations. Technical Paper 1: September 1941*, National Bureau of Economic Research, New York, 1941.

Walsh, Myles E., *Understanding Computers: What Managers and Users Need to Know*, Wiley, New York, 1981.

Ward, Richard, *International Finance*, Prentice-Hall, Englewood Cliffs, NJ, 1965.

Wonnacott, Ronald J., and Thomas H. Wonnacott, *Econometrics*, Wiley, New York, 1970.

Woy, J. B., *Commodity Futures Trading: A Bibliographic Guide*, Bowker, New York, 1976.

Zellner, Arnold, *An Introduction to Bayesian Inference in Econometrics*, Wiley, New York, 1971.

PERIODICALS

Commodity Research Bureau Chart Service, NY.

Commodity Research Bureau Yearbooks, NY.

Federal Reserves of St. Louis, *U. S. Financial Data*, St. Louis, MO.

Index